Victorian Architecture
in London and Southwestern Ontario

SYMBOLS OF ASPIRATION

Nancy Z. Tausky

Ian MacEachern

Lynne D. DiStefano

NANCY Z. TAUSKY and
LYNNE D. DiSTEFANO

VICTORIAN ARCHITECTURE

in London and Southwestern Ontario

SYMBOLS OF ASPIRATION

Photographs by Ian MacEachern

UNIVERSITY OF TORONTO PRESS

Toronto Buffalo London

Canadian Cataloguing in Publication Data

Tausky, Nancy Z.
  Victorian architecture in London and
  Southwestern Ontario

  Co-published by London Regional Art Gallery.
  Bibliography
  Includes index.
  ISBN 0-8020-5698-9

  1. Architecture, Victorian – Ontario – London Region.
  2. Historic buildings – Ontario – London Region.
  3. London (Ont.) – Buildings, structures, etc.
  4. Robinson, Tracy, Durand and Moore (Firm).
  5. London Region (Ont.) – History.   I. DiStefano,
  Lynne Delehanty.   II. London Regional Art Gallery
  (Ont.)   III. Title.

  NA747.L6T38 1986   720′.9713′26   C86-094842-0

All modern photographs are by Ian MacEachern. Photographs of architectural drawings and other period illustrations are by Ian MacEachern, with the following exceptions: 3, 4, 5, 6, 7, 10, 11, 12, 18, 21, 34, 35, 78, 89 by James R. Ingram; 113 by Lynne D. DiStefano; 36 Metropolitan Toronto Library; 9 Public Archives of Canada.

Robert Ballantine adapted from the architectural drawings the floor plans illustrated in 63, 66, 130, 191, and 209.

Most architectural drawings, other archival materials, and works of art in this book are from the Regional Collection, the D.B. Weldon Library, the University of Western Ontario. The other period illustrations were obtained from the following institutions and individuals: 160, Archives of Ontario; 36, Baldwin Room, Metropolitan Toronto Library; 38, 109, 111, London Historical Museums; 1, 27, London Regional Art Gallery; 8, 60, 82, London Room, London Public Libraries and Museums; 117, Photographic Conservancy of Canada; 9, Public Archives of Canada; 19, 26, 29, 171, 172, 174, Ronald E. Murphy, Architect; 113, the Shute Institute; 18, 87, 119, Stratford-Perth Archives; 46, Strathroy Middlesex Museum; 3, 4, 5, 6, 7, 10, 11, 12, 21, 35, Thomas Fisher Rare Book Library, University of Toronto; 34, University Archives, University of Toronto; 2, 15, University Art Collection, University of Western Ontario; 13, Don H. Hensley; 116, Katherine D. Holth; 168, John H. Moore.

The drawing of Malahide Castle (14) by Francis Wheatley is reproduced with the permission of Thames and Hudson.

This book is co-published with the London Regional Art Gallery, and is made possible by generous funding from the National Museums of Canada, the Canada Council, the Social Sciences and Humanities Research Council of Canada, the Government of Ontario through the Ministry of Citizenship and Culture, the Ontario Arts Council, the D.B. Weldon Library at the University of Western Ontario, Brescia College, London Historical Museums, John Labatt Limited, the Blackburn Group, and members of the Moore family.

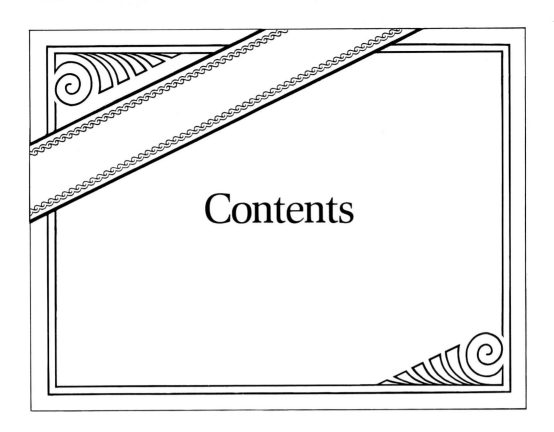

Contents

To our parents,
John and Helena Zwart and Carolyn Calthrop,
who developed our interests in history
and taught us to love old buildings

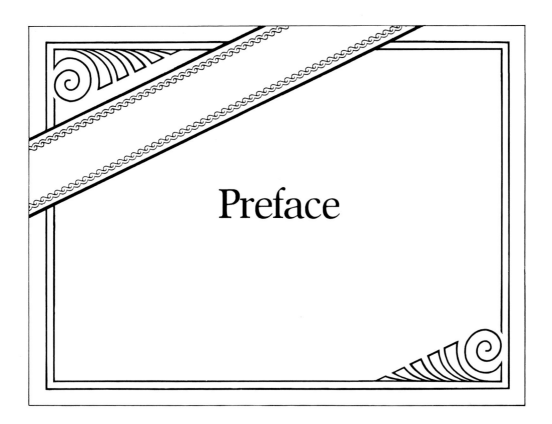

Preface

THROUGHOUT LONDON'S FORMATIVE YEARS, its boosters continually measured the town's often heralded 'progress' in terms of its architectural accomplishments. Its courthouse was 'the finest building in the province,' according to the *Sun* in 1832. The *Free Press* noted with satisfaction in 1870 that 'London is pushing ahead architecturally.' Twelve years later, the newspaper boasted about an 'even more elegant variety of residences.' This book examines what 'pushing ahead architecturally' meant in London and the surrounding districts of southwestern Ontario.

Our examination is focused upon the work of a single distinguished architectural firm. Founded by William Robinson in 1857, the firm played a crucial role in the development of the area's architecture throughout the Victorian period, a consideration that alone could have justified our interest. We were also guided by the presence at the University of Western Ontario of an unusual and valuable collection of documents. The Murphy-Moore Collection contains hundreds of architectural drawings, as well as specifications, daybooks, and numerous other records pertaining to the firm's early history. It provides a rare opportunity to gain an appreciation of the individual qualities of several talented regional architects and to understand the ways in which they affected one another through several generations of partnerships.

Our study places the achievements of the firm in perspective by describing as many as possible of the broader influences in its work. In the opening chapter architectural styles are traced back to their ancient roots; subsequently, the various Victorian fashions in architecture are discussed and related to similar developments in other areas of the period's intellectual life. The second chapter explores what it meant to be an architect in the nineteenth century, in Canada and elsewhere, and examines the materials and technologies available to the architect. The development of London as a community and the effect of civic values upon the firm's work are analysed wherever relevant. We hope that the variety of approaches may prove useful to those who seek to study the Victorian buildings of other towns in other regions.

One of our aims in undertaking the project was to foster more enthusiasm for preserving Victorian architecture, and our research has intensified our awareness of the need for an active and informed approach to the conservation of nineteenth-century buildings. A depressingly large number of the firm's major works have been demolished; a greater number have been irrevocably damaged as period buildings by inappropriate additions and alterations. Our own aspirations will be fulfilled if the book helps future preservationists appreciate the integrity of Canada's Victorian heritage.

This book is the result of efforts by many different people over its eleven-year gestation period. Ronald E. Murphy, the current inheritor of Robinson's firm, made the project possible when in the late 1960s he donated his company's early records to the University of Western Ontario as the Murphy-Moore Collection. In 1975 Stephanie L. Sykes mentioned the existence of the collection to Lynne DiStefano. Three years later Lynne prepared an exhibition on the architecture of George F. Durand for the London Historical Museums.

Discussions between Lynne and Nancy Tausky at that time led to plans for a broader project comprising this book and the circulating exhibition 'Symbols of Aspiration,' which opened at the London Regional Art Gallery in May 1986. The authors shared the historical research and architectural analysis necessary for both undertakings. Lynne assumed most other curatorial and managerial responsibilities and wrote the captions and glossary for the book. Nancy organized and wrote nearly all the text.

Ian MacEachern's excellent photographs, especially commissioned for the project, have made an outstanding contribution to the book.

The other major contributor, to whom we are extremely grateful, is Thomas E. Tausky. He wrote and researched the three general social histories of London, subtitled 'London Grows Up,' 'Recreation and Culture in the Durand Era,' and 'Stability and Change in the Moore Era.' He also made invaluable suggestions about the manuscript on a day-to-day, page-to-page basis, did considerable research into the history of individual buildings, and compiled most of the footnotes.

Among those whose contributions to the project were critical is Sandra DeBoice. She typed numerous drafts and redrafts into the word processor at the London Regional Art Gallery with miraculous speed, and her cheerfulness was a constant source of inspiration.

We are grateful to several organizations and individuals who contributed to the funding of the exhibition and book: the National Museums of Canada, the Canada Council, the Social Sciences and Humanities Research Council of

Canada, the Government of Ontario through the Ministry of Citizenship and Culture, the Ontario Arts Council, the D.B. Weldon Library at the University of Western Ontario, Brescia College, London Historical Museums, John Labatt Limited, the Blackburn Group, and John H. Moore and family.

We sincerely thank our co-publishers, the London Regional Art Gallery and the University of Toronto Press, and particularly Paddy O'Brien, project co-ordinator for LRAG, and University of Toronto Press editor Prudence Tracy for their support and patience. Catherine Frost who copyedited the manuscript for the Press made numerous valued improvements and William Rueter's design for the book provided an attractive and appropriate setting for its content. We also wish to acknowledge the special contributions of Brenda Wallace, former director of LRAG, who initially approved the idea of the exhibition; former historical curator in residence, Ann Davis, who co-ordinated many aspects of the project during its early stages; and Nancy Poole, present director, who sustained the Gallery's support of the undertaking.

Among the many individuals who helped us, Robert G. Hill, Stephen A. Otto, and Douglas S. Richardson deserve special thanks for their encouragement, suggestions, and generous sharing of material and experience.

Guy St-Denis's extensive and skilful historical research made an especially significant contribution to the project. Over the years many other research assistants scoured newspapers and city directories for relevant material, and we thank Elizabeth A. Elliott, Patricia M. Grace, Susan Boyd Hall, Janine M. Love, Arnold W. Nethercott, Catherine M. Pagani, and Rebecca M. Vogan for their careful work.

We are obliged to University of Toronto photographer James R. Ingram for photographing materials from Toronto. We are grateful to David Dudley and Geoffrey Morrow for their conservation of the architectural drawings, and to Walter Eldridge for his conservation of the period photographs.

We are deeply indebted to the staffs of numerous archives, libraries, and museums. None was more generous and cheerfully helpful over a sustained period than Edward C.H. Phelps, Regional Collection, D.B. Weldon Library, The University of Western Ontario, and his colleague, John H. Lutman. Important information was obtained from Christina Cameron and her colleagues in the Architectural History Division, National Historic Parks and Sites Branch, Parks Canada. We also appreciate the assistance of James Anderson and Carolynn and Lutzen Riedstra, Stratford-Perth Archives.

We gratefully acknowledge the kind co-operation of the many archivists and staff members from the Archives of Ontario; Canadian Baptist Archives, McMaster Divinity College; Diocese of Huron Archives, Huron College; Diocese of London Archives (Roman Catholic); The Guild Inn; London Historical Museums; London Life Insurance Company Archives; London Room, London Public Libraries and Museums; Metropolitan Toronto Library; Public Archives of Canada; Presbyterian Church in Canada Archives, Knox College; Separate School Archives, The Msgr Feeney Centre for Catholic Education; Special Collections, D.B. Weldon Library, The University of Western

Ontario; The Thomas Fisher Rare Book Library, The University of Toronto; United Church of Canada Central Archives, Victoria College; and the University of Toronto Archives.

We are very appreciative of the information about buildings provided by many other persons and institutions, and we regret that we are unable to cite each individual contributor. We are also grateful to the people who gave us information about the architects – especially to the descendants and friends of George F. Durand, John M. Moore, and Fred Henry.

Our families have supported us with love and encouragement through long months of postponed conversations, interrupted meals, and dining room tables covered with notes, photographs, and books. Our spouses have done more than their usual share of cooking, errand-running, and child-rearing, and to Tom and Joe we are most grateful. Our children have accepted their sometimes disorganized home life with tolerance and understanding, for which we extend a special thanks to David and Laura, Matthew and Andrea. Jane Vogan has earned our gratitude as a dedicated and self-sacrificing babysitter for the young Tauskys.

Notwithstanding this long list of well-deserved thanks to those who have assisted us, we, of course, accept full responsibility for the book's shortcomings.

NANCY Z. TAUSKY
LYNNE D. DiSTEFANO
September 1986

Victorian Architecture
in London and Southwestern Ontario

SYMBOLS OF ASPIRATION

Colonel Talbot's 'Somewhat Gothic' Courthouse

I N 1878 ARCHITECT THOMAS H. TRACY completed the design for an addition to the most venerable building in his native town of London, Ontario: the half-century-old courthouse (fig. 1), a castle standing guard over its own Thames. As a member of London's most prestigious architectural firm – Robinson, Tracy, and Durand – Tracy was already making significant contributions to the city's future well-being. Particularly important projects that year included London's first waterworks system and its first public high school. In contrast, the courthouse improvements required more concern with the past than the future. The addition was to be in what a local newspaper labelled the 'primitive style' of the original building, 'by special request of several old citizens,' for whom 'reminiscences of former life were kept real by the sight of the old Court House.'[1] Tracy's design was remarkably faithful in spirit and even in detail to the original structure. Nevertheless the remodelled courthouse featured a new shape and a new façade, and ultimately it was the 1878 structure that would stand as the reminder of the city's 'former life.'

LIEUTENANT-GOVERNOR SIMCOE AND THE 'METROPOLIS OF ALL CANADA'

Both London's past and the courthouse that represented it were in some ways unusual. First, London had existed in theory for several decades before it existed in actuality. In 1791, on being appointed lieutenant-governor of the newly formed Upper Canada, Colonel John Graves Simcoe began to

1   *The Gaol and Courthouse*, watercolour on paper, by George Russell Dartnell, c. 1835

consider a site for the province's capital.[2] Worried that both Niagara and Detroit were vulnerable to an American invasion, Simcoe was eager to place a military base far enough from the border to be protected, but sufficiently accessible for quickly mobilized resistance. His desire to locate the capital in such an unsettled backwoods was also related to economic concerns: he considered farming potentially more profitable and more conducive to settlement than fur trading, and a western capital would encourage westward settlement in Upper Canada. With these issues in mind, Simcoe made a preliminary study of maps, first in the Home Office in London, England and then in Montreal, which persuaded him that the forks of a river called La Tranche might suit his purpose. A reconnaissance of the area in the summer of 1793 found the forks the fulfilment of Simcoe's dreams. As Major Littlehales recorded in his diary of the expedition, Simcoe judged the situation 'eminently calculated for the metropolis of all Canada.' The river offered an easy route to Lake Erie and Lake St Clair; a short portage bridged the forks and a water route to Lake Ontario. The soil was 'luxuriantly fine,' a 'pinery' and 'other timber on the heights' were 'well calculated for the erection of public buildings,' and the Indians would find an 'equitable' market for pelts in the new town.[3]

   Simcoe saw his new capital as the centre of an ideal community. He was a staunch British patriot who regarded his appointment as an opportunity for creating a model British society in the new world. He had been a bitter loser in the Revolutionary War, blaming the American victory on poor British leadership rather than American determination, and he felt that his transplanted England might prove so alluring as to make the misguided rebels regret their wanderings and return home to the Empire. As Mrs Simcoe's account of her husband's visit to the forks, based on his own journal, reveals, there was a strong patriotic dimension to his explorations. The party dutifully sang 'God Save the King' before falling asleep in front of a huge fire provided by the Indians. More significantly, and predictably, Simcoe decided to name the envisioned capital New London.[4] La Tranche had already been re-christened the Thames.

Simcoe arranged to have some 3,850 acres reserved for the capital of Upper Canada.[5] He remained faithful to his vision of the new London until illness forced his return to England in 1796, but his dream never materialized. In 1797 the Duke of Portland, the British secretary of state, informed Simcoe's successor that, 'on mature reflection,' he had decided to locate the capital at York.[6]

Though their raison d'être disappeared, the crown reserve and the name chosen for Simcoe's capital-designate remained. Indeed, later legislation regarding nomenclature elaborated on the concept of London city. The London District was formed in 1800, encompassing most of the area bounded by Lake Erie on the south, Lake Huron and Georgian Bay on the north, and lines approximately even with the present day Simcoe on the east and Grand Bend on the west. The act describing the London District also placed the future town of London in Middlesex County. Later, the two townships bordering the forks of the Thames were to be called London and Westminster. By the early 1800s nomenclature alone gave a good deal of importance to a town that was, as yet, no more than a thwarted dream. Lord Selkirk, visiting the site in 1804, entered a note on the incongruity in his diary: 'Sunday 3d June – left our encampment and stopt a few minutes at the Forks, in the great city of London – where there was a Chippaway Bark Whigwham.'[7]

The great city did not become even a fledgling village until 1826, when the still unsettled site was honoured with the title of District Town. Thus, while most cities grow more or less naturally from agrarian or mercantile roots, London began as the administrative and legal centre of the huge London District. The first building planned for the village was a stately home for the courts rather than a log cabin, and early patrons of the courts found that they had to travel several miles, to Swartz's tavern in Westminster, in order to find a place to stay.[8]

COLONEL TALBOT'S 'PRINCIPALITY'

The town's real, as opposed to its imaginary, beginnings were supervised not by Simcoe, but by a man who had been in Simcoe's entourage on the 1793 visit to the Forks, Colonel Thomas Talbot.[9] A landed aristocracy had been part of Simcoe's plan for his new England: to facilitate this end he made land grants of up to 5,000 acres available to military officers, members of the executive and legislative councils, and other leading citizens. Talbot carried Simcoe's intentions to an extreme, eventually claiming over 45,000 acres and controlling a much larger area that he regarded as his fiefdom. Because he exerted such a strong influence over London and the huge 'Talbot Tract,' his interests and methods deserve special notice.

Thomas Talbot was a younger son of Sir Richard Talbot, an Anglo-Irish baron whose fiefdom at Malahide, near Dublin, had been in the family for 600 years. Thomas spent his early years at Malahide Castle. At the age of eleven he was appointed an ensign in an Irish regiment, thus embarking on what was apparently planned as a lifelong military career. Though retired on half pay at the age of twelve shortly after being promoted to the rank of lieuten-ant, four years later he became an aide-de-camp to the Marquis of Buckingham, Viceroy of Ireland, and on Buckingham's recommendation he was enlisted by Simcoe as his private secretary when Simcoe came to Canada in 1791.

Talbot seems to have fulfilled this role with the dash of the perfect courtier and the tact and reliability of an elder statesman. He was lively, cheerful, and entertaining. Mrs Simcoe had high praise for his supervision of her social duties: he was 'au fait in all those points which give weight to matters of no importance.'[10] Governor Simcoe found him a trustworthy diplomat in more serious matters: later, recommending Talbot to the colonial secretary, Simcoe credited him with skill and generosity in handling delicate negotiations between the Indians and the Americans. An early biography contains an account of the nesting instinct which overcame Talbot while accompanying Simcoe on the 1793 expedition to Detroit: 'Early in the evening, on arrival at the spot so deservedly called Port Talbot, the Colonel had a tent speedily erected at the top of the Hill, turned host at once, met the Governor at the tent door, and with the dignity so natural to him, invited His Excellency to the Castle of Malahide, saying "Here, General Simcoe, will I roost, and will soon make the forest tremble under the wings of the flock I will invite by my warblings around me." '[11] Since the biographer is getting the story third-hand at least, its veracity is open to question. But the exuberance shown here characterized most of Talbot's actions, and the lively metaphor illustrates the wit and colourful diction that suffused many of his speeches and made him capable of being such charming company.

Talbot's plan for an Upper Canadian Castle of Malahide was postponed. In 1794 he left to assume the captaincy of an Irish regiment, then fighting against the French in Holland, and he spent the next six years in the army, gaining the rank of lieutenant-colonel. On Christmas Day in 1800 he suddenly sold his commission and shortly afterward sailed for Upper Canada.

The man who returned in 1801 was no longer the model young gentleman. Whether disappointed in love, frustrated in his career, or somehow disillu-sioned with the general temper of English society, he threw off the trappings of civilization with a vengeance, and took a defiant delight in assuming the clothes and practices of backwoodsmen. Writing to the Duke of Cumberland in 1801, just a few weeks after taking up residence in Upper Canada, he bragged, 'I am out every morning at Sun-rise in my smock frock felling and burning the Forest to form a farm; could I but be seen by some of my St James's friends when I come home to my frugal supper – as black as any chimney sweeper – they would exclaim, "what a dam'd block head you have been, Tom" – but I say, no, as I actually eat my homely fare with more zest than ever I did the best dinner in London.'[12] The 'Castle of Malahide' he eventually constructed at Port Talbot was simply a log cabin which he replaced in 1833 with a larger and more refined log cabin, possessing many comforts but displaying the insistently rustic quality that characterized the clothes and demeanour of its owner. When Anna Jameson visited Talbot's home in 1837, she found that the front door led into a hall filled with 'sacks of wheat and piles of sheepskins ... heaped in primitive fashion,' various gardening tools, and, hanging from the rafters, a dead wildcat.[13]

Though assuming peasant manners, Talbot in no way conceived of himself as possessing a peasant's status. He referred to Port Talbot as the 'capital' of his 'principality,' and to the settlers within his domain as his 'subjects.'[14] Since Simcoe's enthusiasm for a landed and titled aristocracy was not inherited by his successors, and the Upper Canada Government of 1800 was not in the business of handing out baronies, Talbot's quest for the land and power that comprised his fiefdom involved a constant struggle with officialdom. With the help of the Dukes of Cumberland and Kent, sons of King George III, and against the wishes of Governor Hunter, arrangements were made whereby Talbot would be given 200 acres of land in Dunwich or Aldborough County for every fifty acres that he granted to a settler. This policy enabled Talbot to amass a personal estate of approximately 45,000 acres.[15] He gained control over a much larger area through his successive appointments as commissioner of various roads. He devised a plan for road-building, modelled on Simcoe's development of Yonge Street, requiring settlers on adjoining lots to clear road allowances before being allowed to pay their settlement fees and receive the patents for their lots. The method was so successful that Talbot eventually became the sole authority responsible for assigning lots and overseeing settlement duties throughout the areas traversed by three 'Talbot Roads': one linking his lands with the rising metropolitan areas to the east, one extending that road to Windsor, and a northern extension into Westminster Township. In addition, Talbot acted as land commissioner in several townships untouched by the road, including London Township.

Initially, at least, Talbot seems to have been motivated by a considerable amount of idealism in presiding over his would-be barony, viewing himself as the protector and benefactor of his 'children.'[16] Simcoe explained to Colonial Secretary Hobart that Talbot 'hoped to develop by precept and example the principles of loyalty, obedience, and private industry' among his settlers, and one anecdote concerning some 'Highland emigrants' who arrived in 1818 shows vividly his efforts in the line of industry:

by way of sealing the contract, [Talbot] treated each of them to a good horn of real whiskey; and while at dinner, the Colonel paced the room, instructing his guests how to build houses, clear land, plant corn and potatoes, with other useful directions; beseeching them to be industrious, sober, and peaceable. At bed time, the Colonel produced a pile of blankets, and requested his guests to make their own bed. One of the party said, 'We never made a bed!' – the Colonel took the mattress, placed it on the floor before the fire, brought the backs of three chairs, to the subservient positions of pillows, spread one blanket, then turned round, and said 'spread the rest of the blankets fairly on top of that, and learn to help yourselves, in Canada.'[17]

Certainly many of Talbot's 'subjects' were keenly enthusiastic about their lord. When Lieutenant-Governor Colborne set out to assess the Talbot settlement in 1829, he found that 'everyone appeared satisfied with [Talbot's] arrangements and appreciated his labours.'[18] From 1817 until his death in 1853 settlers around St Thomas held an annual dinner and dance in Talbot's honour, and the Scottish traveller James Brown reported that London regularly vied with St Thomas over which could hold the most impressive anniversary celebration: 'In the town of London there have been gay balls in honour of the event, at which townspeople and country folks of all parties, joined by the officers of the garrison, have kept it merrily up, and the old man himself ... tripped about as lightly as any.'[19] One aspiring poet of the area, Adam Hood Burwell, wrote an epic on 'a theme, whose dignity should summon forth / The best, and boldest powers of mental worth.' The ostensible theme turns out to be the Talbot Road, a subject understandably dear to the poet's heart, since his father, Mahlon Burwell, had been the surveyor of the entire project. One might expect that Mahlon Burwell would be the epic's protagonist. Instead, the hero is Colonel Talbot, who is treated, like Milton's God, as a creator bringing form out of chaos:

> For Talbot Road, say first, what master hand
> This work projected, and its order plann'd?
> Bade the wild woods their rudest forms resign,
> And springing beauty o'er the desert shine?
> 'Twas *Talbot* – he, with ardent, patriot mind,
> The noble plan, philanthropic, design'd.[20]

Also like Milton's God, however, and for more reason, Talbot found that power could not necessarily command either friendship or obedience. Complaints against his rule were many, varied, and from all quarters. Some settlers were unhappy at getting only fifty acres out of the 200 granted to Talbot. Others found him capricious in assigning and reclaiming lots; since his only method of recording locations was to write a recipient's name in pencil on a large map, his rubber eraser became a formidable and greatly dreaded weapon. On the other hand, the government complained that Talbot's settlers were too ready to put off paying their fees and getting an irrevocable title to their land. Last, but certainly not least in importance, was the clash in political views between Talbot and some of his settlers. Many of them came from the United States, and they retained enough of the old loyalties to resent wholeheartedly Talbot's claims to aristocratic privilege.

The strain of these hostilities gradually tempered the colonel's enthusiasm and benevolence. Already in 1824 one of his friends described his state in pathetic terms: 'The enthusiasm which gave energy to his early efforts is worn out, and he is tied for life to a scene now becoming irksome to him, because having expended all his money, and unable to get it back, he cannot afford to live in England.' Anna Jameson found him 'alone – a lonely man' in 1837. Sir Francis Bond Head's observation in the same year shows how far his public image had deteriorated from that of the paternal benefactor: 'this estimable and gentlemanly personage is looked upon rather as a wizard than a man.' Owing, perhaps, to the violence of one particular Scots settler, Talbot had insulated himself from any display of his applicants' more vigorous feelings by seeing them only through a window. 'When he feels disposed to listen to them,' reported Head, 'he opens a small compartment of his window which he closes and secures the instant he has delivered his reply.'[21]

He ended his days out of favour with the Reform government and, more tragically, exiled from his beloved Port Talbot. In an effort to provide an heir for his life's work, he invited his nephew Richard Airey to live at his estate. It is perhaps not surprising that the Aireys felt impelled to turn the colonel's cabin into what even the visiting Lady Emmeline Stuart-Wortley could consider 'a comfortable country seat,'[22] but in their case the differences in taste were indications of deeper antipathies. In 1850, three years after Airey's arrival, Talbot fulfilled his bargain with his nephew by giving him the title to half of the estate, including the cabin / country house, and bequeathing the rest to George Macbeth, a young neighbour who had been in Talbot's employ for eleven years. The Colonel died on 5 February 1853, in the London home of Macbeth and his wife.

THE NEW DISTRICT TOWN

Though many miles away from his beloved Port Talbot, London could lay some claim to Talbot's affections. It was one of the most thriving towns in the Talbot Tract, and Colonel Talbot had been in charge of superintending its settlement some twenty-five years before.

Westminster Township had been opened to settlement as early as 1810, when Simon Zelotes Watson, a Montreal surveyor, was encouraged by Talbot to bring settlers there from Lower Canada and the United States. The collaboration between Watson and Talbot was short-lived, and Talbot was eventually given sole responsibility for making locations in Westminster. London Township also received its first settlers around that time. In 1808 Joshua Applegarth was allotted a thousand-acre tract of land on the forks for the purpose of growing hemp. With the exception of William Montague, who came to assist Applegarth in 1817, no one else settled in London Township until 1818. In that year there began an influx of Irish immigrants, who came under the somewhat ineffectual leadership of Richard Talbot, a distant relative of the colonel. The township grew rapidly over the next few years, and the population numbered 1,104 by 1825. The crown reserve for London had been reduced to 2,370 acres by 1818, and some encroachments, including the lands first claimed by Applegarth and Montague, had been made even on this reduced area. But in January 1826 the government instructed Talbot to make no additional locations there. London was finally to become a town.[23]

Until 1826 the district town had been Vittoria, nestled in the south-eastern corner of the huge London District. For many residents of the district, the trip to Vittoria over primitive or non-existent roads was difficult and time-consuming. Magistrates trying to hold local courts often found the makeshift sites prone to disruption. When the courthouse at Vittoria burned in 1825, residents of Middlesex County campaigned vigorously and successfully for the removal of the district town to a more central location. On 30 January 1826 the legislature of Upper Canada passed acts declaring London the new district town; providing for the survey of a town plot, with four acres to be reserved for a courthouse and jail; appointing commissioners to be responsible for the erection of the courthouse and jail; and authorizing the commission to borrow £4,000 to cover the expenses of the new building, with the understanding that district householders would later be taxed to repay the loan.

The five commissioners were Thomas Talbot, Mahlon Burwell, James Hamilton, Charles Ingersoll, and John Matthews, of Lobo. All but Ingersoll met at St Thomas on 6 March 1826, where they unanimously elected Colonel Talbot president of the commission, and agreed to insert notices in four newspapers requesting 'plans and estimates for the erection of a Jail and Court House, in one building,' to be submitted by 1 June. The only stipulations, aside from cost, were that 'the foundation and cells ... be of stone and the upper part of brick,' with 'particular attention ... given to a free ventilation throughout the whole building.'[24]

Despite the 1 June deadline, the work of the commissioners was delayed by the tardiness in designating the courthouse site. Talbot had definite ideas about the best location for the town plot, and, very probably, for the courthouse. On 7 March, the day after the first meeting of the commissioners, he informed the governor's secretary that 'the situation in every respect most eligible for the Town is immediately in the Fork,' and added, 'If he [Lieutenant-Governor Maitland] should see fit to leave the selection of the spot, for the Court House, to my judgement, I will do the best that I can.'[25] Talbot's suggestion for the town site was accepted. By the end of June Burwell had completed a survey of 240 acres, covering the area bounded by Wellington Street on the east, North (now Queens) and Carling streets on the north, and branches of the river on the south and west. The still uncleared streets bore the names of British and Canadian dignitaries, including, of course, a central north-south thoroughfare named Talbot Street. There was also a north-south street named Ridout, but the surveyor-general was slow to claim the honour, apologizing in October for his delay in forwarding Burwell's plan to Lieutenant-Governor Maitland.

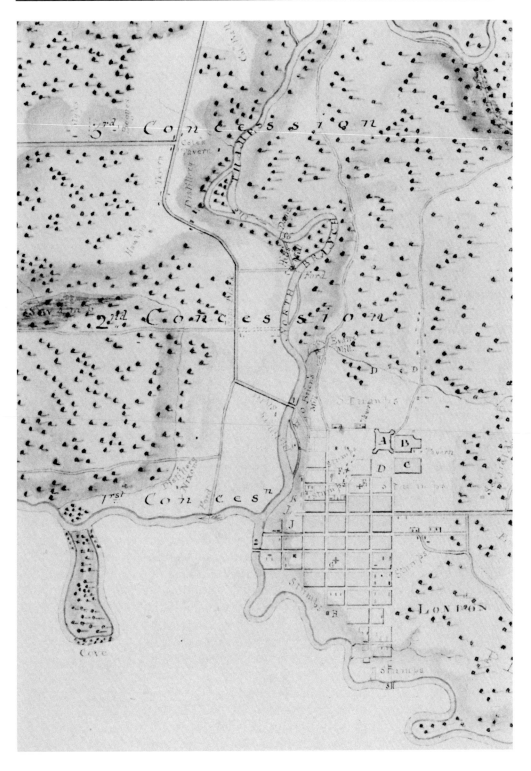

2   *Sketch of Part of the London Township,* watercolour on paper, by 'Nath. Steevens. Lt. xx Regt.,' 1850, detail

It was not until the following spring that the commissioners could meet again to consider the proposals for the courthouse. On 7 April they adopted the plans proposed by 'Mr John Ewart of the town of York,' one of the most talented architects then in Upper Canada. A loan finally procured, construction on the castellated courthouse (fig. 8) began in 1828, and the furnishing of the building was completed in 1831. Meanwhile, a building designed to house the district school served as a temporary courthouse. It was erected on the corner of the courthouse site during the winter of 1826–27 and later moved across King Street to fulfil its original purpose.

The government was also slow to decide whether lots in London should be sold at public auction or granted on the payment of fees, according to the older practice. A week after awarding the contract to Ewart, Talbot wrote to Secretary Hillier expressing his hope that a decision would be made soon and volunteering 'to undertake the superintendence of the Town, as I fear if the lots are located at York, there will be much speculation, imposition, & delay.' Two months later, Talbot's polite and restrained request had been replaced by open irritation about the government's indecision: 'By the delay in not arranging any system about the Town Lots in the Town plot of London, I can assure you, that there will be much mischief – as vagabonds are now taking possession of the best lots, & putting up little Log Huts on them. Individuals have built such descriptions of Huts on 3 or 4 lots and fancy that they are to hold them in consequence.'[26] In the middle of August Talbot received authority to locate settlers in London, following his usual method.

London had begun attracting settlers as soon as it was appointed the district town. Peter MacGregor became London's first resident early in 1826 when he erected a log house at the corner of King and Ridout streets to serve as a tavern and hotel. By 1828 he had a competitor in Abraham Carroll's Mansion House, but MacGregor countered by replacing his cabin with a much more pretentious structure, probably the 'large inn' described by Alfred Domett in 1834, 'with a portico of white wooden pillars as high as the house in front.'[27]

Predictably enough, the new town also attracted merchants and construction workers, the courthouse itself necessitating a sizeable labour force. Architect Ewart built what must have seemed a mansion to house the 'mechanics' imported to work on the courthouse: 'a frame house 50 by 30 feet, and 23 feet high, with a wing 30 by 16 feet and a back kitchen 30 by 22 feet,' complete with 'a barn and stable, 50 by 30 feet,' a walled garden, and an orchard.[28] Ewart had brought as his foreman Thomas Parke, who became a prominent London citizen; in 1833 he was elected a member of the assembly, and he later became surveyor-general.

Another major contingent of early settlers consisted of the court officials, although a surprising number of the men in this category chose to remain living in Vittoria, making the uncomfortable journey to the frontier town only when necessary. One important officer, Sherriff Rappalje, never came at all, consistently sending his son to act as his deputy.

London was undoubtedly not the most comfortable place to live, but the settlers put a good deal of energy into building the town. One observer noted, around 1830, that 'the town is quite new, not containing above 40 or 50 houses, all of bright boards and shingles.' In 1835 Edward Allen Talbot was able to brag in his *Freeman's Journal*, that the town contained 'about 200 dwelling houses, furnished and inhabited, and nearly 100 frames not yet enclosed.' He goes on to list five churches, several schools, and numerous shops and industries, concluding 'that no town in British North America has advanced so rapidly, or can boast a greater number of respectable families.' Talbot particularly commends the 'greatly improved' streets, some with 'well-constructed side-walks.'[29]

Apparently, however, the streets needed improvement. Alfred Domett, a Cambridge student who decided to take his Grand Tour in Canada, had not spoken so favourably of London streets in 1834: 'We crossed the river on a wooden bridge, entered the main street, if it may be called so – consisting of a wide road without footpaths, pavement, or any such accommodations for man or beast, stumps hardly yet eradicated.' Two years before, in 1832, the polluted water in swampy areas, such as the block on Richmond Street between North and Dundas, had contributed substantially to a serious outbreak of cholera in the young city. In 1837 John Sandfield Macdonald, then an apprentice lawyer who had come for the Assizes, found himself stuck for 'the dullest period of my existence' in a place nearly beneath his contempt; 'London is a small place & the houses with one or two exceptions, not worth the looking at. To be sure there are a few neat little cottages, but most of the buildings in the Town are unfinished, having been commenced, but never finished even to admit of holding tenants.'[30]

Always dominating this chaotic scene, like Camelot plunked down on a set for Billy the Kid, was Ewart's towered and battlemented courthouse. Most early commentators rightly called it 'handsome.' The enthusiastic Edward Allen Talbot claimed that it 'is allowed by strangers to be the finest building in the province,' and Mrs Jameson observes that the 'large and stately edifice ... seemed the glory of the townspeople.' Interestingly, however, those writers who fancy themselves as particularly discerning in architectural matters seem curiously tentative about giving the imposing structure a stylistic label. Talbot admits it to be 'not strictly Gothic.' The Reverend Mr William Proudfoot, a Presbyterian minister, describes it as 'a kind of Gothic,' and goes on to suggest, in opposition to the general view, that this 'clumsy and uninteresting' kind of Gothic would be better left unexecuted: 'Surely the Canadians might send to Europe for plans of their public buildings.' The cosmopolitan Mrs Jameson seems more favourably inclined towards the building, but the style so mystifies her that she has to rely on the opinion of a more knowledgeable acquaintance: 'As for the style of architecture, I may not attempt to name or describe it; but a gentleman informed me, in rather equivocal sense, that it was *somewhat gothic*.'[31]

In one sense, the commissioners had sent to Europe for their plans. John Ewart had been trained in Scotland, and he had worked in Edinburgh and

London before emigrating to North America around 1816.[32] His design for the London courthouse used forms and motifs that had been popular in Regency England, adapting them to the particular requirements of a public building in the Canadian wilderness. By surveying early nineteenth-century attitudes towards architecture, we can see why Jameson was confused, her friend equivocal, and Proudfoot downright disgruntled. Such a survey also helps explain why later architectural forms developed as they did in Britain and in the North American part of its empire.

ARCHITECTURAL TASTE: AN ENTHUSIASM FOR THE PAST

A profound enthusiasm for the past prevailed in the early, and late, nineteenth century. The historical novels of Sir Walter Scott, imbuing the English and Scottish past with a spirit of romance and adventure, were extraordinarily popular. *Waverley*, set in early eighteenth-century Scotland and published in 1814, sold 6,000 copies in six months. So widespread was its influence that a merchant in London, Canada called his mansion 'Waverley Hall' in the 1840s. Bulwer-Lytton's *The Last Days of Pompeii* (1834) made that buried town into what one modern architectural historian has labelled a 'popular cult.' Lord Macaulay complained that novelists were appropriating the historian's duty in making the past come alive, and himself set out to write a history that would rival the novels in popularity: 'I shall not be satisfied,' he confessed, 'unless I produce something which shall for a few days supersede the last fashionable novel on the tables of young ladies.' He succeeded. The first two volumes of his *History of England* (1848) sold 22,000 copies in slightly over one year; by 1875 volume I alone had sold 133,653 copies. Even sartorial fashions felt the influences of history. In the first two decades of the century, women wore dresses with a high waist and clinging skirts, similar to those seen on the statues of antiquity. Later, they wore elaborately puffed or slashed sleeves modelled on Elizabethan garments and ruffs called 'betsies' after the Tudor queen. Not surprisingly, architecture also adopted historical styles.[33]

This interest in history was encouraged by two rather different currents in eighteenth-century thought: the sentimental concern with melancholy feelings, and the more scholarly interest in antiquarian pursuits which arose during the same period.

The eighteenth century was generally untroubled by metaphysical uncertainties: Alexander Pope's confident assertion that 'Whatever is, is Right' spoke for his age. Within this relatively comfortable milieu, however, a number of writers became interested in exploring the darker regions of their own psyches. In Gray's 'Elegy Written in a Country Churchyard,' for example, the narrator eventually imagines his own death, burial, and epitaph: 'He gave to Misery all he had.' Such dismal visions seemed most readily inspired by a correspondingly dismal setting, and at least as conducive as graveyards to thoughts of human mortality were the outward and visible signs of architectural decay. The hero of David Mallet's *Excursion* (1826) had encountered terrors in 'an awful *Pile*, ... where *Ruin* dreary dwells.' Almost a century later the tradition of feeling sad near ruins had become such a commonplace that Thomas Love Peacock could satirize it by pointedly providing his lovelorn hero with all the necessary props: 'The terrace terminated at the southwestern tower, which, as we have said was ruinous and full of owls. Here would Scythrop take his evening seat, on a fallen fragment of mossy stone, with his back resting against the ruined wall, – a thick canopy of ivy, with an owl in it, over his head, – and the Sorrows of Werther in his hand.'[34]

The sentimental movement became most often associated with Gothic ruins, those being the ruins most evident in England, and, by extension, with Gothic architecture in general. Horace Walpole used various medieval trappings to create the melodramatic mood of *The Castle of Otranto*: Manfred's son is 'dashed to pieces, and almost buried under an enormous helmet, ... shaded with a proportionable quantity of black feathers'; Isabella flees through the 'several intricate cloisters' that form the 'lower part' of Manfred's castle.

Although genuine age undoubtedly made its contribution to the *de mortuis* theme inspired by medieval buildings, enthusiasts were willing to construct new Gothic structures where no old ones proved convenient. Even ruins could be conterfeited. Thomas Whately recommended Tintern Abbey as a suitable model for 'fictitious ruins,' claiming that it suggested 'every idea which can occur in a seat of devotion, solitude, and desolation.' In addition to ruins, Gothic follies, gatehouses, hermit cells, and even battlemented cowsheds gained considerable popularity as garden ornaments. On a larger scale, neo-Gothic churches and country houses began to appear, fanciful rebels against the established classical style. Horace Walpole built his own Castle of Otranto at Strawberry Hill. However, his attempt to re-create 'true rust' and 'barbarism' was so greatly tempered by his insistence on 'modern refinements in Luxury' that Strawberry Hill, like other eighteenth-century castle houses, completely lacks the frightening and provocative desolation of a good ruin.[35]

Until the latter part of the eighteenth century, most experiments in sentimental gloom had about them a comfortable, somewhat playful quality. Writers found sweetness in sadness; like Lady Elizabeth Seymour, they appreciated scenes of 'glorious horror and terrible delight.' Eventually, however, this neat system of emotional checks and balances gave way to the full-fledged glorification of emotional intensity that characterized early nineteenth-century Romanticism. Wordsworth claimed that 'all good poetry is the spontaneous overflow of powerful feelings.' Shelley, yearning for the freedom of the wind, experienced the full misery of his earth-bound state: 'I fall upon the thorns of life! I bleed!'[36]

Just as the range of interesting emotional experience widened, so too the architectural sources of inspiration became more varied. The melancholy attractions of Gothic ruins were acknowledged in Wordsworth's *Prelude*, where a wren sang 'so sweetly 'mid the gloom' of a ruined abbey. But the monuments of antiquity proved at least as interesting as those of England. Byron found in the ruins of Rome an overwhelming tragedy. He applied the Gothic imagery of moonlight and darkness to a Classical setting, using it to suggest cosmic destruction rather than titillating horror:

> Chaos of ruins! who shall trace the void,
> O'er the dim fragments cast a lunar light,
> And say, here was or is, where all is doubly night?

Keats, on seeing the sculptures that once adorned the Parthenon in Athens, can barely comprehend 'such dis-conceivéd glories of the brain.' Coleridge's famous 'pleasure dome' in Xanadu was based on an opium dream inspired, in turn, by a book about the medieval Chinese emperor Kublai Khan.[37]

The architecture of the early nineteenth century clearly reflected the romantic fascination with a wide range of antiquities. The Gothic style was no longer relegated to the fringes of architectural fashion. The classical styles became more varied, imitating the diversified ruins of different ancient cultures. A cottage at Brighton sprouted arcades, minarets, and domes, to become the Prince Regent's own oriental pleasure palace.

While some eighteenth-century romantics were still seeking the pleasures of melancholy amid Gothic ruins at home, others were pursuing the advancement of learning by recording the antiquities of distant lands. In the 1750s a number of expeditions, often led by architects and equipped with good draughtsmen, set out to explore, measure, draw, and describe the architectural treasures of the ancient world. Back home the drawings and descriptions were published in fine folio volumes that acquainted the world at large with the true nature of antique art.

Probably the most ambitious and influential of these undertakings was the expedition organized by the painter James Stuart and the architect Nicholas Revett, who spent the years between 1751 and 1754 recording the monuments of Greece. Stuart and Revett were following in the wake of other recent investigators, but they considered the earlier accounts 'rather calculated to raise our admiration than to satisfy our curiosity, or improve our taste.'[38] The records produced in their five-volume *Antiquities of Athens* (1762–1830) were scrupulously accurate, based on exact measurements and faithful attention to detail.

In their insistence on accuracy, Stuart and Revett were part of a new generation of classicists. The discoveries about ancient Greek architecture led to an interest in Grecian ruins in Italy that had previously been disregarded, and similar attentions were bestowed on newly discovered Roman ruins. Robert Wood and James Dawkin produced *Palmyra* in 1753 and *Balbec* in 1757, illustrating and describing the late Roman ruins in Turkey. Jealous of these efforts, which he claimed to be 'false as hell,' Robert Adam took time off from his broader study of Italian architecture to gather the material for his *Ruins of the Palace of the Emperor Diocletian at Spalato in Dalmatia*, published in 1764. William Chambers, who was to become Adam's main rival as an English architect, published *Designs of Chinese Buildings* in 1757, two

3   'A View of the Eastern Portico of the Parthenon,' from James Stuart's and Nicholas Revett's *The Antiquities of Athens*, volume II, 1825

years after the appearance of Richard Pococke's equally exotic *Travels in Egypt*. By 1819 recording Classical monuments had become so fashionable that the French Gourbillon could complain, 'There is not a temple standing, not a temple lost, not a god, not a marble, not a stone, which has not been quoted, described, praised, baptized, debaptized and measured in every way.'[39]

The ancient buildings of England were by no means neglected during this period, but the aims and inspirations of the researchers at home seem to have been subtly different from those of the adventurers abroad. Although some substantial pioneering works had been produced in the late seventeenth and early eighteenth centuries, the mid-century, during which there was remarkable activity in the realm of Classical scholarship, produced relatively little on England's medieval monuments. When the interest in Gothic subjects revived, it was strongly influenced by the sentimental literature of the day, and the illustrated books published later in the century tend to emphasize atmosphere at the expense of detail. It was not until 1808 that the *Gentleman's Magazine*, a popular journal which devoted a good deal of space to views of Gothic architecture, included detailed scale drawings of such an influential building as Westminster Abbey. John Britton, whose popular *Architectural Antiquities* appeared between 1807 and 1826, still claimed in 1812 that 'the greater number of readers require variety, picturesque effect and general views.' By 1814 he recognized the need for a more systematic approach and accurate details to please 'many architects and men of science,' but only his last volume was clearly aimed at this discerning audience.[40]

While the Romantics made the past seem alluring in its remoteness, the antiquarians made at least the material circumstances of ancient life seem more accessible. Increasingly, architects or patrons who wanted a particular style of building could draw on detailed archeological knowledge of size, details, and modes of construction, rather than having to depend on vague impressionistic allusions to an era. Moreover, the research had revealed the great variety in ancient styles, and the early-nineteenth-century mind exulted in the heterogeneity of its new-found knowledge, savouring the differences between architectural eras and priding itself on knowing what they were. Loudon's popular *Encyclopaedia of Cottage, Farm and Villa Architecture* (1823) contains a brief discussion of various styles 'well known by architects'; it includes 'Grecian architecture of the Romans,' 'Modern Roman, or Italian,' 'Chinese,' 'Hindoo,' and 'Indian Gothic' (also called 'Arabian,' 'Saracenic,' or 'Moorish'). His sample buildings provide further refinements of terminology. There is an inn in 'Italian Gothic,' an 'Anglo-Italian' villa, an 'Old Scotch' villa, quite different from the 'Mansion in the style of the Scotch Baronial House of the Sixteenth Century,' and, rather confusingly, a villa in the 'latest style of pointed architecture.' Nor is Louden completely bound by the past: his eclecticism is sufficiently wide-ranging to include a 'German Swiss' style cottage and several villas modelled after various railway stations. Indeed, modelling one's creations on particular buildings or particular types of buildings was much in the vogue: John Plaw included in his *Ferme Ornée or Rural Improvements* (1800) a 'Design for a Farm House ... Having the Appearance of a Monastery.' The individual pavilions at Thomas Jefferson's University of Virginia (built between 1821 and 1826) used motifs from Diocletian's Baths, the Temple of Fortuna Virilis, the Theatre of Marcellus, and other Roman structures.[41] The architecture of the early nineteenth century was blatantly based on the last century's learning, and its erudition was meant to be recognized.

It is against this background that Anna Jameson's uncertainty about the style of the London, Upper Canada, courthouse can be understood. Mrs Jameson was not given to admitting uncertainty on many issues, but anyone in the know realized that assessing architectural styles was a matter for connoisseurs. Her friend's arch classification of 'somewhat gothic' is admittedly rather disappointing; in an age of 'Indian Gothic,' 'Italian Gothic,' 'Scotch Baronial,' and 'Norman,' 'Early English,' 'Decorated,' and 'Perpendicular Gothic,'[42] his reply seems both less imaginative and less informed than Mrs Jameson might have wished.

THE CLASSICAL TRADITION AND THE COURTHOUSE

The gentleman is right, if rather dull; for by the standards of the 1830s the courthouse is only 'somewhat Gothic.' It has some features of a Gothic castle, superimposed, in a manner typical of its time, on a building whose design

4 'The Five Orders of Architecture with their Pedestals,' from Isaac Ware's
A Complete Body of Architecture, 1756

is indebted to a complex tradition of classical architecture. It shows the
immediate influence of the Palladian and Neoclassical movements of eighteenth-
century England. These in turn received their inspiration from earlier eras;
the Palladians looked back to the revival of Roman architecture in the Italian
Renaissance; Neoclassicism was inspired by the archaeological researches
of the eighteenth century. Like other examples of nineteenth-century revival
styles, the courthouse can be appreciated only when one recognizes the long
history of classical and Gothic traditions on which it relies.[43] These two crucial
influences will be examined in turn.

Classical architecture has its foundations in the architecture of ancient
Greece. Greek buildings were based on an elementary principle of construction: a vertical post supported a horizontal beam. Over the course of several
centuries, however, both the post and the beam underwent a process of
refinement and definition. The beam became an entablature, consisting of an
architrave, frieze, and cornice, apparently descended from the girders, joists,
and eaves of their wooden ancestors. The posts evolved into three basic types
of columns, originating in Doris, Ionia, and Corinth, respectively, and distinguished largely by their capitals (fig. 4). The Doric was the simplest, consisting of unadorned moldings around the shaft. The Ionic capital featured a spiral
scroll, the Corinthian a less pronounced scroll and rows of acanthus leaves.
Even the exquisite Parthenon, like most Greek temples, consisted structurally
of a low-pitched roof resting on a horizontal entablature, supported on all

four sides by a continuous colonnade, with a shallow gable, or pediment, at each end.

Each style of column, combined with its own distinctive entablature, represented an order, and each order had an individual character derived largely from its proportions. The robust Doric required the thickest shaft, and the delicate, ornate Corinthian the most slender. When the Roman Vitruvius described the orders in the first century AD, he saw 'the proportion, strength and grace of a man's body' in the Doric order, and 'feminine slenderness' in the Ionic. He compared the Corinthian to 'the slight figure of a girl,' an image later abused by the Renaissance Englishman Sir Henry Wotton, who vented his dislike of the ornate order by saying it was 'decked out like a wanton courtezan.'[44] These orders with their attendant emphasis on proportion were to form the basis of all later classical architecture.

The Romans, inheritors of the Greek architectural tradition, greatly enlarged the technical repertoire of the builder. Their main contribution to the art of construction was the development of the semi-circular arch. To build such an arch, wedge-shaped stones are arranged on a properly shaped piece of scaffolding, called centring, which supports the lower elements until the keystone is in place; once that has been accomplished, weights above the arch actually make it firmer, so that the arch is able to carry large loads. The load-bearing capacities of the arch and the Roman invention of mortar and concrete made possible the erection of buildings several storeys high. The arch also presented new possibilities for covering a large area with a roof. A series of intersecting arches meeting in the same centre is called a dome. A series of arches built one behind the other will create a tunnel with an arch-shaped ceiling, called, appropriately, a tunnel or barrel vault. The disadvantage of the barrel vault is that it causes a rather dark interior: because an arch exerts continuous pressure towards its sides, the barrel vault needs to be supported by very thick walls which can be pierced only with caution and difficulty. The Romans solved this problem with the groin vault, created by two intersecting barrel vaults. With the groin vault, the thrust is concentrated in the four corners of the vaulting bay, and windows can be inserted safely in the walls between the corner supports.

Although the development of the arch sometimes made columns superfluous as a means of support, the Romans clung to the esthetic tradition developed by the Greeks, adapting the Greek orders to suit their architectural needs. One popular Roman form, for example, was the triumphal arch (fig. 5), usually erected to honour a victorious military commander. Surviving examples of this genre feature one large central arch, sometimes flanked by two smaller arches, supporting a superstructure with an explanatory inscription and appropriately symbolic sculpture. But the dominant decorative elements are the columns and entablatures that frame each arch and even appear to support the inscribed block. Though structurally unnecessary, the order still controls the proportions and influences the form of the entire structure.

Certainly the Romans did use columns for support as well as decoration.

5   Arch of Constantine, Rome, illustration published in Luigi Canina's *Gli edifizj di Roma antica cogniti per alcune reliquie descritti e dimostrati nell'intera loro architettura*, volume IV, 1851

They built round and rectangular temples surrounded by columns in the Greek fashion. They built large halls – for baths, basilicas, villas, and palaces – in which columns supported a vault or a dome. Often the column formed the side of an arch, with its capital or entablature acting as the impost from which the arch springs. Even in these instances, however, builders chose to use columns not because they had no other choice, but because the orders represented true beauty and elegance.

While revering the esthetic principle of Greek architecture, the Romans did 'improve' the orders. They generally made the Greek columns more slender and the capitals more ornate, and they added two new orders to the established canon. The Tuscan is even simpler and heavier than the Doric; the Composite elongates the spectrum of possibilities at its other end, combining the Ionic and the Corinthian to form an order more ornate than either (fig. 4).

During the fourth and fifth centuries Rome and the western part of its massive empire succumbed to attacks from Germanic tribes. The immediately succeeding centuries lacked the political and social stability and the cultural milieu necessary even to preserve the legacy of Roman architecture; most monuments of antiquity were gradually destroyed and the esthetic principles upon which they were based forgotten. It was only in the fifteenth and sixteenth centuries that several Italian architects set out to rediscover the true nature of their classical heritage and published their findings.

6   Palazzo Porto, Vicenza, Italy, from Giacomo Leoni's *The Architecture of A. Palladio; In Four Books*, book II, 1715

The most influential of these treatises were undoubtedly *The Four Books of Architecture* (1570) by Andrea Palladio, who, like many of his contemporaries, thought that 'the ancient Romans vastly excelled all those who have been since their time.' Palladio's work is very practical in its orientation. Though eager to make some theoretical points, he is always careful to show how theory can be put into practice. Asserting that 'beauty will result from the form and correspondence of the whole,' he provides detailed drawings of each of the orders, with measurements and proportions indicated, and he gives formulas for determining the harmonious dimensions of rooms, doors, and windows. Palladio's style is formal, correct, and rational, following what he sees as the example of Nature. Thus columns, like trees, should be 'thicker at the top than at the bottom,' and the rooms of a house should be arranged like the parts of the human body:

But as Our Blessed Creator has ordered these our members in such a manner, that the most beautiful are in places most exposed to view, and the less comely more hidden; so in building also, we ought to put the principal and considerable parts, in places the most seen, and the less beautiful, in places as much hidden from the eye as possible; that in them may be lodged all the foulness of the house ... I approve therefore that in the lowest part of the fabric, which I make somewhat underground, may be disposed the cellars, the magazines for wood, pantries, kitchens, servants-halls, wash-houses, ovens, and such like things necessary for daily use.

The state apartments were to be on the floor above, the *piano nobile*, for 'upper appartments are wholesomer to live in, the floor being at a distance from the damps of the ground; besides as it rises it is more agreeable to be looked at, and to look out of.'[45]
    Palladio's ideas on the disposal of rooms follow a precedent that was well established by his time, and contemporary architects in Rome had developed a format for the exterior façade of an urban *palazzo* that reflected each storey's interior function. The utilitarian ground floor featured a relatively plain and often rusticated surface; the surface of the *piano nobile* was more elegant in its smoothness and more distinguished in its ornamentation. Palladio used this pattern in his various designs for the Palazzo Porto in Vicenza (c. 1549). The version included in *The Four Books of Architecture* (fig. 6) shows a rusticated ground floor, an especially ornate *piano nobile* where engaged Ionic columns alternate with pedimented windows, and a simpler attic storey with its characteristically smaller windows. Palladio's application of the Roman pattern is somewhat misleading here, however, because he copied the ancients in making the ground floor of the Palazzo Porto a living area.[46]
    That Palladio felt it necessary to include only half of the façade in his *Four Books* clearly indicates his period's insistence on symmetry. The drawing is rather curious in some other respects. Though published after the Palazzo Porto was constructed, the drawing shows a façade more ornate than it actually was; recumbent figures and garlands decorated only the end and central bays of the built edifice, and there were fewer standing statues.

This emphasis on sculptural details is typical of a contemporary architectural movement now called 'Mannerism,' though most of Palladio's own work falls outside its domain. An attitude of playful irreverence towards the Classical forms, inspired largely by the work of Michelangelo, had become apparent in architecture. The results are described as 'mannered' because they call attention to the shapes themselves, using them in ways that deprive them of their original meaning: pediments are broken; window surrounds are designed to make windows look further recessed than they are; entablatures are subtly changed; familiar shapes are so manipulated as to give them a more sculptural, three-dimensional quality. Moreover, surfaces are often covered with sculptured designs, such as garlands, scrolls, strapwork, busts, or human figures. As Mannerist tendencies became more extreme, Mannerist became Baroque, a term that initially meant strange or odd, and came to be applied to architecture that luxuriated in powerful expressions or contortions of classical forms. Baroque architecture is emphatically sculptured, using large-scale, three-dimensional decorations, moulding entire walls into unexpected curvaceous shapes, creating and controlling interesting vistas. John Summerson, comparing architecture to language, describes Mannerism as 'an affectation,' and Baroque as rhetoric, 'in the sense of grandiloquent, contrived, persuasive oratory.'[47]

Throughout Europe the Renaissance of the fifteenth and sixteenth centuries produced a revival of interest in Greek and Roman thought. As part of this movement the Italian revival of Classical architecture gradually spread northwards, sometimes blending with an established local form to produce a structure undreamed of in Rome, ancient or modern. In the Loire Valley of France, for example, a Romantic attachment to the medieval castle led to the Renaissance chateau, a structure with the moat, towers, turrets and symmetrical plan of late medieval castles, adorned with classical pilasters, carvings, and balustrades.

Classicism in architecture did not reach Britain until the reign of the Stuarts; then in the course of one century it ran through all its phases. Inigo Jones became surveyor of the king's works in 1615. He had travelled in Italy, carrying his own copy of Palladio's *Four Books* and making extensive marginal annotations as he went, and the buildings he designed, such as the Queen's House at Greenwich, are very disciplined and refined essays in the Palladian manner. Despite his influential position, Jones's style did not become popular beyond the court. The style usually associated with the term 'Jacobean' is indebted to Flemish Mannerism rather than to Roman antiquarianism. Ornate sculpture and strapwork infiltrated the Elizabethan Great House, and Jacobean architecture features profuse ornamentation and a correspondingly crowded massing of exterior elements. The Baroque had a rich but brief life during the Restoration. In London Christopher Wren designed St Paul's Cathedral and a series of remarkable steeples for the parish churches that had to be rebuilt after the Great Fire of 1688. Sir John Vanbrugh and Nicholas Hawksmoor created, among other marvels, Blenheim Palace (1705-24) as a highly original national monument honouring the Duke of Marlborough.

The accession of George I to the British throne (1714) facilitated the development of strong ministerial government. The Act of Settlement had decreed that, after Queen Anne's death, the crown would pass to the German House of Hanover rather than to the son of the banished James II. Since the first two Georges never fully appreciated their good fortune, spending most of their time and emotional energy on Hanover, the Whig ministers were able to assume more of the duties and privileges of leadership, including patronage of the arts. Thus, the arbiter of architectural taste for the first half of the eighteenth century came to be Richard Boyle, Lord Burlington, a member of the Privy Council, lord high treasurer of Ireland, and an enthusiastic gentleman architect.

Burlington had visited Italy on the Grand Tour, already becoming fashionable as part of a young man's education; his experiences there prepared him to be an enthusiastic supporter of a movement heralded by two books published in 1715, the year of his return to England. One was the first English translation of Palladio's *Four Books*; the second was the first volume of *Vitruvius Britannicus*, written by a Scottish architect named Colin Campbell. Campbell's ostensible aim was to prove the high quality of British architecture by publishing drawings of the most worthy buildings; in his view these ranged from structures by the most well-known classical architects of the previous century – Jones, Wren, Vanbrugh, and Hawksmoor among them – to unexecuted designs by Campbell himself. Campbell's criteria, however, were fairly narrow. He preferred 'antique Simplicity' to the 'wildly Extravagant ... Designs' of the more flamboyant Baroque works, but, despite his allusion to Vitruvius, he preferred the Renaissance 'Restorers of *Architecture*' to the ancients themselves. He particularly admired 'the great *Palladio*, who has exceeded all that were gone before him.'[48] Burlington was so impressed by *Vitruvius Britannicus* that he put himself under Campbell's tutelage, and in 1719 he rounded off his education with a second trip to Italy, undertaken with the express purpose of studying Palladio's buildings and collecting his drawings. One of Alexander Pope's 'Epistles,' addressed to Burlington, lauds the new 'Palladianism':

Erect new wonders, and the old repair;
Jones and Palladio to themselves restore,
And be whatever Vitruvius was before.[49]

The town house in Whitehall that Campbell designed for Lord Pembroke (c. 1724; fig. 7) illustrates the Palladians' debt to their master. Strong horizontal lines divide the building into the traditional three levels: a raised basement, the *piano nobile*, and an attic storey that breaks with convention by holding a 'magnificently finished' gallery overlooking the Thames. The building resembles a *villa*, or country house, by Palladio in having a central portico as its most prominent feature, but it draws on the Roman *palazzo* for its particular

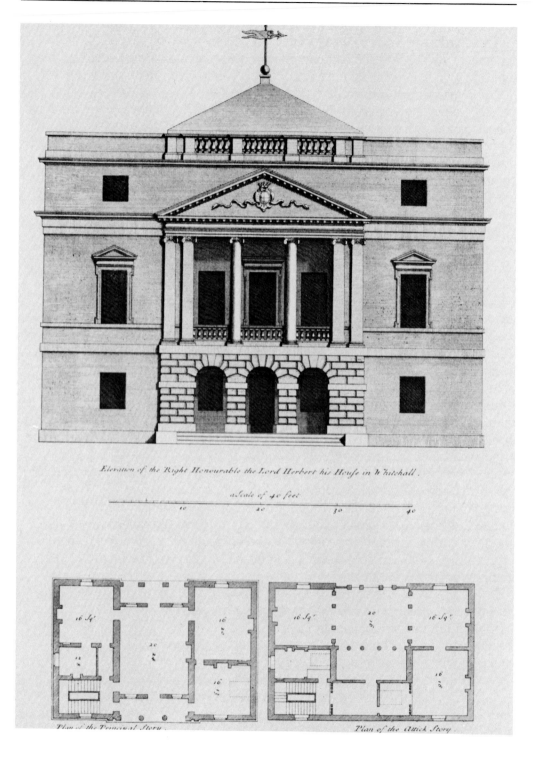

Elevation of the Right Honourable the Lord Herbert his House in Whitehall.

a Scale of 40 feet

Plan of the Principal Story.   Plan of the Attick Story.

7   'Elevation of the Right Honourable the Lord Herbert [Pembroke] his House in
Whitehall [London, England],' from Colin Campbell's *Vitruvius Britannicus; Or the
British Architect*, volume III, 1725

organization: a rusticated arcade leads into the ground floor entrance; above, an Ionic order and a balustrade adorn a loggia, or porch, accessible from the *piano nobile*. The building as a whole demonstrated the 'Simplicity,' 'Regularity,' 'Beauty,' and 'Majesty' that Campbell and Burlington, the British Vitruvii, decreed.[50]

The history of architecture in Upper Canada begins with the Palladian style.[51] Soldiers and governors brought from Britain their understanding of the latest architectural fashion; the Loyalists came with their memories of American versions of Palladianism. Since settlers often had to wait years, or even decades, before erecting buildings with any claim to grandeur, the style thrived in Canada until well into the nineteenth century. Because most 'Georgian' buildings in Upper Canada were relatively modest, they often used simplified Palladian forms such as those found in James Gibb's *A Book of Architecture* (1728), where, for example, the central portico may be reduced to a pedimented projection; or they applied the concepts of regularity and symmetry with no allusion to the more specific parts of a Palladian building.

The archeological investigations that took place from the mid-eighteenth century on showed that Greek and Roman architecture was more varied than Vitruvius and the Renaissance writers had acknowledged it to be, and the Neoclassical movement that these researches provoked looked more directly to the works of the ancients for inspiration. Robert Adam's observations of Roman ruins led him to deduce that 'the proportions of columns depend on their situation'[52] and gave him a broad repertoire of new forms later to be incorporated in his own architecture: oval rooms; concave surfaces; the motifs found in his delicate, Wedgwood-like interior designs; and the intricately manipulated wall planes that became a prominent feature of his exterior designs. Often, for example, he set doors and windows in blind, recessed arches, while pilasters, string courses, or entablatures protruded from the wall. Adam liked shallow surface treatments, so that the recesses and projections were very slight. But because he minimized other textural effects, working with smooth walls and often eliminating window moldings, the variations in planes created a distinct pattern, just as double layers of matting board can surround a picture with a frame within a frame.

While the ruins of Imperial Rome were encouraging greater lightness and delicacy in architectural forms, the newly discovered buildings of Greece struck some viewers as disappointingly heavy. When Goethe first saw the Greek ruins at Paestum in Sicily he found the 'crowded masses of stumpy conical columns ... offensive ... and even terrifying.' William Chambers, Adam's contemporary and main rival, saw architecture as a progressive art in which the Greeks were more proficient only than their predecessors, the Egyptians, and thus were deserving of 'little or no Notice' from the sophisticated critics of the eighteenth century. He observed that the Lysicrates Monument had the 'Form and Proportions of a silver Tankard excepting that the Handle is wanting,' and he judged the Parthenon less impressive in size and style than 'many of our Parish Churches.'[53]

Chambers's progressive theory of art ran against an influential current in

8   London District Court House, London, as originally designed in 1827 by John Ewart; photograph by John Kyle O'Connor, 1875

the eighteenth-century stream of thought. Philosophical arguments in favour of man's essential goodness developed as a corollary the theories that civilization corrupts and 'savages' are noble. The corresponding architectural theory, labelled 'rationalism,' was put forward most convincingly by the Abbé Laugier in his *Essai sur l'architecture* (1753), where he presented the primitive 'rustic cabin' as 'the model upon which all the magnificences of architecture have been imagined.'[54] He argued further that many of these magnificences, including most of the established classical vocabulary, should be discarded. Ideally, a building should be reduced to its essential elements. This theory underlay the widespread evidence of simplification one finds in Neoclassical architecture. Engaged columns may be reduced to plain pilaster strips, or entablatures between storeys to simple unadorned string courses.

The respect for the primitive intrinsic in Laugier's theory also serves, rather paradoxically, to elevate the authority of Greek architecture on the grounds of its age alone. Unlike Roman ruins, however, those of Greece offered little inspiration for the plan of an eighteenth- or nineteenth-century building; the temple seemed a rather specialized form. The British solution was generally to apply Greek columns and porticoes to structures otherwise owing little to Greece. In the United States, where its republican associations made the Greek Revival a national obsession, the impracticality of the temple plan was in no way daunting, and buildings of all sorts were forced into its mould. Canada borrowed from both countries. In Britain the Neoclassicism based on Roman forms preceded the Greek Revival, and in the United States the Greek Revival temporarily eclipsed other styles. In Canada, Roman and Greek revivals

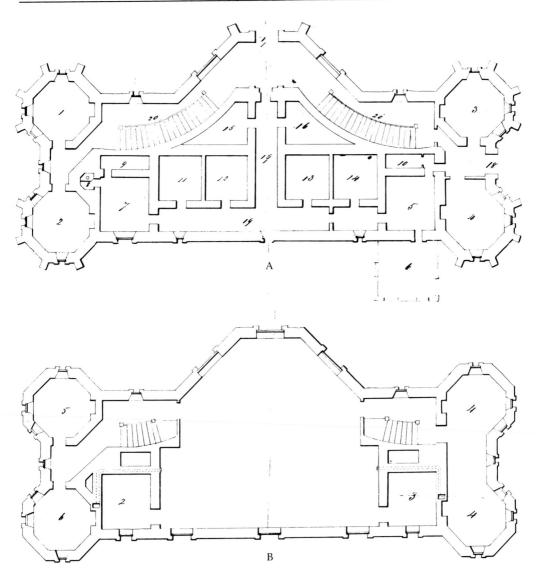

9   London District Court House, London, ground (A) and second floor (B) plans submitted to colonial government in 1839

appeared simultaneously around 1820, and both enjoyed a long and happy life extending into the 1860s.[55]

Ewart's design for the London District Court House (fig. 8) was very much the product of the classical tradition as it was interpreted by the eighteenth and early nineteenth centuries. Constructed of brick faced with stucco, it had the smooth surface typical of Neoclassical architecture. The plainness of the string courses and of the door and window surrounds accentuates this smoothness, but these features project just far enough from the wall to give the sense of layered surfaces beloved by Adam and his successors. The river façade was dominated by a large, protruding, polygonal bay. Again, the arrangement was common, a development from Adam's interest in oval and circular shapes. The courthouse bay extended upwards to the top of the building, creating in effect a massive fifth tower. Plans submitted to the colonial government in 1839 (fig. 9) show that the ground floor of this imposing bay accommodated the main entrance hall, with two curved flights of stairs forming an elegant approach to the courtroom above.[56]

The town side of the London courthouse depends on the Palladian tradition of the earlier eighteenth century, though the Palladian ideas are treated in the simplified, abstract fashion often found in Neoclassical structures. Underlying the arrangement of elements on the courthouse façade is the *palazzo* format. The tall, pointed windows adorn the *piano nobile*, where the stately courtroom is located. The shorter windows below are set in the utilitarian basement level, apparently used here to jail felons and debtors, while more dangerous villains were placed behind the small windows of the attic story. The pointed windows pull one's eye towards the centre of the building, just as a classical portico would, and, in fact, the battlements directly above rise towards the centre in a manner faintly suggestive of a pediment. Finally, the overall dimensions of the courthouse, approximately fifty by fifty by a hundred feet,[57] reflect the Palladian concern with clearly controlled proportions; indeed the measurements of Palladio's façades are sometimes based on the same 1:2 ratio.

THE GOTHIC TRADITION AND THE COURTHOUSE

The courthouse is nevertheless 'somewhat Gothic.' Since the towers, battlements, and pointed windows all point clearly towards medieval sources, the teasing part of this phrase is still the 'somewhat,' even after one has noted the strongly classical character of the building. The full explanation of the term lies in the new understanding of Gothic architecture that was just beginning to be widely influential: the realization that the Gothic style, as it developed between the twelfth and sixteenth centuries, was basically functional; that the Gothic forms had structural as well as decorative importance.

The Gothic style had its roots in what is now called Romanesque architecture,[58] a label alluding to the vestiges of Roman tradition that endured throughout the centuries pejoratively referred to as the Dark Ages. The main repositories of classical learning during this period were the monasteries, and the focus of their architectural efforts was, of course, the church.

The monks followed Roman Christians in adopting the basilica as a model. Romanesque architecture also made liberal use of the Roman round-headed arch – for windows, arcades between naves and aisles, and barrel and groin vaults in naves and crypts. Columns did continue to be used with some frequency, supporting an arcade, embedded in a moulding, or embellishing a pier; vestiges of a classical capital, especially of the Corinthian, appear in numerous Romanesque churches. But their entablatures have disappeared,

10   'West Front of Castle-Rising Church [Norfolk, England],' from John Sell Cotman's *Specimens of Architectural Remains in Various Counties in England, but Principally in Norfolk*, volume I, 1838

their shafts are usually thicker than classical decorum would have sanctioned, and their capitals may feature shapes and designs unknown to Rome. The full implications of the orders were forgotten or ignored.

What dictated the important decorative and structural themes of the Romanesque church was not classical propriety, but Christian devotion. The wall and ceiling surfaces of Romanesque churches were often covered with bright, gilded paintings, depicting scenes from the great story of salvation. The shape of the church was altered to meet increasing liturgical needs: transepts held special participants in the service; the apse became longer to hold a choir and subsidiary chapels; higher ceilings contributed to a sense of awe and mystery. These changes were mirrored in the building's external appearance. Looking at a Romanesque church from outside, one can tell how long the nave is, how many transepts there are, how many chapels branch off from the apse and transepts, and how much room is reserved for the choir and altar. Externally as well as internally the Romanesque church took on a character of its own: massive; dominating its setting; its uneven silhouette, broken by various kinds of towers, clearly indicating its liturgical function.

The appearance of the Romanesque church also revealed a good deal about the way in which it was built, and it developed new structural techniques that were eventually to become decorative in themselves. A consideration of the way in which a Romanesque doorway was constructed illustrates the point. Since Romanesque walls were very thick, elaborate centring was required to build an arch that would go through them. If one built a relatively slender arch in the middle of the wall's thickness, however, that arch could act as the centring for slightly higher arches in front of and behind it. This process could be continued until the complex of arches reached the necessary depth. Thus the Romanesque doorway came to consist of a series of concentric arches, fanning out from the lowest section. A similar technique solved a like problem in relation to the ceiling vaults. Moulded arches, or 'ribs,' built along the intersecting lines of a groin vault could then support the other vaulting stones in that bay. The rib could be carried right down the wall of the church to the floor, accentuating the vertical thrust of the building and, simultaneously, calling attention to the way in which the structure was engineered.

These structural elements achieved greater prominence in the style we now label Gothic. During the twelfth century there were built in and around Paris a number of churches that possessed a character distinctively different from that of their Romanesque predecessors. From Paris the style spread throughout Europe, partly because of the theological influence of the University of Paris and the School of Chartres, and partly because the new churches embodied attitudes rapidly gaining currency throughout Europe.[59]

One way in which Gothic churches differed from Romanesque was in their utilization of structural elements for decorative purposes. The concentric arches were more elegantly moulded and the lines of ribbing multiplied, so that a cross-section of a supporting pier, like the ribbed vaults, created an intricate geometrical pattern. Another distinguishing aspect of the new style was its yearning for light. The style made its first appearance in the rebuilt apse of the church at the royal Abbey of St Denis, consecrated in 1144, where the large stained glass windows enabled the Abbé Suger to admire 'a sanctuary ... pervaded by a wonderful and continuous light.' Christianity had always associated light with God, but the theme took on a special fascination during the last centuries of the Middle Ages. God was light, suffusing and nourishing his creation, unifying all things. One thirteenth-century lyric, partly in English and partly in Latin, prays that the Virgin Mary, who is 'brighter than the

11   'Salisbury Cathedral Church [Wiltshire, England], View from the South Transept, Looking N.W.,' from John Britton's *The History and Antiquities of the Cathedral Church of Salisbury*, 1814

dayes light' and was able to counteract Eve's eternal night by bearing 'the day / *Salutis*' (the day of Salvation), will bring all people to Christ '*In luce*' (in light).[60] Where the Romanesque church provided a bright painting of God, the Gothic church was to be permeated by natural light, sometimes diffused by stained glass.

Of the technical features that made the Gothic style possible, the most important was undoubtedly the pointed arch. The disadvantage with the Roman groin vault was that it required square bays: the intersecting vaults needed to have identical diameters in order to reach identical heights. A vault built with a pointed arch could reach the necessary height from openings of any width, thus permitting rectangular bays. The thrust of the vault could thus be concentrated in a greater number of points, each of which could use a correspondingly more slender support. Used in conjunction with the flying buttress, by which part of the thrust was deflected to a pier beyond the external wall, the pointed arch made possible the large windows that define the Gothic cathedral and also allowed the elaboration of complex vaulting designs, which, reflected in the mouldings of piers and arches, transformed the entire church into an intricate stone sculpture.

Gothic architecture developed along distinctive lines in different countries. The evolution of English Gothic is usually measured in three stages, defined by the style of the windows and the character of the masonry. Early English churches (c. 1175–1300) usually have lancet windows and simple ribbed vaults. The larger windows of the Decorated style (c. 1250–1350) are supported by stone mullions shaped into fairly ornate designs, and the vaults contain more ribs. The Perpendicular style (c. 1350–1550) is aptly described by its name: the windows, now taking up most of the wall space, feature repeated vertical mullions, rising right to the top of the arch. Less closely spaced horizontal mullions produce a grid-like effect, enriched, especially near the top of the arch, by relatively simple tracery. The piers also have a strongly vertical thrust, generally unbroken by capitals, brackets, or courses. Both window and vault, on the other hand, feature shallower arches, and the ceiling introduces new wonders in the art of vaulting, such as the ornate webs of fan-vaulting in the chapel of King's College, Cambridge.

For all their importance in the development of a style, stone vaults were a luxury affordable only to the major cathedrals and the wealthiest parish churches. Most parish churches had timber roofs,[61] but they imitated their stone betters in two somewhat contradictory ways. Sometimes they displayed moulded and carved beams to emphasize the decorative aspects of the structural elements themselves. In other places the wooden ceilings tried to reproduce the effects of stone vaults; one may find a ceiling painted with ornate designs, or even a network of wooden ribs pretending to be stone.

The church was not the only significant architectural form of the medieval period. One other type of building that was to prove especially influential was the castle.[62] Castles sometimes employed a few of the Romanesque and Gothic forms developed in the churches, such as windows reflecting current

12   'Houghton in the Dale Chapel [Norfolk, England],' from John Sell Cotman's
*Specimens of Architectural Remains in Various Counties in England, but Principally
in Norfolk*, volume I, 1838

ecclesiastical styles, but the way in which the castle most resembled the cathedral was that it, too, allowed its form to be dictated by its function. In England, for example, fortresses with a walled circumference replaced the Norman keep when a garrison rather than a family needed protection inside. This curtain wall was heightened as a defence against the large trebuchers, developed towards the end of the twelfth century, which could project stones over a low wall. Towers were set at intervals in the wall to act as buttresses or to provide a view of any mining activity along its base. The parapet was sometimes built out, or machicolated, so that enemy forces could not scale the wall. The battlements along the top of a wall or tower provided openings, or crenels, for shooting arrows, and solid merlons behind which the archers could hide. Ultimately, a fortification demanded qualities diametrically opposed to the requirements of late medieval devotion: a castle needed thick walls, small windows, and an appearance of strength rather than delicacy.

The medieval tradition proved particularly persistent in England. From 1399, when Henry IV usurped the throne, and throughout most of the next century monarchs were so occupied in clinging to power that they had no opportunity to initiate massive building schemes. During the Wars of the Roses (1453–85), the medieval castle could once again prove its worth as a fortress. Henry VII's ascent to the throne initiated a long period of relative stability, when classical influences might have been felt more strongly in English architecture had not Henry VIII's break with the Catholic Church effectively cut off contact with Rome. Under Queen Elizabeth I strong nationalism combined with Protestantism to produce a Renaissance architecture based more on England's own medieval past than on Italy's Classical heritage.

Most Tudor buildings continued to use the forms and techniques that were already common in late fourteenth-century England.[63] The large windows associated with Perpendicular Gothic were often featured in both domestic and ecclesiastical architecture; bay windows and oriel windows continued to be popular. Arched windows were often placed within rectangular stone frames, the flat outline echoed in the hood-mould above. The rising mercantile and yeoman class erected large houses, using medieval techniques such as half-timbering (where the strong timbered framework was exposed to view, with plaster, brick, or wattle and daub used to fill in the interstices); gables, often numerous, were usually decorated with barge-boards, carved and ornamented like those on late medieval houses. Grander houses of the early Tudor period differed more in materials than in spirit. Even Cardinal Wolsey's Hampton Court was modelled on late medieval university architecture, and after Wolsey, in a vain attempt to keep his head, presented the palace to Henry VIII, the king added a great hall with a magnificent Gothic timber roof.

The main Tudor contribution to late Gothic architecture was a matter of emphasis rather than overall direction: the period's love of intricate patterns was reflected in its enthusiasm for devices such as the decorated barge-board, or in the way it elaborated on the designs intrinsic to certain modes of construction. In half-timbered houses, for example, the timber could be shaped into complicated patterns of rectangles and circles; vari-coloured bricks could be used to cover a house with a net of diamond shapes.

The tenaciousness of late Gothic architecture in England, has led some historians to question the term 'Gothic Revival' used in relation to buildings of the eighteenth and nineteenth centuries. But that period's widespread ignorance about the real nature of Gothic architecture contends against the argument for a continuous Gothic tradition. In many quarters the style was held in great contempt because of what were thought to be its barbaric origins, an idea promulgated by sixteenth-century Italian fictions such as the discussion of Gothic architecture in Giorgio Vasari's *Lives of the Artists* (1550): 'This manner was invented by Goths, who, after the destruction of the ancient buildings and the dying out of architects because of the wars, afterwards built – those who survived – edifices in this manner: those men fashioned the vaults with pointed arches ... and filled all Italy with these damnable buildings, so that their whole method has been given up, in order not to let any more be built.' Attempts to place the style in a less denigrating perspective concentrated exclusively on what were seen as decorative features, particularly on the shape of its windows. Thus by 1762 Thomas Warton had distinguished the 'round arches, round-headed windows, and round massy pillars' of the 'Saxon style' from the later 'Saracen fashion' of pointed arches, which had been a legacy of the Crusades. In regarding these structural features as mainly decorative, the eighteenth-century antiquarians were attributing to Gothic buildings the principles of Classical architecture: windows were to the former what the orders were to the latter. Two enthusiasts, the brothers Batty and Thomas Langley, even designed Gothic orders, complete with moulded columns and capitals and entablatures that used Gothic motifs.[64]

Because Gothic elements were regarded simply as alternative forms of decoration, they were often applied to buildings that were classical in every other respect. Such was obviously the case with the London District Court House. It boasted the four towers of the traditional dream castle, machicolated battlements, pointed windows, and even some low buttresses on the towers. The building also has a hint of the heaviness associated with a medieval fortress, caused largely by the relatively low and broad proportions of the towers and the thickness of the window frames; this sense of weight suggests strength as well as romance, and reminds one that the courthouse was also a jail. As we have seen, however, these medieval elements are imposed on a building that is classical in its dimensions, symmetry, and the basic arrangement of its façades. It is, essentially, a Neoclassical country house dressed up, in the fashion of the times, to look somewhat like a medieval fortification. But the medieval elements are meant to be seen rather than used. The buttresses are too small really to support the building, the machicolations too shallow to prevent an enemy's scaling the wall, the merlons too short to hide an archer.

The relationship between Gothic style and structure had become the subject of scholarly treatises only in the early years of the nineteenth century.[65] In

1814 an English architect named George Saunders published an account of the importance of the pointed arch in constructing a vault. Thomas Rickman, in his *Attempt to Discriminate the Styles of English Architecture* (1817), was able to distinguish 'English' from Grecian architecture on the grounds that 'English styles regard not a few parts, but the conception of the whole building,' while 'a Grecian building is denominated Doric or Ionic merely from its ornaments.' It was Rickman who introduced the labels 'Early English,' 'Decorated,' and 'Perpendicular' still used to classify the phases of English Gothic. But it was not until the decades immediately following the erection of the London courthouse that research on the principles of Gothic construction really began to flourish. William Whewell's *Architectural Notes on German Churches* (1830) expanded Saunders's observations on the functional significance of the pointed arch, and Robert Willis isolated the 'mechanical' from the 'decorative' aspects of Gothic structure in his *Remarks on the Architecture of the Middle Ages, especially of Italy* (1835).

The brilliant and eccentric Augustus Welby Pugin injected a spirit of impassioned religiousness into the subject, turning the matter of analytical inquiry into an emotional, moral issue. A converted Roman Catholic, Pugin argued in *The True Principles of Pointed or Christian Architecture* (1841) that 'pointed' architecture was the only style appropriate for churches of the 'true' faith; he also insisted that the style necessarily resulted from certain modes of construction or specific liturgical demands. Pointed architecture perfectly fulfilled the two 'great rules' for excellent design: '1st, that there should be no features about a building which are not necessary for convenience, construction, or propriety; 2nd, that all ornament should consist of enrichment of the essential construction of the building.'

Five years earlier, in 1836, Pugin had published his enormously controversial *Contrasts*, where facing illustrations of modern and medieval buildings aimed at proving the superiority of the latter, on the grounds of their attractiveness and of the moral and spiritual superiority. Combining humour with didacticism, he also provided contrasting title pages, and the modern one, obviously meant to appear plain and unimaginative next to its companion, featured samples of Gothic edifices in 'the new square style,' similar in approach to Ewart's courthouse. Pugin was later to object to the use of the castellated style in any modern context, since it no longer served its original defensive function.[66] If Anna Jameson's friend was really up on current architectural trends, he would have known in 1837 that the old approach of applying Gothic details to classical buildings was becoming somewhat suspect.

It is possible, though not probable, that Ewart's courthouse did reflect some awareness of the new research in its interior design. The courtroom extended the entire depth of the building, and, according to Edward Allen Talbot's eulogy in *The London Sun* of 7 July 1831, it possessed considerable elegance: 'The Court room is finished in a very superior manner. The windows, which are six in number, and truly Gothic, are surrounded by eliptical arches, supported by pillars nearly 20 feet high. Arches also spring from four of those pillars, which passing across the angles of the room, make the ceiling an octagon, and, ornamented as it is, it adds much to the beauty of the room.' Talbot's description gets higher grades for enthusiasm than for clarity, and a reader cannot be certain whether the 'octagon' was an imaginative way of perceiving an authentic quadripartite Gothic vault or, perhaps an ingenious Regency variation on classical vaulting. Elliptical arches sound more classical than Gothic, and Ewart was most likely following the practice defended by Humphrey Repton in his *Inquiry Into the Changes in Landscape Gardening* (1806): 'it is unnecessary to retain the Gothic character within the mansions, at least farther than the hall, as it would subject such buildings to much inconvenience.'[67]

ARCHITECTURAL TASTE: THE PICTURESQUE

That a landscape architect like Humphrey Repton should at all interest himself in the interior and exterior design of buildings is the result of a second important movement in early nineteenth-century thought: the formulation of a new esthetic theory revolving around the idea of the 'Picturesque.' One thread of philosophical thought throughout the previous century had concerned itself with the nature and causes of 'pleasure.'[68] Joseph Addison's 'Essay on the Pleasures of the Imagination' (1712) had introduced the topic, listing the Great, the Uncommon, and the Beautiful as the three external sources of pleasure. According to Addison, the Great, or vast, leads to the contemplation of infinity and so facilitates religious devotion. The Uncommon surprises, satisfies curosity, and inspires new ideas, thus encouraging learning. Beauty, which can be found in gay colours, symmetry, and proportion, or, rather vaguely, 'in the Arrangement and Disposition of Bodies,' leads to Joy and the desire for propagation.[69]

Of the many eighteenth-century elaborations of Addison's ideas, by far the most influential was Edmund Burke's *A Philosophical Enquiry into the Origin of Our Ideas of the Sublime and Beautiful* (1757). Burke rejected Addison's concept of the Uncommon as a principal source of pleasure on the grounds of its omnipresence and its impermanence. His discussion of the Sublime relies largely on the perceptive insight that there can be pleasure in pain: 'Whatever is fitted in any sort to excite the ideas of pain and danger ... is a source of the *sublime*; that is, it is productive of the strongest emotion which the mind is capable of feeling.' Beauty, in Burke's view, is a more limited phenomenon: beauty is 'that quality or those qualities in bodies by which they cause love, or some passion similar to it.' Love is only a sense of 'satisfaction,' however, rather than a deep passion; the latter would be Sublime.[70]

In the last decade of the century Addison's category of the Uncommon was resurrected by one of Burke's disciples, Sir Uvedale Price, but under a new name, the 'Picturesque,' drawn from a different field of esthetic inquiry. A vogue for the Picturesque had developed earlier in the century. It involved evaluating scenes on the basis of their resemblance to pictures, especially those by well-known landscape painters such as Nicholas Poussin (1594–1665) and Claude Lorrain (1600–82). It also involved efforts to make country estates into the

13   Tintern Abbey, Monmouthshire, Wales, from William Gilpin's *Observations on the River Wye, and Several Parts of South Wales &c. Relative Chiefly to Picturesque Beauty; Made in the Summer of the Year 1770*, 1782

same sorts of landscapes by arranging plants, and even hills and rivers, to form suitable contours, and by designing and siting buildings as appropriate adornments for such landscapes. Ideas as to the particular qualities that made a scene Picturesque remained relatively vague until the 1780s when an English schoolmaster named William Gilpin published a series of travel accounts and essays in which he tried to isolate the essential ingredients of the Picturesque, and somewhat modified the term's meaning in the course of sharpening it. According to Gilpin, its most important characteristics were roughness, ruggedness, and intricacy. Moreover, wild nature was preferable to a landscape tamed by human interference; even 'the formalities of hedgerow trees, and square divisions of property, are disgusting to a high degree.'[71]

The three theorists who most persuasively developed Gilpin's ideas were Price, his friend Sir Richard Payne Knight, and Humphrey Repton. Though Repton was the only professional landscape architect, all three writers shared the earlier interest in garden design. But they were issuing a corrective, based on Gilpin's definition, as to what should be involved in making a scene Picturesque.

Price provided the most systematic and comprehensive treatment of the new approach, giving the topic two new dimensions that greatly broadened its significance. His 'Essay on the Picturesque' made a place for the Picturesque in Burke's esthetic scheme, comparing the Picturesque to the Sublime and the Beautiful, and attributing to it at least as much importance. Where the Sublime is vast and uniform, the Picturesque emphasizes intricacy and variety. Where Beauty depends on smoothness and regularity, the Picturesque is rough, irregular, and shaggy. Moreover, Beauty is associated with youth, that period when nature has attained, but not passed, a state of perfect completion. The Picturesque depends on age and decay. 'Among trees,' writes Price, 'it is not the smooth young beech nor the fresh and tender ash, but the rugged old oak or knotty wych elm that are picturesque.'[72]

Moreover, in his 'Essay on Architecture and Buildings,' Price applied the qualities of a picturesque scene directly to buildings. Though he inherited the broad outlines of most of his arguments, he gave them a fresh emphasis and a new interpretation that were to prove highly influential. Among the major tenets of Picturesque architecture, developed largely according to Price's ideas, were the following four claims.

First, a building should blend with the landscape. Price criticizes the common practice of building tall, thin houses in the country: 'So tall, so stiff, some London house you'd swear / Had changed St James' for a purer air.'[73] Country houses should be designed to look interesting from all sides, and the reverse was also true: people inside a house should be able to look out onto appealing views. Moreover, houses should provide easy access to the garden. Formal rooms were moved to the ground floor, French doors became popular, well-placed windows became essential. While Price and most other writers on the Picturesque were concerned with rural buildings, their emphasis on siting and surroundings was applied by architects such as John Nash to urban buildings as well.

Both in order to blend with the landscape and in order to be picturesque in itself, a building should feature the irregular and rugged outlines, the intricacy, and the elements of surprise and novelty that one finds in nature. The idea that the same qualities could make both buildings and landscapes picturesque had been effectively presented by Robert Adam in his explanation of his concept of 'movement' in architecture:

Movement is ... the rise and fall, the advance and recess with other diversity of form, in the different parts of a building, so as to add greatly to the Picturesque of the composition. For the rising and falling, advancing and receding, with the convexity and concavity, and other forms of the great parts, have the same effect in architecture, that hill and dale, foreground and distance, swelling and sinking, have in landscape. That is, they serve to produce an agreeable and diversified contour, that groups and contrasts like a picture, which gives great spirit, beauty, and effect to the composition.[74]

What differs in Price's view is the list of particular qualities necessary to make either a building or a landscape Picturesque. He speaks less of 'convexity and concavity' than of sharp angularity: 'Whatever is sloping has, generally speaking, less of grandeur than what is abrupt or perpendicular.' Where Adam's 'movement' suggests a continuous rhythm, Price lauds that which is sudden, abrupt, or broken. Thus it is difficult for regular classical buildings to be Picturesque: 'The chaste and noble style of Grecian architecture does not admit of a number of sudden breaks and variations of form.' The desirable irregularity in buildings could be caused by purposeful asymmetry or even random additions, 'because they are built of various heights, in various directions, and because those variations are sudden.'[75]

Third, Picturesque structures should be, or should look, old; they should show, or seem to show, the scars and accidents caused by passing time. Thus the theory of the Picturesque reinforced the period's interest in revival styles.

Finally, there is an element of purposeful deception in Picturesque art: it is, after all, art designed to look like nature as perceived in art. Buildings are designed to look old; Price argues that landscapes can be carefully planned to look, but not be, wild: 'Without having water-docks or thistles before one's door, their effect in a painter's foreground may be produced by plants that are considered as ornamental.' Repton quoted Burke's argument about the sublime to justify his own enthusiasm for deceptive *stratagems*: 'No work of art can be great but as it deceives; to be otherwise is the prerogative of nature only.'[76]

One might have expected the Picturesque to have little influence in Upper Canada, where the very desirability of clearing land and attaining one of the rectangular lots so detested by Gilpin rendered trees a foe and landscape planning an unaffordable luxury. And, according to Anna Jameson, this seems to have been the case: 'A Canadian settler *hates* a tree, regards it as his natural enemy, as something to be destroyed, eradicated, annihilated by all and any means. The idea of useful or ornamental is seldom associated here even with the most magnificent timber trees, such as among the Druids had been consecrated, and among the Greeks would have sheltered oracles and votive temples.' However, early travellers, who could afford to take a more distant view of pioneering hardships, often saw Canada through eyes practised in discerning Picturesque qualities. The *Ancaster Gazette* of 1827 contained one visitor's impressions of London: 'I was much pleased with the delightful situation of the town, commanding as it does a most extensive view of the richest, most fertile and most thickly settled part of the province, besides a delightful prospect of both branches of the picturesque River Thames.' And some of the more genteel settlers did try to impose Picturesque qualities on their wilderness homes. Catharine Parr Traill intended 'to leave several acres of forest in a convenient situation, and chop down and draw out old timbers for firewood, leaving the younger growth for ornament.'[77]

The influence of the Picturesque is also evident in many of Canada's buildings, including the London District Court House. Considerations associated with the Picturesque obviously influenced the choice of site. From the courthouse, one could see the view admired by the writer for the *Ancaster Gazette*. Persons approaching London by either branch of the Thames or by the road from the south would find the courthouse a striking focal point: it was set about twenty feet back from the brink of a hill rising above the river valley. To anyone with an eye acclimatized to the Picturesque, the site would have demanded a castle. Price had declared castles 'the most picturesque *habitable* buildings,' and the fiery William Lyon Mackenzie had shown a surprising sympathy for the architectural symbols of feudalism when viewing the Thames near Lobo, a few miles downstream from London: 'The Thames here much resembles some romantic scenery I have beheld on the banks of the Tweed – the square towers only are wanting, but they may be fancied when beholding the log castles.'[78]

Albeit a castle of sorts, though with octagonal towers, the London District Court House conveys more of Adam's movement than of Price's abruptness. The towers and bay, placed fairly close together, march around three sides of the building in a continuous succession of angular planes. The town façade does break the pattern, however, and the battlemented towers create an uneven skyline that would have appealed to Price.

The courthouse is also deceptive, in the Repton-approved manner. Its smooth stucco surface is grooved to make it look like cut stone. The fact that the rectangular windows get smaller as they move higher enhances the illusion of height, an impression also aided by its setting. Finally, although the courthouse was quite wide, it was also shallow. By expanding the building's width at the expense of its depth, Ewart was able to make the building appear, especially when seen from the river, a much more massive guardian of the law than its measurements proved it to be.

ARCHITECTURAL TASTE: SYMBOLISM

In its choice and treatment of a revival style and in its application of Picturesque principles, the London District Court House was a typical Regency building. Yet there was one glaringly unusual aspect of the 'somewhat Gothic' style used here: it was applied to a courthouse.

Until about 1820 the Gothic style had been employed in England mainly for garden ornaments and houses of various pretentions. The commissioners of the Church Building Act (1818), aiming to remedy a severe shortage of urban churches, decided on economic grounds to build most of the new churches in a simplified Gothic style. Civic buildings, however, were not Gothic. Even devoted enthusiasts of the Gothic style advocated 'Grecian' for civic architecture. John Carter had admitted that 'the Grecian certainly best suits ... public buildings; such as palaces, courts of justice, exchanges ... & etc,' and Francis Goodwin was only echoing established opinion when he wrote, in 1833, 'For civil purposes, public or private ... the town hall, exchange or senate-house; the Greek, Roman or Italian styles are universally admitted to be applicable.' Certainly this was the predominant feeling in Canada, where all courthouses and town halls built before the London District Court House, and most for some time afterwards, were in a classical style. Three years before submitting plans for London's buildings, John Ewart himself had designed the Neoclassical Home District Court House and Jail in York.[79]

When Charles Barry's Perpendicular Gothic design was chosen in 1836 to replace the British Houses of Parliament that had burned down two years before, the decision sparked a barrage of criticism from outraged classicists, even though the new building had to incorporate the fourteenth-century Westminster Hall, which had survived the fire. The commissioners responsible for the new Houses of Parliament defended their choice on rather different grounds, however: 'The peculiar charm of Gothic architecture is in its associations; these are delightful because they are historical, patriotic, local and intimately blended with early reminiscences.'[80]

In emphasizing the 'associations' of a style, the commissioners were presenting the kind of argument that their contemporaries would find convincing. Thomas Jefferson stood 'gazing for whole hours at the Maison quarrée like a lover at his mistress,' not so much because he was taken with its physical charms as because he saw in the architecture of the Roman republic a fitting symbol for his own country's republican aspirations. Despite Jefferson's attempts, it was Greece rather than Rome that inspired the American imagination with the concept of a symbolic national architecture: what the architect Benjamin Latrobe described as the new Greece 'in the woods of America' was seen in the style of almost every farmhouse and public building constructed there between the mid-1820s and the mid-1830s. Though the issue was never so clearly resolved in Britain, that country was also searching for a national style during the early nineteenth century, and fervent Gothicists vehemently opposed looking abroad for a model. 'We are not Italians,' fumed Pugin, 'we are Englishmen.'[81] (Like most of his contemporaries, he overlooked the French derivation of the Gothic style.)

Undoubtedly the 'somewhat Gothic' style of the London District Court House was chosen because of its symbolic associations. Unfortunately, there is no extant record giving the reasons for the choice, and now one can only make informed guesses.

Legend has long held that the courthouse was built to resemble Malahide Castle (fig. 14),[82] and certainly there is a family resemblance between the town side of Ewart's courthouse and the west side of Thomas Talbot's ancestral home. In both cases a long sweep of wall, broken only by doors or windows, separates two relatively broad towers. Both buildings are battlemented, though the configurations of the crenellations differ, and the windows of the towers at Malahide, eighteenth-century additions, feature the same kind of tracery one finds in the Gothic windows of the courthouse. The resemblance does not extend to any other details. Likely Ewart felt free to elaborate upon what may have been a rather vague suggestion, giving the courthouse a more complex character of its own.

It is clear that Ewart was obliged to submit to some dictates from the commission. The newspaperman Edward Allen Talbot expresses one complaint in his otherwise glowing report of the new courthouse: 'it fronts the river instead of the town ... With this single defect it does great credit to its builder, Mr Ewart, of York – and what does him still greater credit, he offered to sacrifice nearly one hundred pounds in order to induce the Commissioners

14   Malahide Castle, County Dublin, Ireland, drawing by Francis Wheatley, 1782, from Desmond Guinness and William Ryan's *Irish Houses and Castles*, 1971

to change the front.' Moreover, in 1827 Talbot recommended to Secretary Hillier that Ewart be given the lot of his choice in London, 'as he appears liberal in his views of building the Gaol & Court House,' meaning, presumably, that Ewart was generally willing to accede to Colonel Talbot's demands.[83]

To Talbot and Ewart the baronial castle would have seemed less incongruous as a symbol of government than it would to their English or American countrymen. James Macauley has observed of late eighteenth-century Scotland that 'the castle was the accepted and understood symbol of a landowner's suzerainty, a notion given reality by the disturbed state of the countryside and by the almost feudal powers of the highland chiefs.' Fred Coyne Hamil describes a similar situation in the Ireland Talbot intimately knew: 'A decadent type of feudalism, lingering on from the Middle Ages, bore heavily on the land. The great nobles lived in castles on their country estates, or in magnificent town mansions, supported by the labour of a tenantry scarcely removed from serfdom.'[84] It was an idealized version of this feudal system, with a powerful and beneficent lord protecting, and being served by, his subjects, that Talbot had apparently once wished to establish in south-western Upper Canada. For Talbot the courthouse was a public assertion of the system of aristocratic privileges in which he believed.

By 1827, however, Talbot had reached the point in his career where he felt threatened by circumstances, and the particular spirit of the times made the courthouse a symbol of defiance as well as an assertion. During the years following the War of 1812 there was considerable discontent in Upper Canada, which festered until it broke out into actual rebellion in late 1837. Grievances were directed mainly towards a system of government that was seen as autocratic and towards the handful of men who occupied positions of authority under the system. In 1824 William Lyon MacKenzie had begun publishing his provocative and popular *Colonial Advocate*, with its vitriolic attacks on the executive's abuse of power. Discontent was especially strong in Talbot's domain, where a large proportion of settlers were American, and in the election of 1824 Talbot had been forced to see two Reform candidates elected in St Thomas (named after the colonel, who mysteriously became canonized in the process), beating out his own protégé, Mahlon Burwell.

Talbot had absolutely no sympathy with reformers. Later, on St George's Day in 1832 he delivered a deservedly famous speech against the demonic 'rebels,' who had 'commenced their work of darkness under the cover of organizing Damned Cold water drinking societies, where they met at night to communicate their poisonous and seditious schemes to each other.'[85] To a man of such strong feelings, the classical architecture that had gained such importance as a symbol across the border would undoubtedly reek too much of democracy. A good baronial stronghold showed where true British subjects should place their confidence: in the established British system of aristocratic power and privilege.

POLITICAL PRISONERS IN THE CASTLE

Both the discontent of the reformers and the recalcitrance of the authorities became more pronounced during the following decade. The advent of Jacksonian democracy in the United States and the passing of the first Reform Bill in England intensified the sense of political stagnation at home in Upper Canada. Mackenzie's diatribes, though often embarrassing to his Reform colleagues in the Assembly, won him a large rural following. Although the growing tensions gave the 1836 election special importance, the widespread accusations of fraudulent practices made the Tory majority highly suspect. Elijah Woodman complained in his diary of the unruly conditions in London, which had achieved the status of a parliamentary riding in 1834:

The magistrates ceased to do their duty and a general riot ensued every day that the polls were open. I attended the election on Saturday ... A procession headed by a negro with a national standard, waving it, and at the same time shouting an offer of five pounds for any liberal heads. This procession turned out to be an Orange mob who commenced beating a number of Liberals who were taken up for dead. Two hours before the polls closed Member Parke had to be rescued by a guard and marched to a place of safety and Member Moore had to make his escape out of town for home. The Liberal poll was secured by two clerks who made their escape into the jail for protection and were locked up.[86]

A widespread financial depression made 1837 a poor time for tempers to cool, and the end of the year saw the overt attack on the government by Mackenzie and his 700–800 followers from the counties north of the capital. When false news of Mackenzie's success reached western Ontario, a force of 400–500 men gathered in Oakland Township under Dr Charles Duncombe to add their support to the insurgent cause.[86]

Though both rebel forces eventually fled in disarray, their efforts had far-reaching consequences. The uprisings in Upper and Lower Canada were to provoke Lord Durham's recommendations for responsible government and a union of the Canadas. More immediately, they resulted in the government's determination to quell rebellious sentiments by jailing as many actual or potential rebels as possible. And this, in turn, led to the defacing of the picturesque main entrance of the London District Court House.

The solicitor-general reported seventy prisoners still in the London Jail in April 1838; 130 others had been released on bail. Later that year, when a group of American patriots crossed the Detroit River, ostensibly to liberate Upper Canada from their oppressors, forty-four of the invaders also ended up in the London Jail.[87] The building had not been designed to accommodate such crowds, and the prisoners' wretched experiences have inspired horrifying tales of underground dungeons. In fact, the existing accounts suggest dreadful ordeals, but in rooms quite consistent with those shown on the 1839 plan. In 1887 Colonel L.A. Norton published a vivid recollection of his experiences fifty years before, likely embellished by time:

Each cell was filled, but that was scarcely a beginning, as there were over six hundred prisoners in the castle. Every hall was crowded full, and there were no blankets or other covering save what the prisoners had on ... Where I was located, in the 'House of Commons' [presumably the top floor], the room was about eighty feet long and about sixteen feet wide ... We were some twenty-five feet from the ground ...; besides, there was a sentinel at every angle of the building, and there being fifty angles, we were well guarded.

Dr Edward Theller recalled being 'marched down [from the courtroom] to the cells ... appropriated to the worst class of felons':

I was thrust into a small cell with three others. This cell was about seven feet square; and in that narrow space were confined four human beings. The only ventilation was through a small diamond-shaped hole in the door ...

The only place for relieving the calls of nature was a corner of our cell, and for many days and nights together we endured the suffocating odour of its fetid exhalations. Day and night were undistinguishable to us, except for a few hours of the afternoon, when the descending sun would cast a slanting ray through the grated window of the corridor, which formed the passage between the double range of cells; or when the jailer or assistant would come his rounds with a lighted candle, to distribute our daily bread.[88]

Such appallingly overcrowded conditions strongly reinforced earlier claims that the London Jail was too small; a new jail was built between 1843 and 1846.[89] An undistinguished brick structure with no architectural affinities to the courthouse, it stretched from the elegant central bay towards the river, thus obscuring the original Picturesque setting and the impressive central tower on the river side of Ewart's building. The addition encouraged some internal changes as well, and the London and Middlesex County Courthouse still possesses drawings, apparently contemporary with the construction of the jail, that show several logical alterations in the plan of the courthouse. Because the original grand entrance now led from the second floor of the jail, a new octagonal tower, containing stairways to the courthouse, is shown on the town side of the building. The old stairways are removed, and the space is used for enlarged cells on the first floor of the courthouse. The new tower was never built, however; without it, the ground floor plan is extremely impractical, and it seems possible that the original stairway was retained until the major alterations of 1878.

'A COMPANY OF HALF-CIVILIZED GENTLEMEN'

Other local effects of the rebellion had positive results. The stationing of a garrison in London contributed to the village's growth in population, and it brought an even greater influx of money. Over $200,000 was spent on barracks during the garrison's first year in London,[90] and fortunes were made by some of those who secured government contracts as provisioners to the army.

In 1841, when Upper and Lower Canada became Canada West and Canada East under the single Province of Canada, Britain loaned the new province £1,500,000 to be used on public works. London's member of the assembly, Hamilton Hartley Killaly, became the commissioner of public works, and, in the time-honoured tradition, he thought first of his own constituency. After his generous expenditures, good plank or gravel roads leading to Hamilton, Port Stanley, Sarnia, and Windsor provided an expanded market for the products of the rich farmland surrounding the village and for the industrial goods that were already being manufactured there. By the late 1840s Elijah Leonard's foundry was already manufacturing steam engines and boilers, and Thomas Carling and John Labatt were operating breweries. In 1847 the village became a town, with a population of 4,584.[91]

London's position as a commercial centre was given an additional boost in the early 1850s, when the railroad arrived. The first train came from Hamilton in 1853, via the Great Western Railway. Three years later the London and Port Stanley Railway reinforced London's link with the ships navigating Lake Erie, and in 1858 a branch of the Grand Trunk Railway reached north from London to Stratford. In 1853 the provincial government recognized London's growing importance by establishing postal service and a custom office in the town. Local authorities, too, began giving more attention to municipal services. A gas system provided street lights in 1854, and a police force and a permanent hospital were established the following year.

By the mid-1850s London bore little resemblance to the muddy, trunk-filled pioneer village of a quarter-century before. Its physical appearance had

15   *London*, watercolour over graphite on paper, attributed to Richard Airey, c. 1845

changed dramatically. Not only were its streets clear and its population larger
(10,060 in 1854), but its buildings were radically different in character. When
James Brown had visited London in 1843, he still found a 'wild wooden place
in the wilderness,' with the houses 'all ... fresh and new-like, as if they had
but come from the carpenter's hands yesterday, or had by magic arisen out of
the woods.' Two years later most of Brown's fresh, wooden town had disappeared, destroyed in the Great Fire of 1845. In an effort to avoid another
such disaster, the town council passed a series of by-laws requiring that no
more buildings be constructed of wood. Thus arose the substantial, sturdy
brick town still evident today. As the *Free Press* repeatedly observed during
the following decades, London 'rose like the phoenix bird, stronger and more
elegant than ever,' having 'passed through the fiery ordeal.'[92]
   The character of London had also changed. Eldon House, the home of the
Harris family, had given a genteel centre to London social life since its earliest
days, but the coming of the garrison had added an aristocratic tone and a
variety of lively activities to London society. Sir James Edward Alexander, in
London as commander of the 14th Regiment during the early 1840s, wrote
lyrically of the 'righte merrie' young soldiers who entertained themselves, and
their fellow citizens, with hunts, picnics, sleigh rides, balls, and theatricals:
'Like Polar voyagers, we ... fitted up a theatre, and turned out a very
respectable corps dramatique.' The newspapers of the 1850s suggest the
presence of a modest literary culture as well. The *Free Press* supported a
movement to found a literary guild in London, partly on the grounds that it

would be satisfying to unappreciated newspaper editors, and the Mechanics' Institute, active since 1841, provided instructive lectures such as that by Robert Cooper on 'What we should and should not Read.'[93]

As the guest of honour at the ground-breaking ceremony for the Great Western Railway, held in October 1849, Colonel Talbot treated the day's event as a symbol of London's remarkable progress:

I thank you, gentlemen, most heartily for the honor you have done me this day. I have witnessed a scene which I can never forget or hoped to behold in this settlement ... I believe I am the oldest inhabitant. I have slept on this spot 55 years ago, when my best friend was a porcupine. We were often excessively hungry in those days, but we all used to declare that we were never so hungry as the night we ate the porcupine. What a change has occurred since then! Now I see different beings around me – no porcupine – no bristles – but in their place a company of half-civilized gentlemen. I wish you, gentlemen, all prosperity, and when I am laid under the sod, may you all go on progressing.[94]

If Talbot were a fictional character, one might find a symbolic meaning in his death in 1853, the year the first train came to London. His guardianship was over; his newborn village had reached maturity. In 1855 London officially became a city.

TRACY'S ADDITION: A NEW FACE FOR THE COURTHOUSE

As the region's population became more dense, the actual area under the jurisdiction of the London District Court House decreased. The size of the London District was reduced in 1837 and again in 1841. The divisions into districts ceased to exist in 1849, after which the London District Court House became the Middlesex County Courthouse. In 1854 part of Middlesex County turned into Elgin County. But by the 1870s even the reduced Middlesex County had a population of approximately 90,000, and the courthouse was again experiencing severe overcrowding. According to the *Free Press* of 9 November 1878, 'Not only was the courthouse proper found to be too small for the holding of the assizes and other courts with any degree of comfort, but the offices occupied by the different officials were very inconvenient and too circumscribed for the proper transaction of business.' A year before the newspaper had reported that 'Chief Justice Harrison charged the jury in unmistakable terms denouncing the courtroom in the most severe language and stating that the jail with all its faults was much preferable to this disease producing room.'[95]

In the spring of 1877 the County of Middlesex and the City of London agreed to collaborate on a substantial addition to Ewart's building. Thomas Tracy, probably representing the office of the city engineer, and Charles Holmes, county engineer, were given the responsibility for planning and superintending the addition and the extensive alterations to the existing courthouse. These appointments followed the usual custom of placing government engineers in

16   Middlesex County Courthouse, now Middlesex County Building, London, front addition in 1877–8 by Thomas H. Tracy, side addition in 1911 by Arthur P. Nutter

charge of civic buildings, but, although the *Free Press* reported already in November 1877 that Holmes and Tracy had 'been engaged for some time past drawing up plans,' the exact nature of their collaboration has not been recorded. Tracy, who practised as an architect as well as an engineer, undoubtedly bore the major responsibility for the design of the new building, while Holmes, known only as an engineer, was likely concerned with the more technical aspects of the project. The specification book used by Tracy's firm credits Robinson, Tracy, and Fairbairne with the actual preparation of the drawings and specifications used in the project, adding that the work must be performed according to these plans and 'to the satisfaction of the County and City Engineers & committees.'[96]

The terms 'addition' and 'alterations' are hardly adequate to describe the radical changes carried out in 1878 and preserved in the recent restoration. According to the *Free Press*, 'with the exception of the walls to the west, north and south, the entire building was torn down.'[97] The specification shows that the process of destruction was more cautious than the newspaper suggests: 'All the work in old building that does not correspond with plans to be taken down carefully.' But an examination of the various sets of plans indicates that very little of the old work did correspond with the new designs.

Essentially, the Ridout Street façade was moved about fifty feet closer to the street, thus changing the former rectangular structure into a building approximately 100 feet square. The new ground floor was devoted to offices

17   Middlesex County Courthouse, towers on north side

and a subsidiary courtroom. The main courtroom still occupied the central section of the floor above, increasing in size as its east wall moved forward, but its orientation was reversed so that the judges' bench was now on its eastern end. The specification instructs the plasterer to run a two-foot-wide cornice around the courtroom and to panel the ceiling; possibly Tracy planned to imitate Ewart in using classical décor inside the building despite the Gothic details outside. At some point, however, either during the process of construction in 1878 or at a later date, a network of rather rough-hewn beams gave a Gothic flavour to the courtroom, at the expense of Tracy's proposed elegance.

Outside, more serious efforts were made to retain the character of the original building (fig. 16). New corner towers match the old ones in shape, dimensions, and style of battlements, thus creating a parade of three identical towers along each side of the building (fig. 17). The stuccoed surface is made to look like stone. The new windows have the same simple stone surrounds found in the old building; towards the centre of the new façade pointed windows feature small panes and tracery reminiscent of those in the original façade. Despite these signs of consideration for Ewart's design, the basic character of his Ridout Street façade was obliterated by the addition of a prominent central tower, emphatically signalling the new orientation of the building as a whole: it now faces the town. Admittedly, the tower is designed to blend with the rest of the structure. Its octagonal turrets echo the corner towers. Its pointed windows correspond with those of the courtroom. However, its stepped crenellations are finer and more ornate than those of the main building. In combination with larger rectangular windows, the tower creates a considerably busier façade. The Palladian serenity of Ewart's front is gone; so too is any resemblance to Talbot's Castle of Malahide.

Instead, the idea of the tower seems indebted to a new symbol of power, the central block of the Houses of Parliament in Ottawa, designed by Thomas Fuller and Chilion Jones and completed in 1866. The parliament buildings were originally intended to serve the Province of Canada, established in obedience to Lord Durham's *Report*. Though it provided the much desired 'responsible government,' the Province of Canada had continually experienced storms arising from other contentious areas. One constant source of discontent was the site of the capital: the question of a permanent location for the seat of government dominated the legislative sessions of 1857. When regionalism proved too strong for any major city in either Canada East or Canada West to win a majority of votes, the matter was referred to the queen, who chose Ottawa. The selection of a site nearly straddling the line between the two Canadas was eminently logical, but the queen's decision won no applause from her representative in the new capital: 'It seems like an act of insanity,' declared Governor Monck, 'to have fixed the capital of this great country away from the civilization, intelligence and commercial enterprise of this Province.'[98] The new capital was in some ways reminiscent of London's early days: elegant government buildings, picturesquely sited on a cliff above a river, surrounded by a raw backwoods town.

The notices advertising a competition for the design of the parliament buildings specified a 'plain substantial style,' a phrase interpreted by Canada's mid-Victorian architects to imply something considerably different from its apparent meaning today. The submitted designs bore labels such as 'Classic,' 'Italian,' 'Norman,' 'Elizabethan,' 'Lombard-Venetian,' 'Civil-Gothic,' and, from one obedient soul, 'Plain Modern.'[99] The term 'Civil-Gothic' is especially interesting in that it indicates the breakdown of the classical monopoly on public buildings, a phenomenon largely influenced by the use of Gothic for the University Museum in Oxford, England (1855–60).[100] The new Civil-Gothic style was very eclectic, however. Canada's parliament buildings combined the Italian Gothic recently made fashionable by the English esthete John Ruskin with the French Second Empire style that was to become the hallmark of future Canadian public buildings.

The new buildings housed their first, and last, provincial parliament in 1866. By the following year the parliament that sat there represented a nation. In a remarkably determined and creative attempt to solve the problems associated with the desire for 'rep by pop' in Canada West, the threat of American invasion during and after the Civil War, the desire for westward expansion, and the necessity of an intercontinental railway, the Province of Canada had disbanded into the two provinces of Ontario and Quebec and joined with New Brunswick and Nova Scotia to form a new federation.

The central block of the Ottawa parliament buildings featured a tower which, though very different in scale and detail from that on the front of the London courthouse, is similar in concept. Both are placed in the centre of a symmetrical façade and draw attention to the main entrance. Both have octagonal corner turrets. More significantly, both serve as porches, with pointed archways in three sides of the ground floor. And, finally, in both towers one finds a continuation of the string coursing and the pattern of fenestration used in the buildings they adorn. With Tracy's tower, the new courthouse announces its allegiance to the Dominion of Canada.

THE THREE FOUNDATIONS OF NINETEENTH-CENTURY
ARCHITECTURAL DESIGN

The three interests that had influenced early nineteenth-century architecture – an enthusiasm for the past, a bias towards the Picturesque, and an inclination towards symbolism – remained powerful influences on architecture until the cataclysmic experience of the First World War. The interest in the past made itself felt in the expansion of history as a scholarly discipline during the course of the nineteenth century, and in the widespread establishment of public museums. The Royal Ontario Museum opened in Toronto in 1914, but it had been in the planning stages since the 1890s.[101] Poets continued to find a source of inspiration in historical matter: Tennyson's *Idylls of the King* (1859) recounts the tales of Arthur's Round Table, and Arnold's *Empedocles on Etna* (1852) has as its hero a Greek philosopher of the fifth century BC. *The Seven Lamps of Architecture* (1849) was 'thrown together' hurriedly, because, as Ruskin explains in a note to his preface, he was frantically trying to copy monuments, in the tradition then established for one hundred years.[102]

The enthusiasm for the past continued to encourage the use of revival styles in architecture, though ideas about the underlying principles of style changed radically from generation to generation. The emphasis on historical authenticity that marked the early revival styles gradually gave way to the flamboyant eclecticism of High Victorian architecture. This in turn provoked a reaction during the last years of the nineteenth century, in favour of somewhat simpler designs.

Architecture also continued to be broadly symbolic. A pervasive sense of decorum linked particular styles with particular kinds of building. Gothic remained a popular style for churches and schools. Financial institutions seemed consistently attracted to the suggestions of control and stability associated with classical forms. The federal Department of Public Works decreed, soon after Confederation, that all public buildings should be in the fittingly imposing Second Empire style. And a later Department of Public Works built armories shaped like fortified castles.

Perhaps the most powerful influence on nineteenth-century architectural design was the theory of the Picturesque. Its enthusiasm for irregularity and ruggedness encouraged a prejudice in favour of asymmetrical designs, with irregular rooflines broken by towers, chimneys, dormers, and turrets. Its praise of roughness produced an increasing emphasis on the use of coarse textures and the play between various textures: buildings featured natural brick, heavily rusticated stone, wooden shingles, and elaborately turned or moulded wood trim. Its emphasis on surprise and novelty led to the delight in intricate detail and copious variety found, for example, in the incised woodwork or ornate terra cotta panels of High Victorian houses. The continuing use of period styles derived some impetus from the respect for age in the esthetic of the Picturesque.

That the theory of the Picturesque should have had such appeal for the nineteenth century is not surprising. The period was one of unprecedented change. The Industrial Revolution created massive social upheavals in England and Europe; change was even more pronounced in Canada, where towns like London could be transformed from crude pioneer outposts to major commercial centres in the course of a generation. Certainly in some quarters the repeated shocks of change brought severe suffering and a strong nostalgia for a static, idealized past. But there was also a spirit in the age that responded positively to the new discoveries and opportunities of the period, and the theory of the Picturesque provided a theoretical justification for this attitude by lauding change as the root of all happiness. 'Men grow weary of uniform perfection,' wrote Price, and Knight explained why, in terms of man's insatiable desire for 'acquisition,' 'The source and principle of [happiness] is ... novelty ... If everything were known, there would be nothing to be learned, if every good were possessed, there would be none to be acquired; and if one were wanting, or there were no evil, there would be none to be done; and consequently all would be dead inaction, or action without motive or effect.'[103] The past was interesting, not because it was idyllic in its permanence, but because it revealed the ongoing processes of growth and destruction. Buildings became broken and decayed, visages were marked by 'warring passions'[104] or hard work, civilizations developed and disappeared. Poets were less likely to find a golden age in history than a mirror of the profound contemporary restlessness. Tennyson made of Ulysses, for example, a character who combined the picturesque marks of age with an unquenchable yearning for new experiences: 'Made weak by time and fate,' he still determines to chart 'that untraveled world whose margin fades / Forever and forever when I move.'

The insatiable restlessness of Tennyson's age has multiple reflections in nineteenth-century architecture: in the variety of styles popular at any one moment, in the speed with which architectural fashions changed, and in the continual creation and adoption of new building materials. Ultimately, it proved responsible for the emergence of a new profession: that of the architect who could use the manifold forms of the past to create symbols of present aspirations.

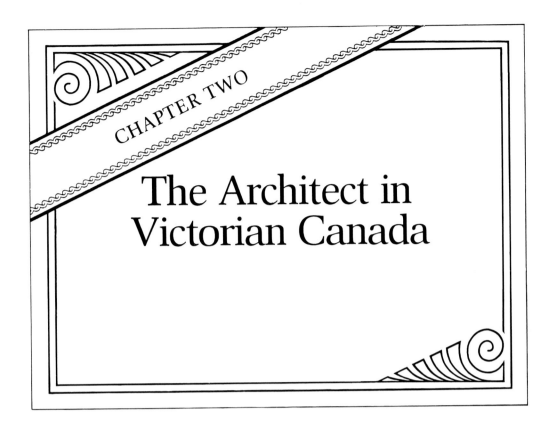

The Architect in Victorian Canada

WHEN DICKENS'S ASPIRING ARCHITECT, Martin Chuzzlewit, sees a plan of a proposed American town called Eden, he rejoices in the professional paradise of his dreams: 'A flourishing city ... ! An architectural city! There were banks, churches, cathedrals, market-places, factories, hotels, stores, mansions, wharves; an exchange, a theatre; public buildings of all kinds, down to the office of the Eden Stinger, a daily journal.' Martin's career seems assured when his fearful query 'I suppose there are – several architects there?' receives the reply, 'There ain't a single one.' Martin decides to start with the market-place.[1]

The description of the imaginary Eden could almost have been applied to the new city of London during the 1850s. Like Eden, London attracted architects eager to share in designing the new town. While Eden turned out to be a disease-ridden swamp, however, London provided a setting where architects' dreams could come true.

London marked its growing importance by erecting two impressive new civic buildings, a market and a city hall, designed and supervised by the first city engineer, Samuel Peters.[2] Though Peters felt himself inadequately paid for his efforts, the opportunity for designing such impressive buildings must have made the position of city engineer especially attractive to his peers. When the municipal council decided to appoint a new city engineer in 1856, they received tenders from six of the nine architects then practising in the town, including Peters. The lowest bidder, W.R. Best, got the job in 1856, but his appointment was short-lived. In 1857 a new appointment was made, this time to William Robinson, who held the position for twenty-one years and arguably became the most influential architect in the city's history.[3]

As city engineer, Robinson was responsible for important civic projects such as the Custom House (fig. 51), Victoria Hospital (fig. 60), a network of schools, and the waterworks system. Since being city engineer was only a part-time position during Robinson's time, he was also able to establish a flourishing private practice as an architect and surveyor, and it was in this capacity that he trained the 'many young men,' who, according to one early history, 'afterwards attained more than ordinary success.'[4] Two of these young men, Thomas H. Tracy and George F. Durand, became Robinson's partners and then his successors. A third, John M. Moore, eventually inherited the business after Durand's death. In the final analysis, Robinson's most significant contribution to the region was probably the establishment of a firm that proved remarkably stable during a period of considerable mobility in the architectural profession, serving as the region's most prominent architectural practice throughout most of a century and designing many of the area's worthiest architectural landmarks.

To a modern observer Robinson's training and qualifications would hardly make him a candidate for such an impressive role. He was an Irish immigrant who, though he had some experience as a carpenter, only started training as an architect at the age of twenty-nine.[5] He served what can at best be labelled an informal apprenticeship under the English-trained Toronto architect Thomas Young and spent two years working, probably as clerk of works, for architect Henry Bowyer Lane. His sole certification was as a land surveyor, and when he entered business for himself in Toronto, it seems to have been exclusively in this capacity. He did not begin to call himself an architect until he moved to London some time after 1852, when he was in his early forties.

From the perspective of his contemporaries, however, the profile of Robinson's career, to be examined more fully in chapter 3, would have seemed entirely natural. The architectural profession was still undergoing its rather prolonged growing pains, and neither the role, the status, nor the requisite training of the architect was as yet fully defined, in either Britain or North America.

THE CONCEPT OF A PROFESSIONAL ARCHITECT

Like most other architectural concerns of the nineteenth century, the idea of the professional architect had a long history, with roots in classical times.[6] But it had played a relatively small role in the history of British building prior to the middle of the eighteenth century: the design of earlier buildings was most often the responsibility of gentlemen-amateurs and master-craftsmen. By 1788, however, Sir John Soane could confidently recommend as a professional standard a role he and many of his contemporaries were able to practice, that of the architect who performed some of the duties previously undertaken by both traditional parties and acted as an arbitrator between them:

The business of the architect is to make the designs and estimates, to direct the works, and to measure and value the different parts; he is the intermediate agent between the employer, whose honour and interest he is to study, and the mechanic, whose rights he is to defend. His situation implies great trust; he is responsible for the mistakes, negligences, and ignorances of those he employs; and above all, he is to take care that the workmen's bills do not exceed his own estimates.[7]

Although this code of disinterested and professional conduct was to serve as the beau ideal of associations of architects over the next 125 years, its definition of the architect's role did not go unchallenged, either within or without the profession.

Soane had placed his description of the architect's role within an argumentative context: 'If these are the duties of an architect,' he asked, 'with what propriety can his situation, and that of the builder, or the contractor, be united?' Proper or not, distinguished contemporaries of Soane such as the Adam brothers and John Nash were speculators and developers on a large scale, and many nineteenth-century architects in Canada chose to follow the less restrictive professional model. John Howard, Toronto's most prominent architect during the 1830s and 1840s, controlled many stages of his massive building schemes: he functioned as architect, surveyor, engineer, speculator, developer, landscaper, landlord, and even lumberman, owning his own mills to cut his own timber.[8] Though Howard conceived of his profession on an unusually comprehensive scale, it was customary for his Canadian peers to combine their architectural practice with some related businesses. Four of the architects who applied in 1856 for the position of London city engineer were also surveyors. John Beattie was a partner of Smith & Beattie, 'ARCHITECTS, MEASURERS & ACCOUNTANTS OF ARTIFICER'S WORK.' W.B. Leather, never one to underestimate his own abilities, advertised himself as 'ARCHITECT, Civil Engineer and Surveyor, LAND AGENT, & C.' But even his open-ended claims were eclipsed by Samuel Peters's boasts about his new partner Thomas Stent, who, in association with Augustus Laver, later designed the east and west blocks of the Ottawa parliament buildings: Stent was 'sole Agent in the Province for the sale of Minton & Co.'s Encaustic Tiles for paving Churches, Hall's Hearths for Stoves, etc., and also for Bowden's brilliant cut Window Glass and patent lever Glass Ventilators.'[9]

While some practitioners diminished the architect's professional status by embracing related business interests, others rejected it on the opposite grounds that architects were artists and thus above practical professional concerns. The most eloquent presentation of this argument is *Architecture, a Profession or an Art?*, written by Norman Shaw and T.G. Jackson in the early 1890s, but the position they espouse had been current for over half a century. Although the concept of the anti-professional artist seems to have carried little weight with the practical architects of Ontario, the idea of the artist-architect did encourage specialization within professional offices, both in Britain and in North America. By the last decades of the century most big

American firms divided responsibilities along lines similar to the arrangement used by Adler and Sullivan (Chicago, 1885–95): Sullivan concentrated on the commercial and engineering aspects of the business, leaving Adler free to deal with matters of design.[10] This specialized approach was also adopted by numerous smaller practices in the United States and Canada, including, to some extent, Durand's and Moore's.

While there was controversy within the profession as to what properly constituted the architect's role, there was doubt outside the profession as to whether he had any distinctive role at all. Many persons who were trained in other pursuits felt themselves fully capable of designing buildings as well. The architect Richard Brown complained in 1842 that it had become the practice of 'the mere builder ... to assume the title architect, without possessing any of the necessary qualifications except that of making mechanical drawings.'[11] And the widespread scepticism about the validity of the architect's specialized role was reflected in the questions addressed to one Daniel Asher Alexander when he was called to witness in a trial in 1817:

> 'You are a builder, I believe?'
> 'No sir; I am not a builder; I am an architect.'
> 'Ah well, builder or architect, architect or builder – they are pretty much the same, I suppose?'
> 'I beg your pardon; they are totally different.'
> 'Oh, indeed! Perhaps you will state wherein this difference consists.'
> 'An architect, sir, conceives the design, prepares the plan, draws out the specifications – in short, supplies the mind. The builder is mainly the machine; the architect the power that puts the machine together and sets it going.'
> 'Oh, very well, Mr Architect, that will do. A very ingenious distinction without a difference. Do you happen to know who was the architect of the Tower of Babel?'
> 'There was no architect, sir. Hence the confusion.'[12]

Architects were generally able to make an absolute distinction between their function and that of the builders, even if the claims they made were not mutually recognized. A much more intimate connection existed between architects, engineers, and surveyors, and the lines of demarcation between these professionals remained rather blurred throughout much of the nineteenth century. Some ambiguity inevitably resulted from their overlapping responsibilities. The architect could best assess workmen's prices and adhere to his client's budget if he possessed the measuring and valuing skills of the quantity surveyor, and the advent of new and complex building techniques required him to possess considerable engineering expertise. The more profound explanation for the close, though sometimes querulous, relationship between these professions lies in their common lineage. In Britain, the birthplace of many Canadian architects and most early ideas about their practice, the surveyor, the architect, and the engineer all inherited roles once in the province of the surveyor alone; pre-dating him, the classical and Renaissance concepts of the architect encompassed the tasks later assumed by the civil engineer.

From Tudor times throughout much of the eighteenth century, in Britain the term 'surveyor' referred to a man performing any of a broad range of tasks; these could include plotting boundaries, valuing or maintaining property, designing buildings, or supervising their construction. The extremely influential Office of Works, which trained and employed some of the most able architects of the seventeenth and eighteenth centuries, was under the direction of a comptroller, surveyor, or surveyor-general; among the holders of this position were Christopher Wren, John Vanbrugh, Lord Burlington, and William Chambers. As architects began to assume a more distinct identity late in the eighteenth century, they were eager to establish the superiority of their calling over that of the jack-of-many-trades surveyor. But their very arguments often betray the confusion surrounding the issue. Architect John Gwynne complained that surveyors 'are so very assuming, that ... they pretend to dictate to the man of science [the architect], and would deprive him of that merit on which only he can form his reputation, that is, his merit as a designer.'[13] Thomas Skaife argued for a 'proper standard' in the architectural profession, so that architects could be distinguished from surveyors: 'A gentleman would then know whom he has to apply to for masterly compositions and undertakings; there would be a visible difference in their professions, though at present they are considered as synonymous.'[14]

Prior to the late eighteenth century the term 'engineer' had been applied solely to military engineers. Following in the tradition of Vitruvius and Palladio, surveyor-architects had considered structures such as bridges and aqueducts well within their domain. But the new technology and growing commerce of the late eighteenth and early nineteenth centuries produced a demand for more complex factories and better communications systems and for the specialists to design them. Some of these 'civil engineers' were architects who chose to concentrate on such projects; others approached the field through technology alone, to the disgruntlement of some architects who evaluated the engineers' encroachment on their territory with jealous condescension. 'In their designs,' claimed W.H. Leeds in 1862, 'there are many violations of architectural propriety, so that it would surely not be asking too much of them to submit to the advice and correction of those that have made the art of design the principal study of their lives.'[15]

Although arguments like Leeds's can still be heard today, the trend towards specialization slowly gained momentum as the nineteenth century progressed. The growing independence of surveyors, architects, and civil engineers can be measured by the attendant growth of professional organizations that could enhance a group's professional status, encourage the development of suitable educational opportunities, and, perhaps, control the membership of the profession.

The civil engineers were the first to form professional groups in England, and their organizations endured. The Society of Civil Engineers was founded in 1771, and the more enterprising Institution of Civil Engineers was organized as early as 1818.[16]

Several short-lived architectural societies preceded the founding of the

Institute of British Architects in 1834. The institute received a royal charter three years later and retained its position as a moderately influential body throughout the 1800s, but it failed to attract a majority of the practising architects until well into this century; even in 1911 its membership included only a quarter of the population it claimed to represent.[17] The controversy about defining the architect contributed significantly to the institute's problems. In an attempt to improve the status of the profession, it excluded from membership any architects practising other trades, such as building or surveying, and emphasized the architect's understanding of design. This idealistic bias inevitably had practical disadvantages for expanding membership. The pure artists among architects had no interest in a professional association, and many who viewed their work as a profession saw it as comprehending related professions as well; as late as 1892 around half of the 1,100 architects listed in the *London* [England] *Directory* were also surveyors.[18] Indeed, the tendency of many practising architects to regard good style as a frill is satirized, none too subtly, by A.W. Pugin in *Contrasts.* A page of mock advertisements includes several for 'PLACES and SITUATIONS':[19]

A YOUNG MAN
WHO UNDERSTANDS SUR-
VEYING WOULD LIKE TO
GO FOR 1 YEAR INTO AN
OFFICE TO LEARN THE
TASTY PART
of the architectural business.

AN ERRAND BOY
FOR AN OFFICE WHO CAN
DESIGN OCCASIONALLY

If the Royal Institute of British Architects was long weakened by being too exclusive, the surveyors may have suffered from the opposite tendency: an overly inclusive view of the profession that impeded a clear sense of identity. Both the Surveyors' Club, founded in 1792, and the Society of Architects and Surveyors, formed in 1834, welcomed representatives of both professions, but surveyors lacked the cohesiveness and sense of professional autonomy to form a thoroughly professional organization of their own until 1868, when the Institution of Surveyors was finally established.[20]

Professional associations emerged more slowly in Canada, and they were less exclusive than some of their English models. Dr W.W. Baldwin, himself a physician, lawyer, and occasional architect, encouraged an audience of architects and builders to form an 'Architectural Society' in 1834, but there is no record to suggest that it took his advice.[21] The earliest known societies were alliances among surveyors, engineers, and architects. In 1849 a group of men representing all three professions met in the office of architect Kivas

Tully to organize what was to become the Canadian Institute. It was initially conceived as a society dedicated to improving the knowledge of its members and advancing the related professions. Very quickly, however, the organization became more academic than professional. A royal charter granted in 1851 describes it as 'A Society for the encouragement and general advancement of the Physical Sciences, the Arts and the Manufacturers in this part of our dominions,' and its broader aims were reflected in its membership. Among the proposed members listed in its first publication (*Canadian Journal, a Repository of Industry, Science, and Art*, volume I, Sept. 1852) were London's two leading citizens, John Harris and Henry Becher; both barristers, they were presumably attracted by the intellectual rather than the professional leanings of the association. William Robinson, then practising as a surveyor in Toronto, was already a member. In 1855 the institute merged with the Atheneum, an established literary society. Its publication of the following year, rechristened the *Canadian Journal of Science, Literature, and History*, reflected an impressive variety of intellectual interests (the aborigines of Australia, research on colour blindness, Longfellow's 'Song of Hiawatha'), but nothing of a strictly professional nature and little on architecture.[22]

Perhaps because the Canadian Institute was seen in some professional circles as too general in its interests, two other organizations for surveyors, engineers, and architects were formed independently during 1859, one in Toronto and the other in Ottawa. The Association of Architects, Civil Engineers and Public Land Surveyors in Toronto seems also to have been largely academic in orientation but with a bias towards architectural interests; one of their main objects was 'the collection and exhibition of Works of Art, Models, and Drawings.' The Ottawa group, called the Association of Provincial Land Surveyors, and Institute of Civil Engineers and Architects, was to share the scientific interests of the Canadian Institute: it had the power to maintain 'Museums, Libraries, Galleries of Art, Reading Rooms, Observatories, Chemical Laboratories, Depositories for Maps, Plans, Models, Documents, and other valuables' and to hold 'Literary and Scientific conversaziones.' But it also had more pronounced professional responsibilities: it could establish 'standards of qualification' for those seeking membership and examine candidates to be certain they met those qualifications. The two organizations merged in January 1862. The merger may effectively have dissolved both groups; for nothing beyond its formation is known of the new association.[23]

Architects first formed their own society in 1876 and 1877, but it, too, proved mysteriously short-lived.[24] It was not until 1889 that they formed an enduring association, when the times seem somehow to have been ripe for establishing professional societies in Canada.

The surveyors led the way with the federal Association of Dominion Land Surveyors, formed in Manitoba in 1882, and the Association of Provincial Land Surveyors of Ontario, organized in 1886. The Engineering Institute of Canada was established in 1887, with headquarters in Montreal, and during the same year a group of Toronto architects formed the Architectural Guild of Toronto. It was the members of this organization who were mainly responsible for founding the Ontario Association of Architects (OAA) in 1889, though the convention at which the OAA was formally established was chaired by Robinson's successor in the London firm, George F. Durand.[25]

While the variety of organizations indicates increasingly distinct professional roles, none of the societies regarded itself as exclusive. In his opening address to the newly formed Ontario Land Surveyors, Willis Chipman observed that 'some few' of them were lucky enough already to belong to the British Institute of Civil Engineers or the American Society of Engineers.[26] The first draft of the OAA constitution did restrict membership to those whose 'sole ostensible occupation' consisted of the practice of architecture, but this qualification was omitted in the final version:

An architect is a professional person whose occupation consists in supplying drawings, specifications and other data preliminary to the material construction and completion of buildings, in exercising administrative control over the operations of contractors supplying material and labour incident to the construction and completion of buildings, and officiating as arbitrator of contracts, stipulating terms of obligations and fulfilment between proprietor and contractor.[27]

London architect John M. Moore was a member of the provincial organizations representing all three related fields.

That there should be some time lag between the development of professional organizations in England and the equivalent progress in its colony is not surprising. Even in the United States, which boasted a much longer history than English Canada, professional organizations for engineers, surveyors, and architects were formed only in the 1850s, many years after their British equivalents.[28] What was unusual in Ontario was the extent to which architects associated themselves professionally with the practical and scientific adjuncts of their work. The early years of the American Institute of Architects were dominated by men whose main interests revolved around their intense concerns with stylistic matters: Richard Upjohn, for example, was an earnest Ecclesiologist; Richard Morris Hunt an enthusiastic product of the Ecole des Beaux Arts in Paris. The Ontario Association of Architects sought to justify itself largely on the grounds that its members were good engineers. The keynote speaker at the organizational meeting of the OAA was Professor John Galbraith of the School of Practical Science, which was about to institute a program for architects. Professor Galbraith stressed the need for a technical education for architects, who, in the chairman's words, 'had so much to do with mechanics.' He also admitted, of course, the importance of 'artistic education' for architectural students, though he felt incompetent to discuss how art should be taught.[29] An address reported in an 1894 issue of the *Canadian Architect and Builder*, the official journal of the OAA, answered 'the vexed question, whether an architect should be an artist or a theoretical mechanic: he must be both; and a man of business, too. An artist may be a thoroughly impractical man ... ; an architect cannot.'[30]

This materialistic bias undoubtedly owed something to the relative newness of the country, but a second important source of influence was likely the unusually high prestige accorded the Canadian Land Surveyor. At a time when neither architects nor engineers had the advantage of any recognized certification or even any organizational backing, the examination and licensing of surveyors was carefully controlled in Canada.

Accurately defined and marked boundaries became a matter of serious governmental concern with the influx of Loyalists eager to claim their allotted grants, and laws designed to regulate the business date from as early as 1785. A 1798 statute gives a startling indication of the importance attached to properly marked boundaries: 'If any person or persons shall knowingly and wilfully pull down, alter, deface, or remove any such monument as aforesaid [indicating a survey boundary], he, she, or they shall be adjudged guilty of felony, and shall suffer death without benefit of clergy.'[31]

Statutes from the same period required that a surveyor be 'duly examined by the surveyor or deputy surveyor general, as to his fitness and capacity, his character, and the sufficiency of his instruments,' and authorized a scale of licensing fees. These statutes were continually revised and made more stringent over the next several decades. An 1849 Act required an applicant to be twenty-one years old; to serve a formal three-year apprenticeship under a certified land surveyor, during which time he should complete a 'course of Geometry, including at least the first six books of Euclid, of plain Trigonometry, Mensuration of Superfices, Plotting and Map Drawing, ... and shall also be sufficiently conversant with Spherical Trigonometry and Astronomy to enable him to ascertain the latitude, and to draw a meridian line'; and to produce references 'as to character for probity and sobriety.' Other statutes, enacted during the following decade, enabled candidates to substitute a university course in 'Civil Engineering and Land Surveying' for part of their three-year apprenticeship and required that a preliminary examination be passed in order to qualify for an apprenticeship.[32]

Most other professional associations in England and North America were eager to establish such standards. In England during the early 1880s both the Institute of Surveyors and the Royal Institute of British Architects made membership contingent upon successful performance in examinations; as soon as the Royal Institute of British Architects included the majority of the profession, it campaigned for compulsory registration. The Western Association of Architects was formed in Chicago in 1884, largely because the American Association of Architects was thought to be insufficiently forceful in promoting issues such as the licensing or registration of architects.[33] An act requiring the registration of Ontario engineers was introduced and defeated in 1899.[34] W.G. Storm, first president of the Ontario Association of Architects, opened the first annual convention with a congratulatory speech in which he exulted, '[We] are now ready to go to the Lieutenant Governor and tell him ... that the public are beginning to call for some guarantee of the ability of persons calling themselves Architects, and that we are prepared to give them that guarantee; that we have discussed the subject in the most exhaustive manner and think we see our way to a state of affairs that will protect the public from incompetent and unscrupulous men.' He went on to delineate the current lack of protection in more precise terms: 'Do not men engage in architectural pursuits without the aid of previous training, pupilage, or any formality whatever except the assumption of a title? – the name put up and the thing is done.'[35]

No nineteenth-century surveyor could get away with that in Ontario. Thus an architect who was also a surveyor had credentials proving that he possessed considerable theoretical knowledge, as well as a sober and honourable character; the surveyorship endowed him with a professional status not yet available to the architect by the end of the century. That the scientific bias of the surveyor should have affected the Ontario architect's perception of his role is hardly surprising – especially in the absence of any clear guidelines as to the special training an architect required. W.G. Storm waxed heavily ironic about misconceptions regarding an architect's education:

Is our profession such a mean acquirement that no special education is necessary? Can a young man 'pick it up' as he would expect to do an insurance agency – a land jobber's or real estate broker's business? Emphatically no! To possess the knowledge to build and the skill to plan and design a building, and to deal with the innumerable questions, scientific, artistic, legal and sanitary, which continually present themselves in ordinary practice, a training as arduous and prolonged as that of any of the liberal professions is necessary.[36]

Unfortunately, neither formal courses nor a well-regulated system of apprenticeship assured the nineteenth-century architect's 'special education.' Certainly, even though anyone could put up a sign and call himself an architect, aspiring architects ideally served a period of apprenticeship. And in England, at least, this apprenticeship theoretically involved a fairly ambitious program of learning, as well as a good sum of money. An early guide to choosing a career, *The Complete Book of Trades or the Parents' Guide and Youth's Instructor* (1842), describes the requirements for entering the architect's trade:

The youth desirous of becoming an Architect should be liberally educated, and in addition to the Latin language, he should be master of French and Italian; have some knowledge of mathematics, geometry and drawing. The premium required with a pupil by a respectable master is from two to five hundred pounds: the youth will also require a considerable sum for the purchase of books, instruments and drawing materials. He must, during his apprenticeship, learn to make architectural drawings from admeasurement, also to sketch picturesque buildings, columns, etc., he must be careful in observing the proceedings of workmen in every branch of business connected with buildings.[37]

An architectural education came quite a bit cheaper in mid-nineteenth-century Ontario. John Howard generally charged £100 for taking on a boy for three years, and the fee seems to have included board, lodging, and, in most cases, laundry.[38]

As Storm's complaints make clear, however, not all architects bothered with a formal training. Even W.B. Leather, who eventually lured William Robinson to London as a partner in his well-respected architectural practice, had no specific education as an architect. Earlier, when applying to superintend the building of St James' Cathedral in Toronto, he had provided an account of his professional background that, perhaps unwittingly, presented his architectural experience as a kind of accidental sideline to his main work: 'I learned my Profession, as Engineer & Surveyor, with my Father & Mother, who are Engineers in Leeds, Yorkshire. I have for many years past been engaged in the practical part, having been Engineer to several Contractors on very extensive Railway contracts in England & Wales ... The last Party, with whom I was ... also built 10 Beautiful Stone Houses ... for which I drew the Designs, & I saw the 10 Executed.'[39]

Moreover, with no system of regulations, even a formal apprenticeship did not guarantee the kind of training an architect required. Its effectiveness depended entirely upon the ability and conscientiousness of the master, and, while some architects took their duties as teacher very seriously, there is massive evidence that the system was often abused. It seems that Dickens's portrayal of Martin Chuzzlewit's master was less exaggerated than one might expect. Mr Pecksniff had hung out a 'brazen plate' announcing himself to be an architect and land surveyor, despite his somewhat meagre qualifications: 'In one sense, and only one, he may be said to have been a Land Surveyor on a pretty large scale, as an extensive prospect lay stretched out before the windows of his house. Of his architectural doings, nothing was clearly known, except that he had never designed or built anything; but it was generally understood that his knowledge of the science was almost awful in its profundity.' Pecksniff's area of real proficiency turns out to be fraud rather than architecture: 'His genius lay in ensnaring parents and guardians, and pocketing premiums.'[40]

One finds numerous echoes of Dickens's caricature in the accounts of Martin's real-life British contemporaries. George Gilbert Scott (1811–78), who did become a notable Victorian architect, recalled his shock on discovering the true abilities of his tutor, James Edmeston:

I had no idea beforehand of the line of practice followed by my future initiator into the mysteries of my profession; I went to him with a mythic veneration of his supposed skill and for his imaginary works, though without an idea of what they might be. The morning after I was deposited at his house, he invited me to walk out and see some of his works – when – oh horrors! the bubble burst, and the fond dreams of my youthful imagination were realised in the form of a few second-rate bricked houses, with cemented porticos of two ungainly columns each! I shall never forget the letting down of my aspiration.[41]

Edmeston turned out to be conscientious, if untalented. George Wightwick was even less fortunate in his five-year term (1818–23) under the surveyor-architect Edward Lapidge: 'No instructions, not even as to the course of my artist-study, were ever given; while the miscellaneous and unsystematized character of the mere office business left me uninformed as to the introductory knowledge necessary to its full apprehension. I expected to find a tutor: I found only an employer.'[42] Canadian masters could be equally negligent. In 1873, three years into his five-year apprenticeship with the Halifax firm of Stirling and Dewar, William Critchlow Harris complained to his brother, 'I wish that old beggar Mr Stirling would come back and take care of his business. He has done scarcely a stroke of work all summer, but left everything to us fellows to break our backs over.'[43]

In the end, each of these discontented young apprentices took on the major responsibility for educating himself. The bitter Mr Wightwick concluded, 'I found, in short, that I had paid my premium for the opportunity of self-instruction – for the advantage of the "run of the office" – for the privilege of serving my master and picking up such information as might lie in my way.'[44] Scott found his employer agreeable if uninspiring: 'Mr and Mrs Edmeston were very kindly persons, and as they had an excellent library, which was my evening sitting room, I had excellent opportunities of ... self-improvement, and I think I took very fair advantage of them. I read much and drew much, and made myself acquainted with classic architecture, architecture from books such as Stewart's Athens, the works of the Dilettante Society, Vitruvius, etc, and with Gothic so far as the scanty means went.'[45] William Harris had to look farther to fill the perceived gaps in his training, which were more practical in nature: 'You see,' he wrote to an English friend, 'that I have not a very good opportunity of learning very much about construction in Halifax. I thought the best thing for me to do would be to get a good book on the subject. I saw one advertised in *The Building News* some time ago which struck my attention.' He asks his friend to send W. Tarne's *The Science of Building* from Liverpool.[46]

William Robinson entered the employ of Thomas Young in 1841, apparently with the understanding that Young would further his education, even though Robinson seems not to have signed formal articles of indenture. Robinson was most directly interested at the time in qualifying as a surveyor, but his choice of Young, a prominent Toronto architect, as his mentor suggests wider aspirations. As was so often the case, however, Robinson was forced to rely on his own intellectual resources, happily abetted by his employer's library: 'although not receiving the promised (but unasked for) instruction from his employer, he had access to his library ... and availed himself of the opportunity each evening, after his day's work, in the study of Euclid, trigonometry, surveying, linear perspective, geometrical building problems, & c.'[47] In using a surveyor's training as the basis for an architectural practice, and in relying on his own self-teaching as the core of that training, Robinson was following a pattern that was perhaps all too typical of his times.

THE ARCHITECT'S LIBRARY

Partly because Robinson's experience was so common, books designed to provide architects and builders with the intellectual tools of the trade were published in great quantity. This practice, too, had begun in the eighteenth century, with sets of instructions designed to raise even the most humble workman's level of competence, if not necessarily his self-esteem: Batty Langley's *The Builder's Jewel* (1757), for example, claimed in its subtitle to comprise 'short and easy rules, made familiar to the meanest capacity, for drawing and working.' Like others of its type, *The Builder's Jewel* consisted mainly of instructions for making the decorative details on classical buildings (columns and entablatures, pediments, panelling, quoins, etc.), though it does discuss some structural matters.

Such 'builder's guides,' as they are now called, tended to become more complex and more comprehensive as time passed. The impressive 578 pages of *Nicholson's New Practical Builder* (1823) are no match for the 1089 pages of smaller print in Joseph Gwilt's *An Encyclopedia of Architecture, Historical, Theoretical, and Practical* (1857), later increased by nearly 300 pages more in Wyatt Papworth's 1867 revised edition. These books contain a history of architecture (Gwilt's thorough treatment includes topics such as 'Druidical and Celtic,' 'Persepolitan and Persian,' and 'Jewish and Phoenician' along with the variations of the Gothic and classical styles), advice on architectural drawing, and practical information on every aspect of construction (the *Practical Builder* has chapters on geometry, carpentry, joinery, timber, masonry, bricklaying, plastering, slating, plumbing, house-painting, and glazing). Some of these self-helps to becoming a builder or architect also include plans and elevations, though such material often forms a small part of the book's general contents. The thirty-seven plates of actual plans in Nicholson's book refer to only sixteen pages of his massive text, though they do try to cover all the basic possibilities. In the realm of domestic architecture, for example, Nicholson provides drawings of a 'First-Rate House,' 'Second-Rate House,' and even of third- and fourth-rate houses, in addition to his more imposing manorial residences in Gothic and classical styles. Asher Benjamin's *American Builder's Companion* (1826) contains plans for five houses, two meeting houses, one courthouse, and a church, all very basic, apparently leaving the particular quantity and form of adornments to the builder's newly educated discretion.

There were also available numerous books that could cater to those who wished to see a greater variety of detailed plans. Following in the tradition of *Vitruvius Britannicus*, many 'pattern books' of the early nineteenth century were designed to fulfil some clearly didactic purpose. John Claudius Loudon rather immodestly hoped his *Encyclopaedia* would extend architectural taste to the buildings and minds of all classes: 'The main object of this *Encyclopaedia of Cottage, Farm, and Villa Architecture*, is to improve the dwellings of the great mass of society, in the temperate region of both hemispheres: a secondary object is to create and diffuse among mankind, generally, a taste for architectural comforts and beauties.'[48] With these ambitious aims in mind, he provides sample dwellings meant to suit the very specific needs of a wide range of occupants: there are patterns, for example, of 'A Dwelling for a Married Couple and One Child, with a Pigsty,' and of 'A Grecian Villa, of a medium Size, for a Gentleman of Fortune.' He also includes compendious notes explaining the particular features of a plan, commenting on the style of an elevation, describing the means of construction and approximating its cost, and prescribing its situation with respect to both landscaping and the direction it should face.

The several books by the American theorist Andrew Jackson Downing have a similar format and somewhat similar aims. He designs houses to satisfy the particular needs of widely differing imaginary clients, by way of illustrating the 'beauty of utility,' or 'Fitness,' but he places more emphasis on their habits than on their class. Thus his *Cottage Residences* (1842) includes 'A Cottage in the English or Rural Gothic Style' for 'families mainly composed of invalids, or persons advanced in years,' and a somewhat more imposing 'Cottage in the Pointed, or Tudor style' is to be occupied by a family who lives 'in a pleasant and social neighbourhood, and are in the habit, occasionally, of entertaining a little party of their friends.'[49] Downing's great passion was landscape gardening, however, and his primary interest in architecture is as a picturesque addition to a view. As a result, he gives extremely detailed instructions for the landscaping and planting around a building, and, instead of elevations, he provides perspectives that show a structure in its suitably picturesque surroundings. His designs proved influential in developing the idea of the suburb, and in promoting the versatile Gothic and Italianate styles of architecture in North America.

Not all compilers of pattern books were guided by altruistic or philosophical concerns. A volume of attractive designs was always a good advertisement for an aspiring architect, and, as the nineteenth century progressed, the publishing of patterns turned into a business as well as an advertisement. Thus a person could find a house he admired in one of *Shoppell's Modern Houses* (issued periodically from the 1880s), and send to the Co-operative Building Plan Association in New York City for a complete set of working plans and estimates. Predictably, the drawings continued to take the form of enticing perspective views, while the descriptions became considerably briefer and more strictly formal.

Architects were not expected to be mere copyists, of course, but the pattern books were one means by which various styles and attitudes gained popular currency. The professional architect would ideally have a knowledge of historical styles based on familiarity with antiquarian researches, rather than on the simple outlines in builders' guides, and his awareness of current ideas about style would be based on recent works dealing with esthetic theory and on news of the most important buildings being designed by his contemporaries. In these areas, too, he could glean information from an abundant number of publications. Records of ancient buildings were continually published in Britain and abroad, and many popular periodicals gave a substantial amount of space to architectural concerns. The rise of professional journals such as the [British] *Builder* (dating from 1842) or the *American Architect and Building News* (begun in 1876) provided useful vehicles for the dissemination of the latest news about construction techniques and stylistic innovations.

A good deal of this literature evidently made its way to Canada. Immigrants undoubtedly brought with them some of the books that had been so popular at home, especially if they had hopes of setting themselves up in a vocation connected with building. Indeed, many writers were particularly concerned with meeting colonial needs. Loudon directed his work to 'both hemispheres.' One William Wilds, a Hertford surveyor, wrote his guide to building cottages (1835) 'For the Use of Emigrants and for the better lodging of the peasantry of England and Ireland.'[50] An 1848 advertisement in a Toronto paper makes it clear that imported pattern books and builders' guides were in some demand then: bookseller Thomas Maclear announces the recent arrival of several 'Architectural Works,' including '*The Five Orders of Architecture*, with Sir Wm Chambers notes ... ,' Nicholson's *Practical Masonry, Bricklaying, Plastering, &c.*, Nicholson's *Practical Carpentry and Cabinet Making ...* , Brooks's *Designs for Cottage and Villa Architecture*, Brooks's *Designs for Public Buildings*, Downing's *Landscape and Rural Architecture*, and Wightwick's *Hints to Young Architects*.[51]

Predictably enough, architects often collected their own working libraries. The heirs of Robert Wetherall, the original architect for Dundurn Castle in Hamilton, put his library on sale in 1846; the sale notice listed books on historical architecture, such as 'Stewart's Athens, 4 Vols'; works by or about some of the more revolutionary architects of the early nineteenth century, including Soane, Piranesi, and J.N.L. Durand; and, in the line of more practical guides, one of Nicholson's volumes. John Howard, Edmund Burke, F.J. Rastrick, F.W. Cumberland, and W.G. Storm are known to have amassed large personal libraries. Cumberland's collection consisted mainly of books recording ancient structures, though there were descriptions of more contemporary buildings as well. John Howard gave his library to the city of Toronto, and an extant listing of its partial contents indicates that he had been collecting relevant periodicals for some time: the 219 volumes mentioned include sixty-one volumes of the *Illustrated London News*, which devoted a good percentage of its illustrations to significant buildings, and thirty-four volumes of the *Builder*, to which he must have subscribed since soon after the magazine's inception. In 1888 the Toronto Public Library held 101 architectural books, including Gwilt's *Encyclopedia*, Loudon's *Encyclopaedia*, Rickman's *Attempt to Discriminate the Styles*, *Vitruvius Britannicus*, two books

18   'Brick Villa No. 2,' from William M. Woollett's *Villas and Cottages; or, Homes for All*, 1876

by the influential English esthete John Ruskin, one by the controversial Frenchman Viollet-le-Duc, and the *Rise and Development of Mediaeval Architecture* by the once disillusioned apprentice, now Sir George Gilbert Scott.[52]

Both the firm founded by William Robinson and the individual architects associated with it seem to have formed libraries, but records of their holdings are incomplete, especially for the Robinson era. The only extant book bearing Robinson's signature is *Tubular and other Iron Girder Bridges* (1850), indicating more about his interest in engineering than about his concern with architecture. Thomas Tracy is known to have owned a pattern book by the Albany architect William M. Woollett. Entitled *Villas and Cottages; or, Homes for All* (1876), it shows twenty-two dwellings (see fig. 18) that do bear some resemblance to works by Tracy and Durand, though their common elements were so popular at the time that one should probably be wary of attributing too much influence to Woollett's book.[53]

Disappointingly, only four of the many volumes in a recent catalogue of the remnants of George F. Durand's library have mainly architectural subjects, and the approach of all four is popular rather than professional, though some of these might have proved suggestive. The Reverend Robert W. Fraser's *Illustrative Views of Interesting and Romantic Parish Kirks and Manses in*

19   Terra cotta medallion, Perth County Courthouse, Stratford, 1885–7, designed by George F. Durand

20   Illustration of keystone in crypt gate, Merseburg Cathedral, Germany, from *Materiaux et Documents d'Architecture et de Sculpture*

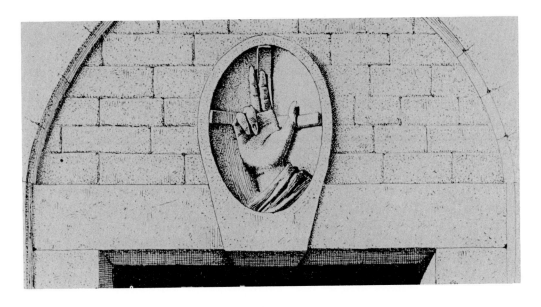

Scotland, for example, shows several historic structures. It seems probable that Durand kept a professional, working library of which, sadly, little record has been kept. He is known to have subscribed to two American journals, the *Inland Architect and Builder* and the *Northwestern Architect and Improvement Record.* And he apparently had bound for himself a large selection of pages from the Parisian journal *Materiaux et Documents d'Architecture et de Sculpture*: his collection, with no title page and a random arrangment of plates, has 'G.F.D.' stamped on its leather-bound spine.[54] The illustrations are mainly of sculptural details from significant European buildings, and Durand evidently found them interesting, in part, as potential models for details on his Canadian buildings. Four medallions on the Perth County Courthouse in Stratford, Ontario, are based on the drawing of a keystone in the twelfth-century gate to the crypt of Germany's Merseburg Cathedral (figs 19 and 20). The terra cotta medallions were made by the Terra Cotta Company,[55] but Durand undoubtedly followed the common practice of providing the design he wished to have moulded.

Durand's version of the design is by no means a mere copy of the image in his source. His strikingly plain model shows what a German scholar inter-prets as the hand of God, raised in benediction. The hand is set against a cross; both are recessed within an oval concavity. Durand's hand emerges from a circular concavity that forms the centre of a rosette; it projects for-ward, as if possessing an independent force enabling it to defy the boundaries of its frame. The blessing hand on the door to the crypt at Merseburg repre-sents the divine mercy that will temper the final judgment of those interred within; Durand places his version of the motif on either side of the two main entrances to the courthouse, presumably as a sign of blessing on those about to invoke the temporal judgment of the law. There is no cross in the courthouse medallions, in keeping with their more secular context.

The library that has been handed down by Robinson's firm also possesses a copy of Rickman's *Styles of Architecture in England* (7th ed., 1881), but it contains no signature to prove whether it belonged to Durand or to one of his successors. The latter is perhaps the more likely alternative, in that most of the collection seems to date from John Moore's time, after 1890. There are numerous books on historical architecture (Moore's partner Fred Henry owned *Examples of Gothic Architecture* (1850) by A. Pugin and A.W. Pugin); specialized building manuals such as the *Pocket Companion containing Useful Information and Tables appertaining to the use of Steel*, as manufactured by the Carnegie Steel Company of Pittsburgh (1903); volumes of four different architectural and building journals emanating from Britain and the United States, respectively; and large files containing illustrations of various buildings clipped from books and journals.

While it is evident that Ontario architects adopted the literate approach to architecture that was typical of their times, they produced little architectural literature of their own. As part of their energetic program to improve Ontario education, Chief Superintendent of Education Egerton Ryerson, and the man who was to become his deputy superintendent, J. George Hodgins, included material on school architecture in their *Journal for Education for Upper Canada* (begun in 1848). In 1857, Hodgins put much of their advice about school buildings in book form, under the title *The School House, Its Architecture*. This edition was heavily influenced by a popular American work, Henry Barnard's *School Architecture* (1841), but an 1876 edition of Hodgins's book, bearing the same title as his earlier work, is much more comprehensive in both its approach and its sources. It treats every aspect of the school's physical make-up, including sites, playgrounds, plantings, hygiene, ventilation, scientific and gymnastic equipment, and a history of physical education extending back to Plato. The book also contains many plans, elevations, and perspectives, designed to make the schoolhouse 'what it ought ever to be – the most attractive spot in the neighbourhood.' His authorities include many American, British, and Canadian sources, and he seems eager to assure readers that some of the plans added to this volume are by Canadians.[56]

A more authentic Ontario pattern book was published, towards the end of the century, by the Committee on Church Architecture of the Presbyterian Church in Canada. The committee was motivated by a desire to improve the quality of Presbyterian church architecture, and the book's 'Prefatory Notes' suggest very high aims indeed. The new churches were to be the enduring monuments to Canada's history: 'England and Scotland are proud of their ancient cathedrals; and although we may not build structures so grand and imposing as these, yet with our abundant supply of stone and wood of the very best quality may we not, by following the laws of architecture, build in such a way that our work shall stand, and meet with the approval of succeeding generations?'[57] The finished book was distinctly anticlimactic. Although the recently established *Canadian Architect and Builder* insisted that 'the [architectural] profession is interested in this movement,' and pointed out that the publication 'should benefit those who have been successful in having their designs illustrated,'[58] individual architects proved curiously reluctant to submit drawings in the committee's competition. In May 1892 the judges appointed by the Ontario Association of Architects wrote to its registrar, W.A. Langton, 'in our opinion there is not a sufficiently large number of suitable designs among them to warrant the committee in publishing a pamphlet.'[59] A pamphlet was produced, containing all of nine designs, by architects in Toronto, Ottawa, Montreal, and Winnipeg. But the quality is mixed, and one suspects that some drawings, such as that by Langton, were requisitioned after the competition. Even the *Canadian Architect and Builder*, wishing to be encouraging, could only damn with faint praise: 'Although they cannot all be declared to be satisfactory examples of church design, the excellence of some is such as to encourage the hope that they will in a measure serve the object the church had in view ...'[60] In the final analysis, the slimness of *Designs for Village, Town and City Churches* (1893) reinforces the conclusion that there was little interest in book production among Canadian architects.

Periodicals seemed a somewhat more congenial medium for the publication of Ontario architects' views. Between 1864 and 1873 the *Canada Farmer* quite frequently interrupted its otherwise steady diet of shop-talk to advise readers about houses, barns, churches, or schools. The plans and elevations were accompanied by a good deal of practical information about siting and building and, more surprisingly, by some emphatic instruction in esthetic matters. One commonly preached dictum was that houses should be tasteful but unpretentious. An article on cottages, for example, described a 'wise man' planning his house:

If his means are limited, he will attempt no ambitious imitation of a particular style, and will not impose upon the public with spurious examples of Italian or Gothic castles. No, he will endeavour to give a cheap cottage a tasteful and truthful appearance. He will have no showy ornaments and expensive carving on the exterior, while the interior is badly planned, meagre and poor. His cottage will be well planned and tastefully built, so that every part will bear the impress of refined judgement, and will afford quite as much pleasure in its way as a spacious mansion; although not the same kind of pleasure, it will be perfect of its kind.[61]

The 'tasteful and truthful' illustrations are of a nicely proportioned log cabin and of what has come to be called an 'Ontario Cottage.' But the *Canada Farmer* opposes excessive informality as much as pretentiousness. A plan for a 'substantial,' if passé, Georgian residence warns against farmyard manners indoors: 'It is the common practice of some of our farmers to take all their meals in the kitchen, this is a habit which marks a low state of society. It should be borne in mind that farming is the natural employment of man, and ought to be made a refined and noble pursuit, and not a mere way of earning a rude subsistence.'[62]

While the *Canada Farmer* dealt occasionally with architectural matters, two London (Ontario) men produced a full-fledged professional journal for a brief period between late 1868 or early 1869 and some time during 1870.[63] The *Canadian Builder and Mechanics' Magazine*, edited by architect Thomas W. Dyas and sculptor Henry A. Wilkins, seems to have maintained high standards. The *Architectural Review and American Builder's Journal* described its contents as 'useful and interesting, original and select' in February 1870. The same journal later excerpted from the *Canadian Builder and Mechanics' Magazine* a very competent, detailed description of the architectural features and the impressive facilities exhibited by the new Deaf and Dumb Institution in Belleville. Sadly, that is the only extant sample of the Canadian magazine's contents. The fact that no full issue of the periodical exists suggests that it had a relatively small circulation as well as a short life.

Another eighteen years passed before a second professional architectural journal appeared, but the *Canadian Architect and Builder*, founded in Toronto in 1888, proved more enduring. It continued as a monthly publication until 1908, when it merged with the *Contract Record* to form a weekly periodical dealing with the same wide range of architectural matters.[64] Like its London

21   Waverley, London, additions c. 1897 by Moore and Henry to building designed in 1882 by George F. Durand, from *Canadian Architect and Builder*, June 1898

predecessor, the *Canadian Architect and Builder* concerned itself with technical as well as artistic aspects of building; one could find articles on drainage or heating systems, as well as analyses of Gothic architecture and illustrations of notable new buildings. Among the several featured designs by John M. Moore's firm was the west front of 'Waverley,' incorporating additions and alterations to Durand's earlier building (fig. 21).[65] In 1889 the journal was adopted as the official organ of the Ontario Association of Architects;[66] thus Ontario architects finally gained a literary voice of their own for the last decade of a very articulate century.

THE NEED FOR AN ARCHITECT

The period's highly literate approach to architecture was only one of several factors helping to make the architect a necessary part of the nineteenth-century building industry. For despite the nebulousness surrounding his role and the poorly controlled quality of his training, the architect did meet a need created by several social and intellectual movements of the times.

One important development involved the reallocation of wealth and the social mobility attributable in England to the Industrial Revolution and in North America to the fluidity of a frontier society. Where patrons of architecture a century before had generally been 'gentlemen,' well versed in architectural matters, the patrons of the Victorian age were likely to be members of the burgeoning middle class, with wealth to spend on buildings, but often without the esthetic background to create tasteful designs of their own. Indeed, the abundant supply of bad taste became one of the period's favourite themes. As part of its campaign against overly pretentious building, for example, the *Canada Farmer* excerpted a story about the fictional Farmer Cheeseman, whose proud new mansion boasted especially garish 'crooked stripes of red, green and yellow' on 'the sides of the fireplaces and mantels, supposed to represent veins in marble,' though 'it would have puzzled a geologist to tell exactly where to classify such a specimen.' The paper curtains portraying famous generals seemed the special pride of the farmer's wife ('Them are the dandies,' she complacently bragged), but were surprisingly makeshift affairs. Even with such sops to their vulgarity, however, the Cheesemans felt uncomfortable in their fine new house, and they built on a kitchen where they 'toasted away' next to the cooking stove, sitting on unpainted chairs at the old pine table. Farmer Cheeseman had copied his house from that of his town cousin, rather than consulting an architect who could have guided his taste and helped him evaluate his real needs.[67] Elsewhere, the *Canada Farmer* strongly encouraged its readers to employ architects, on economic as well as esthetic grounds:

we would ... advise those who contemplate building not to grudge the expense of an architect. His professional skill will, in all probability, ensure better taste and good keeping in the main design and all the features of the building, as well as greater convenience in the arrangements; his knowledge of the trade may protect you from some of the tricks of the contractors, and in this and other ways he will effect a saving in the total expense that will generally more than cover the amount of his own professional charges.[68]

The redistribution of wealth was only partly responsible for creating the new clientele. A re-evaluation of the concept of architectural merit found the most humble abode worthy of esthetic considerations. As J.C. Loudon explains, in the introduction to his *Encyclopaedia*, 'The efforts of Architects, in all ages and countries, have hitherto been, for the most part, directed to public buildings, and to the mansions of princes, noblemen, and men of wealth; and what have hitherto been considered the inferior orders of society, have been, for the most part, left to become their own architects.'[69] Loudon presents himself as an architect for the masses as well as the relatively elite, and periodicals like the *Canada Farmer* display the same attitude when they show a log cabin with architectural merit. William Robinson's contracts included cottages as well as mansions.

The architect's field expanded, not only in the direction of more humble structures, but even more dramatically towards specialized building types, indebted in different ways to the social and scientific developments of the age. The coming of the railroad led to the erection of magnificent stations; it also promoted commerce, and the large market halls and exhibition buildings that allowed a productive society to vaunt its wares. Industrialization required complex factories. The combination of urban problems and a widespread emphasis on social conscience led to the multiplication of service

22   Gould & Stratfold advertisement, from *London City Directory*, 1886

institutions such as prisons, asylums, hospitals, and public schools. Pumping stations, gasworks, and, eventually, power plants were required to provide municipalities with current domestic comforts. Specialized knowledge was required to design any of these structures. Ideally, the designer of a school understood the current pedagogical theories, and the architect of a prison knew the contemporary arguments in favour of a radial plan.[70] When John M. Moore designed a new London factory for the Battle Creek Toasted Corn Flake Company in 1912, he made copious notes on every step involved in manufacturing cereal. The eighteenth-century builder could work with long-established precedents. His successors needed to assimilate and apply up-to-date technical information on a variety of subjects.

The task of planning a building during this period was also complicated by the exceedingly wide range of materials that became available. Technological developments had so transformed transportation and communication that, even in provincial communities such as London, Ontario, builders were no longer dependent exclusively on locally produced materials. The abundant wood and clay of the region did literally provide the basic building blocks of its structures, but a Toronto newspaper reported soon after the Great Fire of 1845 that some new London buildings were featuring 'Cleveland stone.'[71] The arrival of the railroad in the mid-1850s made imports even more accessible. The first *London Directory*, of 1856–7, contains advertisements for Thomas Stent's 'Patent English Brilliant Cut & Ornamental Glass' and for Lionel Ridout as an 'Importer of and Dealer in Fancy and Heavy Hardware,' including 'Iron, Steel, Nails, &c.' By 1886 William M. Dwyer, proprietor of the Victorian Park Marble Works, was making mantels and headstones out of granite from Queenston, South Renfrew, or New Brunswick.[72] Something of the complexity of contemporary trade patterns is indicated by the practices of 'Gould & Stratfold, Plain and Ornamental Plasterers.' According to the typically glowing account in *The Industries of Canada* (1887), this firm's 'business productions' were 'freely circulated throughout the Province.'[73] That some of these productions were manufactured elsewhere, however, is suggested by the advertisement Gould & Stratfold placed in various London City Directories throughout the 1880s and 1890s (fig. 22); the design shown there, an impressive ceiling ornament concocted of elegant cartouches and rustic branches, birds, pumpkins, and corncobs, originated with a Detroit firm.

While specialized building types and imported goods did much to substantiate the architect's role, technology's main contribution to his importance lay in the development of new building materials and new structural techniques. During the Victorian era there was what one architectural historian has called a 'revolution' in the art of building.[74]

THE ARCHITECT'S MATERIALS

The material that dominated the structural revolution of the nineteenth century was iron. When Rudyard Kipling used 'cold iron' as the basis for a religious allegory in 1910, he was relying on the assessment of current technology as well as the superstitions of ancient folklore:

> 'Gold is for the mistress – silver for the maid!
> Copper for the craftsman cunning at his trade.'
> 'Good !' said the Baron, sitting in his hall,
> 'But Iron – Cold Iron – is master of them all!'[75]

Wrought iron is in fact more ancient than Christianity, and cast iron antedates some of the fairy stories that Kipling uses: it was discovered that iron could be shaped, or wrought, many centuries before the birth of Christ, and the art of casting molten iron in moulds had been known in medieval Europe. But the processes used were laborious and expensive. What made iron influential in the nineteenth century was the invention of cheaper and faster methods of processing it. The first significant step towards making iron more accessible in England was Abraham Darby's use, in 1709, of coke rather than charcoal in blast furnaces, a useful development where the availability of coal far exceeded that of wood. By the turn of the nineteenth century, cast iron was occasionally being used as a structural material, mainly in mills, where fireproof columns and beams were especially desirable. Cast iron is relatively brittle, however, and is weaker under tension than is wrought iron. A technique for converting the mass-produced cast iron into wrought iron began to be widely used in the second quarter of the nineteenth century; called the 'puddling process,' it had been patented by Henry Cort in 1784, and involved using iron oxide to draw off impurities, particularly carbon, from melted pig iron. In the St Pancras Railway Station (1863) in London, England, wrought-iron girders proved capable of spanning an area 243 feet in width, free of any supporting columns. By then, Sir Henry Bessemer had invented a method for producing steel on a large scale by blowing oxygen through molten pig iron. But steel came into its own as a construction material only in the 1880s, when steel beams became commercially available, and the use of steel frameworks for 'skyscrapers' was pioneered in Chicago.[76]

Two very different manifestations of the nineteenth-century interest in science proved especially instrumental in encouraging the development of iron buildings. One was the fascination for exotic plants that overtook the upper classes and necessitated the building of greenhouses; the other was the growth of the railroad and the attendant need for stations with large-span roofs. But it was a building constructed to pay homage to an even broader display of Victorian industry and ingenuity that most startled, impressed, and influenced the Victorian public: the Crystal Palace, designed by Joseph Paxton to house the Great Exhibition of 1851. A three-tier structure covering a floor area that measured 1,848 by 408 feet, its glass walls and roof were supported by iron girders and thin iron columns, creating a streamlined sky-blue grid that barely acknowledged the boundary between outdoors and in.[77] It perfectly exemplified what the *Canadian Architect and Builder* was later to recommend as 'realism' in architecture: 'a building should appear to be what it is ... in this century; in the material of which it is built.'[78]

Although a regiment of Crystal Palaces acknowledged the influence of Paxton's building, the wares displayed beneath its airy canopy revealed other sides of Victorian taste, and these predilections dictated different architectural uses for iron. Exhibits of both architecture and furniture drew upon and reinforced the current vogue for historical styles. A.W. Pugin created a 'Medieval Court.' A thirty-foot-high cast-iron dome was so admirably executed in a Neoclassical style that, according to one modern writer, 'it might have been designed by Chambers.'[79] Works throughout the exhibition tended to be highly associative or blatantly symbolic, in keeping with established trends. One of Canada's exhibits was a table cut from 'a tree which made 27,000 feet of available timber.' A contemporary judge 'liked the emblematic beavers carved round the edge of the table; but not the same animals crawling like rats on the cross bars of the legs.'[80] A chair from Ireland made its symbols more prominent as well as more complex: one arm was a recumbent hound described as 'Gentle when stroked,' the other a hound sitting up alertly and labelled 'Fierce when provoked.'[81] Thus the exhibition celebrated the richness of the historical world in a wealth of concrete images, relegating the abstract simplicity of its building to the utilitarian sphere of railway stations, greenhouses, bridges, and exhibition buildings.

More conventional types of buildings generally hid iron columns within a masonry wall, or shaped the iron into forms traditionally assumed by other materials. Whole façades were cast in iron and made to look as if they were built of wood or stone or marble. Daniel Badger, whose Architectural Iron Works in New York City sent entire fabricated storefronts to Halifax, Brantford, and Peterborough before 1865, was predictably enthusiastic about the adaptability of iron: 'It must be evident that whatever architectural forms can be carved or wrought in wood or stone, or other materials, can also be faithfully reproduced in iron. Besides, iron is capable of finer sharpness of outline, and more elaborate ornamentation and finish; and it may be added that it is not so liable to disintegration, by exposure to the elements, as other substances.'[82] Because iron could be shaped into so many different forms, it was liberally used for the smaller and more delicate ornaments essential to High Victorian architecture: hinges, fountains, fences, railings, and the crestings that frequently perched on the period's steeply pitched roofs.

Until the 1890s most iron and steel used in Ontario had to be imported from England, the United States, or Quebec. Most of the several attempts to mine and smelt iron in Ontario were short-lived, despite the ready supply of charcoal and several substantial ore deposits. The most successful of the early iron entrepreneurs was Joseph Van Norman; he ran the Normandale Iron Works on Lake Erie from 1820 to 1847, making a fortune which he subsequently lost on ironworks at Marmora and Houghton. No other companies achieved any enduring success until the establishment of the Hamilton Blast Furnace Company in 1895. This foundry added steel to its repertoire in 1900, and by 1907 there were two companies making iron or steel in Hamilton and five elsewhere in Ontario. Even then, however, the Bureau of Mines estimated that approximately one-third of the pig iron used in Ontario was imported from the United States and Great Britain, 'not necessarily because the foreign iron and steel can be laid down in Ontario more cheaply than it can be manufactured here, but because the demand for this material far exceeds the native supply.' The industry prospered until, rather surprisingly, the First World War caused a radical reduction in demand.[83]

Though little iron actually was smelted in Ontario until the end of the nineteenth century, there were numerous foundries that melted down imported pig iron or scrap iron and recast it in various moulds. Elijah Leonard, whose father came from a long line of Massachusetts ironmongers and had moved north to manage the Normandale plant, established a foundry in London in 1838. He imported pig iron and eventually coke from Buffalo to produce stoves, ploughs, and various other iron products, though he later specialized in railway cars and more elaborate sorts of agricultural machinery. The major stove manufacturer in town came to be McClary's, which started as a manufacturer of tinware in the early 1850s.[84] The number of foundries increased as the century progressed. One particularly ambitious enterprise was the London Steel Works, as described in the *Dominion Mechanical & Milling News* of February 1884:

The London Steel Works are a new industry ... under the same general management as the [Ontario] Car and Car Wheel Works ... It is the first, and at present, the only steel works and steel rolling mill in the Dominion ... The steel workers and rolling mill men ... are from Sheffield and Pittsburgh, and are giving to the Company the benefit of much practical knowledge and many years experience ... With this establishment so centrally situated, and having a capacity for producing 8 tons steel, and 10 to 12 tons bar iron daily, our Ontario trade should be well provided for ...[85]

Despite such optimism, the London Steel Works seems to have made little impact, even on London records.[86]

Though used for numerous kinds of machines and implements, iron seems to have played only a minor role in London's architecture before the 1870s. William Robinson had designed a local 'Crystal Palace' in 1861 (fig. 41), but it resembled its English prototype only in name and function; a rather inventive adaptation of the Neoclassical style, it was constructed mainly of wood and brick. Robinson's conservative choice of materials was undoubtedly influenced by the city's need for economy in the early 1860s, but any conspicuous use of structural iron might well have met with some local controversy. In 1875 an informed and far-sighted Board of Works persuaded the City and County Councils to erect a prefabricated wrought-iron bridge across the Thames at Blackfriars Street. The structure was ordered from an Ohio firm. Widely used in the United States, iron bridges were still a novelty in Canada, and the city Board of Works felt it necessary to stage a test of the bridge's strength before its formal opening. Numerous city officials and a considerable crowd of ladies and gentlemen gathered to watch as 'ten loads of gravel ... weighing in the aggregate about 40 tons, [were] driven on the bridge ... Thereafter, the teams drawing the loads were trotted over, and afterwards the loads were drawn over two abreast, with the effect of showing that the bridge was firm and secure, not a movement of the main arches being visible.'[87]

From 1878 on, Robinson's firm regularly used iron tie rods to reinforce wooden girders and iron columns to support church balconies; in the Grand Opera House (1880–1; fig. 101), cast-iron columns supported two tiers of balconies. At about the same time, Tracy and Durand used exposed wrought-iron beams and rafters to support the roof of a 'mammoth skating and curling rink'[88] (measuring approximately 175 by 75 feet) built as a privately owned enterprise on Queens Avenue. A well-thumbed copy of the *Carnegie Steel Book* of 1903 suggests that Moore and Henry were using imported steel beams with some frequency during the first decade of this century, though Moore seems to have designed steel frame structures only in the 1920s.

London buildings more frequently employed iron in non-structural ways, such as fences and crestings or as fireproof coverings for exposed surfaces. As early as 1868 Robinson specified a galvanized iron roof for the office of H.C.R. Becher on Carling Street. He excluded the roofing from the materials to be provided by the contractor; it may be concluded that the galvanized iron could not be supplied locally.[89] Five years later the town's resources had improved. The local hardware manufacturers S.& A. McBride could execute the much more complicated ironwork on W.J. Reid's Crystal Hall (fig. 58),

23   George F. Durand's design for 'Pulpit Platform and Railing,' addition, c. 1887, to St Andrew's Presbyterian Church, London

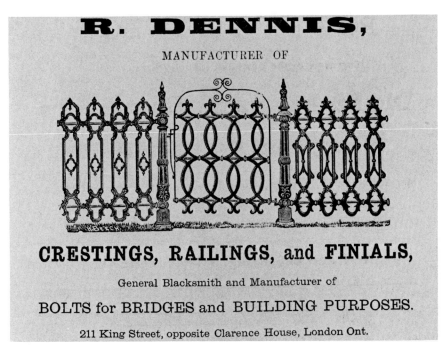

24   Rowland Dennis advertisement, from *London City Directory*, 1883

aptly named in that the façade exhibited large expanses of 'the best English plate glass' and the interior was devoted to Mr Reid's glass and crockery business. The building's roof, cornices, and elaborate window trim – bases, arches, columns, crestings, and finials – were all of galvanized iron, so that 'not an inch of woodwork is anywhere exposed to the attack of fire from neighbouring buildings.' Though less completely devoted to iron than the complete iron fronts sent out by companies such as Mr Badger's, the Crystal Hall was apparently regarded as an unusual achievement for its time: according to the *London Free Press*, 'Several scientific men from a distance have visited the building within the last few days, and speak of it as being second to none in the Province, Mr Scott, the Dominion Architect of Ottawa, among the number.'[90]

When George Durand prescribed a particularly delicate and ornate wrought-iron railing for the pulpit area of St Andrew's Presbyterian Church (renovated c. 1887; fig. 23), he could have relied on the considerable talent of the local blacksmith Rowland Dennis, who by the late 1880s had produced a variety of ornamental fences, railings, and crestings (fig. 24).[91] It is impossible to know whether the actual design of the wrought-ironwork to adorn St Andrew's new interior was created by Durand or by a competent artist-craftsman like Dennis. The firm's usual practice with cast-iron crestings was to specify 'approved patterns,' but wrought iron was not dependent on pre-cast moulds and could easily be custom made according to a design provided by the architect. That Durand himself may have assumed responsibility for the chancel of St Andrew's is suggested by his habitual concern with the decorative details of a structure (he designed both terra cotta panels and furniture for the Perth County Courthouse), and by the close integration of wood and ironwork in the St Andrew's design (the identical capitals in both materials, the identical widths of the panels, and what one might paradoxically call the sunflower rosettes, to name just a few of the unifying elements). In any event, the new pulpit area of St Andrew's must have been an impressive testimony to the decorative richness and elegance of what was also the century's most utilitarian material.

The technology of iron affected other building materials as well, in more or less direct ways. Paxton's Crystal Palace, like other iron frame buildings, required a great deal of glass – 900,000 square feet, to be exact[92] – and it helped accelerate the developing enthusiasm for that material. The Canadian London possessed two Crystal Palaces, one Crystal Hall, and one Crystal Block; all had in common a substantial amount of glass, if not much iron.

New kinds of furnaces and new techniques made possible the production of larger panes of glass.[93] Sheet glass, made by blowing a long cylinder, splitting it along one side, and flattening it while still hot, could be cut into pieces as large as three by four feet, and most London houses built between 1860 and the First World War used at least a few windows of about this size. Beginning in the 1830s even larger 'plate glass' windows were made in England by pouring molten glass on an iron slab with edges raised to the desired thickness.

Size was not the only virtue a window could possess: bevelled, etched, pressed, enamelled, stained, and leaded windows all attested to the widespread fascination with 'art glass.' In 1883 the *Free Press* used the prosperity of London's single stained-glass factory to make a rather smug comparison with the boorish old days:

The manufacture of stained glass in Western Ontario owes its inception to the foresight of Mr R. Lewis of this city, who, some fifteen years since, opened an establishment here at a time when the prospects were anything but bright for a remunerative return from the capital invested. Since then the taste of the populace has undergone a wonderful change, and in many districts where church edifices have been erected, the building has not been deemed complete without two or more of the windows being of stained glass. In dwelling houses, also, many fine lights have been inserted, and the demand keeps pace with the cultural advancement of the people.[94]

The records kept by Robinson's firm support the newspaper's assessment of the growth of interest in stained glass. One of Lewis's first important commissions in London was St Andrew's Presbyterian Church (fig. 49),[95] designed by Robinson in 1868. Ten years later many houses listed in the firm's specifications book had coloured glass in the fanlights and sidelights of the front entryway and in the upper panels of front and vestibule doors. For the Murray house (1878; fig. 95) Durand specified a skylight with a 'figured glass panel' in the centre and a '6 inch border of stained glass.'[96] By the 1890s most of the firm's houses featured front windows, as well as doors, designed to hold art glass in some panels.

A sudden expansion of local producers suggests that a burgeoning of London interest in art glass occurred at the very end of the century. Although Lewis expanded into larger business quarters in 1883, he attracted no competitors until the late 1890s, when Hobbs Hardware set up a plant for manufacturing 'mirrors, leaded glass windows, stained glass, and other art-glass work.'[97] The factory employed over sixty workers in 1906; one of its artists, Henry St George, was among four men who established independent works near the turn of the century.

Some window glass was manufactured in Canada at various points during the century, but there is no evidence that it reached London. Hobbs imported the glass that was cut and leaded in its factory; one of the Crystal Hall's claims to admiration was its English plate glass; and many of the firm's buildings were to have windows of 'good German sheet glass.'[98]

The development of iron technology also had a substantial impact on wood construction: the availability of machine-made nails made viable a new method of framing. Except in primitive log cabins, the framework of early wooden buildings in North America generally consisted of heavy timbers connected by means of mortise and tenon joints. During the Chicago boom period of the 1830s, the 'balloon frame' was developed as an easier and faster alternative to the 'timber frame.' Given its name by its detractors because it was so lightweight, the balloon frame consisted of two-by-four-inch or two-by-six-inch studs nailed at regular intervals to the sill and to a horizontal plate along the top of the walls. The new method quickly gained popularity across the United States, and Thomas Ritchie claims, in *Canada Builds*, that it reached Canada by 1870.[99] But Robinson's firm at least seems to have embraced the new system rather tentatively. The comprehensive specification book used by the firm between 1877 and 1883 contains very few wooden houses. An early example, by Robinson, Tracy, and Fairbairne, applied principles of the balloon frame (it had uniform studs and joists, the latter placed at regular sixteen-inch intervals, and used 'wrought nails'), but the architects retained the heavy sill (ten inch by ten inch) and corner posts (six inch by six inch) of the traditional timber frame structure. For another, somewhat later, house, Tracy and Durand still required six-by-six-inch corner posts, though the specification otherwise conformed to the usual pattern of balloon framing. Nevertheless, until early in this century, that method seems to have been used sparingly by members of the firm; the vast majority of their buildings had solid or hollow brick walls,[100] probably because brick was cheap and readily available in the area until early in this century. When rising prices after the First World War made brick veneer an attractive option, the balloon frame came to be used more frequently. After the late 1890s the Western Wire and Nail Company produced cheap nails right in London,[101] and the many city saw-mills had long been turning out the requisite standard sizes of lumber.

The development of more sophisticated sawing machines affected not only the frame structure of a building, but also its decoration. The scroll-saw, fretsaw, and jigsaw could produce the various 'gingerbread' trims found on Victorian houses, and the treadle lathe facilitated the turnings so liberally

25   Robert D. McDonald House, London, designed c. 1910 by Moore, Henry, and Munro, portico

26 Roman Corinthian capital, from *Illustrated Catalogue of Composition Capitals and Brackets*, The Decorators Supply Company, June 1909

used on furniture legs, balusters, and finials. London possessed numerous planing mills where such embellishments could be produced. An 1884 newspaper article on J.C. Dodd & Son describes them as contractors and manufacturers of doors, sashes, mouldings, band- and scroll-sawing, brackets, stairs, newel posts, hand rails, balusters, 'and all manner of descriptions in fine interior woodwork.' The *Advertiser* went so far as to claim that 'the planing mills of a city speak louder for its growth and that of its surroundings, than any proclamation from the pen of statesman or philosopher.'[102] Among the many proclaimers of the city's growth was A. Cole, 'Wood Turner and Sawyer,' who produced the usual newel posts, balusters, and so on in 1887 but made 'a leading specialty of re-turning billiard and bagatelle balls.'[103]

The enthusiasm for the ornate and whimsical decorations that the new machines could create lasted throughout the Edwardian period, but their production, like that of other building parts, became increasingly standardized and specialized. A London man who studied a particular form of Italianate door found that, of around fifty doors on houses dating mainly from the early 1870s, no two had the same measurements or proportions.[104] By the turn of the century, mail-order books such as the *Universal Design Book* of 1904, sold in both the United States and Canada, made it possible for retail dealers to order an astounding variety of ready-made items in specified sizes: doors, blinds, window and door frames, mantels, mouldings, porch and stair-hall designs (the latter coming complete with the necessary panelling), store fronts, brackets, columns and pilasters, and more. This particular catalogue is not known to have been used in London, but at least one of its suppliers issued a catalogue that was. John M. Moore and his partner, J. Vicar Munro, ordered the 'composition' capitals for the McDonald house (c. 1910; figs 25 and 220) from the Decorators Supply Co. of Chicago. The exterior columns featured 'Roman Corinthian' capitals, modelled on the Pantheon (fig. 26);

inside, one leaps seventeen centuries to the 'modern French Ionic' of Versailles.[105]

The one material that depended on local manufacturers during this period was brick. As late as 1903 the Bureau of Mines reported that 'the multitude of small brick-yards in the main supply the wants of village and rural communities, whose market is preserved to the local makers by reason of the heavy cost of transporting so weighty a material.' Larger suburban plants catered to town and city dwellers.[106] It was this necessary reliance on the home-made product that proved largely responsible for the distinctive appearance of Victorian buildings in south-western Ontario.

The dominant brickmaking material in the large part of Ontario that lies south and west of Ottawa is Erie clay, a relatively clear clay formed in the lakes that covered much of the area during the glacial period. Bricks manufactured from Erie clay burn to a colour often called 'white' in technical literature, but possessing a yellowish buff colour in reality. The exception to this rule is the upper layer of the clay if it is exposed to the surface. The colour of brick depends on the proportions of iron and lime in the clay from which it is made. When Erie clay is exposed to the weathering effects of rain and snow, the soluble lime is washed away while the iron remains, imparting a red colour to bricks made from Upper Erie, or red-top, clay. A study carried out by M.B. Baker in 1906 for the Bureau of Mines found that 'the whole of Western Ontario is covered by a mantle of Erie clay which varies in depth from 1 foot to 130 feet, and in many places is no doubt thicker still ... It is usually found in deep banks of a stiff, tough nature, and is commonly known as "blue clay." ' A slightly earlier report had already commented on the 'abundance of clay' in the province: 'A taste for brick has thus been fostered, and the substantial appearance of such cities as Toronto and Hamilton is in decided contrast to the flimsiness of many frame-built American towns.'[107] As an 1851 article in the London *Free Press* reveals, brick houses were clearly regarded as signs of affluence:

Reader: perhaps like ourselves, you can neither afford the time nor money to visit the World's Fair ... ; perhaps nearer home we may find instructive proof of the progress we are making ourselves.

Mount your buggy then for a drive ... As you travel along, comfortable brick houses face the road, and give you the best idea of the thriving condition of the farmers. The old log house, perhaps, is tenanted by the porkers, or is used as a barn; showing not only the success which has attended the farmer's labours, but that the success is participated in by additional comfort to himself and his stock.[108]

Artist James Hamilton handsomely portrays some clay banks near London in a painting that dates from about 1860 (fig. 27), but one cannot be certain these are banks of Erie clay. The London brickyards operating in 1906 used a quite different and rarer form of post-glacial, sedimentary clay labelled Lacustrine, which probably represented 'an expansion of the old Thames drainage basin.'[109] However unique its source, the brick made from Lacus-

27   *Clay Banks*, oil on canvas, by James Hamilton, c. 1860

trine clay resembled that made from Erie clay in colour – even, it seems, to the point of producing red bricks if exposed to weathering. The granddaughter of one of the Edwardian brickmakers in London presented to her brother a brick from the Masuret house (designed by Durand c. 1884; fig. 129), along with the following note: 'The bricks for this dwelling were made and supplied by your grandfather, the late John Walker, whose initials were stamped on every brick. Ironically, the bricks for this house were the only red bricks ever manufactured as his land, in the Adelaide-Cheapside area, only contained one small vein of red clay and was completely exhausted after this making – and all other bricks in this yard were white.'[110]

Though the basic material remained the same throughout the nineteenth century, there were significant innovations in the ways bricks were made. A settlement provided itself with brick as early as possible; Ezra and Nathan Griffiths were making bricks just outside the London reserve in 1816 and bartering the number needed for a chimney in return for a cow.[111] When London became the District Town, brickmaking operations were established near the forks of the Thames to supply material for building the courthouse.[112] As the city grew, so many brickyards appeared along what is now Commissioners Road that it came to be called Brick Street. These were mainly cottage industries, where brickmaking was a fairly primitive operation. The usual procedure was for the clay and water to be mixed in large troughs by teams of oxen, after which the clay was pressed by hand into moulds, left to dry in the sun, and finally fired in temporary brick kilns. The first machines used to simplify the process were pug mills for mixing, or tempering, the clay, and in 1846 a London District man named David Jacobs Ellis patented a machine, driven by one horse, that could also place the clay in moulds.[113] But London's growth over the next several decades required more efficient operations, with steam-driven engines. Numerous machines were invented for tempering clay and moulding bricks, and, while they varied greatly in design, the processes they employed generally fell into three categories: soft mud, stiff mud, and dry press. Soft-mud machines mixed the clay with water and placed it in moulds.[114] The stiff-mud process, predictably enough, required less water and forced the clay through a rectangular orifice, thus producing a continuous column of clay that needed simply to be cut at regular intervals. The dry-press method used considerable pressure to mould pulverized dry clay or shale into the proper shape. In 1868 the London Pressed Brick Company greatly impressed the *Free Press* reporter with 'the process of brick making by the aid of steam machinery,' whereby '25,000 bricks are readily turned out in a working day of ten hours.'[115] The machine being used, one of 'Sword's Patent Brick Machines,' constructed in Adrian, Michigan, seems to have combined aspects of all three processes. Its basic approach was that of the soft-mud method: 'the body of the machine is a large wooden cylinder, in which work a number of steel knives. The clay is channelled in at the top, and as the knives revolve the clay descends into highly finished steel moulds.' The clay was quite stiff, however: it 'is shovelled direct from the bank into barrows, and is wheeled and cast into the machines just as it is, with the exception of a little sand thrown on when the clay is damp, or a little water if too dry.' Pressure was exerted in shaping the brick: 'These moulds pass over two wheels, and by the aid of a mechanical contrivance the clay is pressed into the moulds very firmly.' The journalist has been soundly coached in the advantages of such pressing:

With reference to the quality of brick made, it is first class, the pressure on the moulds being the same, a uniform standard of brick is secured, and owing to the high pressure, the clay is more solidified than hand made brick. This fact is proved by a comparison of weight, the patent pressed brick weighing, when burnt, from three-quarters of a pound to one pound more than ordinary brick. It is evident that a wall made of pressed brick must be firmer than that with the ordinary article, and as the brick is closer packed in the manufacture, it follows that the cold cannot penetrate so easily, and therefore a building would be warmer when composed of this material.

Despite its pride and its name, the London Pressed Brick Company was not turning out the bona fide article, as a local competitor was quick to make known. Two days after the *Free Press* printed its eulogy of the company, the *Advertiser* carried a notice about 'another brick machine ... designed on the principle of what are known as "dry clay" machines – differing materially from that of the one now in use by the London Pressed Brick Manufacturing Company which uses tempered clay.' This second machine is intriguing. It was designed by a London miller named Henry Fysh and built to his specifications by a Brantford foundry.[116] Unfortunately, the *Advertiser* seems never to have fulfilled its promise of an analysis of the machine's success. By 1875 a Mr Darville of London was manufacturing brickmaking machinery.[117]

As mechanization increased, the cottage industries along Brick Street gradually disappeared,[118] and the centre of brickmaking operations moved to the northern part of the city. In 1875 all three brickyards listed in the classified section of the city directory were located on Adelaide Street between Grosvenor and Victoria Streets. During the decades between 1890 and 1910 there were generally five or six plants in the same area, and one or two in the vicinity of Pipeline Road (now Springbank Drive). According to Mr Baker's report of 1906, all these yards used a soft-mud process, and all were highly mechanized, with permanent kilns. His description of the London Brick Manufacturing and Supply Co. in the Adelaide Street area shows how much things had changed since the days when oxen worked the clay and the sun dried the bricks:

The section of clay is dug ... hauled in dump cars and dumped into a Raymond machine ... It is a very powerful machine with a good pug-mill attachment, and makes six brick at a time. These brick are dumped on pallets which are piled on cars carrying three hundred and thirty brick at a load. These cars are run into long tunnels, through which a blast of hot air is forced by a fan. The cars all enter at one end of the tunnels, which is also the cooler end, so that the green brick get least hot draft while they are wettest. As the dry brick are taken from the opposite or hotter end of the tunnel, each car moves down one length, so that at the end of forty-eight hours each car of brick is dry; the cars are then run into the large open up-draft kilns, three in number. These kilns have permanent side walls in which are placed the fire arches. Each kiln has twenty-five arches and is capable of holding five hundred thousand brick.[119]

The same period also brought innovations in brick construction, albeit less radical ones.[120] The earliest brick buildings possessed a solid brick wall, usually twelve to sixteen inches thick, but the advantages of the hollow brick wall came to be widely recognized after the middle of the century. Consisting essentially of two thinner walls separated by a hollow air space, it provided insulation that was badly needed in the Canadian climate, it prevented dampness on the inside wall, and, of course, it required fewer bricks. The inner and outer layers of the wall were tied together by bricks set perpendicular to regular courses, or by strips of iron or steel. Robinson used a variation on the usual formula for the wall of the Becher office (1868): there, the outer layer of the front wall was two bricks thick, and the inner layer one brick thick, giving the wall as a whole a thickness of eighteen inches. John M. Moore used hollow wall construction right through the Edwardian period. Even the plans for the R.D. McDonald house (c. 1910; fig. 219) show a thirteen-inch hollow brick wall.[121]

Brick veneer made its appearance in London as early as 1889, but it seems not to have been widely used in London until after the First World War, when the brick industry was influenced by the post-war economic milieu. Brick was no longer cheap then. The Bureau of Mines report of 1909 had already bemoaned the demise of 'the era of cheap brick,' but it was complaining of cost increases that were minute compared with those of the next decade. In 1911 the average price for common brick was $7.90 per thousand; in 1920 one paid $13.92 per thousand 'at the works.'[122] Moreover, it was no longer assumed that bricks would be supplied locally. The building depression of the war years had forced brickyards to close down, and those that were left tended to consolidate into large-scale operations that could compensate for the cost of transporting a heavy product by the advantages of mass production, advanced technical expertise, and sophisticated merchandizing techniques. In London there was at most one plant in operation during the war, and the three or four that struggled back into business afterwards were bought up by Phinn Brothers around 1923.[123]

Though Phinn Brothers ran a sizeable operation, a glance at London buildings of the 1920s shows that the local firm was not supplying most of the face bricks used in town. Imported red bricks had already begun to be regarded as prestigious towards the end of the nineteenth century, when pressed brick, made from shale, had come to be admired for its strength, regularity, and smoothness. The grand homes built for John Labatt and Benjamin Cronyn Jr in the early 1880s had used pressed red brick from Hamilton or Toronto. The Bureau of Mines had reported in 1904 that pressed brick was in demand 'for better-class houses in the cities, fronts, etc.'[124] Before the war, however, the necessity of transporting pressed brick made it a considerably pricier commodity for Londoners. Moreover, it was not universally admired. Toronto architect Frank Darling complained in 1897 that one 'could not get a pretty wall out of it. The beauty of a wall constructed of the old brick was that when the sun struck it there were no two places in it that looked alike.'[125] Such an attitude came to fruition in the vigorous demand for 'rug brick' after the war. Its purposely roughened surface, made by scratching the sides of the stiff-mud brick before it was fired, combined with its 'autumnal' colours to recall the more primitive hand-made bricks of a century before.[126]

It is possible, too, that some contempt for the traditional buff brick joined with the current fads to reduce its use. In a study commissioned by the Ontario Department of Mines in 1930, Robert J. Montgomery observed that 'cream-coloured bricks' in the province 'have stood the test of time as well as the red, and some brick men contend that they stand weather better; but they discolour badly when exposed to dust. The brick are porous and absorb the dust, and cleaning is difficult. Cream-coloured bricks when used in the country away from factories and railways give very delightful architectural effects and a pleasing appearance even after years of exposure.'[127] Quite possibly the more venerable bricks about town made the local product less appealing than it might have seemed a few decades before.

The writer of an earlier Bureau of Mines report (1905) had complained that, rather unjustly given their economic importance, 'a bed of shale or a bank of clay makes no such appeal to the imagination as does a gold or silver mine.'[128] In his calculations of clay's impressive worth, the author views the basic building brick as only one of several significant items. Others included sewer pipe, drain tile, paving brick, and specialized forms of brick such as terra cotta. 'Terra cotta lumber,' as it was called, consisted of hollow, porous bricks, produced by a stiff-mud process, into which nails could be pounded as if they were wood. In 1891 the Montreal Terra Cotta Lumber Company proudly advertised its product's superiority to the common wooden variety of lumber, describing it as 'Fire Proof, Sound Proof, Vermin Proof and Damp Proof.' Terra cotta was also important as an ornamental material: it could be pressed in plaster of paris or steel moulds to form capitals, friezes, panels, and medallions, such as the rosette on the Perth County Courthouse. Terra cotta was never made in London. As the demand for bricks of Erie clay diminished, the area came to specialize in the production of drainage tiles.[129]

A few communities in south-western Ontario, such as St Marys and Guelph, could rely on a nearby supply of stone as the major building material, but, like brick, stone was too heavy to be economically transported in quantity. Although St Marys is merely twenty-five miles from London, only two London buildings are thought to have been faced with St Marys limestone, and one, St Mary's Church, was based on plans initially intended for a church in St Marys.[130]

For situations where stone was considered essential, however, its patrons were willing to transport the most desirable sort over considerable distances rather than rely on the St Marys product nearby. The Custom House (1870–3; fig. 51) had a foundation of St Marys rubble stone but employed harder Ohio stone for the rest of the building. The Becher office (1868) also used St Marys stone for its foundation and Ohio stone for doorsteps, window-sills, and keystones. The Benjamin Cronyn Jr house (completed 1882; fig. 111) had window heads and sills of 'Buff Ohio Sandstone.' The Simcoe Street School (1889) had basement walls and 'handsome dressings' of brown Credit Valley sandstone, though the journalist describing the school for the *Advertiser* clearly possessed reservations as to just how handsome some of the dressings were: 'Over each of the main archways are what is purported to be the likenesses of ex-Chairman Sharman and Chairman Wright, of the Board of Education, but it would take a rather acute observer to recognize the faces of either of these gentlemen in the stone cutting.'[131] It seems that marble and polished granite came from even farther away. The Bureau of Mines report for 1905 is rather scornful about the lack of energy displayed in developing Ontario's own resources in that line:

It is passing strange that in a country so well provided with granite as Ontario, conveniently situated, too, as much of it is for shipment by water, practically none of the native material is made use of by our stone-cutters or monument-makers. Very much of the polished granite seen in our cemeteries and adorning the fronts of business blocks is turned out of the stone yards of Aberdeen, Scotland, but is really brought in the rough to that place by sea from Sweden and Norway. What Scandinavia does not furnish us, via Scotland, is sent by Massachusetts, Vermont and Quebec, but one will look almost in vain for shaft or pillar for which a domestic origin can be claimed.[132]

Slate began to be used as a roofing material in London during the 1870s and continued in demand until the First World War.[133] It was popular partly because it was fireproof and relatively weather resistant, and partly because the patterns that could be formed by using different colours of slate complemented the other kinds of elaborate ornamentation then fashionable. But the fact that it needed to be transported from Vermont, Quebec, or eastern Ontario made slate an option for only the more substantial buildings, and even some of them chose cheaper wood shingles, often shaped and painted to imitate the pattern of slate. As has already been noted, galvanized iron was frequently used for roofing commercial buildings. When the roof was flat, tarred and gravelled felt provided the better alternative; indeed, William Robinson considered this mixture sufficiently attractive to cover the visible bottom layer of the roof over his Crystal Palace (1861; fig. 41).[134] The asphalt roofers who advertised in the 1897–8 *London Directory* likely applied a tar and asphalt mixture to flat roofs, though some experiments with the predecessors of today's asphalt shingles had then taken place in the United States.

By the turn of the century Portland cement concrete offered a formidable challenge to stone in many of its traditional roles. The ever vigilant Bureau of Mines reported in 1904 that 'quarrymen look askance at the new material which is replacing their product in bridge work, foundations and construction work of various kinds, contending that it will prove less durable, and more liable to destruction by frost when exposed to the action of water. Time only will show whether these imputations are warranted, but in the meantime there is little doubt that cement for many uses is pressing hard upon stone.' In one sense, concrete was hardly new. The Romans had made cement, using lime from volcanic ash, and 'the success with which [their] structures ... have resisted the wear and tear of the elements down to the present day' had already made the Bureau of Mines optimistic about concrete's durability.[135]

The technique for making cement had been forgotten after the dissolution of the Roman Empire. In 1756 the English engineer John Smeaton rediscovered that some limes, if burned and mixed with water, would harden and stay hard when dry, and hydraulic cements, made from rocks possessing such lime, began to be used in various kinds of construction. But the development that gave concrete a real edge over traditional materials occurred nearly seventy years later, in 1824, when an English bricklayer named Joseph Aspdin devised a method of making cement by mixing clay with carbonate of lime. Since the concrete formed with the addition of sand resembled stone found on the Isle of Portland, he named his invention Portland cement. It was mainly Portland cement that threatened the eminence of the older materials and assumed its own place as a major structural element. Concrete proved a durable, fire-proof, and easily installed material, eliminating the need for highly skilled workmen. Its main weakness, a low tensile strength, could be overcome if it were reinforced with iron or steel rods. The Bureau of Mines, implicitly siding against the quarrymen, described reinforced concrete as 'the only form of construction that is really permanent.'[136]

Hydraulic, or natural rock, cements were manufactured and used in Canada after the middle of the nineteenth century.[137] The specification book shows that houses built by Robinson's firm had concrete basements in 1878, but concrete began to exert a visible effect on London buildings only during the first decade of this century. Cement blocks were used for the foundations of houses, with those showing above ground rusticated to look like stone. After 1907 the blocks were manufactured in London. The mounting shop of McClary's new factory (1904), designed by John M. Moore and Fred Henry, was one of the first all-concrete buildings in Canada, an honour shared with a store in Halifax erected during the same year and reported in the same issue of the *Canadian Architect and Builder*. In 1911 Moore and Munro employed the recently developed Kahn system of reinforcement, featuring steel rods with projecting fins, to strengthen the concrete walls of the Fireproof Warehousing Company near the corner of Richmond and Piccadilly streets.[138]

The period's innovations in the materials and methods for constructing the exterior shells of buildings were accompanied by equally startling developments in interior comforts. A local plumber was already advertising 'Hot and Cold Shower Baths and Water Closets' in 1857, but it seems unlikely that many people were taking advantage of such amenities.[139] There was a marked note of wonder in the *Advertiser*'s account of the bathrooms in Hellmuth's new Collegiate Institute (1864–5; fig. 43): they were 'provided with hot and cold water, which can be brought on by merely turning the taps.' A versatile engine in the basement pumped water up to the taps, drove a sawing machine that cut firewood, and filled a tank on the roof from which water flowed to a fountain on the grounds.[140] The manse of St Andrew's Presbyterian Church (1871; fig. 50) had some form of indoor plumbing, but nothing is known about its accoutrements or means of functioning. The specification book gives quite complete details, however, for the plumbing facilities at the Murray house (1878; fig. 95). The house featured a basement laundry, ground-floor water closet, a scullery with an enamelled iron sink, and an elegant second-floor bathroom with a 'copper-trimmed' bathtub in a 'black walnut casing' and a 'Wedgewood ware marbled basin' with 'marble top and sides.' The house was connected to the new city water system; it apparently used rain-water collected from the eavestroughs as well. A steam-operated force and lift pump pushed water from an underground cistern to a lead-lined tank in the attic, over the second-floor bathroom. Water was heated by a boiler in the kitchen so that all taps were provided with hot and cold water. This scheme was only slightly varied in houses built by Robinson's firm well into the Edwardian period. Some houses had separate tanks for soft and hard water. Others had more basins and bathrooms. The London Club (1880–2; fig. 103) was connected to a sewer on Richmond Street.[141]

Hellmuth's Collegiate Institute featured gas lighting, likely provided by the recently revitalized City Gas Company. It is improbable that most London residences had parted with their oil lamps by this date, but it is clear that all houses built by the firm between the late 1870s and the turn of the century were routinely equipped with gas lighting. The Arva Methodist Church (1898; fig. 202) was lighted with acetylene.[142] The London *Free Press* reported in 1886 that an electric light company was making plans for 'affording illumination for the citizens,' and by 1889 there were two electric light companies in town.[143] Nevertheless, even the firm's most substantial houses used gas lighting well into this century. The Leonard house (1893–4; fig. 189) took advantage of the new amenity, using both gas and electricity for lighting. Possibly electricity was regarded with some suspicion; for even as late as 1910 the McDonald house (fig. 220) still relied on both systems. (The McDonald house also used gas logs in some of its fireplaces.)[144]

Although many Victorian houses boasted numerous fireplaces, and the cast-iron stoves so abundantly produced in London could heat rooms most efficiently, various forms of central heating came to be common during the last half of the nineteenth century. Hellmuth's well-furnished Collegiate Institute was equipped with steam heating in 1865: a boiler in the basement produced steam that was then sent throughout the building in cast-iron pipes. The Bishop's Palace (1870–2; fig. 53) was heated with hot air produced by a coal-burning furnace and circulated to the rooms above by virtue of its lightness. The London Club (1880–1) relied on hot water flowing through a series of coiled pipes, or radiators. Most houses designed by the firm between 1878 and the mid-1890s were equipped with a hot-air system like that in the Bishop's Palace; thereafter, hot water or steam heating came to be preferred.[145]

The North American enthusiasm for central heating was then, as now, a common cause for complaint on the part of British visitors: 'Casual visitors are nearly suffocated by it,' wrote one, 'and constant occupiers are killed.'[146] Contemporary scientists offered some support for the claim. One theory held that hot metal literally burnt the air and made it unwholesome. But the hot air was generally thought to be less dangerous to health than were a building's inhabitants. The knowledge that the human body used oxygen and expelled carbon dioxide led to a theory that 'breathed over' air was harmful. 'Man's own breath is his greatest enemy,' wrote Philadelphia engineer Lewis W. Leeds in the 1860s.[147] Both dangers probably influenced J. George Hodgins's concern with ventilation in Ontario schoolhouses: 'in every school-house without proper means of ventilation, there is a slow and subtle poison, which enters the blood and brains of the pupils, and saps the very foundation of life.'[148]

The evil of inside air made adequate ventilation a major concern of the architect. High ceilings, transoms, and grilles between rooms constituted early attempts to create a healthy flow of air. The Smead system, used by Tracy in the Simcoe Street School (1889), went a step further by assuring a constant supply of fresh air. The system was similar to that found in modern forced hot air systems, where hot air flows through ducts from the furnace, and cold air is led back through separate ducts. In the Smead system, however, the furnaces heated fresh air from outside, while the used air was led into 'foul air rooms' from which it dissipated. 'By this means,' noted the *Advertiser*, 'the air can be changed in a room about 10 times in an hour.'[149]

It was the ability to solve problems such as those concerning drainage and ventilation that led architects to see themselves as practitioners of preventive medicine. In his address to the first convention of the Ontario Association of Architects, President W.G. Storm lauded the importance of the architectural profession partly on medical grounds: 'while to the physician is entrusted the care of the patient after disease has found a lodgement in the system, the architect has charge of the construction of the homes of the community which, from want of a thorough knowledge of sanitary and other kindred matters, may become the hot bed of foul and fatal diseases carrying misery and death throughout the whole neighbourhood, instead of being the health-giving homes of a happy and prosperous community.'[150]

THE ARCHITECT AT THE END OF THE NINETEENTH CENTURY

By the end of the century architects were acutely aware of the complexity of their work. W.E. Doran, an architect from Montreal, complained rather peevishly about the manifold obligations of his job:

the Law says [the architect's] work must be perfect – not only his own work, but he is obliged to see that the work of every cheap Jack whom the cupidity of his client obliges him to employ shall be perfect; he must be omniscient; he must know before-hand the nature of every kind of material used in construction, its power of resistance to strains of every description, to time and to weather, the nature and strength of all cements and mortars, the value of all paints and pigments, he must be proficient in sanitary science, in all manners and fads of heating and ventilation, in all the details of electrical appliances. In a word, he must be master of all the arts and sciences to a certain extent, and then his powers of observation must be limitless; he must foresee against all possible flaws in materials, all willful or unintentional delinquencies on the part of builders.[151]

New esthetic movements and a century's prodigious research on historical styles made mastering the arts as demanding as dealing with the scientific concerns Doran resented.

This proliferation of information was regarded as affecting the architect's role in two ways. First, it encouraged specialization. As Doran rightly prophesied, 'the day of the specialist is coming, and soon the all round man will be regarded as a quack.'[152] Second, it seemed to concerned architects that adequate education had to be mandatory for anyone entering the profession.

After its formation in 1889 the Ontario Association of Architects sought to improve architectural training by setting up stringent educational standards for new members, and seeking to gain legislation that would allow only its members to call themselves architects. Applicants for membership would be required to be over twenty-one years of age; to have completed a five-year period of study with a qualified architect, or three years with an architect in addition to a course at the School of Practical Science; and to have passed a set of qualifying examinations. Four examinations would be necessary: a preliminary examination, two intermediate levels, and a final examination. The topics to be covered were exceedingly comprehensive, ranging from 'History of Architecture' and 'Characteristics of Styles' to 'Mathematics,' 'Structural Iron Work,' and 'Architectural Jurisprudence.' As important as the examinations themselves were the drawings to be submitted in advance. At the first intermediate level students had to prove their facility at working with historical styles, submitting 'Two sheets of the Orders of Architecture, two sheets of the Early English, Decorated and Perpendicular Periods, ... one sheet of Mouldings and Ornament, embodying examples of each of the above Periods.' The second intermediate requirements put more emphasis on technical matters: one sheet, for example, had to show 'Detail Construction of [a] Roof-truss' and two others 'Stone, Brick, and Iron Details.' By the final level students were expected to submit a complete set of architectural drawings, including details and specifications.[153]

The association seems to have been united in enthusiasm for the proposed legislation and confident that its goals were near realization. In December 1889 President Storm predicted 'a new era in Canadian Art' as a result of their legislative efforts: 'our children and children's children will proudly point to a Canadian Architecture worthy of the name.'[154] In March 1890 the *American Architect and Building News* commented rather jealously on the imminent passage of the Ontario Architect's Act: 'The Provincial Government considers the matter of such vital importance to the public that their houses should be carried out under the direction of competent men, and that all buildings of every kind should be properly constructed and supervised, that they have taken it up, made it a Government measure, and this practically insures its passage this session. Did ever any country or part of a country enjoy such an enlightened government?'[155] Such optimism was premature. The act was passed in 1890, but in so emasculated a form that it proved virtually powerless. Instead of allowing association members exclusive rights to the designation 'Architect,' it gave them the title 'Registered Architect,' thus conferring such a subtle element of distinction that it was certain to be lost on the general public. The association agreed to the change, hoping that, once legislators had got into the habit of regulating the architectural profession, they would strengthen the act in succeeding sessions. But three subsequent efforts failed, in 1893,

1896, and 1897, and the association surrendered the attempt. It was not until 1931 that, after a great deal of dogged lobbying by the OAA, the government passed an act making registration and an approved level of education a prerequisite to calling oneself an architect.[156]

Without the backing of legal enforcement, the OAA was forced to lower its own standards and content itself with lesser gains. After 1897 membership again became voluntary, though the association continued its educational efforts by offering classes and setting examinations for students, presenting papers for its members, and, most importantly, by continuing to sponsor the *Canadian Architect and Builder*. A significant further advance in professional organization was the affiliation of the OAA with the Institute of Architects of Canada, formed in 1907 and granted the prefix 'Royal' in 1909.[157]

Despite the profession's concern with the architect's education and the introduction, in Toronto and Montreal, of university courses on architecture, there was still no effective control over the matter even by the Edwardian period. One Mr Lemasnie complained in 1902 of the difficulties facing the many self-educated students: 'And what will become of the student who attempts undirected to read, mark, learn and inwardly digest as much of this [architectural] history as his poor brain can safely bear. I am afraid he will be in the position of the farmer who read through Dr Johnson's dictionary and failed to discover the plot.'[158] Undoubtedly the student architect's best hope throughout the nineteenth century and into the twentieth was to find a teacher like the ideal master described in the *American Architect and Building News*, who attends seriously to his pupil's education without the spurs of legal regulations, and who 'wishes to do his best for him, and help him to do the best he can for himself.'[159]

THE EVOLUTION OF WILLIAM ROBINSON'S FIRM

William Robinson seems to have been a man who would gladly learn and gladly teach. While working for a builder in Toronto, he taught 'geometrical drawing and the various problems connected with their work' to the workmen, at their request.[160] Later, he taught geometrical drawing at the Toronto Mechanics' Institute, and, later still, he was the drawing master at Hellmuth's Collegiate Institute in London. But his talents and inclinations as a teacher seem to have found their most productive outlet within the confines of his own office. An early history of the city's architects lists ten men who learned their profession from William Robinson. Among them are Thomas W. Dyas, who published *The Canadian Builder*; Richard Purdom and Richard P. Fairbairne, who made careers in the department of public works in Toronto, Fairbairne becoming deputy minister; Richard Wright, who joined the staff of the Dominion Architect in Ottawa; and, of course, Thomas Tracy, George Durand, and John Moore, who became partners in Robinson's own firm.[161] The history of that firm suggests that Robinson inspired in his students a respect for the professional ideal of the times, with its insistence on accurate

engineering, fair business dealings, and tasteful design. He also seems
to have inspired loyalty to his ideal of sound teaching, so that a succession
of well-trained Londoners could grow into the succession of partners who
made his firm prominent over many decades. In fact, the firm is still
in business, though this study concerns itself only with its history prior to
the First World War.

To speak of a single firm during that period is in some ways misleading.
Probably both Durand and Moore thought of themselves as possessing independent businesses. No single building, person, purpose, or even name
gave the successive partners a consciousness of working for the same organization. Official company names as indicated in city directories, in tender calls,
and on drawings, are less indicative of a single firm than of a series of more
or less casually formed partnerships:

1857–73	William Robinson
1873–6	Robinson and Tracy
1877	Robinson, Tracy, and Fairbairne
1878	Robinson, Tracy, Durand and Co.
1879	Thomas H. Tracy
1880–2	Tracy and Durand
1882–9	George F. Durand (or, at times, Durand and Moore)
1890–1	Fred Henry ⎫ working separately John M. Moore ⎭
1892–1907	Moore and Henry
1908–10	Moore, Henry, and Munro
1911–13	Moore and Munro
1914	John M. Moore

Such a list tells only part of the story, however. Tracy and Durand were
apprentices together. Part of Fairbairne's apprenticeship overlapped with the
period when Tracy was Robinson's partner. Moore was articled to Robinson
and Tracy and continued working for Tracy and Durand after Robinson's
retirement. His association with Durand came to a bitter end in 1888, when
he sued Durand over disagreements concerning Moore's status in the office
and his share of profits. The dispute shows that Moore held a special
position in Durand's office, though in Durand's view, at least, it fell short of
a real partnership. Fred Henry served a kind of double apprenticeship,
simultaneously training as an architect under Durand and a land surveyor under
Moore. He then became assistant city engineer under Tracy, who had resigned
as Durand's partner when, in 1882, Tracy's role as city engineer was designated
a full-time position. Henry returned to Durand's office in 1889 and took over
the business after Durand's death later that year. J. Vicar Munro was inden-
tured to Henry some years before he joined Moore and Henry as a partner.
These men had long-standing, interrelated professional ties and, obviously, a
strong tendency to work together. Given the continuity of influences and,

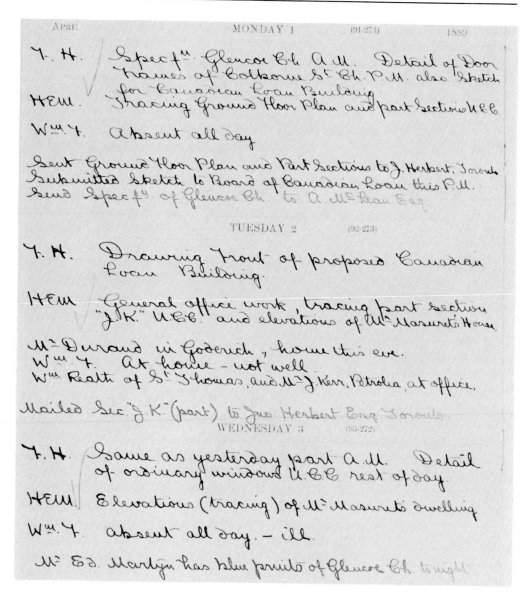

28   George F. Durand's daybook, entries for 1, 2, and 3 April 1889

significantly, of records in this series of practices, it is fitting and productive to consider their cumulative professional history as the history of a single firm.

There were substantial changes in business and organizational practices over the period, owing largely to the increasing demands created by the new technology. Since more complicated directions needed to be provided for builders, architectural drawings, like contracts and specifications, became more detailed.[162] Robinson seems customarily to have produced one set of drawings for a building, with floor plans, sections, and elevations all on a single sheet of paper or linen. His elevations are sometimes enlivened by hints of a setting and of three-dimensionality. The side and front elevations of Christ Church, for example, are set on a brown strip of ground and surrounded by blue sky (fig. 42). Shadows fall away from the buttresses and darken the chancel. The drawings of Durand's era make a clear-cut distinction between working elevations and perspectives. The elevations are insistently flat, and they occupy an undefined space, while the perspective drawings provide buildings with richly imagined, idyllic settings. Following the norm for this period, the church at Walton (fig. 97) is given surroundings that are physically inviting and also suggest an attractive social world: men visit; a child plays, accompanied by the friendly dog of the established stereotype. The increasingly informative floor plans and sections of Durand's era are often relegated to separate sheets of their own, and numerous tracings denote the increased need for independent working copies. Company records make it clear that Durand's office also produced blueprints. The drawings made in Moore's firm after the turn of the century carried even more technical directions, and they were more consistently drawn to a quarter-inch rather than an eighth-inch scale. The delicate watercolour tints used in the earlier drawings to denote materials were later replaced by coloured inks.

Architectural drawings were the subject of considerable professional interest during this period. Architect Percy Nobbs spoke in 1904 on the 'development of draughtsmanship' over the last century, attributing it to the influence of measured drawings on the one hand and the pressures of competitions on the other.[163] The OAA organized an exhibition of architectural drawings as a major feature of its first annual convention[164] and placed a heavy emphasis on drawing as part of a student's education. Yet there seems to have been relatively little connection between an architect's professional prestige and the quality of his drawing. Existing daybooks from Durand's period (fig. 28), listing the activities assigned to each member of the staff, show that Durand himself spent a great deal of time away from the office, engaged in the promotional or supervisory aspects of the firm's work, while a staff ranging in number from two to five laboured steadily at the drawing board. This situation was by no means unusual. Speaking to the OAA in 1900, W.A. Langton observed, 'When an architect sues for his fee and his drawings are brought into court as evidence of the work he has done, the opposing counsel at once proceeds to make the discovery that the drawings have not been made by the architect at all but by a draughtsman.' Langton goes on to consider the vexed question of the architect's responsibility for a design he does not draw. He observes that the American architect H.H. Richardson evolved a highly personal style, yet he himself usually provided only sketches of floor plans as the initial basis for his draughtsmen's efforts:

some big works had possessed the mind of the head draughtsman with ideas of grandeur. He was at a table near me designing the entrance to a house at Albany when Mr Richardson passed and, after looking over his shoulder for a moment, said, 'C'est

29 'Graeme's Dyke,' Harrow Weald, Greater London, England, 1870–2, architectural perspective drawing by R. Norman Shaw, from R. Phene Spiers's *Architectural Drawing*, 1887

la delicatesse qu'il faut maintenant mon ami,' (it is refinement we want now) and went away. It was delicatesse he got. The fenestration of this house was in charge of another draughtsman whom Mr Richardson kept rubbing out his windows all morning until they came right and were accepted with the remark 'there is nothing like rubbing out.'[165]

Langton obviously considers Richardson's practices rather extreme, but his discussion shows that, even in more typical offices, the draughtsmen played a crucial role in producing the final working drawings.

Perspectives, on the other hand, came frequently to be the province of specialists. R. Phene Spiers noted in *Architectural Drawing* (1887) that 'as a rule it is found more convenient to have large perspective drawings prepared away from the office by architects and artists who have made it their special avocation.'[166] Despite the fact that Durand himself was an accomplished artist, the daybook shows that he had one of the watercolours he submitted to the OAA exhibition, a perspective of his design for Upper Canada College, drawn by such an expert: 'Saturday, January 12 Rec[d] from "American Architect" via Detroit the water color Perspective of College executed by E.A. Dean'[167]

Certainly practices varied from time to time and office to office. Durand's other offering to the OAA exhibition was his own watercolour perspective of the Labatt house (1882–4; fig. 116).[168] Fred Henry was sufficiently interested in drawing to obtain Spiers's book,[169] an extremely comprehensive volume with illustrations that inspire a high level of performance. The complicated angles of Graeme's Dyke, for example, provide matter for a demonstration of R. Norman Shaw's skill at pen-and-ink perspectives (fig. 29). In 1912 perspectives required in Moore's office were executed by one of his draughtsmen, Donald Hennigar.[170] Nevertheless, while good drawing was greatly admired, the really essential aspects of the architect's role were mainly intellectual: he combined the ability to envisage plans and designs, leaving draughtsmen and builders to give them tangible, visible forms.

While it is impossible to know exactly what roles the firm's architects played in producing designs, the daybooks reinforce stylistic evidence in suggesting that their functions became more specialized as the period progressed. Robinson and Tracy seem to have worked quite independently, if amiably, within the context of their partnership. One can make an intelligent guess by looking at one of their buildings as to which partner was its designer; their individual styles seem distinctive, despite some obvious cross-influences; and newspaper reports make it clear that most commissions were undertaken by a single architect rather than carried out as a collaborative effort. In contrast, most of the designs that came from Durand's office bear a common stamp, suggesting that Durand kept firm control over the artistic dimension of work bearing his name. Characteristic touches from both Tracy and Durand in the earlier buildings imply collaborative efforts. The arrangement Durand made with Moore after Tracy's departure seems to have involved a clear division of responsibility rather than collaboration: Moore was to 'look after all Surveying and Engineering work,' but his role as a designer was apparently limited to executing Durand's ideas.[171] Moore continued to apply the principle of a division of labour when he headed his own business. By 1912 Moore had so arranged his office that he had two employees, including his son O. Roy, dealing mainly with buildings requiring considerable technical knowledge; and two others, including Munro, working on buildings where artistry in design was a more major consideration.[172]

Despite the increasing specialization in architectural practice between 1860 and the First World War, the differing talents of the various architects, and the fashionable shifts in styles and materials over these years, there are some strong threads of continuity in the firm's work. All the firm's members attended to sound engineering, but Robinson, Tracy, and Moore showed a particular interest in the technical side of their work. Moreover, all shared certain broad attitudes towards building design: a respect for balance and unity; a sense of restraint; careful control of details; and the flexibility, openness, and curiosity required to adapt to stylistic innovations. There were also numerous signs of more specific kinds of influence. Sometimes the firm's designs comprised reinterpretations of earlier buildings. The tower of the Presbyterian Church in Dorchester (fig. 176), designed by Moore, handles details in a manner reminiscent of Durand's Roman Catholic Church in Petrolia, and it is tempting to trace elements in both back to some of Robinson's work (figs 49 and 70). The

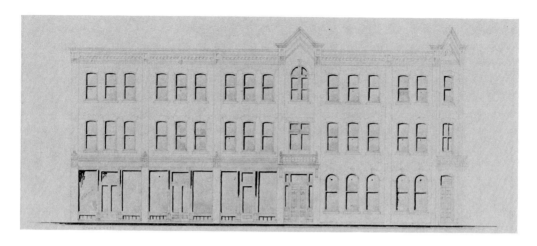

30 'Hotel & Stores for D. McRae Esq.,' Glencoe, designed c. 1890 by John M. Moore

format for most of the public schools designed by Tracy and Durand is modelled on Robinson's King Street School. On other occasions elements of an older work are simply reused. The design Moore employed for numerous village hotels, such as D. McRae's in Glencoe (fig. 30), is just a slightly simplified version of Tracy's Grigg's Hotel in London (fig. 83), built eleven years before. The Whiskard house (fig. 186), by Moore and Henry, has porches and a bay that strikingly resemble equivalent features on the double house Durand designed for Thomas Parker (fig. 165).

The firm retained a consistently high reputation, gaining many of the most important commissions in London and in a broad area around it. Robinson designed churches in Barrie and Dresden, near Chatham; Durand was the architect of the Perth County Building in Stratford, Victoria Hall in Petrolia, and Upper Canada College in Toronto. Moore provided plans for a rectory as far away as Windsor.[173] Ultimately, Robinson's influence spread, directly or indirectly, well beyond the boundaries of his adopted home. He could also claim most of the credit for turning London itself into an 'architectural city' that far surpassed the Eden of Martin Chuzzlewit's dreams.

The Robinson Era

WILLIAM ROBINSON

STILL A YOUNG MAN, just turned twenty-seven, William Robinson first came to London as a labourer engaged to help build barracks for the garrison stationed there after the 1837 Rebellion. Though that stay lasted less than three years, two interesting documents attest to Robinson's interest in both his temporary home and his own intellectual development. That his name is first on the members' list of the London Mechanics' Institute (5 January 1841) suggests that he may have been instrumental in its revival that year; he was later elected its assistant recording secretary.[1] He also drew one of the earliest existing maps of London (fig. 32), though as yet he had no formal qualifications as a surveyor. Dated '1840 & 1841,' it shows the streets as they were envisioned and named in the ambitious 'New Survey' of the late 1830s. Drawings in the map's margins also indicate something of his personal aspirations.

These vignettes are unique. It was fashionable, especially on larger maps made before the middle of the nineteenth century, for the inscription to be surrounded by a fairly elaborate scene of the area being depicted (Indians hunting on a map of America, for example, or a fisherman on a map of Newfoundland). Later in the century one finds a variation of this practice on maps of towns or cities: rather than scenes from life, there are drawings or photographs of major buildings. The images on Robinson's map lack the customary realism and direct relevance to the subject. Instead of scenes of

31 William Robinson (1812–94), from *Annual Report of the Association of Ontario Land Surveyors*, 1915

London, he depicts a scroll draped over a broken column, and a curious fowl who seems to be a peacock. The illustrations appear to be earnest but naïve exercises in drawing, relying largely on stylized and traditional motifs. Although the architectural elements in the sketches are competently done, the flora, fauna, and people are often quite crude. Nevertheless, two of the drawings reveal a bent towards originality and a sense of humour that reward a detailed consideration.

The complex of images surrounding the inscription has a venerable iconographical history, extending back beyond Poussin's *Et in Arcadia Ego* (c. 1630).[2] Poussin's painting depicts three Arcadian shepherds and a shepherdess happening suddenly upon a tomb in their idyllic world; the words of the title, 'Even in Arcady, there am I,' are to be understood as the threatening pronouncement of Death. Among the many later works to feature variations on this theme, Robinson's sketch must rank as one of the most bizarre. The usual iconographical elements are all there: the sarcophagus and urn, the dead branch in the midst of luxuriant growth, the figure pointing to the tomb, and even the Arcadian sheep. But the tomb is rather improbably labelled 'London, Canada West,' and the mourner is an impotent-looking Britannia. Presumably some kind of satire is intended, though its exact nature is now impossible to gauge: Was Robinson a confirmed Tory who predicted doom from the union of the Canadas and the spectre of representative

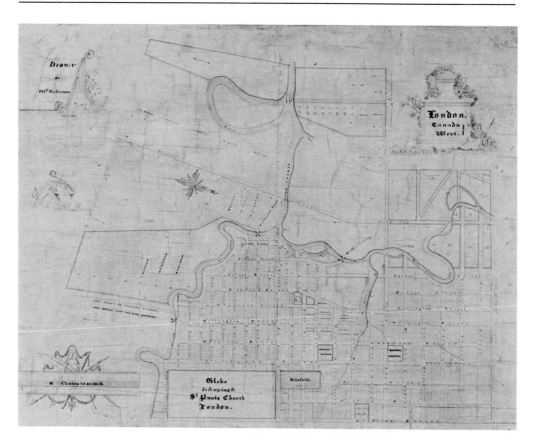

32   *London, Canada West*, map by William Robinson, 1840–1

33   *London, Canada West*, detail showing a young surveyor

government? Was he simply finding London dull? Though too vague to be particularly effective, the vignette does reflect an inventive and informed mind.

Another drawing (fig. 33) shows a young surveyor leaning on a globe, with his survey spread out before him and his compass in his hand. The artist has not quite met the challenge offered by the youth's exaggerated pose, but his cheerful face and extravagant position are none the less expressive of great pride in the vocational world he commands. What is especially interesting about the young man's face is its resemblance to that of its creator: it possesses the same round chin, slightly bulbous nose, and triangular shape found in one of the much later photographs of William Robinson. The picture of the young surveyor seems to be an idealized self-portrait; together with the map, it comprises the earliest tangible evidence of Robinson's hope of becoming a licensed surveyor. The sketches also hint at broader artistic interests.

THE ROBINSONS OF NEW ROSS AND ROSEGARLAND

Relatively little is known about the training already undergone by this aspiring young surveyor or about his life prior to 1839. The single source of information about his early years is a biography in Goodspeed's *History of the County of Middlesex* (1889).[3] The biography is gratifyingly detailed, and its unusually chatty tone suggests that it was based on an actual interview with its subject. Unfortunately, as is often the case with personal conversations, it assumes information that is not always supplied, and thus it frequently proves tantalizing rather than definitive.

William Robinson was born on 27 March 1812, in New Ross, County Wexford, Ireland. He had an uncle, John Davis, who 'was educated at Trinity College, Dublin, for the Episcopal ministry,' and 'took quite an interest in the education' of his nephew William. Other formative influences were found in his immediate family. An older brother, John, was a surveyor, and it was his example that first encouraged William to consider that profession. His father, James, seems to have had some connection with building. We are given the intriguing information that James 'removed from New Ross to Rosegarland, to superintend the erection of buildings in the interest of his brother John.' Rosegarland had been the seat of a barony already in the Middle Ages, and considerable building was done on the estate during the eighteenth and nineteenth centuries.[4] But it is not at all clear what position John held in relation to this construction (architect? estate steward?), nor is James's precise vocation known (was he a contractor? a building surveyor? an architect?). A later passage in Goodspeed's biography reaffirms the implication that William grew up in an environment concerned with building, but it provides no further illumination: 'his theoretical knowledge of building ... was greater than his practical, owing to his opportunity of seeing mechanics at work, occasionally using tools, copying estimates, etc.' After moving to Canada, James turned to farming and left architecture and its related professions to his sons.

William emigrated to Canada in November 1836 with his parents, sister, and three brothers. After the family settled on a farm in Burford Township, about thirty-five miles east of London, William spent five years engaged in odd jobs connected with building. He obtained employment as a carpenter for one year in Hamilton and then for eighteen months in Brantford, and in 1839 he moved to London. There he seems to have determined on a more professional course, and probably early in 1842 he moved to Toronto in order to obtain the training necessary for becoming a land surveyor.

TRAINING IN TORONTO

Robinson did eventually obtain his licence and practise as a land surveyor, but the remarkably circuitous route he followed towards attaining his goals prepared him for a career as an architect and engineer as well. He spent his first two years in Toronto in the employ of Thomas Young. Young agreed to instruct Robinson in land surveying, but, if Goodspeed's account can be trusted, the arrangement did not constitute an official apprenticeship: Young is clearly referred to as Robinson's 'employer'; the instruction was 'promised (but unasked for)'; and, as mentioned in chapter 2, Young's only direct service as a teacher was to open his library to Robinson. Whatever the precise terms of their arrangement, however, Robinson's decision to work with Young at this point suggests the breadth of his interests. Thomas Young had established a name for himself as an artist and architect. He had spent several years as drawing master at Upper Canada College, and his very accomplished *Four Views of the City of Toronto* (1835–6) had been among the first prints issued by Nathaniel Currier. He had gained recognition as an architect when he won the enviable commission to design King's College (Upper Canada's first university, later to become the University of Toronto) in 1837. He was also a land surveyor and, from 1840 to 1842, Toronto's first city engineer.[5]

King's College was undoubtedly the main topic of interest while Robinson was working in Young's office. Though the design had been drawn and tenders solicited five years before Robinson joined Young's staff, the Rebellion and the appointment of an unsympathetic governor had postponed construction. It was only when Sir Charles Bagot replaced Sir George Arthur as governor of Canada West that the project was resumed in 1842, and building was in progress for the duration of Robinson's employment with Young. Already in the late 1820s a design for the college buildings had been procured from an English architect, Charles Fowler. These drawings formed the basis for Young's design.[6] That he significantly reduced Fowler's plan is remarkable given the ambitious scale of his own scheme: the college was to consist of three separate buildings connected by covered walkways and surrounding three sides of a forecourt roughly double the size of a football field. Only one of the smaller subsidiary blocks was ever built, but, as Young's drawing (fig. 34) shows, it was still monumental in composition as well as size. It followed the usual British formula for Greek Revival buildings in applying an archeologi-cally correct portico to a building that was otherwise relatively simple in shape and decoration. The King's College façade recalled a perfect Greek

34   King's College, Toronto, designed c. 1837 by Thomas Young

Doric portico, with two engaged columns *in antis* supporting an entablature
with a plain architrave, and a frieze with the requisite triglyphs and metopes.
Eighteenth-century researchers had made the shocking discovery that Greek
Doric columns, such as those of the Parthenon, had no base, and Young
carefully followed his classical model in this respect. The Greek Doric was
an austere and massive order, and the formal purity of the college's façade
enables one to understand Ruskin's later reflection, 'The Doric manner of
ornament admitted no temptation, it was the fasting of an anchorite.'[7]
    Even when not bound by another architect's concept, Young seems to have
had a feeling for simple, crisp, and monumental forms, though, like most
architects of his time, he could design in a number of styles. Other projects in
progress during Robinson's tenure with Young were the vaguely Egyptian
obelisk that won first prize in the competition for a new monument at
Queenston to honour Sir Isaac Brock (1843), a Greek Revival church in
Streetsville (Holy Trinity Anglican Church, 1842–3), and the second Gothic
courthouse in Canada West, built in Guelph to serve Wellington County (1842–
4; fig. 35). Like the London District Court House, the Wellington County
building followed the Regency fashion in applying Gothic motifs to what was
essentially a classical structure. Its detailing did make the Guelph courthouse
look like a cross between a miniature medieval castle and a Tudor manor
house: it had square towers with crenellated parapets, drip mouldings,
lozenge-shaped window panes, and pointed arches in the doors. One would
be hard-pressed, however, to find an actual historical model for its irregular

35 'The Court House, Guelph, Ont.,' 1842–4, designed by Thomas Young, from
Canadian Illustrated News, 21 February 1874

parapet, which emphasizes the central section in the classical manner. Moreover, the Gothic features are applied with a classical sense of restraint,
regularity, and symmetry, and the dimensions of the façade are based, in rather
complex ways, on carefully calculated mathematical proportions.[8]

   Robinson's training with Young seems to have formed or reinforced a
sympathy with the classical tradition that was to affect all his own architectural
designs. He would follow in many other of his mentor's footsteps as well.
In addition to becoming a prominent architect, he would be a drawing master
(at the London Collegiate Institute), a land surveyor, and city engineer (in
London).

   Although he apparently influenced Robinson in a great number of ways,
Young's proficiency in alienating professional and personal contacts suggests
that he may have been a difficult employer. In 1840 he had been forced to
resign as architect for the Huron County Jail because of disagreements over
his fee, exacerbated by John Howard's spiteful indictment of both Young's
charges and his reliance on a clerk of works for on-the-job superintendence.[9]
Young separated from his wife in 1841. In 1843 he lost his job as city engineer
after arguing with the city about his pay, and disagreements between himself
and the contractor for King's College, John Ritchey, were so profound that
architect Henry Bowyer Lane had to be called in as an arbitrator. Young's

business problems increased as time went on, and he died a poverty-stricken alcoholic in 1860, when he was around fifty years old.

Robinson eventually defected to one of Young's opponents, though not, it seems, as an act of rebellion. According to Goodspeed's comprehensive account, Robinson considered going to New York after leaving Young's office, but, passing Mr Ritchey on the street, he was offered a job as assistant to the builder's head foreman. He accepted and spent the next two years (c. 1844–6) in Ritchey's employ. The experience was probably profitable. During those two years Ritchey held the contracts for some of Toronto's most celebrated building projects: major additions to Osgoode Hall, the Church of St George the Martyr, the Bank of Montreal on the corner of Yonge and Front streets, and the Provincial Lunatic Asylum.[10]

In 1846, however, Robinson temporarily forsook the art of building to pursue his old interest in land surveying. After studying with an unidentified surveyor for some months, he passed the requisite examination in Montreal and received his licence to practise, the Honourable Wm Henry Boulton and the Honourable W.B. Robinson, both political and spiritual heirs of the Family Compact, acting as his sureties for the $2,000 fee.

The licence was immediately shelved while Robinson took advantage of another excellent opportunity for improving his knowledge of building and architecture. In his journal for 29 January 1847, John G. Howard recorded, 'called at Mr Lane's office on my way home and recommended Mr Robinson to him as a Clerk. He agreed to take him, having buildings to erect at Hamilton.'[11] Lane was a young, English-trained architect who arrived in Canada in 1841 and quickly gained a number of impressive commissions, including the Market House and City Hall at Front and Jarvis streets and two buildings Robinson would have known through his work with Ritchey: the Church of St George the Martyr, and the major expansion of Osgoode Hall, which made it a monumental public building. Then, in November 1847 Lane abruptly abandoned his meteoric career in Upper Canada and returned to what his biographers have described as 'England and obscurity.'[12]

Robinson evidently shared in the meteor's last glow, though Howard's journal is imprecise regarding his capacity. Given Robinson's experience and talents, it seems likely that he was employed as clerk of works: Goodspeed's *History* describes his position at this time as 'Superintendent of buildings.' Howard's entry rather suggests that Lane was planning to use Robinson's talents on his Hamilton projects. If so, Robinson may well have supervised the erection of the portico Lane was adding to the south façade of Dundurn Castle, or Lane's elaborate remodelling of the mansion's interior. But it is by no means certain that Robinson was in Hamilton, and Lane was also engaged on some substantial Toronto buildings during his last year: Holy Trinity Church; the designs for Homewood, a charming Gothic house for George Allan; and Lawton Park (fig. 36), a residence in the Regency style for one Colonel Carthew.

36   Lawton Park, Toronto, designed c. 1847 by Henry Bowyer Lane

Robinson was definitely working on the latter building in 1848 and 1849.
He seems to have been acting as clerk of works after Lane's departure, paying bills, keeping accounts, and trying desperately to settle the feud between
the contractor, a Mr Smith, and the extremely obdurate Colonel Carthew.[13]
A rather curious report, in Robinson's hand though not necessarily in his
voice, gives a thorough, impassioned, and blatantly biased account of the
dilemma. Lane had abandoned the colonel's house at an inopportune stage,
leaving only some rather general plans (the front elevation and floor plans)
and a few scribbled lines by way of specifications. This abdication in itself
had posed problems for the contractor and his workmen, and Colonel Carthew had enhanced them by adding a series of expensive afterthoughts to his
original scheme, and by procuring much of the woodwork from a demolished
mansion. He apparently expected to save money through this stratagem, while
in fact it necessitated a great deal of unpleasant extra labour: 'workmen
detest to be employed at the patching, fitting, glueing, working out pieces of
moulding by hand ... and they would prefer even if they had a certain amount
for doing it, to get out a new set.' Carthew and Smith agreed on 24 May
1848 to accept a valuation by John Howard, but Howard was slow to come
forth with his judgment, and Robinson was forced to plead the urgency of
a settlement: 'Probably by this time you may know the amount of Mr Smith's
bill, if so you would much oblige me by inserting it in this note and returning
it. My anxiety to know is my excuse for troubling you.' Howard's analysis of
'the just and fair value' of the work is dated 'March 3rd, 1849,' by which time

a personal tragedy had caused Carthew to lose interest in his beloved mansion. He had commissioned the house and bought the six acres surrounding it in anticipation of his approaching marriage. According to legend, however, his fiancée was killed or critically injured while visiting her future home, and Carthew sold the property without ever inhabiting it.[14]

The documents connected with the Smith-Carthew dispute are interesting here less because of the episode itself than because of what they suggest about Robinson's position. Clearly he was still performing many of the clerical jobs that would have fallen to him as Lane's clerk of works. If Robinson actually composed the very detailed report as well as copying it, however, he must have entered Smith's employ as a labourer instead of retaining the supervisory position he held under Lane. Complaining of the nearly four months required to finish the great double staircase in the main hall, the writer of the report suddenly turns defensive: 'I know the workmen [have] not failed in doing their duty, being one of them myself.' Whatever his status, Robinson was evidently not yet ready to present himself as an architect. Indeed, the detailed report complains of 'the time spent by … [Smith's] men in preparing their own drawings.'

Robinson nevertheless seems to have regarded his work on Lawton Park as finished after seeing the financial dispute settled, and in the spring of 1849 he finally put his surveying licence to use. He completed the survey of the Toronto–Owen Sound Road and then formed a business partnership in Toronto with Charles Rankin, a land surveyor whose interests do not seem to have extended towards either architecture or civil engineering. Robinson and Rankin worked together until Rankin moved to Owen Sound in 1851.[15] Robinson carried on the business until 1852, when a serious illness forced him to end his Toronto career and return home to his father's house in Burford.

A CAREER IN LONDON

While in Burford, Robinson received letters from W.B. Leather suggesting a partnership in London. Robinson eventually accepted the proposal, and near the beginning of 1853, when he was in his early forties, he moved to the town to which his energies would be devoted for the rest of his life.

As mentioned above, William Beaumont Leather had been trained as a land surveyor and civil engineer in England. In 1850 he deserted his first wife, married a second (without bothering to divorce the first), and moved to Toronto, where he spent a year in partnership with the man who became Canada's most renowned engineer, Sandford Fleming, the inventor of Standard Time, and chief engineer of the Canadian Pacific Railroad.[16] In the following year Leather moved to London, where he seems very quickly to have established himself as a man of some competence. In April 1853 Samuel Peters, then town engineer, and Leather were appointed as the architects on the Building Committee for the Town Hall and Market House, though it seems that Peters actually designed both buildings. Leather had important

37   Post Office, London, 1858–60, designed by William Beaumont Leather,
photograph by John Kyle O'Connor, c. 1875

projects of his own: 'a magnificent pile' at the corner of North and Ridout
streets for A. and T.C. Kerr of Hamilton, and 'a spacious Hall to accommodate
2,000 people' for the Sons of Temperance.[17] Unfortunately, neither these
structures nor illustrations of them survive.

There are, however, several photographs of a building that was designed
by Leather at a later date: the London Post Office of 1858–60 (fig. 37), an
extravagant edifice that must have served as a dazzling image of the central
government's presence in a city suffering from a severe financial depression.
Its initial cost was an astronomical $33,750. Although the *Free Press* was
somewhat awed by the annual cost to the public, it seemed generally content
that the 'zeal, industry, and integrity' of the Post Office employees would
be rewarded with their increased 'comfort.'[18]

Leather's design was fittingly flamboyant, in the mannerist style of the later
Italian Renaissance. The *Free Press* reporter seems to have been impressed and
overwhelmed by Leather's learned attitude towards his composition: 'We
have been furnished by the accomplished architect ... with a detailed description of the exterior of the building but, it being couched in the phraseology of
the profession, the explanation would not be understood by the general
reader.' One suspects that it was not understood by the reporter, either, though
he does call attention to the 'attached Roman Doric columns' on the ground
storey and the 'attached Corinthian columns above,' and he rightly notes the

'vast quantity of "rusticated" work ... throwing in bold relief the plain portions of the columns.' Underlying Leather's compositions is the format of the *palazzo*, with its rusticated ground storey, its elegant *piano nobile*, and the smaller attic storey windows above. Leather has elaborated the plan in numerous ways. Paired engaged columns rise through the top two storeys. Where the end bays project, the exposed corners are adorned as Corinthian pilasters, peeping from behind the engaged columns. Sculpted garlands cascade down the window frames. The façade would be altogether impressive, were it not that its cornice seems too light. As it is, the concentration of heavy, double columns makes the building look too intense, like Atlas straining to hold up a golf ball.

Unfortunately, Leather's practical building knowledge seems to have lagged behind his understanding of style, and the opulent Post Office was besieged by continual problems with leaks and poor heating. By 1867 the many necessary repairs had raised the cost of the building to $40,526.06.[19]

It is difficult to imagine the architect of this outspoken and sloppily constructed edifice collaborating with the careful and reserved William Robinson, and, largely owing to the fact that records for this period in London's history are sadly incomplete, nothing is known about their work together until 1856. In that year they were appointed, with Peters and Stent, to test a proposal for supplying water to the city.[20] Their firm was also one of the applicants making bids for the position of city engineer.[21] Their partnership, however, seems to have been fairly casual. The *London City Directory* for 1856–7 listed the firm 'Leather and Robinson' in its classified section, but each partner also ran a completely independent paid advertisement for himself alone. Robinson's advertisement faced that of his painter brother, and the identical type faces and sizes of the two ads might encourage a reader to expect a family partnership, where one brother dealt with exterior and the other with interior design.[22]

By May 1857 Robinson had set up a completely independent practice as a land surveyor and architect, and later that year he was appointed city engineer.[23] That position had become extremely controversial during the preceding year. Samuel Peters had angrily resigned over what he considered inadequate pay for his services; further, he had walked off the job with all the official maps showing sewer lines and street elevations, refusing to return them until the city met his demands. Unfortunately, a dearth of extant newspapers for the crucial period makes it impossible to know whether the mayor fulfilled his threat to prosecute Peters, but the episode understandably encouraged the municipal council to think seriously about the mutual obligations binding the city and its engineer. A special report by the Committee on General Improvements recommended that the engineer be paid a percentage of the cost of the work he did for the city, and that he 'be directed to attend in the City Hall during business hours.' Most council members considered this stipulation excessive, however, so the motion that eventually carried required that the city engineer be in City Hall for one hour each day.[24] Robinson appears to have prevented any further conflicts by diplomatically renting space in City Hall for his private architectural practice.[25] He seems to have been diplomatic in other areas as well, since he enjoyed a long and peaceful career as an architect and engineer at a time when relations between engineers, architects, their patrons, and members of the building trades were often quite volatile.

He held the post of city engineer until 1878. The terms of payment changed over the years (in 1873 he received a salary of $300 a year),[26] and the responsibilities came to occupy a larger share of his time. But the position retained its part-time designation, and Robinson's private architectural practice flourished alongside his public post.

Even had he not carried on a private business, Robinson would have made a substantial contribution to London's appearance in his role as city engineer alone. In addition to overseeing highly visible engineering projects such as bridges and roads, he had several responsibilities related directly to building. Throughout Robinson's tenure the city engineer functioned as building inspector, seeing to the safety of all structures erected in the town.[27] More significantly, he was also responsible for the erection of a wide range of municipal buildings, including schools, market stalls, an exhibition building (1861; fig. 41), immigrant sheds (1873), a hospital (1874–5; fig. 60), a police station (1873), and a pump house (1878; fig. 74).[28] His firm became involved in the reconstruction of the Middlesex County Courthouse (1877–8; fig. 16), because Robinson was city engineer. Moreover, federal commissions seem routinely to have fallen his way. He designed the Custom House (1870–3; fig. 51) and the Militia Buildings (c. 1876; figs 65 and 68), and it is tempting to suspect that Leather received the Post Office commission (1858; fig. 37) through Robinson's influence. His private practice enabled him to add houses, churches, stores, factories, and out-of-town municipal buildings to his list of achievements.

By the time of his retirement in 1878 Robinson had designed many of the region's most admired buildings; he had trained many of the town's young architects, including those who would carry on the work of his firm; and he had a business that was prosperous enough to support three partners besides himself.

The years of Robinson's London practice bridged important transitions in the city's social climate and its physical appearance. London passed through years of financial crisis, followed by the slow recovery of prosperity and confidence, and the buildings that reflected its growing prosperity came increasingly to be shaped by a new complex of attitudes towards architectural design.

LONDON GROWS UP

The coming of the railroad in 1853 prompted dreams of growth that could never bear any resemblance to reality. Land speculators as far away as Strathroy and Komoka bought, surveyed, and sold lots well beyond the boundaries of today's London. When the bubble burst in 1857, Amelia Harris at Eldon house was quick to notice the social consequences. She wrote in her diary for 1857 [entry of 14 October]: 'The commercial distress is making a great change in the prices of everything. Rents are reduced more than a third. [13 November]: Times are quite as dull in Toronto as here; necessity has forced economy, everyone is trying to see how cheaply they can live; no word of balls, dinners or parties.'[29] By early 1859 a soup kitchen was established in London, serving 2,948 quarts of soup in the month of February. The town's brewers were among the donors who supplemented public funds: John Carling subscribed $100 and John K. Labatt gave 1,000 pounds of flour.[30]

No doubt to Robinson's dismay, conditions were slow to improve. Looking back in 1865, the London *Free Press* observed: 'we all know that in 1860, '61, business was greatly depressed.'[31] On 20 July 1860 the *Free Press* supported a proposal to replace the full-time police force (which had cost the city an extravagant $3,720 the previous year) with part-time constables because 'in these times of municipal distress, it is well to look at matters from a pecuniary view.' On 16 March 1863 H.C.R. Becher noted in his diary, 'The country has had many years of depression following the false inflation of 1855–56–57, and it is not over yet.'[32] The coming of better times was signalled by the 1864 starting date for three financial institutions: the Canadian Bank of Commerce (which came into being in London and Toronto in that year), the Merchant's Bank, and the Huron and Erie Savings and Loan Society (later to become Canada Trust).[33]

The London of the early 1860s was no longer the lively little garrison town it had been before the coming of the railways, but neither was it the ambitious and progressive small city it was to become within a decade. Its callowness as a community emerges in several bizarre episodes of the period.

On 12 September 1860 the Prince of Wales (later to be Edward VII) was entertained by London's quarrelsome high society. 'The Londoners gave him a royal and enthusiastic welcome,' Amelia Harris told her diary but added, 'There has been a great rumpus among the ball committee.'[34] If his vivid account is to be believed, Henry Becher was the innocent victim of the Prince's would-be partners and their outraged husbands: 'An old friend is nearly ready to set me up and wants to fight a duel with me because his wife does not dance with the prince soon enough ... Two gentlemen follow me about the ballroom intimating that I am a damned scoundrel etc. I receive these assurances with a smiling face as if they were paying me compliments ... '[35]

Demonstrations of loyalty to the prince were doomed to be unlucky. In 1863, safely in England, he married Princess Alexandra. A ball was held at the Tecumseh Hotel in honour of the marriage, and in the lobby of the hotel London's colourful mayor, Frank Cornish, encountered Major Bowles, senior officer of the garrison. His Worship was 'much intoxicated,' the *Free Press* reported; 'he attacked Major Bowles and finally tore the Crimean medals from his coat and flung them around him.' The London *Prototype*, claimed that 'the affair arose out of an alleged slight of [Mayor Cornish] by [Major Bowles], in refusing the former admission to the ball-room.' It was also rumoured that Major Bowles had been too friendly to Mrs Cornish. But in the *Free Press*'s view, 'no sort of provocation had been offered.' That newspaper, never a friend to Cornish, turned to sarcasm in commenting upon the attack on Bowles: 'perhaps the inspector general, when he next visits us, may find himself suddenly assaulted and divested of his medals.'[36] To avoid this embarrassment, Sir Fenwick Williams, commander-general of British forces in North America, took the unusual precaution of withdrawing most of the garrison from London, after city council refused to apologize for its pugilist.[37]

London residents were no safer in their beds than in the leading hotel. A gentleman who came to be called 'Slippery Jack' was a frequent nocturnal visitor: 'If the people were asleep he would go into their bedrooms and tickle their feet or gently pull their noses.' Twenty years later, it was claimed that two people played the role of Jack, one of them a member of the 'Hellfriars Club' (the name is perhaps a corruption of the 'Hellfire Club' of eighteenth-century England), an organization that devoted some of its energies to putting up posters satirizing the 'mushroom aristocracy' or *nouveaux riches* of the community.[38]

A more serious danger to the city was posed by the apparent threat of American invasion. No less than three times in the 1860s a war scare arose. At an early point in the American Civil War an international incident was created when the navy of the North removed two Confederate agents from a British ship. Amelia Harris reported that 'war is almost inevitable'; Becher, more appreciated now, lectured 'a great crowd' at city hall on 'International Law.' Three years later, in late 1864 and early 1865, London, this time without its redcoats, again faced the prospect of war. Amelia Harris was even more alarmed: 'the country will be over-run. The thoughts of such a possibility keep me from sleep.' A genuine panic was created in 1866 when the Fenians, fanatical Irish-Americans bent on punishing Britain, actually invaded Canada. Mrs Harris was present at a somewhat unusual St Paul's Cathedral service: 'There was great excitement during the service ... the bugle sounded, and then half of the congregation left. After another short interval the bell rang an alarm. There were very few left in the church ... As no one in the church knew what the cause of all the alarm was it was very exciting.'[39] No Londoners came to harm at the front, and a week later a grateful city rewarded its heroes with a public banquet at a cost of $357.[40]

Fears of American belligerence were prominent in the movement towards Confederation. London's two newspapers, the *Free Press* and its rival the *Advertiser*, were ultimately united in supporting the project, though the *Free Press* was initially opposed to it. When the great day, 1 July 1867, finally came, the *Free Press* grumbled that 'it is to be regretted that no fitting celebration will be made here.'

A more thrilling event had occurred the previous year – the apparent discovery of oil in London, following upon earlier strikes in the region. Mrs Harris sent out her son on a reconnaissance mission: 'Edward drove there with

Mr Hicks, the chief owner of the well. When they came within a quarter of a mile of the well they found that the oil was a fact and then Edward said it was the funniest scene he ever beheld, singing, dancing, drinking with the chorus of "Oil, Oil." ' Becher, his good friend Amelia reported, 'tried to sham coolness ... but was in as great a frenzy as any of us.'[41] Unfortunately, it soon emerged that Mr Hicks had thoughtfully provided from an oil can the liquid he later claimed to have discovered.[42]

The oil boom of the surrounding area nevertheless played a role in the economic recovery of the late 1860s. The historian Fred Landon reports that 'at one point in the city's history, all that section lying south of York street and east of Adelaide street was taken up with refineries' and associated industries. Imperial Oil was founded in London in 1880. But partly because of citizens' objections to the smell, the refineries gradually disappeared.[43]

The city's prosperity came to rest on other foundations. As a transportation centre London was strengthened by the building of the London, Huron and Bruce Railroad, supported by $100,000 in civic money. When the line was officially opened on 11 January 1876, there was 'a grand celebration ... 800 people dine and speechify at city hall.'[44] A wide range of local industries arose or expanded their operations. Among these enterprises were the Carling and Labatt breweries, the McClary Manufacturing Company (stoves), C.S. Hyman tanners, McCormick Manufacturing Company (biscuits), several furniture companies, and large-scale cigar makers. From early times London had established itself as a retail centre for the surrounding agricultural district; by the 1870s the city was beginning to look to wider markets for wholesalers' operations.[45]

The greater prosperity was clearly reflected in the city's appearance. Successful merchants and industrialists liked to build houses that displayed their wealth, and increasing civic pride produced various projects to make London as a whole more impressive and beautiful.

Looking back upon the city's development from the perspective of 1888, the *Advertiser* recalled the era 'some fifteen or eighteen years ago, when the fever for parks struck London.' The fever in reality affected some citizens more than others. A debate raged for several years about the proper use of lands acquired from the federal government in the early 1870s. A pragmatic faction wanted the whole vast area chopped into building lots. The case for civic idealism was eloquently stated by John Carling, London's leading Conservative politician for decades: 'It was not merely the city of today that they should look to, but to the city it was likely to become 40 or 50 years hence ... Let us go to work and provide an expansive pleasure ground, a breathing place for the citizens, where they and their children may assemble and breathe purer air.' In the end, a compromise was reached: some of the land was sold off, and the rest became Victoria Park. For some years after the park became civic property it was more picturesque than beautiful, since the local burghers were 'very fond of allowing their cows, horses, pigs and geese to roam at large.' By the end of the 1870s, however, the park had been 'planned, levelled, sodded and laid out in a tasty manner.'[46]

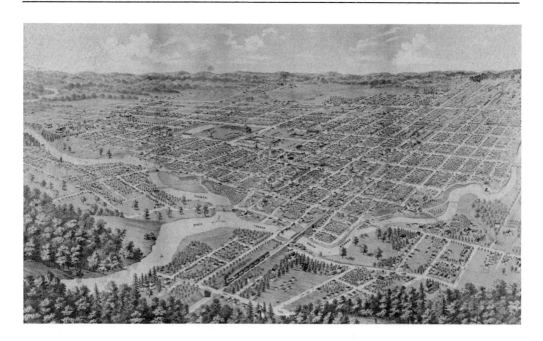

38 'Bird's Eye View of London, Ontario, Canada, 1872,' lithograph delineated by E.S. Glover and printed by Strobridge & Co. Lith. Cin.

One hopes that Lord Dufferin, the governor-general of Canada, did not have to stumble over too many pigs when he formally dedicated Victoria Park, on 27 August 1874. His Excellency seized the occasion, somewhat surprisingly, to compare the New World London very favourably with the British capital: 'While in certain respects you are behind hand, in others you are infinitely superior to Old London.' The new London, Lord Dufferin suggested, benefited from not having the poor, the pollution, and the prostitutes 'by which, I regret to say, the streets of the British capital are contaminated.'[47]

London newspapers were in no doubt about the virtues of their city in general and their architecture in particular. As early as 5 July 1869 the *Free Press*, reflecting upon public buildings, private homes, and churches, commented that 'London is pushing ahead architecturally.' The *Advertiser* noticed in 1870 that 'the buildings now going up are more elaborate than those of yore. Taste and refinement are evident in the designs.' The paper set an ambitious goal: 'We want to see London the handsomest city in Canada.' A year later the *Free Press* boasted that 'no city of its proportions in America ... has made more substantial progress than our good city of London within the past twelve months' – the word 'progress' would be echoed over and over again in the newspapers' building reports of the next decade. In its 1871 article the *Free Press* noted approvingly that home ownership now lay within the grasp of the lower orders: 'What a happy state of things is this, when hundreds of our citizens, the judicious and thrifty mechanic as well as the merchant and manufacturer of capital, possess means for investment in substantial homesteads.' In the following year the *Advertiser* chose to place its emphasis on

39   Richmond Street, London, with the Custom House and Bank of British North America on the left, and the Bank of Montreal, Merchant's Bank of Canada, and Post Office on the right, photograph by John Kyle O'Connor, c. 1875

building materials: 'old and almost worthless frame buildings are constantly being replaced by costly and beautiful structures of brick.' The newspapers were not shy about informing their readers as to exactly how costly these beautiful structures were. A. McBride's 'well designed two story brick residence' on Colborne street cost him $4,000 in 1874, with Robinson and Tracy as his architects; in the same year Nicholas Pollard had to content himself with a $500 house on Hill Street, constructed of the despised frame.[48] Shops as well as houses were becoming more 'costly and beautiful.' The financial district that had developed along Richmond Street by the early 1870s was particularly elegant (fig. 39).

A development eagerly noted by the newspapers of the 1870s was the expansion of the 'suburbs' – East London, London South, and London West. In March 1873 the *Advertiser* reported that 'all the city's architects are more or less engaged preparing and designing plans for suburban and other residences of rich appearance, large proportions and costly style.' In April 1876 the same newspaper asserted that 'a quiet drive through our suburbs will surprise any one who has not kept track of the operations of the past few years.' Four months later Amelia Harris took such a drive in London South and confirmed the newspaper accounts: 'a good many very nice houses have been built. The old homes are all changed.'[49]

Lord Dufferin, during his 1874 visit, had contemplated the 'great advance' of London with a 'deep feeling of exultation.' Comparing the appearance of the city with what he had seen less than two years before, he noted that 'new buildings appear to be springing up in every direction, and fresh streets, wider and more imposing than those which satisfied your early ambition, have been laid out.' His Excellency may have preferred the 1874 arrangements, since in 1872 he had been taken to inspect an oil refinery. In 1874 he notified the civic authorities in advance that he desired 'to forego the pleasure of a visit to the London asylum.'[50]

THE WORSHIP OF GOTHICISM

Though Robinson was eventually to share in the city's prosperity (and to have a hand in the new buildings, the wider roads, and the asylum), the poor economic situation must have made his first few years of independent practice, in the late 1850s, quite bleak. An admittedly incomplete list of his buildings includes only two items for the years between 1857 and 1860: a grist mill in Delaware and a frame schoolhouse on Talbot Street in London.[51] A spate of commissions in the early 1860s heralded the coming of better times.

Already in the buildings of these years there are evident some stylistic biases that were to remain in force throughout Robinson's career. Where given a choice, as with the Exhibition Building of 1861 (fig. 41) or stores erected in 1864 and 1865, respectively, he used styles derived from classical architecture. But for buildings with religious connections he apparently felt impelled to use Gothic. His churches are all Gothic. He designed a Gothic building to serve as the Anglican Synod House (1864–7).[52] The (Anglican) Collegiate Institute (1864–5; fig. 43) was in a Tudor, or late Gothic, style. The Bishop's Palace (1870–2; fig. 53), also greatly indebted to Tudor architecture, has a distinctly Gothic doorway. An awareness of the factors that made Robinson perceive an inviolable link between Gothicism and religion is central to an appreciation of his work, although he chose to disregard some of the major trends of the times. In addition to placing his achievements in perspective, a survey of major developments in church architecture indicates some of the broader changes in the period's taste. It helps explain why most London buildings of the 1870s were 'more elaborate than those of yore.'

The first decisive links between church architecture and the Gothic style were forged in England by the commissioners of the Church Building Act (1818), a measure designed to remedy the appalling lack of churches in rapidly developing urban areas. The commissioners were more concerned with economy than with style, and their recommendation that the churches be Gothic was based mainly on the fact that classical churches needed expensive stone porticoes. The commissioners' advice was followed, and 174 of the 214 so-called 'commissioners' churches' were nominally Gothic.[53] These churches have been widely denigrated, often deservedly. But some of the feeling against them has been based on dogmatism rather than taste. Their Gothicism, like that of other churches of their time, consisted mainly of applied details, in the Regency manner. They had pointed windows, possibly a tower with battlements or pinnacles, and perhaps some light buttresses, but the proportions and shape of the buildings were often still those of the Georgian church, and the tower rose from the centre of the façade as it did in a typical Georgian design. The discovery of Gothic structure, already discussed in chapter 1, was soon to make Regency Gothicism of all sorts not only rejected but despised.

A.W. Pugin, who so emphatically insisted on the marriage of structure and form, also argued that Gothic architecture alone was truly Christian. Greek temples, 'suited only for ... idolatrous rites,' could never form suitable models for churches, while 'An old English parish church, as originally used for the ancient worship, was one of the most beautiful and appropriate buildings that the mind of man could conceive; every portion of it answered both a useful and mystical purpose.' It followed for Pugin that every portion of an ancient church should be present in a modern one: a tower for bells, a chancel 'set aside for sacrifice,' chapels, a sacristy, and 'a southern porch for penitents and catechumens,' to name a few of the most fundamental requirements. Gothic details applied in lieu of the 'true principles' were 'a mere disguise' or even 'a great profanation.'[54]

Pugin's love of Gothic architecture led him in 1834 to shock his friends and parents by renouncing the Church of England and adopting Roman Catholicism. But at roughly the same time as Pugin was considering apostasy in order to worship in Gothic surroundings, John Henry Newman and other Oxford churchmen were writing the first of several tracts that would bring the ritual and mysticism of Catholicism to Anglican worship. The arguments for liturgical reform put forward in the Oxford Movement were soon taken up by a group of men at Cambridge, but The Cambridge Camden Society (est. 1839) was especially concerned with the restoration and erection of buildings suitable for ritualistic services.[55] Owing to the strong Protestant influences of the preceding centuries, the Anglican church had become emphatically non-ritualistic, and those parts of the church intended for liturgical purposes had been, to use one of the society's favourite terms, 'debased.' The society's journal, the *Ecclesiologist*, reported that 'the ancient Font [at a church in Northamptonshire] was taken as a *horse-trough to the vicarage*, and has now disappeared,'[56] and altars seem frequently to have substituted for coat racks. The chancel and choir were often walled off and used for storage space or Sunday school classes. New churches were usually just simple rectangular structures that provided a good view of the pulpit, with galleries around the back and side. The Cambridge Camden Society (later the Ecclesiological Society) set out to bring back the chancel, the font, the altar, and the other liturgical accoutrements of the medieval church.

The Ecclesiologists also had strong opinions, resembling Pugin's, about the style proper for church architecture. As one detractor summarized their views, 'Thou shalt not worship the grandeur of Egypt, nor the beauty of Greece, nor the grandeur of Rome, nor the romantic delicacy of Mohammedanism, nor the plastic varieties of Italy – but thou shalt worship only GOTHICISM! Through its mysterious vistas and lengthened arcades alone shalt thou hope to reach the high altar of Christ!' In fact, their precepts were even narrower. They insisted that the only appropriate style was Decorated Gothic, representative of the period before 'decay and debasement began,' although exceptions could be made for the outposts of civilization. Drawings of Early English churches were sent to the United States, New South Wales, and New Zealand on the grounds that its simplicity made Early English easier for colonial builders to copy. Indeed, New Zealand was even allowed to use the Norman style, 'because ... its rudeness and massiveness, and the grotesque character of its sculpture, will probably render it easier to be understood and appreciated by [native artists].'[57]

Although the Ecclesiologists were given to emphatic statements of their views, they were not opposed to changing them, and certain principles of design evolved over the years, especially in relation to parish churches. One should enter the church through a porch, and a tower, if there were one, should be placed to one side.[58] The solidity and simplicity of medieval parish churches came to be greatly admired. An 1854 issue of the *Anglo-American Magazine* (Toronto) echoed a thought that had been made popular by Ecclesiological writings: 'we admire the [cathedral] only as the sublime canonization of art, while the [parish church] appears to us the spontaneous creation of nature.'[59] In an effort to accentuate their naturalness, churches came often to be given a rustic quality, with the help of characteristics borrowed from the rural cottage or its Regency derivative, the *cottage ornée*. The church's proportions became lower and broader, eaves projected over the walls, interior beams might be purposely rough-hewn. The walls were to be massive as well as low. The impression of massiveness could be achieved by emphasizing the expanse of the wall's surface: windows became smaller and buttresses fewer. The *Ecclesiologist* favourably contrasted 'simple massiveness' with decorated 'meagreness.'[60] Since it was mandatory that the constructional materials be allowed to show, the main interest in the wall surface lay in the masonry itself, and its components could be chosen so as to provide colour and design. Thus varicoloured stone and brick could be laid in contrasting horizontal courses or even used to form elaborate designs on the 'simple' surface.

The dictates of the Ecclesiologists were widely accepted, both within and without the Anglican church, and at home and abroad. Thus in 1854 the *Anglo-American Magazine* praised a Brampton church by Mr Hay in terms of the Ecclesiologists' criteria: 'We have here ... a substantial looking edifice with low walls and high pitched roof, giving a bold and fearless outline, expressive at once of dignity and humility, to which the low-roofed porch adds effect. The tower stands as it ought, upon its own base. It is a massive structure, indicative of strength.'[61]

Indeed, their ideas are strongly and rather incongruously reflected in one

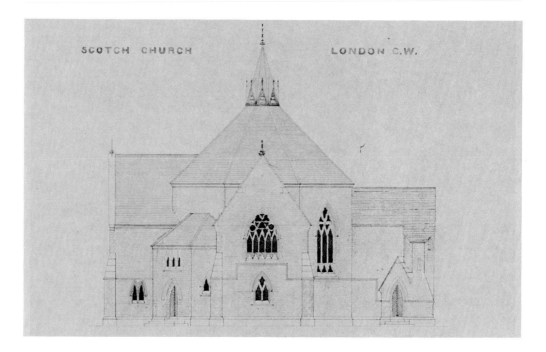

40   'Scotch Church London C.W.,' designed in 1859, drawing signed 'Fuller Messer & Jones'

of Robinson's first major commissions. In 1859 and 1860 he acted as supervising architect for St James Presbyterian Church in London (fig. 40), a very distinguished structure designed by the Toronto firm Fuller, Messer, and Jones.[62] Certainly no self-respecting Ecclesiologist would ever have approved the octagonal shape (which caused the building to be dubbed locally the 'Pepperbox Church'); an octagonal church in London, England (1858) had been judged by the *Ecclesiologist* as 'thoroughly suitable for Cushing's American Circus,' though the journal later admitted that 'a plan of this shape will accommodate a very large number of people with an almost uninterrupted view of [the] pulpit.'[63] This was an important consideration for the members of St James. They were adherents of the Established Church of Scotland, and their services were strongly oriented towards preaching and just as strongly opposed to the papist overtones of ritual. (Fuller's design was in fact modelled on a Scottish church.) But the Scotch Church, as it was also called, nevertheless possesses the solid, weighty, somewhat chunky quality that came to be praised by the Ecclesiologists. The bare surfaces of the walls are given a good deal of prominence. The irregularity of the stone quoins imparts a deceptively crude, or rustic, appearance to the church. And the windows are even in the approved Decorated style.

The Scotch Church seems to have been influential in several significant ways. The contact established during its construction between Thomas Fuller and William Robinson formed the beginning of a long relationship between Fuller and Robinson's firm. The shape of the church may have encouraged

Fuller's use of a polygonal plan for the Library of the Canadian Parliament Buildings. It also likely affected one of Robinson's important commissions in 1861, his octagonal exhibition building (fig. 41). But it did not have much effect on Robinson's churches.

Since most of Robinson's church commissions were for Presbyterians or low-church Anglicans, one would not expect him to feel much interest in meeting the most stringent of the Ecclesiologists' requirements. But it is a testimony to the pervasiveness of their influence that Robinson's work does bow to the most fundamental of their dictates. His Anglican churches usually had chancels, albeit they were too shallow by Ecclesiological standards, and Christ Church, London (1862–3; fig. 42), has a south porch that Robinson may well have intended as the main entrance.[64] Otherwise, he made relatively little distinction between Anglican and Presbyterian churches. He used the lancet windows of Early English Gothic in his simpler designs, such as those for Christ Church, London, and Christ Church, Dresden (1867; fig. 47), but the preferred Decorated style appears in the more ambitious St Andrew's Presbyterian Church (1868; fig. 49). He did call attention to the buildings' structural elements, with relatively prominent buttresses on the outside and exposed beams inside, and the latter are usually quite rough. Trinity Church in Barrie (c. 1864) had an open timber roof instead of the plaster ceiling usually found in Robinson's churches.

However, though he accepts the inevitability of certain concessions to the Gothic style, Robinson's real sympathies, even in church-building, are with the classical tradition. With the exception of the Strathroy Presbyterian Church, where Tracy or Fairbairne may have had some hand in the design, all Robinson's churches have façades of a pre-Ecclesiological type. They consist of three bays, with a prominent entrance in the centre. Both Trinity Church in Barrie and St Andrew's Presbyterian in London have centre towers. Robinson's other church façades are all variations on the theme expressed in Christ Church, London.[65] There may be two windows rather than three above the door; the buttresses may extend upwards into pinnacles; an Anglican church at Wingham (1868–9) features a bell-cote over the gable. There is often an attractive simplicity about these churches, but they are never plain in the sense admired by the Ecclesiologists, and they appear substantial rather than massive. Though their values may appear somewhat old fashioned from an international perspective, they form handsome specimens of church types then still current in Canada. Henry-Russell Hitchcock, probably the leading authority on nineteenth-century architecture, claims that 'most of the Neo-Gothic in Canada up to [the 1860s] is more properly to be called Early rather than High Victorian.'[66]

IDEALS IN HIGH VICTORIAN ARCHITECTURE

The Ecclesiologists were undoubtedly responding to the period's shifting tastes while also helping form them. John Ruskin's influential essays about architecture give some insight into the shift in values that lay behind what we call High

Victorian architecture, as they consistently appeal to a building's 'masculinity': stone and mortar render 'the style of architecture ... more masculine and more scientific' than does cement; 'just, upright, and manly principles' act as a guide to architectural merit.[67]

What has been called the 'Victorian cult of manliness' had become the established faith by Ruskin's time.[68] The force of masculinity must have been even stronger in mid-century London, Ontario, where the enthusiasm for bachelorhood sparked a controversy in the local press. One Belinda argued strongly about what she felt to be her rights, but her arguments fully accepted the period's claims regarding masculine supremacy: 'How much more pleasant are the smiles of a loving wife and the prattle of a miniature duplicate of oneself, than stinking smoke, bad wine, and sentimental novels!'[69]

Certainly size in itself was a crucial part of the Victorian image of manliness. Tennyson's Sir Walter Vivian is in many ways a model gentleman:

No little lily-handed baronet he,
A great broad-shoulder'd genial Englishman,
A lord of fat prize-oxen and of sheep,
A raiser of huge melons and of pine,
A patron of some thirty charities ... [70]

It is not surprising that massiveness should be thought a virtue in architecture as well, though Ruskin complained that English builders failed miserably in this respect: 'all that we do is small and mean, if not worse – thin, and wasted, and unsubstantial ... Until that street architecture is bettered, until we give it some size and boldness, I know not how we can blame our architects for their feebleness in more important work ... An architect should live as little in cities as a painter. Send him to the hills, and let him study what nature understands by a buttress, and what by a dome.'[71] Thus it was not only parish churches that were to be massive, in England or in Canada. Already in 1855 the Montreal firm of Hopkins, Lawford, and Nelson expressed contempt for Lane's decade-old design for Osgoode Hall: 'The style of architecture of the present building is inappropriate to the purpose of Courts of Law from its too great lightness, and we consider that for such a building as the Law Courts, perhaps the most important [building] in the place, a more massive and more imposing style should be adopted.'[72]

Massiveness was by no means the only architectural expression of masculinity, however, or even the most important of the new architectural virtues. Buildings were also praised because they were 'assertive,' 'vigorous,' 'robust,' 'strong,' 'muscular,' or they had 'character.' The prolific English architect and architectural critic Robert Kerr defended the Gothic style for its 'spirited and substantial vigour'; people might not sympathize with the excessive enthusiasms of some confirmed Gothicists, 'but all this does not deprive muscularity of its undoubted power.' More confident than Ruskin about the works of his own country, he used the same set of virtues to distinguish English from French architecture: 'For muscular power the one side of the channel, for more feminine grace the other.' This at first sounds like an acknowledgment of equal though different advantages, but the scale tips as the weighing continues. The Parisian villa is 'elaborately polished rather than thoughtful'; French projections tend 'towards feebleness as compared with the bold and heavy work of the English school.'[73] All this architectural strength was generally thought to reflect the moral fibre of a building's creators. As Mrs Gaskell's fictional manufacturer, John Thornton, noted, 'We are of a different race from the Greeks, to whom beauty was everything. Our Glory and our beauty arise out of our inward strength.'[74] This concept forms the basis for much of Ruskin's thought in *The Seven Lamps of Architecture* where, for example, an architect's integrity is seen as essential to the 'truth' of his construction.[75]

The vigour, muscularity, assertiveness, and strength associated with masculinity and moral strength had various architectural manifestations. One was the appearance of dramatic textural effects, to which brick and roughly cut stone made significant contributions. Another was the prominence of bright colour, which could be applied to buildings, as with paint or gilding, or could be intrinsic to the building materials themselves. For, as Ruskin explained, 'external colouring must pass away ... the hues of our cathedrals have died like the iris out of the cloud, and the temple whose azure and purple once flamed above the Grecian promontories, stand in their faded whiteness, like snow which the sunset has left cold.'[76] Inspired by the medieval buildings of Italy, Ruskin advised layering materials of various colours so that human constructions suggested 'the natural courses of rocks, and beds of the earth.'[77] Such polychromatic layers became the norm in High Victorian Gothic buildings, but more intricate effects were also common, especially in window heads or in the area below the cornice. In France, where buildings were not always as effete as Kerr claimed, vigour was expressed in the profusion of rich sculptural effects and elaborate ornamentation associated with the Second Empire style. And, indeed, English Gothic was also often decked out with a wealth of pinnacles, finials, towers, oriel windows, and buttresses, blatantly rejecting the 'plain simplicity' so prized by admirers of the medieval Gothic church.

All these factors – texture, colour, mass, a profusion of ornament, or its decisive absence – contributed to a building's 'character,' but perhaps the most significant implication of this favoured term lay in its suggestion of individuality, or even of eccentricity. Victorian architects sought to make their buildings original, the outward and visible symbols of their own creativity.

The intensity of the High Victorian architect's determination to be inventive was perhaps the characteristic that most distinguished him from the architects who preceded and followed his era. He lived in a period of unparalleled invention and productivity in the fields of science and commerce, and the generally derivative nature of the arts struck many critics as an inexplicable humiliation. Tennyson, who was long intrigued by the stories of Arthurian romance and was eventually to compose his own epic cycle of Arthurian poems, worried at an early stage about the validity of such an enterprise. In 'The Epic' (1835), a young poet named Everard is said to have burned 'his epic, his King Arthur,' because 'He thought that nothing new was said, or else / Something so said 't was nothing – that a truth / Looks freshest in the fashion of the day.' And Everard, defending himself, asks, 'why should any man / Remodel models?'[78] The emphasis Pugin and the early Ecclesiologists had placed on historical authenticity gave way in many quarters to a search for a fitting 'fashion of the day.' The architect James Savage complained as early as 1836 that 'the imitation of styles is a valuable discipline for a pupil, but it is a confession of incapacity in a professor ... All imitation is essentially affectation – the shew of a quality not really felt. If attempted seriously, it is puerile.' He went on to argue that architectural style should mirror the times that produced it.[79] Kerr develops the same idea at greater length in his *The Gentlemen's House* (1864). A 'bewildered' client has just had listed for him some of the styles he can choose for his house, 'just as you choose the build of your hat,' and he objects, politely but insistently, to the whole idea: 'But really ... I would much rather not. I want a plain, substantial, comfortable *Gentleman's House*; ... I don't want any *style* at all ... Look at myself; I am a man of very plain tastes; I am neither Classical nor Elizabethan; I am not aware that I am Renaissance, and I am sure I am not Medieval ... I am very sorry, but if you would kindly take me as I am, and build my house *in my own style – the style of the passing moment –* ' Kerr concludes that such a request simply cannot be met at the time and goes on bitterly to explain why: 'We live in the era of *Omnium-Gatherum*; all the world is a museum. To design any building in England nowadays is therefore to work under the eye, so to speak, of the Society of Antiquaries ... Our *Style of the passing Age* ... exists in bewilderment. Much learning hath made it mad. The character of the nineteenth-century in English architectural history will be simply this; – An inconceivable appetite for relics of the Past was at once its virtue and its vice.'[80]

Already in the 1840s some architectural theorists were exploring a possible avenue to using an 'appetite for relics of the Past' as the basis for a new style, appropriate to the passing age. On becoming professor of architecture at University College (London, England) in 1842, T.L. Donaldson described the growing practice of eclecticism: 'We are wandering in a labyrinth of experiment, and trying by an amalgamation of certain features in this or that style of each and every period and country to form a homogeneous whole with some distinctive character of its own, for the purpose of working it out into its fullest development, and thus creating a new and peculiar style.'[81] The editor of the *Builder* recommended a similar approach in 1845: 'An original style, characteristic of the age, might be provided by a complete investigation of every style of architecture, and the adaptation of all beautiful features which do not militate with each other.'[82] The principle of eclecticism increasingly gained followers on both sides of the Atlantic. By 1876 the *American Architect and Builder* was forced to acknowledge that 'eclectic design' required 'serious consideration,' because 'it is so prominent, and shows so much tendency to prevail throughout Christendom.'[83] That it had reached London, Ontario by that year, in theory as well as in practice, is indicated by the *Advertiser*'s comments on the Congregational Church (fig. 79) designed by Thomas Tracy: 'The architecture is that of the later Norman': there is a 'dwarf tower with Mansard roof'; and, by way of very high praise, 'The style is peculiarly its own.'[84]

Certainly the eclectic approach and the emphasis on masculinity were largely responsible for the new look of many mid-Victorian buildings, but a third important factor was the period's reliance on a greater range of historical, and contemporary, models. Where early Victorian interest had focused on medieval English and ancient Classical structures, the architecture of the mid-century looked towards medieval and Renaissance buildings on the continent. Ruskin's enthusiasm for the medieval buildings of Italy and France made them popular as Gothic exemplars. Kerr's fictional architect offered German and Belgian medieval modes as well.[85] Napoleon III made contemporary Paris a glittering cultural and social centre, with the result that his ambitious architectural projects were widely imitated: most influential were Visconti's and Lefuel's additions to the Louvre, using motifs derived from the seventeenth-century palace. There was also an increased interest in buildings of the Italian Renaissance, including not only those in the serene and correct 'Palladian' mode, but in addition the more eccentric and mannered works of the High Renaissance in Italy. One modern architectural critic, Peter Collins, attributes the sudden flowering of interest in this period partly to the fact that 'so few Antique buildings remained to be studied.' But the Renaissance Revival was less archeological in its orientation than previous classical revivals had been, and Collins later admits that the real appeal of Italian Renaissance forms lay in their 'immense adaptability': they 'allowed an architect to select – and to invent for himself – such compositional and decorative forms as might be considered suitable for the occasion.'[86] Italian farmhouses, often several centuries in the making, could also inspire highly inventive imitations.

ROBINSON'S CHARACTER AS AN ARCHITECT

The earliest secular buildings that Robinson himself is known to have designed were in the classical styles that had reigned in the early part of the century. His public buildings relied on the Neoclassical tradition. The exhibition building of 1861 had entranceways modelled on the Roman triumphal arch. The plans of his early town halls, at St John's (now Arva, 1869) and Strathroy (c. 1867–70; fig. 46), were based on the Greek temple. The earliest house that can definitely be attributed to him, a small rural cottage north of London (1867), was of the type now widely known as an Ontario Cottage, actually a simple Regency house with one storey, a centre hall, symmetrically placed windows, and a hipped roof; the few distinctive features of Robinson's early cottage, such as the front entryway, were Georgian in character, although the very slightly arched heads of the windows and doors presage new stylistic predilections. Already in the mid-1860s much of Robinson's work had begun to assume a strongly Italianate character. If, as was usually the case, the newspaper's description of the Crystal Block (1865; fig. 45) reflected the architect's views, Robinson's interest in Italianate styles was indeed closely related to their 'immense adaptability': 'The style of architecture is after no peculiar school or model, although perhaps many hints have been derived from the ... Italian. But generally speaking the Block has been designed and erected with more regard to substantiality and adaptability to mercantile pursuits than to ancient architectural beauty, which it is now-a-days the vanity of designers and builders to try to imitate.'[87] Around 1870 Robinson began to make frequent use of the mansard roof associated with the French Second Empire style, but, in keeping with the fashion for eclecticism, he very effectively placed it on buildings that possessed none of the baroque quality otherwise associated with the style, such as the Tudor Bishop's Palace (1870–2; fig. 53), the Renaissance Revival Custom House (1870–3; fig. 51), or the Italianate Crystal Hall (c. 1873; fig. 58).

Loosely used, the term 'Italianate' covers a variety of sources, ranging from the urban *palazzi* of the Italian Renaissance to the villas and farmhouses of rural Italy, more or less casually imitated. Italian rural buildings had already gained some popularity as models in the late eighteenth century, by virtue of their picturesque appearance in the works of popular landscape painters such as Claude Lorrain. Ruskin was still to find them highly picturesque in 1837, when he began the series of articles entitled *The Poetry of Architecture*. There he gives a vivid description of the 'lowland cottage' of Italy. It has a nearly flat roof, whose edges 'project far over the walls, and throw long shadows downwards,' thus protecting the upper windows from 'the strong and constant heat of the Italian sun.' A 'graceful irregularity' contributes to the 'marked character' of those houses, for which the marked character of the Italian seems responsible: 'The modern Italian is completely owl-like in his habits. All the day-time, he lies idle and inert.' He prefers 'patching up a ruin to building a house,' with the result that most dwellings comprise various irregular additions to an ancient structure, 'and the habitations of the lower orders frequently present traces of ornament and stability of material evidently belonging to the remains of a prouder edifice.' Thus one frequently finds well-proportioned and richly ornamented windows. These cottages usually appear in clusters, and at least one of them usually features a square tower, which serves 'to destroy the monotony, and contrast with the horizontal lines of the flat roofs and square walls' of the group as a whole.[88]

Imitations of these dwellings in the English-speaking world copied many of their distinctive features. The roof of an Italianate house has a shallow pitch and broad eaves. The windows are rectangular or they have round or segmental arches, often with elaborate heads and keystones. The plan may be irregular, and a square tower may vary the outline of the composition. But these new buildings have none of the 'not unpleasing mixture of grandeur and desolation' that Ruskin found in the originals. Italianate houses aimed at grandeur alone. Samuel Brees specified that his *Rural Architecture: A Series of Drawings in the Italian Style* (London, England, 1843) was 'for the use of gentlemen building.'[89] Andrew Jackson Downing praised the villa as 'the most refined home of America – the home of its most leisurely and educated class of citizens,'[90] and Samuel Sloan observed that 'its appearance at once bespeaks it the abode of the wealthy and refined.'[91] These refined homes typically had some characteristically Victorian touches: cornice brackets with elaborate incised ornamentation or turned pendants, and a decorative frieze with ornate woodwork or brickwork.

From the late 1860s on, all Robinson's houses have an Italianate character. His more substantial homes, such as the Kent house (c. 1875; fig. 222), were symmetrical, with a centre hall plan much like that of the Militia Office (c. 1876; figs 65 and 66). In some later examples, there is a small gable over the centre bay. Only one of the houses designed by the firm during this period is known to have had a tower: Belvedere, built for wholesale and retail grocer William Simpson Smith on his Westminster estate, possessed the usual symmetry, but it had an imposing five bays and a centre tower. That the Smiths considered Belvedere an inordinately important structure is indicated by the fact that they had a cornerstone-laying ceremony, though the event seems to have been treated with an appropriately light touch: the stone apparently contained only the names of those present inscribed on parchment, and it was laid by the Smiths' youngest son.[92] Another frequently used plan was narrower and deeper, with a side hall. Normally, houses featuring this arrangement had a two-storey elevation with three narrow bays across the front and possibly a centre gable. Durand's design for the Dunn house (c. 1885; fig. 134) represents a late example of this type. Essentially the same floor plan (fig. 63) was used for the very different sort of elevation represented by the houses designed for Alexander Johnston (1874; fig. 61) and Henry Johnson (c. 1880; fig. 62), where the front façade has a gable roof and a bay window. As the Johnston cottages indicate, the Italianate style became too popular to remain the preserve of the rich. Even the smaller Ontario Cottages designed by Robinson took on Italianate features.

Italianate houses aspired towards elegance inside as well as out. The more 'refined' examples had high ceilings, elaborate wooden and plaster mouldings, and spacious rooms. These usually had marble mantels adorning coal-burning fireplaces, though in one, the Fraser house (1877),[93] there was a cast-iron mantel shaped to look like marble.

While Italian farmhouses inspired the design for Victorian houses, the urban *palazzo* format that had been influential throughout the eighteenth century often formed the model for self-consciously conservative public buildings and financial institutions. Robinson's designs for both the Custom House and the Huron and Erie Savings and Loan Society (1870–1; fig. 57) are derived from the *palazzo*. Since Victorian architects tended to be less rigidly academic than their eighteenth-century predecessors, however, there developed a popular commercial style that was only very loosely related to its *palazzo* prototype. Robinson's Crystal Block and Crystal Hall are both highly innovative and experimental in their approach to the form; the firm's designs for the row of buildings stretching up Richmond Street from the Grigg House (fig. 84) show variations on what became its usual format for commercial blocks, with round- or segmental-arched windows regularly placed between piers and with cornices of decorative brickwork.[94]

Though he used currently fashionable styles, Robinson's designs were selective in their allegiance to the broader trends of the times. His works rarely possess the massiveness or even the assertiveness of most High Victorian architecture. His taste was decidedly attuned to the lighter and less strident values that the early Victorian period had inherited from eighteenth-century classicism. He preferred uniform colour to polychromy, symmetry to asymmetry, and relatively flat surfaces to pronounced sculptural effects. He also preferred clearly articulated surfaces to the challenge of an uninterrupted wall: he habitually used features such as pilaster strips and string courses to frame the bays and windows in his architectural compositions. Nevertheless, while eschewing the heaviness and aggressiveness admired by his age, Robinson was obviously very much attracted by its eclectic and inventive approaches to architectural design. The best of his works have a distinctive and attractive 'character,' combining considerable originality with a quiet good taste.

For the bolder, more outspoken designs favoured by the times, one must look to the work of Robinson's students. Thomas H. Tracy and George F. Durand were apprentices with Robinson during the 1860s, and, after various experiences in the wider architectural world, both returned to join him as partners. Tracy came back to London in 1873 and worked with Robinson for over five years; Durand returned in 1878, the year of Robinson's retirement. For the last two years of Robinson's career, Richard Purdom Fairbairne was also a partner.[95] He had apprenticed with Robinson from 1872 to 1876; after leaving the firm he went to work for Kivas Tully in the provincial Department of Public Works. That he eventually became deputy minister validates the firm's assessment of his talents, but regrettably virtually nothing is known of the work he did in London. Fortunately, both Tracy and Durand left behind an impressive legacy of Victorian showpieces.

ROBINSON'S CHARACTER AS A MAN

In both their reserve and their competence Robinson's buildings seem accurately to reflect their designer. Goodspeed's *History of the County of Middlesex* describes him as a man who 'is quiet and unassuming, and the embodiment of honor.'[96] Other contemporary references show that he was greatly respected for his competence, diligence, kindness, and generosity.

He was evidently very dedicated to his family. Although his will shows him comfortably well off at the time of his death (he left over $15,000), he boarded throughout his career with his brother Frank, a painter and decorator; after 1875 they occupied a relatively modest two-storey Italianate house on the south-east corner of Horton and Waterloo streets. Though Robinson bequeathed more to Frank's children than to his other relatives, a long list of nieces and nephews received some of their uncle's carefully enumerated possessions. In addition to money, the especially prized articles included three watches, a relief globe, a five-volume Bible, fourteen volumes on the natural history of birds, electric batteries, and a collection of stereoscopic views. One Howard Robinson was to have 'his choice of my two violins and the best violin bow.' Robinson died in his adopted city on 10 October 1894. At his request he was buried alongside his parents' graves in a family plot in Norwich Township near their Burford home.

Robinson's concern for his adopted city was demonstrated, not only by his professional contributions, but also by gifts such as the gymnasium he donated to the Union School, 'being a firm believer in the benefit it would be to his pupils,'[97] and the generous legacies he bequeathed to various city charities. These included two temperance unions, three old peoples' homes, the Protestant Orphans' Home, 'City Hospital South,' Christ Church, and, to Bishop Baldwin, $1,000 'to be expended on extreme poverty cases.'

From his perspective and that of his contemporaries, his greatest contribution to London was the designing of a city waterworks system. Its completion coincided with his retirement in late 1878, and the eulogies of William Robinson at his retirement banquet were liberally mixed with eulogies of the waterworks. One exchange is particularly revealing:

Ald. Campbell, after alluding to his intimate acquaintance with Mr Robinson during a long series of years, said the longer a man knew him the better he would like him, but like all good men, it was very hard to get acquainted with him. When, however, you do, he is found to be a perfect treasure ... In conclusion, he hoped that Mr Robinson, during his approaching visit to Ireland, would pick up with a bouncing Irish girl and make her his wife ...

Ald. Egan, after referring in a humourous vein to the concluding remarks of the previous speaker, said no man could have been more devoted, sincere, or honest to his wife than Mr Robinson and himself were to the water-works scheme. If we had been married, the probability is that we would not have succeeded so well in perfecting the system of water works ... We were wedded to the scheme.[98]

Provincial Exhibition Building, 1861
North-east corner Central Avenue and Wellington Street, London (demolished)

The Provincial Exhibition was an annual event organized by the Provincial Agricultural Association for Canada West. From 1846 to 1857 it circulated to a variety of towns (including London, in 1854), but in 1857 the association decided that the fair would rotate among only four cities in the future: Toronto, Kingston, Hamilton, and London.[99] In recognition of this honour Toronto spent almost $21,000 on an iron and glass 'Crystal Palace' for the fair of 1858.[100] When London's turn came in 1861, the city was eager to provide impressive facilities of its own. But the severe financial slump of the preceding years made economy a major consideration, and the city had to content itself with a building of brick and wood rather than iron.

Though he used conventional materials, Robinson did succeed in providing a practical, distinctive, and very distinguished Crystal Palace for under $9,000.[101] He seems to have been among the first architects in Canada to adapt the then fashionable octagonal shape to an exhibition building: it was also used in Hamilton (1860) and Ottawa (1874–5).[102] Both of the latter structures have only an octagonal core, however, with radiating spokes. Robinson's more compact design consists of a series of octagonal layers, rather like an octagonal wedding cake, except that where wedding cakes generally rise in uniform steps, the irregular layers of the Exhibition Building form a graceful parabolic curve. Neoclassical details give the structure a character that is dignified enough for a civic building and festive enough for a fair. On the upper tiers Doric pilasters alternate with round-headed windows; at the ground level visitors entered the building through simplified triumphal arches, with monumental doorways eight feet wide and fourteen feet high.

Inside, displays were located on the ground floor, measuring 186 feet from angle to angle, and in a gallery the outer wall of which corresponded to the building's second tier, while the inner wall supported the third tier. At the octagon's core one had a clear view of the roof and the cupola, 'not intercepted by any timbers to the height of eighty-seven feet.'

It is interesting to speculate on the possible sources of Robinson's unusual conception. Owing largely to the influence of Orson S. Fowler's *A Home for All* (1848), the octagon had achieved some popularity as a house form during the 1850s. Fowler strongly recommended octagon houses on the grounds that they were lighter, better heated and ventilated, cheaper per square foot, and more closely aligned with the ideal spherical forms of nature than were square or rectangular shapes. Robinson was gaining more direct insight into the potential of the octagon form through his work on the Scotch Church (1859–60; fig. 40). Another, less exalted, source may possibly have inspired the series of concentric layers: the drawings of circular stables in Loudon's *Encyclopaedia*.[103]

Stables would have been an appropriate influence in that the London *Free*

41 'London, Ont. – Western Fair Building and Grounds,' from *Canadian Illustrated News*, 30 October 1875

Press considered livestock 'first in importance' at the 1861 Exhibition. Predictably, farm machinery and horticultural products are also prominently featured. More surprising is the attention given to carriages; both the *Free Press* and the judges were especially partial to an 'open top buggy' with an 'elegantly carved body' in the 'form of a sea shell.' Other displays under the general heading 'Arts, Manufacturers, Ladies' Work, &c' included furniture, stained glass, 'decorative house painting,' 'Machine-wrought Moulding,' 'Machine-wrought Flooring,' specimens of 'Turning in Wood,' 'Veneers from Canadian Woods,' corn brooms, wash tubs, and architectural drawings.

The 1861 fair grounds were located on property that had recently been vacated by the garrison, just north and north-east of what is now Victoria Park. After the successful 1865 Exhibition on the same site, local politicians urged that a London fair be made an annual event. When the first 'Western Fair' was held in 1868, however, it had to share the facilities with the garrison, reinstated in London to ward off the Fenians, and the Exhibition Building itself was off limits to the fair-goers.[104] The building regained its old status after the garrison's departure later that year and continued to house both Provincial Exhibitions and Western Fairs until 1887, when the fair grounds were moved to their present location at London's Queen's Park.[105]

Christ Church (Anglican), 1862–3
138 Wellington Street, London

When the Diocese of Huron was formed in 1857, St Paul's Cathedral was the only Anglican church in London. In 1862 steps were taken towards establishing a second church, at the foot of Wellington Road, just within the city's southern limits. The *Free Press* saw the church as a boon for 'numbers of the inhabitants of London who for years have experienced inconveniences in having no place of worship near at hand, or in not being able to secure seats in St Paul's church.'[106] Overcrowding at St Paul's undoubtedly contributed to the decision to found a second church, but new churches were designed to increase the flock as well as to accommodate the faithful, and a church in the south would balance the new Huron College in the north as a reminder of the Anglican presence in the expanding parts of the city.

The Reverend Mr G.M. Innes, appointed by Bishop Benjamin Cronyn to organize the new parish, must have been a very dedicated man. He worked without a salary;[107] he himself raised $500 in Britain towards the cost of the new church; and he evidently had to face some trials from the more unruly members of his gathering congregation. Later, from his more exalted position as Dean of Huron and Rector of St Paul's, he recalled his first year in London:

The congregation worshipped ... in the old public school house on King Street and an ... outdoor service was held on Thursday afternoons on the ground on which Christ Church now stands, which had been donated by Bishop Cronyn. These outdoor services were well attended but the boys were frequently very troublesome. The stump of an old tree was the pulpit; this was hollow at the base. On one occasion the boys filled this with dried leaves and while the sermon was proceeding a lighted match was introduced and the preacher had to descend ignominiously and was greeted with shouts and laughter of the said boys.[108]

The efforts of the Reverend Mr Innes were strongly aided by the members of St Paul's, especially 'the ladies' committee,' which raised enough money to build the $4,000 church debt free, largely through subscriptions ranging in amount from 25¢ to $200.

The *Free Press* reported that the design was 'after an early period of pointed architecture, economy of construction being a leading feature.' Lancet windows were cheaper than those with tracery. Robinson, however, turned enforced simplicity into an elegant orderliness. The three lancet windows that dominate the central part of the façade are echoed in the east wall of the shallow chancel. The tripartite division of the west front indicates the interior divisions between nave and aisles; the exterior buttresses are aligned with interior columns. The south porch, though possibly a concession to one of the

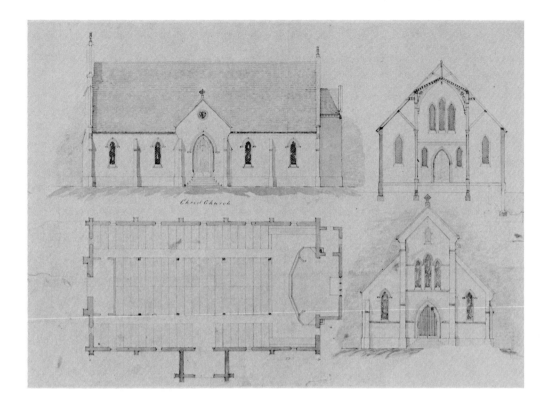

42   Christ Church, London, architectural drawing showing front elevation, south elevation, floor plan, and section

Ecclesiologists' favourite demands, is carefully centred in the side wall in a manner quite opposed to their taste – and most unusual in any era. Inside, octagonal wooden columns support pointed arches that run parallel to the length of the church, while rather rough wooden beams and rafters span the nave and aisles. J. Furneaux Jordan's comment on Exeter Cathedral, that its nave seemed a 'stone forest,'[109] could well be applied here in a modified form. For the tall columns, branching out into arches and braces far above, do rather suggest a woods. But there is nothing of a forest's mystery in Christ Church. With the relative slenderness of the columns, the wide span of the arches, and the clear light coming through windows that were originally leaded but stained only in some borders, the comparison is rather to a grove in a carefully designed garden.

The church expanded during the next few decades. A church hall was built in 1879, and sometime prior to 1887 a gallery was added.[110] Apparently the congregation did borrow money for these improvements. William Robinson bequeathed $800 to Christ Church to be used for lifting its mortgage; he left an additional $300 to be invested and the interest used 'for Tract distribution' in the church. A funeral service for its architect was held in Christ Church before his burial in Norwich township.[111]

The Collegiate Institute, 1864–5

North side St James Street between Wellington and Waterloo streets, London (demolished)

The London Collegiate Institute first opened its doors to the 'sons of gentlemen,' as its prospectus defined them, in 1865. Two years later the school was rechristened Hellmuth Boys' College, after the man mainly responsible for its foundation, an energetic and rather enigmatic Anglican clergyman named Isaac Hellmuth. Hellmuth had grand ambitions for his school: it was to provide a primary and secondary school education 'second to none that can be obtained upon the continent' and 'equal in efficiency to the best institutions of England and Germany.'[112] Despite Hellmuth's prodigious efforts, however, the school failed to prosper. In 1877, just twelve years after its auspicious opening, the college closed, though it was immediately reincarnated as Dufferin College, with the man who was then headmaster assuming ownership of the school and renting space in the building.[113] Meanwhile, Bishop Hellmuth was modifying his original vision by arranging for the building's use as the first home of the Western University, subsequently to become the University of Western Ontario. Although the university managed to survive, its first quarters proved impractical, and the building designed for the best school on the continent spent its final days as a warehouse for drainage tiles.

Isaac Hellmuth was a converted Polish Jew who came to London in 1862 as the first principal of Huron College, then exclusively a theological school. It was only the first of several schools he would help establish in London. The idea of a boys' school, at least, was already in his mind when he drafted the Huron College constitution: among the school's objectives, as he saw them, was the foundation of 'a preparatory Collegiate School.' When it appeared, however, the Collegiate Institute was designed to do much more than to prepare boys for a theological training. The initial cost of the building was an astronomical $66,000, over four times the cost of Huron College, and it was designed to offer the very best staff, program, and facilities available. Hellmuth's high aims for his school are indicated by the quality of its first headmaster: the Reverend Mr Arthur Sweatman was a Cambridge mathematician who went on to become Bishop of Toronto and later Primate of Canada.[114]

Sweatman presided over a surprisingly comprehensive program of studies. The Collegiate Institute had a 'Classical Department,' which taught Hebrew as well as Greek and Latin, but it also possessed an extremely comprehensive 'Modern and Scientific Department,' in which pupils would study 'less Latin and Greek, and more Mathematics, Modern Languages, English Literature, History, Geography, ... Composition, and Book-keeping,' as well as Drawing (under the mastership of William Robinson) and a wide variety of science courses. Upper Canada College also introduced science into its curriculum at

43 'The Hellmuth College at London, Ontario, Canada West,' from *Illustrated London News*, 19 February 1870

about this time. However, while Upper Canada College hired a lecturer in chemistry and physiology for $300 a year, Hellmuth introduced courses in 'Physical Science, Chemistry, Natural History, Geology, Mineralogy, Experimental Philosophy, and the Use of Instruments,' and he spent $3,000 on scientific equipment.[115]

The school's curriculum seems the perfect fulfilment of the ideas put forward by Egerton Ryerson, then chief superintendent of schools, who considered the British concentration on Latin and Greek too narrow for a Canadian education; likely Hellmuth and Ryerson were basing their ideas on some of the same continental models. In other respects, too, the Collegiate Institute sounds like a textbook illustration of the theories promulgated by Ryerson and his deputy minister, J. George Hodgins. As Hodgins was later to explain, in his 1876 edition of *The School House*, a variety of trees were useful as lessons in botany: 'while enjoying their shade, the inquiring pupil might learn their names, classes, and uses.' The Collegiate Institute's grounds were to be planted with 'every variety of trees, including maple, spruce, balsam, cedars, chestnuts, mountain ash, tulip, poplars, willows, etc.' Ryerson was a strong advocate of athletic training, particularly gymnastics. The Collegiate Institute was to have a well-equipped gymnasium, as well as a cricket field, racket court, swimming pond, and skating rink.[116]

The building that was to house the Collegiate Institute (fig. 43) was apparently to be as exemplary as the school's other components. Certainly it was impressive in terms of size. It provided dormitories for 150 students and separate apartments for the instructors, along with the requisite reception rooms, sitting rooms, classrooms, kitchen, and dining hall. It also housed a 'well-fitted library,' a museum, and, incorporated into the eastern wing, a four-storey residence for the headmaster. In addition, as mentioned in chapter 2, the building featured the latest in technological comforts: it had central steam heating, gas lighting, and indoor plumbing that provided hot and cold water.

Unfortunately, Robinson's design for the building was not the architectural paragon Hellmuth might have expected. The *Advertiser* had characteristically glowing words for the appearance of the building: 'the effect is bold and graceful; the whole design is one of tasteful simplicity. All superfluous orna- ments have been avoided, and the plain excellence of the structure is exhib- ited.'[117] A modern viewer might be inclined to describe the building as ungainly rather than graceful, and as bare rather than tastefully simple, but it is interesting in terms of Robinson's development as an architect.

The Collegiate Institute is nominally in the Tudor, or late Gothic, style considered appropriate for Anglican schools. Included among its several Tudor and Gothic motifs are the cross gables, the rectangular drip moulds, the pointed windows, and the finials. But these motifs are used in a somewhat half- hearted fashion. They seem superimposed on a building that is largely classical in feeling, with its symmetry, its string courses and simulated quoins, and a lantern featuring a heavy entablature. Although the two traditions could be effectively combined, Robinson's design here suffers from an excessively restrained and even mechanical approach. The overly spare decoration creates an impression of austerity; the identical proportions of the three bays that project in front prove monotonous. There is also an awkwardness about the building's proportions that appears in some of Robinson's other work of this period and seems, as here, to be a product of the high basement frequently used as an economical means of providing extra space. There were other practical reasons for raising the basement of the Collegiate Institute: a flight of stairs could give more dignity to the main entrance, and, on the school's site, a higher basement could diminish the risk of flooding. But Robinson had not yet developed the bolder, more imaginative approach, the appreciation of verticality, or in this case the more extensive Gothic vocabulary, that would let him exploit the additional height.

In making his building too tall, Robinson unwittingly created an appropriate symbol for the college. It ultimately failed to meet the initial expectations of its founder, but there is little evidence to explain why. Apparently the school prospered for its first few years. That some serious problems existed by 1871 is indicated in a letter from Ryerson to his daughter Sophia, mistress of Eldon House in London. Commenting on the Reverend Mr Sweatman's application for the position of high school inspector, Ryerson wrote, 'It is thought that there must be some "screw loose" in connection with Hellmuth College, or he would not be a candidate for such an office. It appears that Hellmuth College only sent *two* students to the University last year; while even the *Whitby*

44 'The Western University, London, Ontario,' from *Illustrated London News*, 23 November 1878

Grammar School sent *nine*.'[118] Sweatman's departure (for a post at Upper Canada College) apparently intensified the school's difficulties, so that it had trouble attracting students and raising even operating expenses. After an initial burst of local enthusiasm, some parents may have decided that the established Upper Canada College was more prestigious. Others may have opted for the public grammar schools, which were steadily improving, instead of paying the hefty $220 per annum necessary for tuition, board, and 'washing' at Hellmuth Boys' College. When the Association of the Professors and Alumni of Huron College arranged to purchase the property for the new university, there were outstanding debts of $22,000, and the school's shareholders were anxious to rid themselves of a financial burden, even though the sale price would not repay their original investments.[119]

The problems associated with Hellmuth Boys' College did not deter Hellmuth from expanding his building program. He seems consistently to have taken a strong interest in the design of his buildings. While working on Hellmuth Boys' College, Robinson was also the supervising architect for St John's Chapel at Huron College, designed by Toronto architect William Kauffman. Hellmuth hired Gundry and Langley, another Toronto firm, to design the Hellmuth Ladies' College in 1868. Displaying even greater ambition, he engaged Gordon Lloyd, a distinguished architect from Sandwich and Detroit, for his last three projects. In 1872, after becoming the second Bishop of Huron,

Hellmuth had plans drawn for a grand cathedral which was to be located on the south-east corner of Richmond and Piccadilly streets. (Only the chapter house was ever erected.) In 1877 Lloyd designed a chapel for the Ladies' College. In 1878 he designed a major reconstruction of the exterior of Hellmuth Boys' College (fig. 44);[120] Bishop Hellmuth apparently thought the building needed to be revamped before it would be altogether suitable for housing a university.

Gordon Lloyd's magnificent revision of the building transforms it from a rather graceless Early Victorian structure to a High Victorian tour de force. He has daringly enhanced the verticality of the building by creating a massive tower over an enlarged central pavilion, by placing spires over the end pavilions, and by heightening the lantern and even the chimneys. He has replaced the bay windows that Robinson positioned on the lower two storeys with oriel windows on the upper storeys, and he has lightened and varied the bottom part of the building with an open arcade. More windows decorate the façade, and horizontal lines of polychromatic brick enliven the walls and counter the height of the towers. Robinson's sober, spare building has been changed into something rich and strange.

Lloyd's revisions were never executed, and the Hellmuth College building never became the glorious home for the university that Hellmuth had apparently envisaged. The new university opened in 1881, with a Faculty of Divinity, composed of the Huron College staff, and a Faculty of Arts. A Faculty of Medicine was introduced in 1882. Only three years later, in 1885, the Faculty of Arts was forced to close for lack of students, and the university building became virtually deserted. The Faculty of Divinity moved back to the old Huron College, and the medical school, finding the lighting and heating in the main building inadequate for its purposes, moved into a five-room cottage on the property.[121] A Faculty of Law, begun in 1885, never did use the Hellmuth College premises, which by then were reportedly in a considerable state of disrepair. In the 1890s a tile company, using sand from the Grosvenor Street quarry, employed the basement of the university building for storage until in 1894 the Star Life Insurance Company foreclosed the mortgage on the property. Soon after it was sold to a contractor, who demolished the building and divided the property into building lots.[122]

While the new university was struggling through its first years, Isaac Hellmuth suddenly and unexpectedly deserted his project. In 1883 he accepted a position as Suffragan Bishop of Hull, ostensibly because his wife's failing health required a milder climate. The move did not turn out particularly well. Both his wife and the Bishop of Ripon, who was responsible for the appointment, died in the following year, and the incoming bishop chose not to reinstate Hellmuth in his new position. Hellmuth spent the rest of his life holding a series of more minor ecclesiastical positions. His decision to leave London when his fondest dream seemed to be taking shape has been the object of considerable speculation and controversy. It has been suggested that the church encouraged his departure; there was some powerful opposition to his plans for expansion, particularly to the cathedral and the university. After he left some questions surfaced regarding his handling of college funds. He had raised close to $100,000, mainly in England, towards the expense of the new university. Critics found it strange that Hellmuth had appropriated nearly $10,000 of this sum to pay for his own fund-raising trips to England, and that funds specifically designated for academic chairs had never been so applied.[123] There seems, too, to have been some misrepresentation regarding the destination of the general funds. Gordon Lloyd's design for the remodelled building was published in the *Illustrated London News* (23 November 1878) above a caption explaining that Hellmuth was in England to procure 'the requisite funds for its completion.' In fact, no start was ever made towards realizing Lloyd's conception. Despite some suspicious circumstances, Hellmuth had warm defenders,[124] and his decision to return to England may simply have represented one more submission to ambition.

None of the buildings Hellmuth commissioned still stands. The University of Western Ontario does remain as a monument to his dreams, and a short road named Hellmuth Avenue runs through the middle of what used to be the Hellmuth College grounds.

The Crystal Block, 1864–5

North-west corner Richmond and Dundas streets, London

The Crystal Block, occupying a long, narrow lot at the intersection of London's two main streets, was built to replace a structure that had been destroyed by fire. Because its owner, a Reverend Mr Palmer of Guelph, was anxious not to let his valuable property stand vacant, construction of the new block began in September, pressed on through the winter months, and was completed in April. The challenging winter building conditions and the unusual design of the building made it 'the subject of much curiosity, speculation, and scrutiny' on the part of London's citizens.[125]

The Crystal Block faces Richmond Street, largely, no doubt, so that its long side could be exploited for more shop fronts. This orientation gave Robinson a chance to design a façade of almost monumental proportions, along what was becoming the city's most fashionable commercial street (fig. 39). His design is an imaginative, interesting, and very free interpretation of the Neoclassical mode. The building was originally symmetrical, with a parapet on both ends (the mansard roof is a later addition). On all three exposed sides the round-headed arches of the ground floor and the more elaborate window heads of the storey above signify the arcade and the *piano nobile* of the *palazzo*. The façade recalls a common Neoclassical pattern, where, usually, an imposing central section is separated from protruding end pavilions by two recessed wings; in the Crystal Block all five divisions are flush with the sidewalk, and blind arcades, two storeys in height, distinguish the end and centre sections. There are several less conventional aspects to the building, which supports Robinson's assertion that 'the style of architecture is after no particular school or model.' The blind arcades have segmental rather than round arches, where large, rough voussoirs alternate with smaller, smoother stones. This striking combination indicates Robinson's growing interest in varied textural effects, evident, too, in the contrast between the banded, brick pilasters and the smooth brick walls between them. The wrought-iron balconies, designed by the architect himself, were singled out for particular praise in the *Free Press* and said to attract 'considerable notice and remark' from passersby. Perhaps the most unusual and intriguing elements of the design were the eight niches that adorned the end and centre sections of the façade. They were to be occupied by marble statues 'of home manufacture,' carrying symbolic associations appropriate to the area: 'In one it is proposed to place a figure suggestive of settler life in Canada, the ideal of this at present being a rough and sturdy labourer leaning upon a stump, which he has chopped partially through, and holding in his hand an axe indicative of the nature of his toil. In another a Canadian Indian robed in his native costume. The others are intended to be occupied in the course of time

45   The Crystal Block (on the left), photograph by John Cooper, c. 1895

as the occasion and its attending circumstances might suggest.' Thus one of
London's first monuments to the age of Italianate elegance incorporated
reminders of its recent, primitive past.

It is not clear how many statues ever did occupy the Crystal Block, but the
building attracted numerous shops and businesses over the last century. It
also housed, during its earliest years, a reading room sponsored by the
YMCA, where young men could 'profitably employ themselves' with 'a good
supply of books, magazines, and newspapers,' or perhaps attend, say, a singing
class. Though its attractiveness is now somewhat disguised by unappealing
store fronts, the building still stands, one of the last representatives of a
handsome Victorian streetscape.

Strathroy Public Building, probably designed between 1867 and 1870

Strathroy (never built)

In 1848 Strathroy, ten miles west of London, had three stores, a blacksmith, a tavern, a grist-mill and a saw-mill. Four years later engineers for the Great Western Railway Company proposed a route through Strathroy, and the arrival of the railroad in 1858 transformed the crossroads. In 1860, with a population of 750, Strathroy was officially designated a village; by 1870, with 3,200 inhabitants, it became a town.[126]

The citizens of Strathroy seem to have been unusually eager to have public buildings suitable for their increasing status. By 1861 they had already built a town hall, and they built another for $500 in 1863.[127] During the election campaign of 1870 one contestant argued that 'we need a new Town Hall and Market House.' In 1872 the council approved a loan for building the third town hall; two years later it passed a by-law approving the expenditure of $2,350 on a combined engine house, firemen's hall, and council chambers, designed by J.H. Cook, who was also appointed to oversee its construction for the princely sum of $35. The most recent town hall was built in 1928.[128]

Robinson's drawing of a building to be erected in the Village of Strathroy, would seem to indicate that interest in a multipurpose building arose even before 1870 and possibly as early as 1867; the 'London, *Ont*' under Robinson's signature indicates a post-Confederation date, but the 'C.W.' on the embossed seal shows that Strathroy officialdom had not yet adjusted to the new nomenclature. In addition to an engine house and council chambers, Robinson's design incorporates an assembly hall and platform, a police office, a lock-up, and a market hall. All this inner diversity is contained in a simple structure loosely modelled on a Greek temple; its gable is treated like a pediment, with the oculus often found in Neoclassical buildings, and the piers simulate columns. However, the narrow recessed bands of the piers and the pronounced brackets of the cornices give the building a staccato-like rhythm, an effect very different from the serenity usually associated with the Greek Revival form. Both features reflect the Italianate influence that was becoming increasingly marked in Robinson's work.

In keeping with the conventional mode, the front elevation of the building was thoroughly symmetrical. The main entrance, which led to the ground floor market and to the assembly hall above, occupied the two central bays. But the rear elevation (fig. 46) was considerably less elegant, owing to the building's ingenious split-level plan. In the back portion of the building the jail and engine house occupied rooms situated slightly lower than the market, allowing the council chambers to be fitted into a kind of mezzanine above.

46   Strathroy Public Building, Strathroy, detail of architectural drawing showing rear
elevation; drawing signed 'Wm Robinson'

Prisoners, policemen, firemen, and councillors could reach their respective
quarters only through a basement-level back door clearly designed for utility
rather than beauty. Perhaps it was the indignity of such an arrangement that
decided the councillors against Robinson's plan.

Christ Church (Anglican), 1867–8

Dresden

Among the thousands who were moved by Harriet Beecher Stowe's novel *Uncle Tom's Cabin* (1851–2) was an Englishman named Thomas Hughes.[129] He determined to become a missionary to escaped slaves and eventually created an Anglican congregation in Dresden, Ontario and its close neighbour Dawn Mills, the home of the real Uncle Tom, Josiah Henson.

Hughes's first Canadian mission was in London. In 1857 he was sent there by the Anglican Colonial Church and School Society to teach in a school for both black and white children that had been established three years before.[130] Under the leadership of the Reverend Mr Martin Dillon, the mission school had proved remarkably successful, not only in educating black students, but also in breaking down substantial racial barriers. Two years after Hughes's arrival, however, the school closed, ostensibly because black students were finally being admitted to the common schools.

Hughes moved on to Dresden and Dawn Mills, villages north of Chatham. A large black population had gathered in the Dresden area, owing to the attractions of the Dawn Institute, a charitable project organized by Henson among others, designed to teach former slaves the skills needed to function in a white society.[131] The Colonial Church and School Society had started a school in Dresden two years before, largely in response to the severe problems experienced by the institute.[132] But Hughes, who had been ordained while in London, now devoted himself to religious rather than educational guidance.

His initial efforts to develop a church in Dresden were frustrated by the strong racial prejudice in the area; the school for whites was off limits as a meeting place, and, later, white landlords were reluctant to sell a site for a church for blacks. What seems to have been remarkable patience and true charity on Hughes's part was rewarded by success in gathering a mixed congregation in Dresden, and in 1867 work began on a church building. Since the congregation was very poor, financing the church depended on charity (£50 from a ladies' committee in England), numerous money-making projects (including a three-day bazaar), and a great deal of volunteer labour. The men of the church cut logs and carried them to the mill; the bricks were made on the farm of Samuel Hughes, the rector's nephew. The result, in Thomas Hughes's own words, was 'a very neat, chaste building.'[133]

Robinson's design for Christ Church, Dresden, resembled his plan for Christ Church, London, though on a much smaller scale. Only two windows are grouped over the main door, but their arrangement is echoed in the side bays and in the window of the main entryway, giving the building a sophistication and liveliness rare in Ontario churches erected for black congregations. Inside, the building is much simpler than the interior of the London church:

47   Christ Church, Dresden

there are no columns or aisles, and even a chancel could not be afforded when the church was initially constructed. But the interior details are attractive, if simple, and Hughes could have felt justifiably proud of his flock's accomplishments.

Sadly, Hughes's diary shows that even before the church was consecrated in 1871 he felt serious misgivings and some despair about his efforts in the area:

May 28th, 1871. A fair congregation at Dresden. No of communicants 14. A very poor congregation at D. Mills, only about 20 present. No of Communicants 4. Felt very much depressed in spirits today. Sometimes think that my work is done in this mission. The change brought about by the great influx of whites has made my work much more trying and difficult than formerly. The unchristian prejudice against colour seems to be ineradicable ... This tries, at times, both my faith & patience ... Judgement O Lord belongs to thee, and in thy hands I leave this matter. But O Lord direct my steps aright. Make the path of duty clear before me. Sustain my drooping spirit. Increase my faith. Give the grace to persevere in the work thou hast for me to do.

Hughes was pleased with the good turn-out at the consecration, but his doubts of the past months were still uppermost in his mind: 'Oct. 11, 1871. Now our church to build [for] which I laboured so long and so hard. O may He, who has enabled me to bring this work to so happy a conclusion, give me grace to persevere in the work he has given me to do. And may his blessed Spirit so bless his word that many lively stones may be added from among the people of this place to beautify his glorious spiritual temple.' Apparently his prayers were answered, for he stayed in his difficult post until his death in 1876. Josiah Henson, summoned to his good friend's sickbed, claimed Hughes's 'last moments were peaceful, and his faith to the last was triumphant. He died as he had lived, a genuine Christian.'[134]

St Andrew's Presbyterian Church and Manse, 1868–9 and 1871

now First-St Andrew's United Church and Farquhar House,
350 and 356 Queens Avenue, London

In 1832 an extremely forceful, energetic, and articulate Presbyterian clergyman named William Proudfoot established himself in London. As he observed in the following year, 'Mr Donaldson from the 10th concession told me that the Methodists and Baptists have exceedingly increased in the township. God only knows, I hope in His Mercy so to bless my labour that they and all who hold errors will not increase.'[135] Unfortunately for Proudfoot, London's first two decades found local Presbyterians divided by the same rifts as those that disrupted the Scotland they had left, and Proudfoot had to count many of his own sect among those misled by error.

Although Proudfoot was a Secessionist, he hoped to combine members of the Established church with members of the Secession Church in a single congregation. He organized such a united congregation in 1833, but by the time its first church building was erected in 1836, several supporters of the Established church had drifted away, and in 1843 they built a church of their own, an attractive but small frame structure costing £500. However, in the same year there was a major split in the Church of Scotland: a long-standing controversy over the issue of political patronage resulted in the formation of the Free Church, which opposed state control of the church. Most of the St Andrew's congregation voted to align themselves with the Free Church; a small number remained with the Established church and organized themselves as the congregation of St James Presbyterian.[136]

By the 1860s all three Presbyterian congregations found themselves able to build substantial brick edifices. Their differences of opinion on other issues did not keep them from using the services of the same architect. Robinson was the local supervising architect for the octagonal St James Presbyterian which opened in 1860 (fig. 40). In 1861 he designed First Presbyterian Church for what had been Proudfoot's congregation. In 1868 and 1869 he was the architect for the very impressive building erected by the congregation of the Free Church.

By 1868 this congregation had grown considerably, both in numbers and in prosperity. The new St Andrew's Presbyterian Church (fig. 49) was to seat 1,200 people and to cost around $22,000, over twice the cost of St James. The building committee took its responsibilities very seriously; interestingly, their recorded concerns are exclusively technical and practical, including issues such as lighting and heating systems, dimensions and gallery supports. There is no mention in the building reports of any concern with style; that aspect seems to have been entrusted to the architect.[137]

48   St Andrew's Presbyterian Church, London, early photograph of architectural
perspective drawing; drawing signed 'Wm Robinson'

49   St Andrew's Presbyterian Church

St Andrew's was the most accomplished of Robinson's forays into the Gothic Revival style. He has made a virtue of the building's height by accentuating the pleasing contrast between the limestone foundation and the buff brick with a protruding stone course. The long windows are well proportioned for the building's height. The porches on each side of the church broaden the building so as to counter its verticality, and seem to anchor it to the ground. The tower, one of Robinson's most masterful achievements, rises gracefully through a series of increasingly delicate stages to an intricate crown of pinnacles (those between the corners are now missing), from which ascends a tall and slender spire. The corner pinnacles of the tower, like those at the corners of the church, are in effect miniature lanterns; the sky shining through their openings increases the sense of lightness at the upper reaches of the building.

The same virtuosity is displayed inside, where a complex of elegant braces, spandrels, and beams arches over the nave. Stencilled glass by Robert Lewis (some of which still exists in the tower) adorned the windows. But despite its open supports and Decorated style, the interior of St Andrew's could not be mistaken for that of an Anglican church. There was originally no chancel; even more revealingly, there was originally no organ (a feature found even in the modest Anglican church at Dresden).

Music was a contentious issue in the church at the time the new building was constructed: the choir and the minister were at odds over an organ. Though the Reverend Mr John Scott won the initial battle, Clarence T. Campbell has claimed that conscience and the opposition together made Scott's victory temporary: 'with prosperity came the growth of modern ideas, especially in regard to musical services. The majority of the congregation wanted an organ. With this Mr Scott had no sympathy. He was no weakling to surrender to what he thought was wrong, but he was not so self-willed as to lead a faction against the wishes of the people, so he resigned his pastorate in 1875.'[138] In 1887 George Durand designed a major addition to the church. It included a chancel area that was to hold an organ loft and choir gallery, as well as the new pulpit and railing discussed in chapter 2 (fig. 23).

The manse (fig. 50), designed by Robinson in 1871,[139] is a perfect architectural complement to the church. Also of white brick, it sits nearly even with the tower and well to the east, thus defining a comfortable amount of space around the church. It is a quiet, Italianate building, with the brackets, round-headed window, and low-pitched roof typical of the style. There were originally round-headed arches in the entryway as well, similar to those found on the Reid cottage; the present door and porch are later additions. The house is fittingly distinguished for a manse, but sufficiently simple not to detract from what was obviously deemed the more important building.

The interior also possesses a certain elegance, accruing from the high ceilings and attractive mouldings characteristically found in Italianate houses, but there are signs here of tasteful economy. The mantels, for example, are wooden versions of a common marble style.

The manse has a centre-hall plan similar to that of the Militia Offices (fig.

50   St Andrew's Manse

66), with a kitchen wing at the back. The plan of the manse is less symmetrical, however, probably because of the special functions it had to fulfil. On the right as one enters the building are a large dining room and a smaller room suitable for the rector's study. On the left, instead of the double parlour one would expect, there is a single living room obviously fit for entertaining or lecturing to large groups.

St Andrew's was to experience another significant stage in its growth in 1938, when its congregation merged with that of First Presbyterian Church. The united congregation that Proudfoot had unsuccessfully tried to form a hundred years before had finally become a reality.

Custom House, 1870–3

North-east corner Richmond Street and Queens Avenue, London (demolished)

The London *Advertiser* greeted news of a possible custom house for London less with gratitude than with a kind of petulant impatience: 'At last our city member has made a move towards having a custom house erected in London ... The want of a suitable Custom House has been long felt by the businessmen of the city and the erection of such a building will occur none too soon to satisfy the demand.' In the period since London had been established as a custom district in 1854, three different temporary offices had served to house the custom facilities.[140]

That a custom house was finally approved for London in 1870 probably had less to do with the volume of business in the city than with Confederation. The new government was eager to establish its presence throughout the dominion, and it chose as one means a major building campaign, concentrating on post offices and custom houses, to help accomplish its aim.[141] The London Custom House was to cost over $32,000.[142]

Because these buildings had an important function as the projection of a national image, their style was to some extent controlled by the Department of Public Works. The department usually provided ground plans and fire-proofing requirements for a building, and it generally stipulated that the building was to be in what is known as the Second Empire style. The local architect was then free to draw his own plans within the parameters established by these directives. His completed design had to be submitted to the Department of Public Works for approval, and the department quite frequently made changes, which were sometimes successfully contested by the local architect. As a result of this process, the final design was usually a joint effort.

It seems likely, however, that the finished design of the London Custom House (fig. 51) was mainly Robinson's own. The local newspaper credits it to him, and the building exhibits the restraint, deliberateness, and refinement that generally characterize Robinson's buildings.

Restraint was not a quality often linked with the Second Empire style, which was usually defined by a mansard roof and a strongly textured, three-dimensional façade. Robinson's Custom House possesses the mandatory mansard roof, but it otherwise comprises an insistently flat treatment of the Renaissance mode. The central pavilion projects forward only slightly. The rustication of the ground floor and the quoins is very light, while the stone facings covering the rest of the building are extremely smooth. The convex mouldings of the first floor windows are recessed so as to be flush with the wall. The pilasters framing the windows of the *piano nobile* are shallow. Even the coat of arms, the most prominent sculptural detail on the building, is carefully

51   Custom House, London, photograph by John Kyle O'Connor, c. 1875

located within the plane of the central projection. As a result, the building seems surprisingly retiring, quietly displaying its graces rather than forcing them upon one.

The building did have many graces to display. Unfairly, perhaps, those that particularly captured the admiration of London citizens were those least architectural in character. There was great demand even for photographs of the sculptor's small models of the coat of arms, and the arrival from Boston of the $1,700 clock and bell was eagerly awaited. The clock dial was to be illuminated at night, and an 'automatic arrangement' was to turn the gas off and on at the appropriate intervals. That this system did not work at first was 'a subject of complaint in the city for months.'[143]

T.S. Scott, chief architect in the Department of Public Works, officially accepted the building for the Dominion on 19 September 1873.[144] By the mid-1880s increased customs traffic had made the original structure inadequate.

52   Custom House, architectural drawing showing George F. Durand's proposed clock tower addition

In 1884 George Durand designed an addition at the rear of the building which nearly doubled its size.[145] At the same time he made drawings for a new clock tower at the front (fig. 52), presumably in an attempt to give the Custom House some of the flamboyance evident in most Public Works buildings of the period.

Essentially, Durand's design raises Robinson's clock tower by setting it on a large, convex base. The coat of arms is enshrined in an ornate baroque pediment that rises above the frontispiece. The proposed new arrangement possesses a good deal of charm on its own, but it is doubtful that it improves Robinson's building. Had it been constructed, its wealth of variety would have detracted from the harmonious simplicity of Robinson's façade.

In the early 1970s, approximately 100 years after its erection, the Custom House was demolished. It has left behind a few traces. The royal arms and the iron cresting now decorate the Benmiller resort complex. The cast-iron fence that surrounds St Paul's Cathedral uses the design originally created for the fence around the Custom House; its beaver motif, like the Second Empire style, was a reminder that London belonged to the new Dominion of Canada.

Bishop's Palace, 1870–2

now St Peter's Cathedral Rectory, 196 Dufferin Avenue, London

The Roman Catholic Diocese of London was established in 1856, a year before its Anglican equivalent, but the first bishop, Adolphe Pinsonneault, did little to aid its development. Pinsonneault came from a wealthy French family, and, except for some years devoted to the study of theology in Paris, he spent his entire life in Montreal. His talents and attitudes were better suited to the established church in Quebec than to the pioneer conditions of his new diocese, and his attempts to recreate Montreal in south-western Ontario proved pathetically misguided. Pinsonneault, whom one historian described as 'an ardent French Nationalist with no love for either the English [or] his Irish co-religionists,' very soon moved the see to Sandwich, where there was a French community. But his antipathy to the British and the lavishness he exhibited on projects such as a $30,000 bishop's palace created problems for him in Sandwich as well as in the rest of his diocese. In 1866 he was asked to resign.[146]

The new incumbent, John Walsh, was a man much better suited to his role, by both his Irish background and his forceful, practical, and efficient character.[147] In January 1868, within two months of acceding to the bishopric,

54   Bishop's Palace, label stop, probably a portrait of Bishop Pinsonneault

55   Bishop's Palace, marble mantel in Bishop's private parlour

56   Bishop's Palace, main interior staircase

he moved the see back to London. There he undertook a successful appeal
for funds in order to erase his inherited debt of $40,000, and he set out to
strengthen his faltering domain. He is said to have possessed a good deal of
personal charm; a nun who once met Bishop Walsh described him as 'real
old-country Irish, stout and jolly, with a hearty chuckle.'[148] A more critical view
is presented in James Reaney's *Handcuffs* (1975), one scene of which is set
in the Bishop's Palace where Bishop Walsh's Conservative political views
influence his opposition to the ill-fated Donnelly family.[149] That his determination could work for the benefit of his diocese is indicated by his success
in raising money, first to clear the debt, and then to carry on a massive building
program. After a trip to Rome in 1876 he summarized the progress report
he had submitted to the Holy See. Since 1868 the diocese had built twenty-
eight churches ('many of them ... splendid and costly structures'), seventeen
'commodious' presbyteries, three convents, an orphanage, a college, and 'an
Episcopal residence, second to none in the Province.' 'In fine,' he observed,
'more than a quarter of a million dollars has been actually expended in
church improvement within the last nine years.'[150]

    The Bishop's Palace in London, costing around $17,000, was considerably
cheaper than Bishop Pinsonneault's.[151] It was a very imposing structure
nevertheless. Robinson's design is remarkably eclectic. The main entrance is
emphatically Tudor and ecclesiastical. It features a pointed Tudor arch,
stained glass windows showing a variety of religious symbols, and an arched

hood-mould with sculpted label stops that apparently portray Pinsonneault (fig. 54) and Walsh. The rectangular hood-moulds elsewhere and the building's H-shape give the structure as a whole something of a Tudor air, but the quoins, string courses, and brackets derive from various classical traditions and make congruous the use of the French mansard roof. A combination of such varied elements could have been bizarre, but in the Bishop's Palace the assorted parts are so carefully selected and balanced that they form a thoroughly unified whole, with a presence that simultaneously suggests piety and power.

The H-plan allowed for the physical separation of the building's various functions. The east wing contained the episcopal offices and most of the facilities of the rectory, including 'a thoroughly equipped recreation-room.' The west wing was devoted mainly to the bishop's requirements, with a 'large and commodious reception-room' on the first floor, and the bishop's chapel and private apartments above. The latter included a spacious and elegant parlour containing an elaborately carved marble mantel (fig. 55). The profusion of fruits and flowers falling from the cornucopias may well symbolize divine grace, though the very robustness of the sculpture evokes a sense of material plenty as well. In the hall linking the wings is a magnificent staircase that provides access to the basement and all three above-ground floors (fig. 56).

The setting of the Bishop's Palace has changed. When built, it stood behind a white brick Gothic church facing Richmond Street. However, Bishop Walsh's plans for establishing the bishopric in London included the construction of a fittingly majestic cathedral in addition to his other projects. St Peter's Cathedral Basilica, designed by Toronto architect Joseph Connolly, was dedicated in 1885.[152]

The Bishop's Palace itself has also undergone significant alterations. An extensive addition to the back of the building was designed by Moore and Henry; the double curving stairway that leads to the front door is a later addition. The building now serves only as a rectory. In 1912 the bishop's place of residence became a handsome Italianate house that had also been designed by Robinson in the 1870s, though a new portico by Moore and Munro largely obscures its original façade (fig. 222).

Huron and Erie Savings and Loan Society, 1870–1

East side Richmond Street between Dundas Street and Queens Avenue, London (demolished)

The Huron and Erie Savings and Loan Society, the ancestor of the present-day Canada Trust, was organized in 1864, one of several such institutions spawned in London during the Victorian period.[153] In June 1870 the *Free Press* announced that the society had 'resolved to erect a first-class building for their own use.'[154] An indication of its high aims is that it intended the building to 'be faced with Cleveland stone.' In fact, they finally settled for using stone only in the numerous and substantial window surrounds, but their new premises still proved impressively elegant. The Huron and Erie Company occupied the ground floor and rented the remaining space to other interested parties. Masonic Lodges chose to use the third floor as their hall.[155]

As with the Custom House just two doors away, Robinson placed a mansard roof on a building that was otherwise indebted mainly to the Italian Renaissance. The Huron and Erie building, however, had little of the high seriousness that characterized its neighbour. There is a rather debonair wittiness about its design, revealed in the superimposition of a curved mansard on a gable roof, in the unexpected asymmetry of the ground floor, and in the variety of window heads; the façade is a virtual sampler of Italianate window shapes.

Presumably Robinson intended no disrespect by his more light-hearted plan. The Huron and Erie firm was one of several financial institutions in which he owned shares at the time of his death.[156]

57   Huron and Erie Savings and Loan Society, London, advertisement from *London City Directory*, 1878–9

Reid's Crystal Hall, completed 1873

South side Dundas Street between Richmond and Clarence streets, London (collapsed)

When the Reid wholesale and retail china company outgrew its Richmond Street premises, its owners planned a new building that would satisfy present needs and 'be commensurate with their rapidly expanding business for some time to come.'[157] Thus their new fifty-foot-wide structure was designed as two complementary stores; the ground floor of the smaller could be rented out if not required by Reid's. It is the building's division into two shop fronts that accounts for its strikingly asymmetrical façade, a phenomenon rare in the Robinson canon.

The design is unusual in other respects, too. One reason that 'several scientific men from a distance ... visited the building' was that it had the cornice and window dressings of galvanized iron already discussed in chapter 2. The ground floor features the round-arched windows found in Robinson's other *palazzo*-inspired designs, but here the arches are of delicate, slender strips of iron, slight interruptions in a plate glass wall. Although the storeys above are of brick and the window surrounds have the proportions of wood, the oriel windows comprise another unconventional element. Such windows were frequently to be found on stores of a later date, as a result of the Queen Anne movement. But, as the *Free Press* rightly observed, in 1873 they were 'a new feature ... in the construction of a business establishment.' They served the same practical purpose as the wide expanse of glass below: to enable passersby to view the enticing wares within. They also added an appropriately domestic touch to a store dealing with household merchandise.

A variety of technical conveniences made the interior as interesting to 'scientific men' as its exterior. An elevator moved goods to and from the upper storeys. 'Speaking tubes' facilitated communications between various departments. The *Free Press* reported, too, that 'the building is constructed ... in a perfect manner,' with timbers that were 'exceedingly substantial, and capable of carrying a tremendous weight.'

Reid's carried an extraordinarily wide range of goods: 'Parisian marble statues and works of art, many of them exceedingly costly'; 'French and German Bohemian vases'; 'French, English and German dinner, tea, and toilet sets'; imported glassware, cutlery, lamps, chimneys, 'granite ware,' and the ' "C.C." or common ware ... generally in use among the humbler classes.' The main floor showroom was elegantly furnished. A 'lofty walnut showcase' extended down the full hundred-foot length of the store. Suspended from the thirteen-foot ceilings were 'chaste and beautiful gasoliers' designed to light the room at night, while reflections in the window threw 'the full blaze of the gas upon the gorgeous spread seen from the street.'

58   Reid's Crystal Hall, London, photograph, c. 1875

Originally, the upper floors were devoted to storage, sorting, and packing. By 1876 a china-painting industry was also located on the premises. A number of London citizens had developed this skill, under the influence and tutelage of London artist John H. Griffiths.[158] By 1889 W.J. Reid and Company had sixty employees, most of whom were women engaged in decorating china. The company also had buyers resident abroad, so as to obtain imported china-ware, and W.J. Reid himself made annual trips 'to visit the leading pottery manufactories of Europe.' Five travellers promoted the company's wares throughout Canada.[159]

In 1907 the building came to a spectacular and controversial end. On 16 July during the course of converting the smaller premises into a 'bowling and billiard palace,' three-quarters of the structure collapsed.[160] Ten people were killed. The accident was eventually attributed to various causes: the many new windows in the east wall, mortar that had been weakened by an earlier fire, inadequate support for the crumbling masonry while the wooden timbers were being replaced by iron beams, and thoughtless shifting of the heavy loads stored on the upper floors. The *Canadian Architect and Builder* implicitly exonerated alterations architect, W.G. Murray, of responsibility, placing the blame instead on London's negligent attitude towards construction safety. The by-laws controlling building inspection were still essentially the same as they had been in Robinson's time, with the city engineer the only official responsible for making inspections and few regulations in force for him to impose. By October 1907 a special committee was at work on a new by-law, and London City Council was taking applications for the position of building inspector.

Labatt's Brewery, 1874 (with later additions)

probably incorporated into present buildings, 150 Simcoe Street, London

Brewers set up business in London almost as soon as the village began to take shape. Labatt's can trace its own history back to one John Balkwill's primitive brewery, established in a log building in 1828. John K. Labatt and one Mr Eccles bought Balkwill's operations, by then located in a store building, in 1847. Labatt assumed sole control of the business when Eccles retired ten years later, and he eventually passed it on to his son, also John.[161] Aided by the ready supply of barley in the area, Labatt's was one of two local firms that by the 1870s had developed their markets well beyond the precincts of London. Labatt's and Carling's erected considerably larger buildings in 1874 and 1875, respectively,[162] in order to meet the increasing demand for their products.

Labatt's chose the opportunity to expand after a fire in March 1874 completely destroyed its old structure. The fire department appeared soon after the alarm was raised by a patrolling policeman, 'but owing to some difficulty,' the *Free Press* reported, 'which did not appear to be understood by the spectators, no water was thrown for about twenty minutes after the scene was reached.' Then the inadequate hose kept bursting. Meanwhile, the fire raged largely unchecked, destroying $30,000 worth of malt alone. The night watchman awakened from his nap in a second floor room just in time to escape.[163]

A new building, three times as large as its predecessor, was underway 'as soon as the remains of the old one had cooled sufficiently to admit of removal.' By June the brickworkers could celebrate the completion of their part of the job with a 'social' at the brewery, where 'the healths of the architect, contractors and others were drank with enthusiasm.'

The *Advertiser* lists 'Robinson & Tracy' as the architects without specifying which partner was mainly responsible, and the building is so utilitarian that an attribution on stylistic grounds is speculative. It seems unlikely, however, that Robinson would have entrusted such a complex commission to his recently acquired junior partner, and the oculi in the gables do suggest Robinson's hand.

59 Labatt's Brewery, London, from *Montreal Illustrated*, 1874

The 1874 building is towards the centre of the illustration (fig. 59). It consisted of the brewery itself (the long building with a cross gable near its centre); the lower appendage, with its own cross gable and cupola, in front of the brewery; and the malthouse, kilns, and ice house directly behind it. To the extent that this complex has a distinct style, it is vaguely Italianate, with windows headed by segmental arches. The grouping does have a picturesque quality that derives less from its 'style' than from its function. The structure was planned to take advantage of its hillside location, so that one end of the building has more storeys than the other. Interesting features such as the cupolas and the louvered third floor were essential for ventilation – to keep the brewery from becoming too hot and to allow for the escape of the carbon dioxide produced during the fermentation of the malt extract.[164] The malt house cupola in the Carling's brewery had a rotating cylindrical bin from which the barley could be shot into the various storage bins, and a similar device may also have been in use at Labatt's. Whatever their precise function, however, the cupolas give the edifice a festive air quite appropriate to a brewery.

The building was designed to produce the English-style ales and porters then prevailing in Canada. The brewery's most popular brand was a version of India pale ale;[165] the European-style lager that is now Labatt's best-selling type of beer was not produced by the firm until 1911.[166] The 1874 plant must have been a technological success, for Labatt's beers proceeded to win medals at major exhibition competitions held in Philadelphia (1876); Sydney, Australia (1877); and Paris (1878).[167] These heady triumphs were then advertised to boost sales.

The expansion of the firm's sales required further expansion of its facilities just a few years after Robinson's building was completed. In 1880 Tracy and Durand designed the relatively small office building near the gate and the wash house and storage areas beyond the main building; in 1882 Durand designed a new bottling centre.[168] By 1884 the complex had assumed the appearance it has in the picture from *Montreal Illustrated* (1894; fig. 59).

The very fact that such a publication contained an illustration of the London brewery (the product of which is 'preferred by connoisseurs and medical men') attests to the importance attached to the firm's expanding operations, the 'principal branch' of which was located in Montreal.[169] Ten years earlier the *Dominion Mechanical & Milling News* had already commented on the widespread popularity of Labatt's ales: 'The sales of the famous Labatt's ales and porters now reach from Winnipeg to Quebec, and there is not a town or city in this vast area of space where the product of the brewery is not found.'[170] John Labatt (d. 1915) was eventually to sell his beer across Canada and in American centres such as New York, Chicago, and Buffalo.[171] The company maintains its head office in London and continues to flourish, though the Labatt family no longer controls the enterprise.

City Hospital, 1873–5

replaced by present Victoria Hospital building, 375 South Street, London

The City Hospital built in 1875 far surpassed previous hospital accommodation in London, and represented a new attitude towards hospital care. Earlier medical facilities had included pest houses, erected at various dates to deal with cholera epidemics, and several inadequate 'general hospitals' housed in rented or hastily built facilities. The immediate predecessor of the 1875 City Hospital was located in a deserted barracks. It functioned as a home for the aged and the chronically ill as well as a hospital; until 1870, when the Asylum was built, the local hospitals had also housed the mentally ill.[172]

The need for a better hospital had long been recognized by city officials. Already in 1863 the city council had vainly requested from Parliament a grant contributing towards the cost of a more substantial civic hospital.[173] It was reported at a meeting of city council on 29 April 1867 that the city engineer had drawn plans for a new hospital: the building was '50 x 100 feet with a balcony at each End 10 feet wide. Estimated Cost from Eight to Ten Thousand Dollars.'[174]

Robinson was ultimately to create enough hospital designs to test a Griselda's patience. In March 1873 the *Advertiser* reported that Robinson was 'at work upon plans for the new hospital to be erected during the coming season in the southern part of the city.' On 18 May 1874 the Council and Relief Committee informed city council that more plans had been submitted. Two weeks later the committee expressed its desire to have the latest information 'as to modern improvements and [the] most approved plan,' and decided to defer any discussion on plans until the city physician had attended a medical conference in Buffalo and visited hospitals in that vicinity. In July the same committee rather mystifyingly advocated 'the use of small brick buildings for hospital purposes in preference to large,' a scheme more likely to be found in England than in Buffalo, and recommended calling for tenders on the plans for small buildings produced by the city engineer. The city engineer must have been overcome with relief when tenders for one of his plans (a single large building) were finally accepted on 24 August 1874. Even at that stage he had been forced to provide optional plans. Contractors submitted tenders for the structure with and without a mansard roof. The councillors decided that civic pride justified the extra $960 expense on the $10,960 contract and opted for the mansard roof and a tower.[175]

The decision was quite possibly influenced by the potential monotony of the building without those appendages. Except for its attractively corbelled cornices and brackets, the hospital has essentially the same format as Labatt's brewery, where piers alternate with arched windows. The extra $960 bought a pleasingly varied, picturesque roofline, with flared eaves, patterned slates,

60   City Hospital, London, photograph from the Egan Albums, c. 1875

moulded chimneys, lugged dormers and crested towers. In typical fashion, however, Robinson made variety subordinate to order: the building is strictly symmetrical, with classical 1:2 dimensions (it measured 36' x 72' with a 30-square-foot wing in back), and the chimneys rise no further than the crest of the roof.

The new hospital was not to be regarded exclusively as a refuge for the indigent and helpless; in addition to the wards for female patients on the third floor and the separate building for the men's ward, there were 'eight nice rooms for paying patients,' to 'be fitted up at different rates, and in corresponding styles, according to the accommodation required.'[176] A hospital for 'paying patients' was a relatively new concept; it depended on several recent developments that had made surgery a more viable medical procedure. Anesthetics came into use in the 1840s. Joseph Lister, in applying Louis Pasteur's theory that germs were responsible for infection, had shown that chances of recovery from surgery improved dramatically if the wounds were disinfected. Lister's experiments were almost immediately reported in Canadian journals, and by 1874 any hospital attuned to 'modern improvements' was prepared for an expanding surgical clientele.[177]

Initially, the standards of the new hospital were highly lauded. In 1876 a provincial inspector described it as 'excellent, both in respect to order and cleanliness.' But the hospital was soon to run into trouble with the province because it continued to provide accommodation for the poor, elderly, and orphaned, who were excluded by the provincial guidelines. Moreover, its custom-decorated rooms for richer patients were seeing little use. In 1878 the Hospital Committee decided to send to surrounding municipalities 'a circular setting forth the advantages of our City Hospital as a curative institution.'[178]

The establishment in 1882 of the School of Medicine, affiliated with Western University, greatly helped the London hospital in its bid for recognition. The new $3,000 wing added in 1883 represented the beginning of the series of additions that is still in progress. In the 1890s several London citizens proposed a new hospital, in deference to Queen Victoria's expressed desire that Diamond Jubilee projects be devoted to helping the sick and suffering.[179] The new Victoria Hospital actually incorporated the Old City Hospital, but Robinson's building fared less well in later reconstructions. In Victoria Hospital's continuing attempt to incorporate 'modern improvements,' only the spirit of its progenitor has survived.

Cottage for Alexander Johnston, designed 1874; completed 1876

469 Colborne Street, London

In 1874 leather merchant Alexander Johnston commissioned Robinson and Tracy to design two adjacent 'cottages,' on Colborne Street, to be used as rental properties.[180] It is impossible to know for certain which architect filled the order. The cottages do not have the pilaster strips that usually frame Robinson's façades, and the combination of bracketed gables and bay windows might well have been inspired by Tracy's work on the Asylum (fig. 78). On the other hand, without their porches the cottages would have possessed the simplicity, or even the austerity, that often marks Robinson's houses. Whichever architect was responsible, it is clear that he designed both cottages. They differ only in their window treatment: the cottage rented by John W. Little (fig. 61) of the prosperous dry goods establishment, Robinson, Little & Company, has round-arched windows; the windows next door have segmental arches.

The term 'cottage' was used during this period to refer to any modest house, though the word carried overtones suggestive of a picturesque rural dwelling. The Johnston cottages combine Italianate features with picturesque irregularity. Brackets and raking cornices support a broad gable in front and another on the side. Bay windows protrude from both gable walls. These cottages also meet the criterion of modesty. Each has only one and a half storeys and inside lacks some of the usual assets of Italianate houses, such as plaster ceiling mouldings and elegant mantels. But the rooms are pleasantly proportioned, and the cottage illustrated is by no means stripped of all tokens of architectural graciousness. Two examples provide proof: an arch supported by moulded corbels leads from a comfortably wide entrance hall into the stair hall, and attractive panelling adorns the interior wall areas beneath the bay windows.

The basic design of the Johnston cottages was used in several of the firm's later plans, including those (c. 1880; fig. 62) for one Henry Johnson, possibly the accountant who lived in London between 1874 and 1882, though he never resided in such a house. An 'H. Johnson' did request plans from Tracy for '2 frame houses' in 1879;[181] those houses and the brick residence illustrated here were probably to be built for speculation or, like the Johnston cottages, as rental properties.

The Johnston cottage and the Johnson house have several features in common: the front gable, the bay window, and very similar side hall floor plans (fig. 63), though the rooms of the two-storey Johnson house are larger. Despite its family resemblance to the Johnston cottage, however, the house in the drawing possesses several characteristics that point to its later date, and

61   Cottage for Alexander Johnston, London

62   Residence for Henry Johnson, London, detail of architectural drawing showing front elevation

indicate the changing fashions in architectural taste: the bracketed cornice has been replaced by a decorative barge-board; there are paired windows above the bay; the roof has a steeper pitch and a more complex outline. The clearly Italianate character of the earlier cottage has given way to the more elaborate and eclectic High Victorian approach that was evident in Tracy's work after 1875 and in the work of his partner George F. Durand.

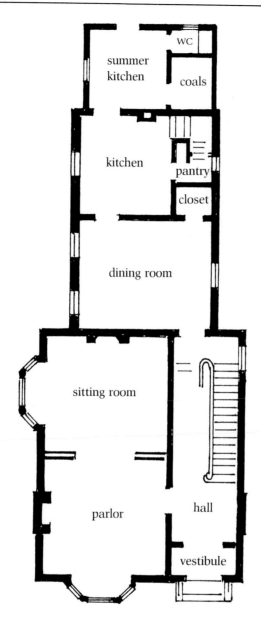

63   Residence for Henry Johnson, ground floor plan adapted from original drawing

David C. Hannah Double House, 1874

367 Princess Street, London

Robinson and Tracy called for tenders on a 'Residence for D.C. Hannah, Esq.' on 22 August 1874; only three months later, on 25 November 1874, the *Advertiser* reported that Hannah's double house was nearly ready for occupancy.[182] David Collins Hannah, then a shipping clerk, occupied half of the building; in 1877 Robert Hannah, presumably a relative, bought and occupied the other half.[183] David was to make a prosperous career for himself as a merchandise and custom broker. He was also active in public affairs: he served as an alderman in 1892 and 1893, and he played an important role in the militia. In 1905, at the age of sixty-four, he moved to a much larger house at 535 Waterloo Street;[184] first Robert, then his widow, and finally his son lived in their part of the duplex until 1937, when the double house was turned into four apartments.[185]

The Princess Street house may not have accorded with David Hannah's expanding prosperity for some time, as the individual quarters were not particularly roomy. Downstairs, two rooms led off a centre hall: the first was quite large and gracious, containing a fireplace with a wooden mantel approximately centred on its outside wall. Behind this comfortable parlour, however, was a rather modest dining-room, and the kitchen in the rear wing was also relatively small.

The façade initially had two front doors, under the two centre windows. The present Neoclassical door and the bay window are twentieth-century additions; the gable also seems to be an addition, though it probably dates from the late nineteenth century.

Despite these alterations, one can see in the building several features characteristic of Robinson's house design. The pilaster strips meet the brick frieze above and the water table below to form a frame around each bay. The brackets are located at the top of each pilaster, giving it the visual impact of a weight-bearing post. At the sides of the building, symmetrically arranged chimneys replace the pilasters. These careful refinements join with the building's setting, well back from the street, to give it a distinctive and elegant air, even on a street still occupied by a number of attractive Victorian houses.

64 David C. Hannah Double House, London

Militia Buildings: Office and Drill Shed, 1875–6

East side Wellington Street between Dufferin and Central avenues, London
(demolished)

The national depression of the 1870s had such an adverse effect on the military budget that when the roof of the Montreal drill shed collapsed in 1873, it was allowed to remain in a ruinous state for fifteen years.[186] Yet a whole new set of militia buildings was constructed in London in 1876. The story behind this coup is long and complicated; London's cause was helped mainly by the fact that the federal government was given the opportunity to pay in land rather than in money and also, probably, by the time-honoured custom of political patronage.

For nearly thirty years the British garrison had occupied the land bounded by what are now Clarence and Richmond streets, Dufferin Avenue, Wellington Street, and Picadilly Street, a massive portion of London's present downtown area.[187] After Confederation defence became a Canadian responsibility; by the end of 1870 only Halifax was garrisoned by British troops. Before that time, as we have seen, militia soldiers played some part in defending against Fenian invasion; nevertheless, Sir John A. Macdonald called them 'holiday soldiers' and claimed that the Fenians did not take them seriously.[188]

Confederation did not improve militia effectiveness. Government austerity forestalled the development of facilities for training the militia, and the buildings that had accommodated the British troops rapidly became derelict.[189] In 1875 Lieutenant-Colonel John B. Taylor, deputy adjutant general of the London District, reported that 'the state of the buildings, stores and works at this station are far from being in a satisfactory condition ... The Drill Shed has been in ruins for the last two years.' He goes on to recommend against repairing them, 'since an agreement made between the Government and the Corporation of the City of London is now being carried into effect.'[190]

The newly appearance-conscious city together with London's most influential Conservative, John Carling, had devised a plan for making a park out of a portion of the old garrison lands. In pursuit of this goal, an agreement was made with the federal government in 1874 whereby London would be ceded approximately twenty acres of the old grounds in exchange for property east of the municipal boundaries called Salter's Grove, on which the city was to erect new militia buildings at its own expense.[191] When Lord Dufferin dedicated Victoria Park in August of 1874, both he and the city council apparently regarded the agreement as a fait accompli. In reality, negotiations were to stretch out over the next two years, during which time the city changed its position as to where the new buildings should be located.

In April 1876 a city delegation proposed to Prime Minister Mackenzie and the minister of militia that the government 'give Salter's Grove back to the city, and the city ... grant the Government the north-east block of the Park.'

65   Militia Office, London, detail of architectural drawing showing front elevation

They argued in favour of this arrangement that money would be spent in the city (no doubt their real motive) and that the buildings would be under the protection of the city police and the fire brigade (this reassuring arrangement had not prevented the previous officers' quarters from burning down the year before). Though Ottawa seemed amenable, council members darkly suspected that local militiamen were blocking the scheme.[192] Nevertheless, the federal authorities did eventually agree to the city's proposed land trans- action, with the provision that the city pay 'not less than $21,600' for the full cost of the new buildings. Alexander Mackenzie, the Liberal prime minis- ter and a former major in the Lambton militia, may have been influenced in his assent by the fact that one of the two city representatives, Colonel John Walker, had stood as a Liberal candidate two years before. The new build- ings were to be erected in the block bounded by Duke (now Princess), Wellington, Great Market (now Central), and Waterloo streets.[193]

Robinson had submitted plans for the new buildings to local militia officers in May 1875, and in July of that year he took them to Ottawa. They were

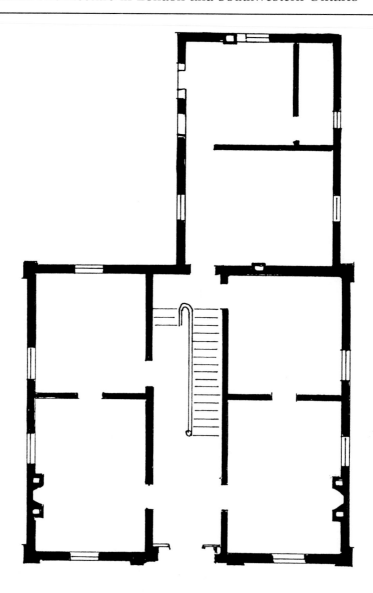

66   Militia Office, ground floor plan adapted from original drawing

approved 'with one exception – they [Ottawa officials] preferred a little less
elaboration.' The design ultimately approved for the militia offices (fig. 65)
was described by the *Advertiser* as 'a neat-looking two-storey building, devoid
of any unnecessary ornamentation.'[194] The scrolled stone heads of the door
and windows were presumably considered necessary; certainly they do impart
an air of distinction to the very attractive structure. Otherwise it is quite simple.
Its corners are marked with pilaster strips rather than quoins and, instead
of the elaborate wooden brackets usually found on Robinson's Italianate houses
by 1876, there is a row of simple brick brackets that strongly resemble dentils.
Its centre-hall floor plan (fig. 66) was one greatly favoured by Robinson;

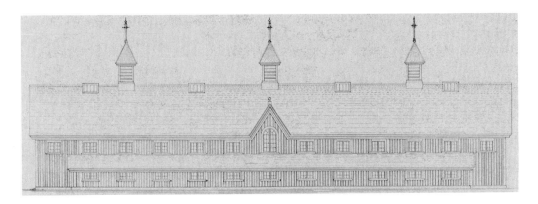

67   Militia Drill Shed, London, detail of architectural drawing showing side elevation; drawing stamped 'Militia & Defense Canada'

68   Return of the Seventh Battalion from the North West (with the Militia Drill Shed in the background), photograph, 1885

where possible, as here, he made the main part of the plan perfectly symmetrical, with the rooms on one side mirror images of those on the other. The domestic design of the Militia Office was apt, in that it did provide living quarters for the deputy adjutant general, the brigade major, the district paymaster, and the provincial shopkeeper.

The relative simplicity of the Militia Offices enabled it to blend with the other buildings, which were mainly in an almost stark classical design, with Italianate touches. In addition to the offices, the new buildings were to include stables for seventy-two horses, a store-house, a powder magazine, and a drill shed.[195] The powder keg was moved from its old site, Robinson drew designs for the stables and store-house, and the government provided plans for a wooden drill shed. City council discovered, however, that the $21,600 they had promised to spend would cover the cost of building all the military structures of brick. Robinson's adaptation of the government's board-and-batten drill shed gave the new brick structure (fig. 68) a very different character from that seen in the drawing (fig. 67). Piers and heavy buttresses emphasize the building's bulk. The vertical lines of the boards are replaced by fairly broad bays. Using brick, Robinson could easily give arched heads to the smaller windows as well as to the window in the prominent central gable.

The scene in the photograph (July 1885; fig. 68) shows the London militia returning from the North West Rebellion. As the return of 'the Warrior Boys of the 7th' drew near, 'the Forest City became fully aroused to a degree of enthusiasm almost unbounded.' The Drill Shed was the central location for these ecstatic tributes. There 'our heroes; received an address from Mayor Becher, who noted that the men missed out on any combat: 'we regret that you should have been disappointed, but this regret is lessened by our joy at your safe return ... bringing with you no maimed or wounded, whose condition we should have to deplore.'[196] A few days later a victory banquet for 500 was served at the Drill Shed featuring, in addition to roast beef, spring lamb, spring chicken, spring duck, leg of mutton, and corned beef and tongue, several 'ornamental dishes,' including the graceful compliment of 'Arch of Buffalo Tongues, a l'Empire.'[197]

Following these triumphs, the militia buildings once again became the subject of complicated debates. John Carling, who had an important role in the early negotiations for the erection of the buildings, was also central to their partial abandonment. As postmaster-general, he passed on to his colleague, the minister of defence, a complaint about the danger of the powder keg. As a landowner, he made available to the city an alternative site. On 23 February 1886, the city signed a contract with the federal government exchanging the militia site near Victoria Park for Carling's Farm, north-east of town.[198] Two years later after an infantry school had been built at Carling's Farm, both the former militia grounds and the remainder of the old garrison lands were sold by auction. Oddly enough, the Drill Shed remained in place and in use until the London armoury was built in 1905.[199]

St Andrew's Presbyterian Church, 1877–8
Strathroy

As soon as a Presbyterian congregation was officially formed in Strathroy in 1863, it bought land to hold a church and manse.[200] But the next few years brought failing membership, futile efforts to attract a permanent minister, and financial difficulties. It required a good deal of courage and help from other denominations for the twenty-three-member congregation to build a church in 1867, at a cost of $2,314. Ten years later the congregation had outgrown its first church building and began work on its replacement.

The official opening of the new structure (fig. 70) was held in December 1877, as soon as the basement could accommodate services. The ecumenical spirit that had helped pay for the first church was still thriving in the town; one James Manson was so impressed by the sight of 'Episcopalian, Sweden-borgian, Methodist and other ministers' speaking from the same platform that he contributed $530 towards the $12,419 cost of the building.[201] The entire church was finished by July of the following year, when a second set of opening ceremonies was held, this time in the 'main auditorium,' where oak pews curved around the pulpit, and, according to the Strathroy *Age*, stained glass windows and mauve walls made the 'general tone of the place ... very church-like.'[202]

The plans were drawn by the firm of Robinson, Tracy, and Fairbairne, and one can easily see the senior partner's typical format underlying the organization of the façade. The plan has a central porch, a string course dividing the porch area from that of the window above, two flanking bays with paired windows similar to those at Dresden (fig. 47), and buttresses delineating the parts of the design. Here, however, this basic design is varied in some interesting ways. A corner tower breaks, or at least dents, the absolute symmetry of the front, and gabled bays at the side play on the idea of transepts. The drawings show barge-boards in the side gables; at some point, either in the planning stage or later, the parapet and pinnacles on the elevation of the façade were replaced by a barge-board as well. These alterations to Robinson's basic design have some ingenious and skilful aspects. The tower is incorporated into the corner of the building so as to fit on the narrow lot. The front barge-board unifies the façade and the side gables; it echoes and thus emphasizes the decorative gables over the roundels; and it effectively frames the triangular window at the top of the gable.

Nevertheless, the restrictions of the lot and the need for a high basement dictated a relatively tall, narrow structure whose proportions do not entirely lend themselves to the relatively adventurous interpretation of the firm's old format. The tower seems squeezed into its alloted space. The barge-board, with its suggestions of rusticity, would look more suitable on a building with broader and lower proportions.

69   St Andrew's Presbyterian Church, Strathroy, detail of architectural drawing
showing front elevation

Though the façade relies on a pattern that Robinson had made part of the
firm's repertoire, it is by no means certain that he was responsible for the
final design of St Andrew's. Indeed, one article in the *Age* specifically credits
'Messrs Tracy & Fairburn' with drawing the plans, and though one suspects
the newspaper may inadvertently have neglected to give the firm's full name,
the tower and pinnacles shown in the drawing do bear some resemblance to
comparable features in Tracy's design for St James', Westminster (1877). The
barge-boards, like other legacies from the *cottage ornée*, were also to appear
on churches by Tracy and Durand. Moreover, it is possible that the firm bore

70   St Andrew's Presbyterian Church

no responsibility for the 'gingerbread' work of the façade. It may have been added during construction, which was supervised by a member of the congregation,[203] or even at some later date. The church very definitely impresses one as the work of many hands; it is less effective as a completely unified whole than as the sum of many interesting parts.

Nathaniel Reid Cottage, completed c. 1878

477 Waterloo Street, London

Nathaniel Reid was a colourful London entrepreneur who established the Crystal Hall (fig. 58). His obituary claims that he 'made and lost several fortunes,' and that at one time he owned 'the whole of the land on which the thriving town of Barrie now stands.'[204] In later life he channelled all his energy into his prosperous china business; the day before he died, he inspected 'improvements lately made' to his warehouse in the company of his son, W.J. Reid.[205]

For some years before his death Nathaniel Reid lost 'the use of his lower limbs.'[206] It seems likely that this handicap influenced his choice of house design. Though his new house has the shape of an Ontario Cottage, there is nothing modest about its decoration or even its size; the only significant way in which it differs from most substantial houses of the period is that all its rooms are on one floor.

From the outside the generous size of the cottage and details such as the wooden frieze hint at its special refinement, but they hardly prepare one for the splendours within. From a roomy vestibule, two doors with etched glass panels lead into a spacious hallway divided by an arch resting on ornate corbels (fig. 73). It is tempting to identify the warrior in the keystone with the building's owner, but no portrait of Nathaniel Reid survives. Whatever his provenance, this warrior was to become a favourite within the firm. He appears in the house Durand designed for Henry Dunn (1885; figs 133 and 134), and again in the Robert D. McDonald House (c. 1910; figs 219 and 220), by Moore and Henry. Seven rooms apparently opened off the centre hall of the Reid Cottage; two, on the right, were quite large and probably functioned as parlour and dining room, respectively. A small room to the left has a very elegant marble mantel with carving as detailed as that around the bishop's fireplace (fig. 55), but much more delicate. Service facilities were located in an extensive rear wing. The graciousness of the house speaks well for the good taste of the Crystal Hall proprietor, as well as for the discernment of his architect.

71   Nathaniel Reid Cottage, London, front entrance

72   Nathaniel Reid Cottage

73   Nathaniel Reid Cottage, upper part of front hallway and doors to vestibule

There are no newspaper references or firm records providing absolute proof that Robinson was the architect, but there are strong arguments in support of ascribing the house to him. Most persuasive are the high praise accorded the Crystal Hall and the many resemblances between the cottage and Robinson's other works: examples include nearly round interior mouldings, the Italianate entryway (fig. 71), the framed bays, and the projecting centre bay, a feature found in many of Robinson's more substantial residences.

Pump House, c. 1877–9

Springbank Park, London

Finding an adequate system for supplying water to London already had been considered by some an urgent issue in the 1850s, but the idea was controversial even then, setting a pattern that was to persist throughout the next two decades. In 1856 several parties, including the *Free Press*, placed their trust in a scheme for piping water from the Westminster Ponds south of London. Mayor William Barker was among the sceptical: 'Messrs Peter and Stent and Leather and Robinson had already reported in favour of the Westminster ponds, and stated that there was an overflow of several million gallons from the ponds. While he knew ... that some of the creeks leading from the ponds were not sufficient to give a cow a drink. Interested parties could get their local engineers to represent anything.'[207] Though experiments at the time supported the mayor's view about the ponds, the scheme was resurrected in 1873 and 1874, when the city council approved the expenditure of over $8,000 for a thorough testing of the area, only to have Robinson verify the conclusion Barker had reached before: 'No springs were there.'[208] On Robinson's recommendation the city hired the province's most highly reputed hydraulic engineer, Thomas C. Keefer, as a consultant on a water system. He concurred in the conclusions already reached by Robinson and Alderman Egan, who was later to chair the city's Fire, Water, and Gas Committee, in recommending a source known as Coombs' Springs, west of London on the south bank of the Thames.[209] When Keefer's $400,000 plan was referred to a popular referendum, however, feeling ran so high that the politicians gave serious consideration to cancelling the election. Mayor Benjamin Cronyn Jr called a special meeting on 11 March 1875 to complain that 'he had never been so abused' as at a public meeting the night before, and to consider appropriate action. The council voted to abstain from more public meetings but to go ahead with the vote.[210] The scheme was roundly defeated, 699 votes to 243.[211]

Strong proponents of a waterworks system, however, believed that its advantages warranted continuing the fight. A good water system reduced the fire hazard (fire engineer Thomas Wastie resigned after the referendum was defeated), provided purer water (chemist William E. Saunders showed that the water from Coombs' Springs was purer than that from town wells), and had the potential to attract those whom Thomas Keefer described as 'immigrants of capital.'[212] When a group of leading London citizens proposed building waterworks as a private company in 1876, the city again raised the issue of a public system. This time, with the help of a provincial ruling excepting non-users from paying rates, the vote in favour of the waterworks carried with a substantial margin.[213] Licking its wounds, the *Advertiser* commented, 'another scheme for waterworks, bountifully sprinkled with religion and politics, but hastily considered and extravagant in its aims was ... carried.'[214]

74   Pump House, London

75   Pump House, photograph, c. 1885

Though still an impressive expenditure, the waterworks proved considerably cheaper than Keefer had predicted. Robinson had made the drawing measurements on which Keefer had based his estimate in 1875 and felt convinced that the work could be done for less. The 1879 report of the Board of Water Commissioners, made by John Carling, observes that 'the result has fully justified the correctness of Mr Robinson's estimates, and the accuracy of his calculations.' Thomas Tracy, who acted as supervising engineer during construction, also had high praise for the accuracy of his partner's calculations: 'though [before the construction] of the works his hydraulic knowledge has been called into question ... I can say with confidence that I have found his estimates safe, his judgment excellent and his knowledge even of details all that could be desired.' The total cost of the waterworks was $325,035.24.[215]

The system was able to utilize the Thames River basin in two significant ways. First, the valley provided a natural watershed for Coombs' Springs. Water was collected in a series of underground drainage tiles which fed into various holding ponds, one of which still exists near Storybook Gardens. From the ponds the water was channelled to the pump house, situated next to a dam. Thus the river provided the hydraulic pressure for pumping the water to a reservoir at the top of a nearby hill. The force of gravity could then drive it through pipes to points all over the city.

The two hydraulic pumps were encased in a pump house (fig. 74) that in most respects could have passed for a typical Ontario Cottage. It was square (thirty-six by thirty-six feet), with a window on each side of the front door (the extra bay on the south side was added in this century). Its only concessions to its utilitarian function were the large double doors on the front and side, its metal (fireproof) roof, and its iron floor and roof girders.

Pump houses of the period frequently assumed domestic forms, but the setting of the London Pump House made its cottage style particularly appropriate. Not only does it resemble local farmhouses, but in its location, perched on the brink of a winding river at the base of the area's highest hills, it provides a fitting adornment within an especially picturesque landscape (fig. 75). Indeed, the pump house and its surroundings were chosen for illustration in *Picturesque Canada*.[216] The building would have been frequently glimpsed from both the road above and from the regular riverboat excursions that landed a few yards away, and Robinson took some care to make his cottage appropriately attractive. Its tall chimneys, steeply pitched roof, and cresting provided an interesting profile; a barge-board and triangular window adorned its gable; the usual pilaster strips hold ornamental brackets, and the windows have stone segmental arches with incised key stones (fig. 76).

Tracy, Durand, and Moore were to use the cottage format for later pump houses. In 1881 Tracy designed a second building on the London pump house site to hold steam pumping equipment as a back-up to the hydraulic power. His building is carefully designed to complement Robinson's; it, too, has the form of an Ontario Cottage, with barge-boards that echo Robinson's, and a plaque shaped like Robinson's window. But Tracy has also expressed his

76   Pump House, one of the original front windows

own stylistic interests: his building features polychromatic brickwork, paired windows, and an uninterrupted surface area. The Stratford Pump House (fig. 119) is another High Victorian interpretation of the Ontario Cottage.

The members of Robinson's firm seem to have found the London Waterworks a stimulating enterprise. Tracy was eventually to specialize in designing waterworks systems in British Columbia; John M. Moore, who was apprenticing in Robinson's office during the late 1870s, was to become the engineer and supervisor of the London Waterworks in the 1890s. For Robinson the planning of the Waterworks comprised a fitting climax to a remarkably productive career. His persistence, technical skill, and architectural ability all contributed to what the *Free Press*, in 1882, called 'the crowning piece to London's great enterprises during the last ten years.'[217]

THOMAS HENRY TRACY

When Thomas Tracy entered an apprenticeship with William Robinson, he was likely acquiring as a mentor a long-standing acquaintance of his family. His parents, John and Mary Brady Tracy, had come to London in 1840 directly from Robinson's own native soil, County Wexford, Ireland. Like Robinson, they were Irish Anglicans and chose to become members of Christ Church (1861; fig. 42) in London.[218] Robinson and the senior Tracys lived in the same Horton Street neighbourhood; after 1872 they resided just a few doors apart on the same block.[219]

Their son Thomas Henry Tracy was born in London on 25 June 1848.[220] He attended London city schools and in 1864 at the age of sixteen began a five-year apprenticeship with Robinson. Though his initial interest was in land surveying, and he was to qualify as a Public Land Surveyor on 8 April 1870, he became attracted to all facets of Robinson's work and eventually produced significant accomplishments in the fields of architecture and engineering.

THE LONDON LUNATIC ASYLUM: 'TRIFLING DEFECTS'

His career got off to a rather ominous start. On completing his apprenticeship in 1869, he went to work for Kivas Tully in the provincial Department of Public Works, a ministry then entrusted to London's parliamentary representative, John Carling. The department was at that time involved in consolidating and improving its mental institutions. Its plan was to have three strategically located asylums: the Toronto Asylum was to be enlarged, and two others were to be situated in the eastern and western parts of the province. It was decided to place the western asylum in London, and Tracy was sent home to act as clerk of works for the enterprise.[221]

The project was enormous. The main building (fig. 78), 610 feet in length, was designed to provide 500 patients with 'health, convenience, comfort and security.' In addition to the main structure, there were two large work-shops, a bakery, a storehouse, two barns, a 'stable and cow house,' a mortuary, a two-storey residence for the superintendent, and two entrance lodges.[222]

Some indication of the project's extent can be deduced from the fact that its cost, approaching $250,000, was a cut-rate figure. Tully explained in 1873 that he had originally recommended a $500,000 budget but had been informed by the legislature that $500 a patient should be adequate. He quoted the Hon. D.B. Wood, provincial treasurer, as one who held representative opinions: 'I have nothing to say against ornamental buildings, exhibiting the highest degree of architectural taste, where circumstances require and warrant structures of that class. But for the requirements of lunatics I think a plain structure ... will answer the purpose quite well.'[223]

Although there is little ornamentation on the building, Tully's design avoids

77   Thomas H. Tracy (1848–1925), from *London and Its Men of Affairs* (1915)

plainness, and indeed achieves a highly picturesque quality, by dividing the massive structure into a series of wings of varying heights, positioned in differing relationships to each other so that from above they form a broad and jagged U-shape. The only actual ornamentation consists of the cupolas that enhance the picturesque roofline; the bay windows that break the long, flat surfaces of the higher gable bays; and the Italianate brackets that provide an interesting variation on the Tudor outline of the building.

The building was completed remarkably quickly. Work was begun early in June 1869; on 9 November 1870, the *Advertiser* reported that the building would 'in a few days be ready for occupation.' The government considered speed essential; so eager was it to close down the asylums at Maldon and Orillia that 120 patients were moved to London from the former on 18 November and 250 from the latter on 23 November.[224]

Less than a month later the superintendent of the Asylum, Dr Henry Landor, wrote Carling complaining of 'wants and deficiencies in nearly every part of the Asylum.'[225] Tully asked William Robinson to provide an independent assessment of the building's condition. Robinson found some 'trifling defects,' which were to be expected 'in so large a building built in a very limited time,' but thought no fault was attached to anyone involved in its construction, so long as the contractor was willing to correct some of the minor problems.[226] The complaints intensified over the following months, however, and by 1872

78 'The Asylum for the Insane, London,' 1869–70, designed by Kivas Tully, from
the *Globe and Canada Farmer*, 14 March 1879

and 1873 both Tully and Robinson were making excuses for the problems
rather than arguing against their existence. Eventually, engineers and architects
from Toronto, Hamilton, and Detroit were hired to assess the problems and
recommend repairs.[227]

It is difficult now to know how to evaluate the various claims. Under
headlines such as 'The Botched Building' or 'How the Builders Bungled its
Construction,'[228] the Liberal *Advertiser* clearly revelled in the discomfiture
of its Conservative political opponents, and the newspaper's testimony must
be viewed with scepticism. The assessors disagreed strongly among themselves about possible solutions for the serious problems, such as improper
drainage, which seem genuinely to have existed; thus mistakes in the original
arrangements for an ambitious and innovative building should probably not
be too harshly judged. On the other hand, both Tully and Robinson had
interests to protect, and their inclination to minimize the deficiencies probably owes something to their respective positions. There seems little doubt
that much of the work was sloppily done, and that underfunding and haste
contributed to poor workmanship. How many problems could have been
avoided by better supervision is an open question.

The clerk of works seems at least to have put a great deal of energy into
his job. On 10 August 1869, the *Free Press* observed that 'Mr Thos Tracy,
engineer of the Department of Public Works is constantly on the grounds, and
at present engaged in laying out the stonework of the western sections.' The
paper commented again, on 19 May 1870, that 'Mr Thomas Tracy, C.E. ...
is constantly on the grounds directing the work, and by his attention to
details does much towards its advancement.' It seems, however, that what
the *Free Press* perceived as attentiveness, others regarded as overwork. Tully
noted in his 1869 report:

When the contracts for the buildings, main drain, fences &c., were awarded for the Lunatic Asylum, London, the amount of work was so much increased that the Clerk of Works could not superintend the whole, which required constant personal supervision, besides making the necessary measurements for progress estimates, working drawings, &c.; it was necessary, therefore, to procure the services of a practical mechanic to act in the capacity of foreman of works during the building season.[229]

That an inexperienced young man (aged twenty-one) who had just completed his apprenticeship should have been placed in charge of a project of the magnitude of the Asylum seems irresponsible. Robinson was undoubtedly right in claiming that 'large buildings like the Asylum require more persons than a clerk of works and a foreman to superintend their erection.'[230]

Tracy stayed with the Department of Public Works until early in 1872, when he, like hordes of other ambitious architects and builders, sought a share in the extensive rebuilding projects necessitated by the Great Chicago Fire of 1871. He worked for a Chicago architect until November 1872. Then, likely at Durand's instigation, he moved to Albany, NY to work under Thomas Fuller on the New York State Capitol. In May 1873 he returned to London and entered into partnership with William Robinson. Since the controversy over the Asylum was then at its height, this arrangement must have had about it the air of a public declaration of faith. Tracy's future career was to vindicate Robinson's confidence in him.

ARCHITECT AND ENGINEER

As Robinson's partner, Tracy was to share the older man's interest in all branches of his profession. The first newspaper reference to Tracy after his return to London reports him to be leading a staff of surveyors 'engaged in defining the location and boundaries of streets.' He developed considerable skill as an architect, as one can see from the buildings illustrated and discussed on the following pages. The city considered Tracy competent enough as an engineer to hire him as Robinson's replacement for a brief period in 1874, while Robinson devoted himself full time to testing the water supply at Westminster Ponds.[231] Tracy was to prove his engineering skill while supervising the construction of the London waterworks. At the banquet honouring Robinson when he retired as city engineer, Robinson's short speech was entirely in praise of his partner and successor. The *Advertiser* reported Robinson as saying 'he felt pleased to think that the Council had chosen Mr Thomas Tracy ... He did not wish to flatter that gentleman when he said that he knew of no one better suited in every way for the position.'[232]

Tracy at first copied his mentor's example in combining his duties as city engineer with private architectural practice. For one year, in 1879, he had his own business.[233] Then, at the beginning of 1880 he was joined by George Durand, with whom he worked for two extraordinarily productive years.

In February 1882 representatives of city council, the Water Commissioners, the Board of Education, and the Separate School Board decided to hire among them a full-time engineer. Tracy's negotiations regarding the position show that he was aware of some personal sacrifice in taking on the new role: 'Mr Tracy said in all fairness the salary should be somewhat higher. It involved his throwing up his business chances, without the assurance that he might not be discharged within six months. He would require a horse, and necessitate a great many expenses which should be taken into consideration.' His prospective salary was raised from $2,200 to $2,400 a year 'in view of what he would have to throw up,' and Tracy accepted the offer.[234]

In doing so he rejected not only the potential for making a substantial private income but also, for all practical purposes, his role as an architect. To some extent this was a matter of circumstance; increasingly, architects for major public buildings were being chosen by competitions. It seems also to have been a matter of choice. As engineer for the school board, Tracy was responsible for designing schools; yet in 1889, when he was actively engaged in plans for a model school, he relied on Durand to design the building's exterior.[235]

Tracy was to stay in close touch with his old firm. When he went off to fight in the North West Rebellion, his position as chief engineer was filled by John M. Moore,[236] who had apprenticed under Tracy and Robinson and continued to work for Tracy and then for Durand. Tracy was welcomed back as a conquering hero and as an economy measure: 'Mr Geo. Birrell stated that the Engineer came home safe from the wars, and was looking healthy: that some extra hard work would not do him any harm and that there was no use of taking any action in the superintendent business just now.' Tracy replied that 'he thought he could manage it,'[237] and Moore went back to private practice. By 1887, however, there was an assistant city engineer, Fred Henry,[238] who had trained in Durand's office and would eventually become a partner in the firm.

On 23 June 1891, the 'London and Environs' column of the *Advertiser* carried the following intriguing item: 'City Engineer Tracy left for Banff NWT on Monday at noon for his month's leave of absence. He will go on as far as Vancouver BC and if the climate proves as invigorating as he expects he will likely accept the position of city engineer which is being held open for him.' It is not clear that Tracy was motivated exclusively by a preference for rain over snow. On the positive side, he was welcome in Vancouver; the council there had offered the job to him by a unanimous vote, and when he arrived at the station, the 9 July *Advertiser* reports, 'Mayor Oppenheimer and J.J. Blake' were there to greet him; 'Several other London friends went to meet him, but were too late.' Another reason may have been that Tracy had been the subject of some London council bickering over his estimates for sewers; he had his warm defenders, but others were still ready to bring up the smell of the Asylum: 'Ald. Taylor mentioned something to the effect that the asylum system was not satisfactory. Ald. Spencer said the asylum authorities were delighted with it. It would pay the alderman to visit the spot.' Apparently, even before the Vancouver position was offered to him, Tracy had attempted to resign his London post. His resignation was accepted on 20 July. The *Canadian Architect and Builder* predicted that London would have trouble finding someone 'with equal ability' to take his place, and that he would 'doubtless leave the impress of his skill upon the future development' of Vancouver.[239]

Among Tracy's contributions to his new home were the development of a water system for that city and the plotting and construction of its major thoroughfares, 'carved out of the forest under his supervision.' He held the position of city engineer for fifteen years. In 1906 he resigned in order to go into private practice as a land surveyor and civil engineer.[240]

Tracy evidently enjoyed the challenge of technological experimentation and civic planning. In 1886 he was eager for a snowfall in order to try out the iron plow he had designed.[241] In 1892 he sent a notice to the *Canadian Architect and Builder* relating his trial in Vancouver of 'bituminous rock pavement ... giving a good foothold to horses,' a venture which, the journal commented, 'will be watched with interest by other cities.'[242] In his capacity as a private consultant, Tracy developed waterworks in several British Columbia towns, including Kamloops and Nanaimo. His Vancouver *Sun* obituary reveals the wider vision connected to this interest: 'He was an earnest supporter throughout of the movement to bring about a Greater Vancouver water scheme. He was a thorough believer in the future of Vancouver, and at every opportunity urged that greater publicity be given to the enormous water power resources of British Columbia.'[243]

SOLDIER, MASON, AND INVESTOR

Thomas Tracy was a man of many interests and accomplishments. In addition to his professional occupations, he had an extremely successful military career, he attained exalted Masonic honours, he played a role in London's cultural life, and he undertook several varied business ventures.

As a youth Tracy won a medal for service during the Fenian raid of 1866.[244] He was a captain and company commander of militia volunteers at the time of the North West Rebellion, returning home with a beard that 'created almost a panic in the minds of tonsorial artists.'[245] It is perhaps not too fanciful to speculate that this experience had some bearing on his later interest in the West. The *Free Press* speculated eloquently upon the impact the expedition would have on its participants' understanding of Canada:

They have become acquainted ... with the fact that this is no common country. That it is not only fertile and happy but that it is of immense extent ... They ... will have gathered during their absence more than they could have possibly done under other circumstances an idea of what Canada is, and have formed some conception of that which it is likely to become, when its vast areas of territory have become peopled. Five thousand of our young citizens can now bear witness to the opportunities that are bound up in the North-west.[246]

Though he was eventually to succumb to the opportunities of the West, Tracy participated enthusiastically in the 1885 homecoming celebrations; his house, part of a handsome Neoclassical terrace on Ridout Street next to the court-house, was mentioned as being especially well decorated for the event.[247] By the time he left for Vancouver, six years later, the esteem in which he was held had earned him the rank of lieutenant-colonel and the overall command of the Seventh Fusiliers. This was the London unit that participated in the 1885 Riel campaign; by late 1889 it had fallen on bad times and evidently needed Tracy's talents for its revitalization.[248]

Tracy's progress through the Masonic ranks was equally impressive. Perhaps this was not entirely coincidental, since there were strong links between the military and the Masons. When only twenty-seven he became master of the prestigious St John's Lodge 209a and served a second term the following year.[249] He subsequently advanced in both of the principal Masonic hierar-chies, the York and the Scottish rites, and eventually became grand junior warden of the Grand Lodge of Canada. This position enabled him to partici-pate in the affairs of the Ontario governing body. The current president of the London Masonic Hall observes that perhaps six Londoners have achieved a comparable eminence in the past 100 years.[250]

When in 1876 the cornerstone of the Mechanics' Institute (fig. 80) was laid in conjunction with a Masonic ceremony, Tracy was involved in the proceed-ings in a triple role: as a Mason, as the building's architect, and as vice-president of the Mechanics' Institute. He was also to serve as a director of the Western School of Art, an organization that grew out of Institute classes.[251]

Although Tracy's full-time job as city engineer kept him from private architectural practice, it did not prevent him from making business investments. Two of these reflect his professional interests. In 1881 he was one of several London citizens who secured a Canadian patent for the Bell Electric Light Company. The following year he invested in the Bennett Furnishing Company, which manufactured furniture for schools and churches. Some years later, in 1888, he became a director of the prosperous Ontario Mutual Insurance Company.[252]

Tracy was to display political talents in Vancouver. He was well over seventy when he was elected an alderman in 1920, securing the second-highest vote total in a city-wide contest. He continued in that office until his death.[253]

Tracy had married Sara M. Bryan from Amsterdam, New York (close to Albany, his temporary place of employment) in 1874. They had two children, a daughter Sara, named after her mother, and a son Thomas Leonard, who shared his father's interests as well as his name. He left a course in engineering at McGill University to volunteer for duty in the First World War and was killed in Flanders on 12 September 1916.[254]

Thomas Tracy Sr died a more peaceful death nine years later, on 31 October 1925. His death was the subject of the major front-page headline in the Vancouver *Sun*, where he was described as a man 'with an enviable reputation for integrity and gentlemanly bearing.'[255] Goodspeed's *History of the County of Middlesex* had noted, while Tracy still resided in London, that he was 'a man well known and universally liked and esteemed.'[256]

TRACY'S CHARACTER AS AN ARCHITECT

Although Tracy's decision to direct his energy towards engineering rather than architecture resulted in a highly productive career, architectural historians must feel some regret at his choice. The handful of buildings that can definitely be attributed to Tracy alone show a remarkable talent in architectural design. Like Robinson, he worked in a variety of styles, but his taste is more clearly inclined towards the High Victorian 'masculine' qualities that held little interest for his teacher. Tracy's work was frequently polychromatic; he liked heavy, robust forms; his buildings sometimes had an almost theatrical quality. At the same time, he was sufficiently versatile to be relatively faithful to the light Regency Gothic of the Middlesex County Courthouse when he designed the substantial addition to that building. He brought to architectural design some of the same creative energy and interest in experimentation that were to make him a successful engineer, and he combined these qualities with an acute esthetic sensitivity that made him, for a time, a stimulating force in his native city's leading architectural firm.

First Congregational Church, 1874–6

South side Dundas Street between Waterloo and Colborne streets, London
(destroyed by fire)

When the members of the Congregational church in London (est. 1838) decided in 1874 to build a larger building, they had its architectural merit very much at heart. Their 'intention,' according to the *Free Press*, was 'to build an edifice which will be a credit to the city and a lasting monument to the enterprise of the denomination.' The church that Tracy designed was well qualified to fulfil their expectations, in a style that the *Advertiser* rightly claimed was 'peculiarly its own': 'Mr Tracy has introduced some novel ideas in his plans, quite different from any existing church structure in the city,'[257] and, it might have added, anywhere else.

The church does use a complex of ideas generally associated with High Victorian Gothic: polychromy (here achieved by contrasting Ohio stone and deep red Brantford brick with the Westminster pressed white brick provided by a member of the congregation), patterned high slate roofs, dormers, and cast-iron crestings. Instead of the usual pointed windows, one finds the round and round-arched windows of the 'later Norman' style (an English version of the Romanesque) and there are other Norman details to complement them, such as the columns flanking the front door, and the sawtooth trim above it. The façade's main claims to individuality start at the level of the unexpectedly bracketed cornice. Below, the two towers are completely identical; above, they resemble each other only in their slightly flared eaves. The tower on the east is rather appropriately labelled 'a dwarf tower' by the *Advertiser*; it has a deliberately stunted appearance, while the other rises through a series of dramatic stages to a height twice that of its companion, enabling it to be 'easily seen from the different parts of the city.' The one tower seems to have been insistently pressed down while the other was forcefully pulled up: even the small dormers of the west tower are elongated. The tension that results powerfully expresses the High Victorian ideal of active, dynamic strength.

The dramatic quality of the façade takes on a new dimension when one perceives that it bore little relationship to the body of the church. The front door led into a stairhall, from which one ascended to an auditorium that was a match in novelty for the building's exterior design. The auditorium itself was oval (and covered by an oval roof approximately as high as the dwarf tower). The raked pews were arranged in a semi-circle. There was a horseshoe-shaped gallery. The gas lighting was indirect. If all this sounds somewhat theatrical, the 'stage' area was purposely unassuming: 'The platform is only slightly elevated ... A simple table and chairs form the furniture.'

79   First Congregational Church, London, photograph, c. 1875

Sadly, what should have been a lasting monument was destroyed
by fire. Only its high tower has endured; it now occupies its own square,
lovingly preserved but, regrettably, dwarfed by the multi-storey buildings that
surround it.

London Mechanics' Institute, 1876–7

229–31 Dundas Street, London

The history of the Mechanics' Institute in London, Ontario and elsewhere in the English-speaking world is the story of an extremely idealistic enterprise that recorded significant successes while failing in its main aim. Originating in late eighteenth-century Birmingham and Glasgow, the movement to educate workingmen did not gather force until the London Mechanics' Institute was founded in the British capital in 1823. During the next two years dozens of British branches sprang up, each with its own library and program of technical and uplifting lectures. By 1853 there were 120,000 members of 700 Mechanics' Institutes in the British Isles. In the words of a historian of the period, 'the right of the people to culture' had been established, but, since it was clerks and shopkeepers who principally enjoyed the facilities, 'Mechanics' Institutes have failed to attract mechanics.'[258]

Upper Canada soon followed the lead of the mother country. The York Mechanics' Institute was founded in 1831. Kingston was next, followed by London in 1835. The first London Institute had forty-nine members when it applied for a government grant in February 1836, but at some point between that year and 1841 the organization vanished.[259]

Fifty-eight people, with William Robinson at the head of the list, made a second, more successful, attempt in 1841. The constitution adopted in that year shows that the London members had absorbed the spirit of the British experiment: the 'power of mind' of the people and thus their 'social and political condition' are to be improved 'through education.' The Library Committee eloquently stated and put into practice their conviction that 'money in the treasurer's hands is a dead letter – expended in books, it speaks, thinks, and acts.'[260]

A co-operative spirit was evident in the construction of an imposing building, first located on the Court House Square, in 1842: 'some members gave money, some materials, and others labour.'[261] In its early days, the Institute was a meeting place for varied activities such as debates, balls, and temperance lectures. Yet, like its British cousins, the London Institute failed to appeal to the class for which it was intended. In 1852 men from the working class constituted only about one-half of the total membership; by 1880, by another standard of measurement, the proportion of working-class members had shrunk to one-fifth.[262] 'Throughout its history,' Eleanor Shaw has noted, 'London's Mechanics' Institute was managed by prominent citizens ... It was a benefit conferred on the working man from above.'[263]

Hard times and the competition of a rival library association sapped the energy of the Institute in the late 1850s and early 1860s; by 1861 it was moribund and remained so for nine years. After the provincial government revived

80   London Mechanics' Institute

81   London Mechanics' Institute, third-storey windows

its policy of awarding grants, the London Institute came to life again, with a reorganization in 1870 and a growth in membership from thirty-nine at the initial 1870 meeting to 581 by 1873.[264]

Credit for government aid must go to John Carling, London's own leading Conservative, who regarded Mechanics' Institutes as 'People's Colleges.'[265] Yet, in London as elsewhere, government policy was at odds with the people's real will. The authorities were determined to encourage technical education, so as to create a skilled artisan class; in London the most popular night courses were art and elocution. The government wanted technical books in the library; over half of the volumes in the London Institute were fiction, a category the government did not recognize.[266]

Despite, or perhaps because of, its disregard of government guidelines, the London Institute was doing well enough to consider expansion a very few years after its revitalization. The laying of the cornerstone for a new building (fig. 80), on Thanksgiving Day, 2 November 1876, proved to be a spectacular affair, owing to the grand Masonic ceremony that accompanied it; over 1,500 'of the brethern collected from all parts of the Western District.'[267]

That Tracy, a Mason and vice-president of the Institute, turned out to be the building's architect was not necessarily a foregone conclusion: a competition for the design was announced in June 1876. Nevertheless, it seems that Tracy may well have had an edge over his rivals. In May the directors had suggested that he examine the Hamilton Mechanics' Institute and also 'public halls in Buffalo' with an eye to garnering ideas for the London building. Tracy's design was accepted on 14 August 'after a tedious discussion.'[268]

It seems to have been understood, in London at least, that mechanics' institutes were to have the architectural stature of full-fledged civic buildings. The structure erected in 1842 had been in the Greek Revival style then considered especially prestigious, with massive Ionic columns supporting a broad pediment. By 1876 the accepted fashion for government buildings was the French Second Empire style. Tracy's design fit into this mode by virtue of a centre tower with a convex mansard roof that has now disappeared.[269] The ornate tower and the four large dormer windows beside it created a very heavy, obtrusive top storey, which in this case had a practical symbolic purpose: to attract attention away from the first-floor stores to the premises of the Mechanics' Institute above. The tower also emphasized the entrance to the Institute, situated between the shops.

The main Institute facilities – a reading room, library, and museum designed to house Stephen Mummery's collection of stuffed birds, fishes, and reptiles – were located on the second floor, along with a hall, featuring a well-equipped stage, that could be rented out to retrieve some of the building's cost. Classrooms, committee rooms, and possibly a gymnasium were planned for the upper storeys.[270]

As was often the case with Robinson's buildings, Tracy's mansard roof and its trimmings were placed above a façade that is essentially Italianate in character. Tracy's design, however, reflects the exaggerated and playful attitudes of the High Renaissance. The capitals of the giant pilasters, for example, stop just short of the frieze, as if to mock their traditional weight-bearing role. The keystones over the windows (fig. 81), at the apex of wooden pediments, are blatantly useless in a structural sense. Yet these keystones and pediments dominate the second and third storeys, projecting assertively from a surface that is otherwise relatively flat, and even delicate, in design. Significantly, the keystones slant downwards. They seem to invite, and also meet, the gaze of those looking up from the street below.

At the 1876 ceremony Colonel Walker stated that 'the directors of the Institute and himself felt deeply the responsibility they have incurred in undertaking to erect this large and commodious building.' That responsibility added up to an $18,000 building debt that eventually felt as heavy as an albatross.[271] Ironically, the Masons and Tracy's firm collaborated on a more severe blow; the Grand Opera House, part of Tracy's and Durand's Masonic Temple, opened in 1882 and destroyed the Institute's hall as a money-maker. The public's appetite for educational courses declined in London and elsewhere in the 1880s, and membership in the London Institute did not grow. The London Mechanics' Institute faded out of existence in 1895, providing as its final act of mass education the nucleus of the new London Public Library's collection.[272]

High School, 1877–8

North-west corner Dufferin Avenue and Waterloo Street, London
(destroyed by fire)

London's new high school reflected both changing educational policies within the province and the city's increasing interest in providing first-rate educational facilities. Prior to 1871 secondary education in Ontario was mainly classical, and grants to grammar schools were determined by the numbers of Greek and Latin scholars.[273] In that year Chief Superintendent of Schools Egerton Ryerson introduced legislation designed 'to secure such an education of youth as to fit them for the ordinary employments and duties of life.' Most high schools were now to teach an English and a commercial course. The better schools, to be designated 'collegiate institutes,' would offer a classical course as well.[274]

London's Board of Education, under the leadership of Benjamin Cronyn Jr, had been eager to see the city's high school qualify as a collegiate institute, but there was no hope of achieving that status until the high school occupied a building of its own, separated from the 'public' or elementary schools. The necessity of building more public schools to keep up with an expanding population had made lack of funds an insuperable obstacle to constructing a high school before 1876. Then, as a by-product of the complex negotiations surrounding the transfer of the old garrison lands, the city was able to sell property and use the proceeds for a high school.[275] The new school became a collegiate institute within a few months of its opening.[276]

The prestigious designation speaks well for the new facilities. There were eight classrooms, most designed to seat forty students, a library, an 'apparatus room,' an assembly hall, and offices for the headmaster. As a result of increased independence and family encouragement, girls had begun attending high schools in greater numbers in the 1870s. They were provided with separate classrooms and their own 'recreation grounds,' divided from the boys' play area by a 'handsome trellis fence.'[277]

Both city newspapers aptly described the style of the new school as 'modern Gothic.' The building could actually serve as a textbook illustration of what architectural historians now call High Victorian Gothic, in that it features all the definitive elements: pointed arches, polychromy, a steeply pitched roof, cast-iron cresting, and a profusion of gables. It is interesting that even though buildings in the 'modern Gothic' style no longer bore much resemblance to medieval or Tudor institutions, 'Gothic' was still considered the appropriate style for schools. All the schools designed by Tracy and Durand during the next few years were to feature the combination of architectural forms found in the High School.

One cannot prove with documentary evidence that it was Tracy who

82   High School, London, photograph from the Egan Albums, c. 1880

designed the High School, but in 1877, when the firm prepared the plans, he was the partner most likely to have worked in the High Victorian Gothic mode. By 1878 the project seems to have involved most members of the firm. George Durand attended a Board of Education meeting to present Robinson's 'neat plan' for an octagonal privy, designed 'in the Gothic style ... in perfect keeping with the main building.' The 'Mr Moore' who provided an estimate for planting trees on the school grounds was probably John M. Moore, then apprenticing in Robinson's office.[278]

By 1889 the increasing demand in London for secondary education required Tracy to design an addition so large that it made the original building into a rear wing.[279] Not surprisingly, however, the new structure was admirably sensitive to the stylistic qualities of the old; even the delicate polychromatic design below the eaves was carried around the new school. When the building burned down in 1920, however, it was generally felt that still further additions had made the school inconvenient and unattractive, and the fire was regarded as a happy event, providing an excuse for rebuilding.[280]

The Grigg House, 1879

332 Richmond Street, London

Except for three stores facing Richmond Street, all the large block that Tracy designed for John McKinnon was given over to a hotel, ostensibly called the American House. From the time of its opening, however, the hotel was locally known as the Grigg House, after its proprietor, and the name was formally changed by 1883.[281] Samuel Grigg seems to have possessed an impressive personality. Contemporary sources described him as 'courteous, polite, and thoroughly attentive to his business,' and 'a most genial and obliging host,' whose 'personal popularity … made the "Grigg House" pecularly attractive and home-like.'[282] By 1879 he had been involved in the hotel business for twenty years,[283] and his experience and charm enabled the Grigg House to rival the established Tecumseh House across the street.

The hotel had attractive facilities as well as a personable host.[284] On the first floor were various public rooms, including a bar, a billiard parlour, a barber shop, and a reading room. A parlour and the frequently commended dining room were on the second floor, along with several two-room suites. Single rooms located on the second and third floors were said to be 'large.'

From outside, the Grigg House had an imposing presence that accorded with its class within. As the accomplished drawing indicates, the ground floor was particularly elegant. Its materials undoubtedly added to the richness of its design: the specifications call for the shop, bar, hall, and office 'fronts' to be of 'grained oak, twice varnished,' though, unfortunately, it is not now clear exactly what is meant by 'fronts.'[285] The upper storeys are surprisingly simple. Their general format was by this time almost routine for the firm's commercial buildings. Most of the buildings extending along Richmond Street from the hotel (fig. 84) were designed by the firm in the 1870s;[286] as one can see, they usually have in common Italianate windows alternating with piers, and elaborate corbel tables that give interest to the upper part of each façade. The corbelling of the Grigg House, however, is considerably less complicated than that of its neighbours. Its relative plainness enables some striking details to stand out. The keystones, for example, are incised with a variety of patterns. The corner where the main entrance was located was dignified by iron balconies and a strikingly imaginative pediment. Another pediment, in the centre of the York Street façade, carried a date stone that was originally intended to contain McKinnon's initials. Modesty triumphed over fame in the final product.

It was Grigg's name rather than McKinnon's that was to be associated with the hotel over the next century. The building was called 'Grigg's Hotel' until 1976, although Grigg himself left the establishment, possibly to do

83   The Grigg House, London, architectural drawing showing York Street elevation

84   The Grigg House and the Richmond streetscape

penance for a misspent life, in the early 1890s. Grigg became a Baptist evangelist, 'a whole-souled energetic Christian worker,' who held audiences 'in rapt attention' while he 'told the thrilling story of his life and conversion.'[287]

Trinity Anglican Church, completed 1879
Birr

The *Advertiser* saw the small parish church Tracy designed for the village of Birr as 'another evidence of the improved taste of the people.'[288] Although its façade had the old centre tower format that Robinson had used, the solid, stocky character of the Birr church did appeal to the period's new tastes. Several features contribute to its impression of weightiness: the heavy buttresses, the relatively broad tower and short spire, the overhanging eaves, and even the shortened arches of the corbel table, surrounding the building like heavy lace.

When one enters the church, however, its orientation seems suddenly reversed. Instead of being borne down by its weight, it seems to be aspiring upwards in the traditional Gothic manner. Originally, the beams and rafters were exposed right to the peak of the roof; the narrow paired windows also contribute to the intense verticality of the interior. Tracy has managed to impress an aura of Gothic mystery even within these extremely small confines.

The parishioners of 1879 were somewhat reluctant to give up their former,

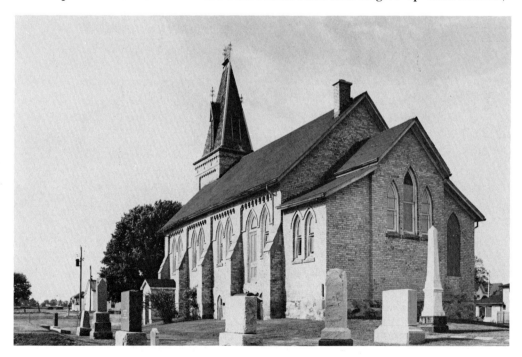

85   Trinity Anglican Church, Birr, view from south-west showing church and graveyard

86   Trinity Anglican Church

smaller, church, because 'hallowed memories' lingered about it – of Archbishop Brough, who had served the parish for twenty-five years, and of many early settlers who 'had been lain to rest' there. Now hallowed memories seem to linger around Tracy's church. It has not been in use since 1972, but an active decision to abandon the building seems never to have been made. Cobwebbed attendance charts still await the next Sunday School class; prayer books are in readiness for the next service. The church stands like a stalwart ghost, keeping watch over the graves that now comprise its only parish.

CHAPTER FOUR

The Durand Era

GEORGE F. DURAND

THE CAREER OF GEORGE F. DURAND ran a course in many ways similar to that of his contemporary and friend, Thomas Tracy. Both were articled to William Robinson during the 1860s; on completing their apprenticeships, both entered employment elsewhere that involved them in overly ambitious and controversial projects; both eventually returned to London, where they formed successful practices as Robinson's partners and successors. The London careers of both men ended within a short time of each other, Tracy's through his move to Vancouver, Durand's through his premature death. Partners for a few years, the two were lifelong friends; Tracy was a pallbearer at Durand's funeral. Yet, for all their close connections, Tracy and Durand were attracted towards very different facets of their common profession. Where Tracy ultimately chose to forsake architecture for engineering, Durand was mainly interested in the artistic dimensions of architecture. The *Advertiser* expressed its local pride, at the time of his death, in asserting that Durand 'was acknowledged to be the best designer in the Dominion.'[1]

George Durand would have gained an early acquaintance with the art of building. His father, James, had established a very successful building and contracting business with John Wright in 1854.[2] Originally from Thurso on the northern coast of Scotland, James Durand was known in London as possessing a Scotsman's 'shrewd judgment' and conscientious 'industry,' qualities that were to make Wright and Durand one of the leading contracting firms in

87   George F. Durand (1850–89), photograph, c. 1888

London, and to bring him success in other fields as well.[3] He sat on the London city council at various times during the 1850s and 1860s, and he made a close race of the elections of 1867 and 1872, won by Conservatives John Carling and William Meredith, respectively. His business enterprises were not limited to building. In 1875 he was one of the original promoters of the Canadian Savings and Loan Company; in 1887 he served as its president. By then he was too busy as a banker, an arbitrator, and an insurance adjuster to give much thought to his building business, which had been taken over by his younger son, Andrew.

That James Durand encouraged George to seek a career in architecture rather than building likely resulted from his early recognition of his elder son's pronounced artistic talent. In 1864, when George (b. 9 July 1850), was fourteen years old, his father wrote to London marble sculptor and drawing teacher J.R. Peel arranging to have him enrolled at Peel's art school.[4] Approximately two years later George began training as an architect, a profession that enabled him to combine the family interest in building with his own interest in drawing.

There still exists a perspective view by George Durand that dates from his

88   Sulphur Springs Bathing House, watercolour and ink on paper, by George F. Durand, c. 1868

student days (fig. 88). It shows the Sulphur Spring Bathing House, the main fixture in a spa opened by Charles Dunnett in 1868.[5] The 'Ontario White Sulphur Springs,' as they came to be known, were at the forks of the Thames River, immediately below the courthouse. Their product was advertised as especially therapeutic for rheumatism, gout, scrofula, 'Skin Diseases,' dyspepsia, 'Nervous Prostration,' and 'female diseases.'[6] Its virtues attracted many Americans in addition to a local clientele during the spa's years of operation in the nineteenth century. The pencilled notations suggest that Durand's watercolour may have been a working drawing depicting one of the firm's more utilitarian but distinctive designs. Its combined cubic and pyramidal forms created an interesting exercise for a student in architectural drawing, and one can see in the perspective of the bathing house the foundations of the watercolour technique, probably learned from Peel, that was praised in Durand's later work: the *Canadian Architect and Builder* judged Durand's watercolour perspective of the Labatt house (fig. 116), displayed at an exhibition sponsored by the Ontario Association of Architects, as showing 'great facility in the handling of the brush.'[7]

THE NEW YORK STATE CAPITOL

After completing his apprenticeship with Robinson, Durand moved from a minor role in a provincial city to a crucial position in one of the largest and most controversial architectural projects of its times, the New York State Capitol in Albany. Durand was hired, apparently as clerk of works, by Thomas Fuller, who had an earlier association with Robinson. Begun right after the American Civil War, during a period renowned for its grandiloquent architecture and extravagant spending, the building was originally budgeted to cost 'no more than four million' and was tacitly expected to cost much more.[8] Thomas Fuller and Augustus Laver, both of whom had previously worked on the Canadian parliament buildings, collaborated with Boston architect Arthur D. Gilman on the original design for the Capitol, an opulent Second Empire structure almost overwhelmed by its remarkably substantial tower (fig. 89).[9] Fuller, who was chiefly responsible for supervising the Albany building, had to deal with numerous criticisms from the project's inception. Objections were raised to the fact that such an important government project was in the hands of a 'foreign architect'; even closer than patriotism to the hearts of Fuller's critics was the issue of money.

In 1874 an Assembly subcommittee reported that the building would likely cost over $10 million. Faced with this realistic assessment, the Legislature still opted to let the building continue according to the initial plans. In the following year, however, a new governor, elected to fight corruption, decided to reform the Capitol project as well as capital politics. An advisory board, ostensibly appointed to provide an objective professional evaluation of the building, consisted of the pre-eminent architects Henry Hobson Richardson and Leopold Eidlitz and landscape architect Frederick Law Olmsted. Their report initiated a controversy that dominated the new *American Architect and Building News* throughout its first year. The board cleared Fuller on one charge. It found no evidence of negligent superintendence, though the wording of its report suggests that the spirit of the times perhaps required an occasional blind eye: 'in view of the difficulty of carrying on such work at the present time and under our present political customs, and in the present condition of the industry, the State must be thought fortunate if the Capitol presents no more extensive and serious marks of imperfect success in superintendence than are fairly borne witness to in these statements.'[10]

The board attacked the building, however, in terms of planning and design: its layout was impractical; the exterior gave no hints as to the arrangement of the rooms within; iron, plaster, and wood were too often substituted for the more dignified stone; the building lacked 'repose and dignity.'[11] The justness of these criticisms may fairly be questioned, in that they are so clearly based on principles quite different from the equally current attitudes actually

89   'Capitol for the State of New York, U.S.,' designed c. 1867 by Fuller and Laver, from the *Builder*, 28 May 1870

underlying Fuller's design. The arrangement of his building was formal rather than 'convenient'; his enthusiasm for using new materials in new ways was as typical of his times as was the Puginesque and Ruskinian enthusiasm for masonry; the yearning and restlessness expressed in the exuberance of the building as a whole, and even more emphatically in what one critic has called its 'tormented skyline,'[12] are completely antithetical to the Board's standard of 'repose.' Nevertheless, even though prestigious architects such as Richard M. Hunt rose to Fuller's defence, Fuller was dismissed in 1876, and Richardson, Eidlitz, and Olmsted became the new Capitol architects. The building was completed in 1897, after other changes in supervision, and at a cost of over $22 million.

Durand was with Fuller in Albany from 1870 to the time of the latter's dismissal. According to letters of recommendation written by Fuller and by two commissioners of the project, Durand very successfully filled the responsible positions he held in relation to the building. Fuller wrote,

Mr G.F. Durand was for upwards of six years my principal and confidential assistant and during that period had chief control of all the works at the new Capitol of this State which was then being erected under my Superintendence; his duties required extraordinary skill and accuracy and although all matters in relation to these works were subject annually to the most severe Legislative investigations requiring some very complicated calculations and detailed estimates, in no case were the services or the evidence or the integrity of Mr Durand called into question.

Commissioner W.A. Rice described Durand as 'the assistant architect of our new State Capitol for several years,' and praised his 'ability,' 'faithfulness,' 'energy,' and 'strict integrity.' Hamilton Harris commented on his 'great merit' as an architect and particularly complimented his 'business talent.'[13]

Despite his deserts, however, Durand's fate in relation to the Capitol was tied to his master's, an inevitability that apparently added to Fuller's sorrows: 'It was a matter of deep regret to me,' he confided, 'that I was not able to retain Mr Durand's services.'[14] Fuller was to spend the next few years in a kind of professional limbo from which he was rescued in 1881 by his appointment as chief architect to the Dominion of Canada. While in that position, he was to remember Durand by awarding him three important government contracts: Durand was supervising architect for post offices in Strathroy and Goderich (fig. 93) and for the Infantry School, now Wolseley Barracks, in London.[15]

DURAND'S RETURN TO LONDON

Durand, too, seems to have spent the years following the collapse of his involvement with the Albany project in a state of some professional uncertainty. After a year or so at a granite works in Maine, he returned to London, where he was briefly employed at the Globe Iron Works.[16] He joined Robinson and Tracy at the beginning of 1878, and he appears to have done very well as a novice partner, carrying out at least three important commissions on his own: a Roman Catholic church in Ingersoll, the impressive Federal Bank in London (fig. 96), and a substantial house for Charles Murray (fig. 95). With the last project he broke with tradition by signing the tender calls himself instead of giving the full name of the firm,[17] a move that would seem to indicate his interest in establishing his own name as an architect. Yet it is not at all certain that he remained with the firm during the following year. After Robinson's retirement Tracy appears to have continued business with few changes in office personnel. John M. Moore, who had been apprenticing with Robinson and Tracy, went on working for Tracy, and Richard Fairbairne remained in Tracy's employ at least through June 1879, when a call for tenders is signed 'Tracy and Fairbairne.'[18] Given Durand's high profile within the firm during 1878, the absence of any references to him during 1879 strongly suggests that he was seeking work elsewhere.

Not until 3 January 1880, when a newspaper advertisement listed Tracy and Durand as partners,[19] is there clear evidence of Durand's further association with the firm; this time his return to the fold was to be permanent. Tracy and Durand worked together until Tracy became city engineer on a full-time basis; after that, Durand headed the firm, entering at times into a semi-partnership with John M. Moore.

Durand settled into a London career at a fortunate time. The years of his partnership with Tracy were tremendously active ones for the building industry in London. When a reporter for the *Advertiser* visited the 'commodious offices' of 'Tracy, Durand and Co.' in November 1880, he found 'a large number of assistants actively engaged in preparing plans, getting out estimates, and giving information to anxious contractors.' The partner he interviewed was in a cheerful mood. ' "The fine weather seems to get everybody thinking of building," remarked Mr Durand,' an especially striking observation given the time of year. In 1882 Durand 'prepared plans for buildings, the gross value of which was $250,000.'[20]

The building scene was not to remain so prosperous. In the fall of 1884 the annual building report in the *Advertiser* admitted that 'This year was not at all a good one.' For Durand, the year seems to have been an absolute disaster: 'Mr Geo. F. Durand said the only house of any consequence which he had put [on order] was that for Mr J.B. Laing on Wellington street; cost $9,000. He had a number of smaller ones, additions, etc, amounting in the aggregate to about $10,000 or $15,000.' At the opening of the 1885 season the *Advertiser* found 'the building trade at a standstill, with no symptoms of revival.' An unnamed 'leading architect' is quoted as saying that 'the only real way to account for the trouble is the hard times.' Happy days were here again in 1886, however, the 'busy builder' taking a 'generally cheerful view of the situation.'[21] Despite a subsequent strike in the building trade, Durand's business flourished for the rest of the decade.

The nature of the firm's work during the 1880s differed in some respects from that of the preceding decades. Its major projects included relatively few commercial blocks, though it provided a great number of new fronts. London's central commercial district, even as it exists today, was quite thoroughly developed by the end of the 1870s. The city's growth was to be concentrated in the areas of public buildings, industry, and housing. The houses designed by the firm during the Durand era covered a considerable range within the upper reaches of the market. A large number of commissions for 'semi-detached villas' or 'double houses' indicates the widespread interest in speculation, but there are fewer tenders for 'three frame cottages,' or, for that matter, cottages of any sort. The more expensive of the firm's houses, especially during the early 1880s, were extremely lavish. Quite a few London families had accumulated considerable wealth, and the spirit of the times encouraged them to proclaim their affluence in ostentatiously large and imposing residences, such as the Cronyn and Labatt houses (figs 111 and 116).

Out-of-town work comprised a larger share of the firm's commissions during the 1880s. To some extent this trend was the natural result of the area's prosperity and London's regional importance. The *Free Press* had noted in 1878 that 'Several of our architects are preparing plans for buildings in towns and villages throughout Western Ontario.'[22] Durand's growing reputation was an added factor. In 1888 he was appointed architect for the new Upper Canada College (fig. 160). The following year, his design for the Toronto courthouse placed second and, according to the possibly biased *Advertiser*, it would have been first if it were not for pressure to choose a Toronto architect.[23]

While it is evident that Durand was responsible for these later designs, several factors make it difficult to be certain as to the division of responsibility between Durand and Tracy during their two prolific years together in the early 1880s. Both men shared a common High Victorian vocabulary; both tended to work in a variety of styles; and relatively little is known of either's earlier work. It is therefore impossible to make absolutely definitive attributions on stylistic grounds alone. The generally consistent quality of the firm's work during this period suggests a strong degree of collaboration. There is some evidence, however, that Tracy tended to defer to his junior partner on important matters of design. For example, although both men were, predictably, involved in the firm's and the city's largest project of those years, the Masonic Temple and Grand Opera House (1880–1; figs 92 and 101), it was Durand who accompanied a Masonic delegation on a tour of opera houses and Masonic halls in the United States, an expedition undertaken to get ideas for the London building.[24] St Peter's Separate School (1881–2; fig. 110) was completed after Tracy had become the official architect for the Separate School Board, yet the *Advertiser* specifically credits Durand with drawing the plans.[25] Tracy later claimed that Durand had designed the Talbot Street Baptist Church (1881–2; fig. 106).[26] It is tempting, on the basis of this lean evidence and the later careers of both partners, to speculate that Tracy increasingly concentrated on engineering concerns, leaving Durand to bear the major responsibility for architectural design.

There is conclusive evidence that Durand attempted to organize his office along such specialized lines after Tracy's departure. At the beginning of 1884 John M. Moore, unhappy with his salary of $800 a year, informed Durand that he wished to leave his employ. According to Moore's testimony, Durand persuaded him to stay 'and look after all Surveying and Engineering work,' with appropriate remuneration. Unfortunately, this agreement was to be the cause of considerable misunderstanding and bitterness over the next few years. The dispute came to a head in April 1888, when Moore finally did leave Durand's office and sued Durand for what Moore believed was his share of the firm's income.[27]

MOORE VS DURAND

The legal examinations of the plaintiff and defendant (respectively dated April and September 1889) are interesting and important for the insights they provide into the relationship between Moore and Durand during the 1880s. But beyond proving Durand's eagerness to delegate engineering tasks, they are maddeningly inconclusive. The crucial agreement of 1884 was entirely gentlemanly, with nothing committed to writing, and the gentlemen involved held quite different interpretations of what was said at the time.

Moore's version has the virtue of being admirably straightforward, consistent, and clear. According to his claim, he was to receive 'all the fees connected with the Surveying and Engineering Department,' and the fees from
'any work in the architectural department brought in through my [Moore's]
influence' and carried out by himself. When not engaged on his own jobs, he
was to help with the general work of the office for which he was to be paid
a 'fair proportion of what was received.' He was to contribute nothing to
office expenses. Moore claims that he had regularly received the fees for his
own work, averaging about $800 a year, but that Durand did not grant
him his 'fair share,' which had never been defined, of the general proceeds.
Although Moore had the books in his custody and recorded all work in the
daybook, he had not prepared an exact statement of the money owed him,
because 'I trusted the defendant to prepare one.'

The evidence is given in differing ways. Moore's testimony is reported in
the form of a coherent if repetitive monologue; in Durand's case, the actual
questions and answers are recorded, and his answers often appear evasive and
inconsistent. Nevertheless, it seems clear that he regarded his arrangement
with Moore in a light that is far less favourable to the younger man. Durand
insists that the 1884 arrangement was meant only to prove to Moore that
he should be happy with $80 a month (Durand's version of Moore's salary at
the time): 'I suggested as there was a diary kept in the office that he should
keep a memorandum of the work he [had] done and he would find ... that
I was paying him all that he was earning. That was the conversation word
for word.' He had never regarded Moore as a partner in the business, although
the firm had at times used the name 'Durand and Moore.' Durand is supris-
ingly blunt as to the pragmatic reasons for this designation. Probably in 1884,
'they appointed me ... engineer of Westminster and I took it with the understanding that Mr Moore was to attend to the whole business.' In November
1887

we were just ... getting out the infantry school advertisement and a friend of mine
wanted to know if some arrangement could not be made whereby parties in town that
were objecting to my having the work, being a Grit, should not be mollified in some
way ... I suggested myself that, Mr Moore being in my employ, his name could be
used in connection with the matter. That would probably let down these parties that
were talking about the matter on political grounds.

According to Durand, it was only when discussing this 1887 arrangement that
he agreed to give Moore 'a fair proportion' of 'the excess' if 'his work exceeded
the amount he had been paid for it.' In Durand's view, any 'fair proportion' had
been balanced by what he saw as Moore's share of the office expenses, but
he had not drawn up a statement to prove his point: Moore 'talked about
a settlement, and I told him the books were there and for him to work out a
statement of what he claimed.'

Given the remarkable ignorance both parties displayed as to the real figures involved, it is impossible to know how the dispute should have been settled. Since the case never did come to trial, no record of an actual judgment exists. The documents do point to some significant facts, however. The most obvious is that business relationships in Durand's office were, for worse rather than for better, based largely on personal trust rather than on the more impersonal contracts of modern business practice. It is also evident that, for all Moore's eagerness and rather convincing claims of partnership, the architectural side of the business was very thoroughly Durand's preserve. Moore displays a disconcerting lapse of memory regarding his own accomplishments: 'I drew original plans on my own account. I can't remember any of them just now. I prepared details of Petrolia Masonic Temple and Town Hall from plans furnished by Mr Durand and was working at many plans all the time. I remember no particular ones just now.' Durand had furnished plans for all the buildings about which he was questioned in relation to Moore's work.

The documents provide more insight into Moore's character than into Durand's. Durand himself admits that Moore was a 'straightforward, reputable, truthful fellow,' and Moore's sincerity and disillusionment are strongly evinced in his testimony. He appears to have accepted the informal and ill-defined financial arrangement in a spirit of trust and wishful thinking. Durand's attitude and his underlying character are harder to decipher. It is evident that he could be imperious, patronizing, and even devious. At the time of the interview he was obviously irritated by the whole matter and not inclined, for personal or legal reasons, to give much credit to his former employee. By September 1889 his mood may have been complicated by various pressing concerns. Not only had the dispute with Moore been building up for over a year, but Durand was also coping with an incredibly heavy work-load, and he had been seriously ill over a period of several months. The legal examination was not calculated to bring out the best side of what appears to have been a complex personality.

DURAND'S OFFICE

Moore's departure must have severely inconvenienced Durand, whether or not he admitted it. Aside from Durand, who necessarily spent a good deal of time away from the office, Moore was the man in charge. In addition to his responsibilities related to surveying and engineering, Moore handled accounts, kept records, and did the more challenging jobs connected with drawing and working out details.[28] At the time of Moore's departure, in April 1888, there were four other men working in the office, three of whom were apparently apprentices. The fourth, Pierce Graydon, seems to have been versatile and experienced, but he was apparently called in only on an occasional basis when the volume of business demanded it. During the rest of 1888 and 1889 there were generally three to five men in the office, but there was a surprising amount of turnover. The only person from Moore's days to remain

90   St Andrew's Presbyterian Church, Glanworth, designed in 1888 by George F. Durand; detail of architectural drawing showing front elevation

for the full two years was Herbert E. Matthews, an apprentice under Durand who was eventually to become the provincial architect of Manitoba.[29] On 30 March 1889 Fred Henry, who had also apprenticed under Durand before becoming assistant city engineer under Tracy, returned to work for Durand, providing experienced and capable help at a time when it was sorely needed.

The daybooks from those years prove that an architect's job was not an easy one. Durand and his itinerant staff handled between them approximately seventy different projects, some of them major. In addition to federal commissions provided by Fuller (two post offices and the Infantry School), these included Upper Canada College (fig. 160), the Petrolia Town Hall (fig. 150), the Canadian Savings and Loan building in London (fig. 161), a hospital in Stratford (fig. 162), high schools in Lucan, Glencoe, and Sarnia, and numerous churches and houses. Admittedly, buildings in the latter two categories did not always call for completely new plans. Church building committees often borrowed the plans of churches they admired with an eye to reusing them, usually with some variants. Thus, the Glanworth Presbyterian Church (completed 1888; fig. 90), for example, strongly resembles the Palmyra Baptist Church (fig. 99), built seven years before. House builders were often equally suggestible. Nevertheless, the members of Durand's staff seemed to need their six-day work week, and they often put in evenings as well.

Durand himself trained his apprentices, prepared the basic designs for each building, and handled most of the field work, which involved a great deal of travelling. During 1889 he began to be absent from the office for another reason as well. Beginning on 18 March, one frequently finds entered in the daybook such comments as 'Mr Durand ill today' or 'D. at home,' or 'Mr Durand at office part A.M.' Durand's health became a matter of public concern. On 27 June the *Free Press* reported, 'the many friends of Mr George F. Durand will hear with satisfaction that he is recovering slowly from his recent severe illness. Mr Durand will not resume his professional duties until he has entirely recovered, and Mr Fred Henry is in the meantime managing his business.' Journalistic optimism was again required on 20 August: 'Mr George F. Durand has returned from his vacation at the seaside greatly improved in health.'[30] By mid-December, however, the daybook entry can no longer be optimistic: 'Monday, December 16. "Doctors pronounced Mr Durand hopelessly ill." ' The story is concluded four days later: 'Friday, December 20. Mr Durand died at 12:15 tonight.' Durand's fatal disease is never defined: the *Canadian Architect and Builder* claims that it was believed to be caused by overwork.[31]

DURAND'S CHARACTER

Both city newspapers asserted that Durand had 'hosts of friends,' drawn to him by his 'excellent qualities' and 'estimable character.'[32] His funeral seemed to prove their claim. The cortege was reported to be one of the largest ever seen in the city: in addition to 'over two hundred' Masons and many

91   Terra cotta panels, Perth County Courthouse, Stratford, 1885–7, designed by George F. Durand

local friends, it included visitors from Detroit, Buffalo, Albany, and New York City and Thomas Fuller from Ottawa. 'The sidewalks were crowded with spectators,' according to the *Free Press*, 'and expressions of sympathy and regard were heard on every hand.'[33]

Compared with Tracy, however, Durand did not lead an especially public life. The *Advertiser*, apparently using information supplied largely by Tracy, observed that Durand 'had ... repeatedly been urged to accept nomination for public office of prominence, but had as often declined, his devotion to his profession and private life being characteristic.'[34] He was a member of St Andrew's Presbyterian Church and was active as a Mason. Otherwise, his interests seemed to be exclusively artistic, professional, and domestic.

Some of Durand's books have been retained by his heirs, but it is not always possible to establish the ownership of individual volumes. Several art books bear Durand's signature; they suggest a wide-ranging interest from the ancients to his contemporaries and from practical guides to books on the philosophy of art. He was apparently eager to give practical encouragement to artists: he served as a director of the Western School of Art[35] and belonged to the Art Union of London (England), an organization created to support worthy artists by purchasing and distributing their works.[36]

Durand regarded architecture mainly as an art and was clearly anxious to be recognized and remembered as an architect-artist. He even 'signed' one of his buildings: a terra cotta panel on the Perth County Courthouse, designed generally to honour the architect's art, shows a tool bearing the particular inscription 'Geo. F. Durand, Architect' (fig. 91). When the Ontario Association of Architects was formed a few years later, signing buildings became a controversial matter; although the Association felt advertising was demeaning to an architect, there seemed general agreement that it might be permissible for an architect to put his name on a building in a 'modest manner.'[37] Placed well above eye level and a small part of an intricate design, Durand's signature was sufficiently modest, an unexpected treat for those who bestow particularly close attention upon the building.

Durand did not take the view that art and professionalism were antithetical. He was an enthusiastic supporter of the idea of a provincial organization of architects. It is proof both of his interest and of the esteem in which he was held that he was chosen to chair the organizational meeting of the Ontario Association of Architects, and he was elected its second vice-president.[38] Unfortunately, he was unable to complete his term. The *Canadian Architect and Builder* gives a poignant account of Durand's appearance at the OAA's November convention:

His friends were deeply pained on that occasion to observe the ravages which disease had made on a constitution naturally strong, and the indications pointing to the early close of a talented and useful life. Yet, as they bade him good-bye at the close of the convention, it was not in the expectation that they were wishing him a last farewell ... In his death, the architectural profession has lost one of its ablest members, and the Ontario Association of Architects one of its most valuable promoters.[39]

The chief mourners of Durand's death must have been his immediate family. He left a widow (née Sarah Parker, the daughter of a prominent Albany builder) and four young children, the eldest of whom was twelve. They at least did not have to face poverty as well as bereavement. Durand's will instructs his executors to liquidate his assets, including the family's relatively modest Italianate house on the south-east corner of Queens Avenue and Waterloo Street, and use the funds to provide for his wife and children. In 1893, when the estate was settled, the assets amounted to $36,420.52.[40] The money undoubtedly proved necessary; for Sarah died only five years after her husband, after 'a long and lingering illness.'[41] James Durand, who was to be the executor of his son's will, did not live to fulfil that role. He died on 14 November 1890, of 'what is commonly termed "heart failure," ' but would have been diagnosed by the *Free Press* as a broken heart: 'it may be truthfully said that the death of his eldest son, George F., the well-known architect some time since, produced a very marked change upon him and from that time he was not the same cheerful, genial man whom everybody liked.' Some indication of the close relationship that existed between George Durand and his immediate family is found in a letter George wrote to his mother from Albany in 1874:

Andrew and Tom Wright arrived here on Wednesday Evening safely having enjoyed their trip so far very much indeed. Andrew has a blister on his little toe caused by his boots but I think it will be better before he leaves here as he is wearing an old shoe of mine ... I hope you and father will certainly get off for your trip this season ... Of course dear parents I should be very much pleased to see you here but do not let me monopolize all your trips. Go in which direction you fancy but please take a trip at all events. I feel it would do you both a great deal of good.[42]

George Durand's business met a fate that might not have pleased him. A report in the *Canadian Architect and Builder* to the effect that Detroit architect Gordon Lloyd would take over Durand's firm was never realized.[43] Fred Henry spent two years on his own, completing the projects Durand left unfinished at the time of his death, and then joined forces with John M. Moore. Thus Moore, still fighting for proper compensation when Durand died, was in effect to inherit Durand's firm. It was perhaps a sign of Moore's willingness to bury an old feud that in 1895 he hired Durand's daughter, Kathleen, as the firm's stenographer.[44]

RECREATION AND CULTURE IN THE DURAND ERA

Durand's active career in London spanned a period in the region's history that was most suited to his talents. The area was sufficiently established and prosperous to have time for the arts and money for building. Durand's lively, assertive, and often lavish designs reflected both the spiritedness and, to some extent, the restlessness of his era.

The last years of Durand's career were plagued by general labour troubles in the building business, as well as by his dispute with Moore. During the economic depression of the mid-decade tradesmen were forced to offer their services for wages that were fifteen to twenty per cent less than before. The revival brought a 'general increase in the price of labour,' which the employers regarded as 'a serious handicap on the upward movement of the trade.'[45] Such was the background to the strikes of 1887, a year when 'labour agitation in Ontario rose to a climax.'[46] The painters went out first, striking for a week in April in order to have their daily hours of work reduced from ten to nine. 'The employers gave in.' On 2 May it was the turn of fifty brick-layers, seventy-five carpenters, and ninety labourers to strike. Construction of the new Western Fair buildings, designed by Durand, was halted. By 10 May the 'boss carpenters' had begun to crumble. Bricklayers, who were seeking a raise from 30 to 33½ cents an hour, were leaving town. Less than three weeks later, the bricklayers got the increase they wanted; 'one of the terms of settlement was that no crowing should be done over the bosses' defeat.'[47] This peaceful union victory was achieved in an era of violent clashes and strike-breaking. The civility of the dispute was all the more remarkable in view of the acrimony that arose shortly thereafter between two less class-divided groups, the architects and the builders of the city.

During the impending strikes, an architect took the opportunity to attack publicly the Builders' Exchange for 'most unfair and arbitrary measures' in attempting to negotiate lower prices with suppliers. Less than a year later the builders not too diplomatically aired their complaints: 'Latterly, however, some of the architects, at least, seem to work on the principle that in order to be a success in their business and maintain their prestige with the general public they must euchre the contractor out of a large proportion of his money, and their judgments have been very arbitrary and one-sided.' The contractors evidently succeeded shortly thereafter in imposing new conditions on the architects. A correspondent of the *Canadian Architect and Builder* explained, 'the principal change ... is that whereas formerly the contractor was bound by the decision of the architect on any matter in dispute, except deductions, now he has the right to appeal from any decision.'[48]

An elaborate ritual to confirm the peace then took place. The 'first annual' builders' banquet was held at Grigg's Hotel (fig. 84) on 4 January 1889. 'The principal object ... was to promote a more hearty feeling of fellowship between all those engaged in the building trade.'[49] In Victorian fashion, 'the assault on ... the many tempting courses' took nearly two hours to complete. Following the toast to 'Our Architects,' Durand and Moore, among others, gave 'spirited speeches,' and 'reference was made to the better regime which had been ushered in.'

Exactly six months later another gesture of good will occurred: a baseball game between the architects and the builders. The architects won, 25-18. Playing right field and batting ninth for the architects was a former Durand partner, Colonel Thomas Tracy; Fred Henry played shortstop; and Herbert E. Matthews was in centre field.[50]

Baseball was a fitting ritual to enact, since it had played so prominent a role in the community life. A recent historian of Canadian baseball has suggested that 'middle-sized urban centres of the time' used the sport 'as a means to enhance their public images.'[51] Certainly, the London Tecumsehs of 1876–7 did their best to go big league. After winning the Canadian championship in 1876, the Tecumsehs boasted several imported American players the next year and captured the championship of the International Association, a rival of the newly established National League. On 27 August 1877 the Tecumsehs defeated the Chicago White Stockings by a score of 4-3 in a game played before 1,500 fans at Tecumseh Park (now Labatt Park). Cap Anson, in one authority's judgment 'one of the very best who ever played,' was thrown out at home plate; his 'cantankerousness had to show itself,' the *Free Press* reported, and 'he disputed the decision.' Fred Goldsmith, the Tecumseh pitcher, had some claim to inventing the curve-ball, and on that day 'puzzled the visitors wonderfully' with his 'scientific pitching.' The White Stockings must have been impressed, for Goldsmith went on to star for them in the 1880s.[52]

According to their own secretary, the Tecumsehs were actually invited to join the National League after the 1877 season. They did not want to give up the chance to play lucrative home exhibition games (a practice contrary to National League rules) and so declined the offer. Shortly thereafter both the Tecumsehs and the International Association fell to pieces.[53]

The Tecumsehs did last long enough to play the Rochesters on Civic Holiday 1878, a day on which the *Free Press* congratulated Londoners for having invented Civic Holiday itself, and expressed the view that 'a holiday is alike essential to the individual and to the community.'[54] The rich diversity of amusements, social and charitable activities, and cultural events available to London citizens in the 1870s and 1880s testifies to the community's acceptance of the *Free Press*'s precept.

Picnics, parades, and public ceremonies of all kinds were always well-attended. In 1860, 3,600 people, or virtually one-third of the town's population, had gone on the civic excursion to Sarnia, while 600 individualists had descended on Port Stanley instead. Twenty years later these mass exoduses had fallen out of favour, but 2,500 persons were at the annual picnic of the St George's Society, held within the city.[55]

Londoners in those years were, to use Samuel Johnson's term, very clubable. The innumerable Masonic lodges no doubt were among the most prominent social organizations, but there were also over a dozen branches of various types of Foresters (Ancient, Independent, and Canadian).[56] The several national societies were confined to those representing the British Isles, since London, as reported by the 1881 Census, contained only a handful of continental Europeans. The Bachelors' Club was formed in 1871, 'having for its aim the promotion of social intercourse and moral improvement.' It was renamed the Brunswick Club in 1879, 'on account of some of the members having ceased to be bachelors and not wishing to give up their membership.'[57]

The 1870s and 1880s were important decades in the development of music, theatre, and art in London. Looking back in 1910, the Danish-born conductor and teacher St John Hyttenauch recalled an ambitious but isolated event in 1863, the 25 February benefit concert, in which selections from *Messiah* and the whole of Mozart's '12th Mass' were performed: 'the church was jammed for the concert which was in every way a success.'[58] In the 1870s, more permanent musical organizations were formed, and the inauguration of several additional concert halls acted as a catalyst. Frances Hines, a student of this moment in London musical history, has observed: 'By 1880, London was firmly established as one of the most active musical centres in Ontario ... Progress had been steady and certainly significant in the forty years prior to 1870, but the following decade stands out as exceptionally productive.'[59] On 7 and 8 July 1875 St John Hyttenauch conducted a performance of the first half of *Messiah* and other selections; he drew some criticism for holding rehearsals at his home on the Sabbath. Two months later he became the conductor for the London Musical Union, an organization that attracted not only musicians, who had two two-hour rehearsals each week, but also eighty-three non-performing members, including the Honourable John Carling and the ubiquitous Bishop Hellmuth. This group lasted for three years; in the early 1880s a new organization, the London Philharmonic Society, took its place.[60]

A remarkable family, the Sippis, dominated London musical life together with Hyttenauch (with whom, in fact, they often performed). Of Italian origin, they had lived in Ireland for generations before arriving in London. Charles Sippi Sr was apparently a gifted violinist. His elder son, also Charles, had an astonishingly diversified career. His first stop in Canada was Port Stanley, where he began practising medicine in 1865. By 1867 he had become house surgeon at Hellmuth College, where he also taught classics, physiology, and English. From 1874 to 1887 he was the manager of Nordheimer's Music Company, and during the same period he was the organist and choirmaster of Bishop Cronyn Memorial Church. In 1887 he was appointed bursar of the London Asylum. Throughout these two decades he was the tenor soloist at every major performance by local artists. In his spare time he served on the executive of both the London Musical Union and the Irish Benevolent Society, and for two years he was the worshipful master of a Masonic lodge.

George Sippi, brother of the younger Charles, was not quite as versatile but had an equally distinguished career. He served as organist and choirmaster at St Paul's Cathedral for thirty-seven years. He played the piano and violin, and was both a scholarly student of church music and a composer.[61] Without the Sippis to teach, perform, organize, and conduct, London's musical life would have been meagre.

Music was given a prominent place in the delirious civic celebrations that followed the safe return of the London militia regiment after serving in the North-West Rebellion campaign. The thanksgiving ceremony at St Paul's Cathedral featured a 'special musical service by the choir under Mr George Sippi's direction.' At the elaborate banquet served in the drill shed Charles Sippi sang 'Let Me Like a Soldier Fall' in what the *Free Press* judged to be 'good form.' A free, open-air band concert given in Victoria Park was a 'manifestation of the people's delight in having the heroes of Clarke's Crossing at home again, and their desire to do them honour.' It is an appropriate reflection of the era's imperialist spirit that the music, 'which was exceptionally good,' began with 'March: Brave British Volunteers' and ended with 'Rule Britannia.'[62]

In order to flourish, both music and drama require adequate physical facilities as well as gifted performers. The city hall, built in 1855 with a seating capacity for concerts of 540, was an important and well-used resource.[63] The two most important later halls, for visiting musical as well as theatrical groups, were the Holman Opera House and the Masonic Hall.

The Holman family had roots in London going back to the early 1830s. George Holman Jr, the son of the first Holman settler, toured North America in the 1850s and 1860s with his talented family, known professionally as the Holman Juvenile Opera Troupe. In 1867 Holman took over management of Toronto's Royal Lyceum Theatre which then, his advertisement proclaims, was 'Crowded Nightly by the Elite.' Holman and his company made frequent appearances in London, and in 1873 he acquired the London Music Hall, located on the second floor of an 1866 Neoclassical building at the corner of York and Richmond streets. Renamed and with an enlarged stage, the

92 'Richmond Street, London,' streetscape showing south-east corner of Masonic Temple and Grand Opera House, from *Picturesque Canada*, volume II, 1882

Holman Opera House began its new existence on Christmas night 1873 with two Offenbach operettas. Thereafter, the Holmans began each annual tour in London. They 'kept up with the latest New York productions,' Hines states, 'and brought Canadian audiences the most current operatic successes.'[64] In the 1880s a series of untimely deaths put an end to the troupe, but the surviving couple remained in London and helped in amateur productions for many years.[65]

An exciting day for London theatre-goers was 18 March 1880; the E.A. McDowell company came to town with their national tour of *H.M.S. Parliament*, a home-grown satire with music and plot borrowed from *H.M.S. Pinafore*. 'It is the only Canadian play,' the *Advertiser* noted, without much exaggeration; the performance was 'one of the most enjoyable ever given in London.' The operetta was presented in the Mechanics' Institute (fig. 80), designed three years before by Tracy; 'the hall was crowded almost to overflowing,' the *Free Press* reported, 'and a more good-humoured, receptive and enthusiastic lot of people it would be impossible to play to.' The script, recently republished, attacks Sir John A. Macdonald's protectionist National Policy, along with his drinking habits and the government's corruption. For the London audience, 'a local "gag" was introduced, where to appease "Mrs. Butterbun" the Captain proposes to give her the contract for dredging the Thames, which drew forth uproarious merriment.'[66]

A more lasting source of entertainment was the Grand Opera House, part of Tracy and Durand's Masonic Temple (1880–1; figs 92 and 101). The impresario was C.J. Whitney, a Detroit businessman who had previously managed the Holman Opera House while the Holmans were on tour. London's Grand Opera House became the first Canadian link in Whitney's theatre chain which eventually included four Ontario houses and several in Ohio and Michigan.[67] On opening night (8 September 1881), the *Advertiser* reviewer admired 'the frescoing on the ceiling, the magnificent chandeliers and gasoliers, [and] the well-executed stage scenery,' while the *Free Press* critic claimed, 'one might well imagine himself transported to some brilliant metropolitan theatre.' The audience agreed: 'such expressions as "This is something like," "Fine, aint it" were to be heard on all sides.'

The play they saw was *Felicia*, an adaptation of a French novel, starring the fiery Rose Eytinge. Felicia conceals from her illegitimate son the knowledge of his birth. He falls in love with a girl whose father forbids the marriage. Curiously enough, the girl's uncle happened to be Felicia's former lover, so, naturally, 'there are painful confessions all round.' After everyone gets over the shock, 'the marriage is accordingly brought about, the young people made happy, and the mother retires from the world to a convent.'[68]

Felicia was no doubt representative of the kind of melodrama frequently presented on the Grand Opera stage. Yet, as Mary Brown has revealed in her performance calendar of the Grand Opera House, the range of entertainments offered to the London public was remarkable. In the opening 1881–2 season, no less than five different minstrel companies arrived, along with O.S. Fowler, a phrenologist, who went on for six nights. On the other hand, lovers of real theatre might well have been pleased by the celebrated actress Mlle Rhea in Dumas's *Camille*, or a performance of Gilbert and Sullivan's *Patience* (first staged in England only a year before, and performed at the Opera House by two different companies). Thomas Keene, the veteran English Shakespearian actor, performed Richard III for a night. Ernesto Rossi, as Hamlet and Romeo, offered a more unusual treat: the acclaimed European actor did his roles in Italian while the rest of the cast spoke English.

Well situated and well served by rail, London was able to attract first-class performers in transit between more major centres. In the 1880s and 1890s Londoners had the opportunity to see Sir Henry Irving and Ellen Terry, James O'Neill (father of the playwright and subject of the latter's *Long Day's Journey Into Night*), Lionel Barrymore as a boy, the celebrated tragic actress Modjeska, Lillie Langtry (the 'Jersey Lily' most remembered in the role of Edward VII's mistress), and on 8 April 1896 Madame Sarah Bernhardt in Sardou's *La Tosca*, a play written for her.[69]

London's most vigorous early era as a centre for painting coincided almost exactly with the Durand years. In art, as in music, a few foreign-born pioneers created and sustained a community interest in their chosen disciplines. An important show was held in the Mechanics' Institute soon after Tracy's building was complete; nearly 400 works owned by Londoners were put on display.

In that same year (1878) art classes that had been given by the Mechanics' Institute since 1871 were reorganized as the Western School of Art and Design; two years later 457 students were enrolled in the school's courses. China painting was strongly emphasized in the school and became a significant form of employment for women.

The Western Art Union was formed, again in 1878, apparently in protest against the centralizing tendencies of the Ontario Society of Artists, begun in Toronto two years before. By 1883 the Western Art Union had a rebellion on its own hands. A group of younger artists, recently arrived in the city, began the Western Art League. Their first president was Frederic Marlett Bell-Smith, a genuinely distinguished and versatile painter who taught art at Alma College and the London high school. 'Much jealousy prevails,' in the London art world, the *Free Press* claimed, and the two newspapers gleefully joined in the bickering. After Bell-Smith left London in 1888, several of his painter-friends drifted away, and, Nancy Poole states, 'London became an artistic backwater.' In 1890 Paul Peel returned to his native city with sixty-two canvases he exhibited at the Tecumseh House Hotel. Not one was purchased.[70]

DURAND'S STYLES

The diversity of the firm's architecture during the 1880s was largely the result of the period's interest in creative experimentation together with the numerous and sometimes conflicting theories as to what constituted architectural design. Probably the most evident trait of High (in contrast to early or late) Victorian architecture was its eclecticism, and yet not everyone favoured an eclectic approach. Part of the controversy surrounding the Albany capitol in 1876 concerned the stylistic changes proposed in the Richardson-Eidlitz scheme. At one point, Eidlitz was asked 'what business' he had grafting a Romanesque top onto Fuller's Italian Renaissance bottom storeys. Instead of defending the mixing of styles, Eidlitz retorted with the specious logic of a determined six-year-old: 'What business had Fuller to put that basement under my building?'[71] The influential *American Architect and Building News* worried, with some cause, that the results of a widespread eclectic approach could be 'like learning to play the violin': 'He who essays an established style, like him who plays a fixed-tone instrument, can by beginning with simple tunes avoid great offence even in his earliest progress; but he who designs eclectically, as he who attempts the violin, must learn not only to play his theme, but to make his notes, and must expect for long years to torture all the sensitive persons who come in his range – and himself if he is one.'[72]

In fact, by this time some architectural tones had already become fixed, and these could act as the harmonic foundations for new melodies: certain eclectic combinations of elements were accepted as congenial. One can glean some insight into Durand's and Tracy's ideas about stylistic categories from the newspaper reports of the early 1880s which used stylistic labels apparently provided by the architect's office.[73] Oakwood (fig. 111) and the Masonic

Temple are said to be in the 'Renaissance' or 'French Renaissance' style; the Bond Street School, St Peter's Separate School (fig. 110), Waverley (fig. 112), and Endiang (fig. 116) are described as 'Gothic'; a store front for Mr Beattie is 'Queen Anne'; the Colborne Street Methodist Church (fig. 159), Upper Canada College (fig. 160), and the Canada Savings and Loan Company (fig. 161) are all said to be in the 'modern Romanesque' mode. An examination of what these terms meant to Durand and his contemporaries can pinpoint the prevailing trends within the eclectic movement and provide a basis for understanding much of Durand's work.

The term 'Renaissance' seems to have represented a relatively free reinterpretation of the classical tradition, with the emphasis placed on its later rather than its ancient phases. Both the Masonic Hall and the Cronyn house would now be categorized as 'Second Empire' on the strength of their French mansard roofs. The façade of the Masonic Hall featured basic classical elements such as pilasters and pedimented windows. The posts of the porch at Oakwood were variations of Ionic columns. Both the Opera House façade (fig. 101) and Oakwood are quite restrained in their classical decoration, however, and one can see signs of Gothic influence in the horizontal lines linking the window heads and in Oakwood's highly irregular plan.

'Gothic' turns out to be a remarkably comprehensive term for the reporters and, no doubt, for Durand. It was applied not only to schools and churches, where pointed arches alone could possibly justify its use, but also to houses such as Waverley (designed 1882; fig. 112) and Endiang (1882–4; fig. 116) where the brackets and some of the windows look suspiciously Italianate. The very inclusiveness of the term 'Gothic' points to the extraordinarily complicated history of the Gothic Revival, as it occurred in England.[74]

We have already noted, in chapter 3, some of the early stages of High Victorian Gothic. The style was closely associated with ideas about architectural 'Truth,' as expounded by Pugin, Ruskin, and the Ecclesiologists. 'Truth' in functional terms was expressed by the provision in churches for proper liturgical functions and in other buildings by sufficiently 'convenient' plans; it was thought that a building's exterior appearance should reflect its interior uses. Equally important was the concept of 'constructional truth,' according to which a building should reveal its means of support and the basic materials of which it was built. In England, where the most common building materials were stone and brick, the development of ideas related to 'constructional truth' was consistent with a growing admiration for qualities intrinsic to masonry such as a sense of heaviness and massiveness. Materials of contrasting colours and textures, used for different courses, emphasized the layering process by which a wall was built. Large sections of wall space were left uninterrupted.

During the 1860s the Gothic style came to assume a more foreign appearance and to lose its ecclesiastical overtones. The medieval buildings of Italy reinforced and guided the enthusiasm for constructional polychromy. The pointed window, the definitive feature of Pugin's 'pointed' style, was sometimes replaced by more Italianate window shapes. The steeply pitched roofs, often with small dormers, and the saddle-roofed towers of medieval France also became part of the developing style. They were frequently adorned with iron crestings. Public buildings, commercial buildings, and even factories began to be Gothic. Thus the Stratford Pump House (1882–3; fig. 119) is by no means an anomaly in displaying all the distinctive features of the period's church architecture.

High Victorian Gothic appealed to a taste for strong and even violent effects. Its practitioners were attracted to bright colours and strong contrasts, sometimes pushing opposing elements into purposely discordant relationships. Forceful effects of all sorts were admired: in 1859 the *Ecclesiologist*, in a highly laudatory article on Butterfield's All Saints, Margaret Street, in London, England, noted that 'the foliage of capitals and string-courses ... is often exaggerated in its coarse but honest originality ...' and even comments, not unfavourably, on 'the deliberate preference of ugliness' observable in the church.[75]

One has no trouble accepting Durand's judgment, relayed through the newspaper reporter, that his schools were 'Gothic.' The Bond (later Princess) Street School, explicitly mentioned as Gothic, was very similar to the Talbot Street School and most of the firm's other public schools; the design for the Roman Catholic Separate School differed only in its third storey, which was never built, and its tower. In each school orange-red bricks were used to create strongly contrasting patterns against the white brick. The patterns took the usual forms of horizontal courses, window headings, and friezes, all designed to stress various structural elements. There are the customary pointed windows and crested roofs, and the Separate School tower has the dormers frequently associated with the style. In the crowding of the roundels in its front gables one can sense something of the deliberate discord sometimes introduced into the period's buildings.

Except for their high-crested roofs, however, Waverley and Endiang are not Gothic in the same way. Both houses clearly draw on developments within the Gothic movement that occurred during the 1860s. Some young architects who had been trained in the Gothic tradition began to design in what they called the 'Old English' style. The term was purposely vague. Its proponents drew on English vernacular architecture of the fourteenth to the seventeenth centuries, without worrying about strict fidelity to any one period. In his *History of the Gothic Revival* (1879), Charles Eastlake praised William Eden Nesfield for realizing, in Cloverley Hall, 'the true spirit of old-world art, without hampering himself by those nice considerations of date and stereotyped conditions of form which in the last generation were sometimes valued more highly than the display of inventive power.'[76]

As we have noted, rural cottage architecture had influenced earlier architects of the Gothic Revival. The new style was distinctive, however, in drawing on a much broader range of architectural motifs: even country mansions came to sport leaded windows, hung tiles, multiple moulded chimneys, elaborate barge-boards, and half-timbered and overhanging gables. Some of the old

Gothic principles were interpreted in new ways. The previous concern for constructional truth now evidenced itself less in insisting that structural elements be revealed than in ensuring good craftsmanship. There was considerable interest in using or reviving appropriate regional techniques. The foreign polychromy was replaced by more traditional masonry or by half-timbering, such as that of Graeme's Dyke (fig. 29) by R. Norman Shaw. The respect for 'convenience' manifested itself not only in versatile floor plans, but in other aspects of design as well. Eastlake praised Shaw's Leyes Wood for its modern comforts, including its plaster ceilings and its combination stained and plate glass windows, from which one could look out more easily than from the usual 'pattern glazing' of a Gothic window.[77]

Though inspired by late medieval rural buildings and adhering, in their own way, to the Gothic Revival's old ideals of truth and convenience, the 'Old English' architects were guided by a new fashion in esthetic taste. They generally viewed themselves as artists, and many of their clients were associated with the arts. They had friends and acquaintances among the later Pre-Raphaelites, with whom they shared an interest in fine detail, and there was a new emphasis on delicacy in some of their work. Warrington Taylor, eventually to become manager of William Morris's crafts firm, complained in 1862 about the massiveness for which some English architects were striving:

all that is huge coarse in French Gothic they seize – but they have no feeling for the poetry of that very insular characteristic 'littleness of English nature', everything English, except stockjobbing London or cotton Manchester, is essentially small, and of a homely farmhouse kind of poetry ... English Gothic is small as our landscape is small, it is sweet picturesque homely farmyardish ... – French is aspiring, grand straining after the extraordinary all very well in France but is wrong here.

The new trend was towards more interruptions in rooflines and wall surfaces, with more space devoted to windows. Eastlake noted that Shaw gave considerable attention to the 'minute details' of a work: 'The wooden architraves, door panels, staircase railings etc, which were once allowed to take their chance at the contractor's hands, or were only selected from a series of patterns submitted for approval, have of late years become to architects the object of as much attention as the plan of a room or the proportions of a façade.'[78]

Charles Eastlake himself unwittingly proved responsible for another chapter in the history of the Gothic Revival. In his first book, entitled *Hints on Household Taste, in Furniture Upholstery and Other Details* (1868), he applied the current interpretations of Truth and Convenience to furniture. Like Morris and his circle, who emphasized the dignity of crafts made in the traditional manner, Eastlake was eager to revive 'the spirit and principles of early manufacturers.' He took into account the suitability of furniture for 'the habits of modern life.' His designs, with their bold, relatively simple outlines, were generally perceived as a lightened form of Gothic furniture. The surfaces, however, were liberally adorned with incised woodwork, and the arms and legs were often elaborately turned. The book was extremely popular. To

Eastlake's chagrin, it spawned in the United States an 'Eastlake' style of commercially manufactured furniture that was often cheaply made and for the taste of which Eastlake claimed he 'should be very sorry to be considered responsible.'[79] Even further beyond Eastlake's worst imaginings were the architectural reverberations of his book. In America, where porches and verandahs were often considered an essential part of a dwelling, the furniture designs provided models for exterior decorative detail, especially for balusters and posts. So popular were the results that the number of porches, verandahs, and balconies on a single dwelling proliferated, and an 'Eastlake' style developed, marked, usually, by a good deal of elaborate wooden trim and an abundance of porch-like appendages. When the *California Architect and Building News* sought confirmation of their view that 'could Eastlake behold some of the extra delineations, he would doubtless cry to the gods to blot out the monstrosities,' he replied, more reservedly, that he could have 'no real sympathy' with such 'extravagant and *bizarre* taste.'[80]

Whether Charles Eastlake approved or not, woodwork in the 'Eastlake' manner, inspired by the work of a recognized authority on the Gothic Revival, seemed to many North Americans a natural and logical extension of the Old English style. Both Waverley and Endiang show Old English influence in their moulded chimneys, decorated gables, and extraordinarily varied rooflines. But it is the 'Eastlake style' of the porches and balconies that gives the houses their most distinctive quality. That Durand thought of these houses as 'Gothic' rather than 'Eastlake' or 'Queen Anne' suggests that he was still thinking in terms of English themes, while in practice relying on their American variations. Modern historians would more likely regard both houses as 'Queen Anne,' comparing them to the American versions of another English style.

Eastlake saw in the work of the 'adaptational or Artistic School' the best hope for the spread 'throughout the land' of the 'noble and expressive language' of Gothicism: 'Architects must learn to sacrifice something of their antiquarian tendencies.'[81] Already, however, the artistic architects were being led by their interest in atmosphere rather than archeology to cross the boundaries of Gothicism into classical territory. They became absorbed in the domestic architecture of the late seventeenth and early eighteenth centuries, for reasons that are well stated by one of the most articulate architects of the late nineteenth century, J.J. Stevenson, in his influential *House Architecture* (1880). First, it was 'a builder's, not an architect's style, the product of traditions naturally developing themselves.' By the late seventeenth century, he argues, builders had been thoroughly trained in the classical style, but they tended freely to mingle classical with Gothic features, 'so as to produce a complex and characteristic English style.' The result was comfortably domestic: 'with their broad white frames and small window panes twinkling in the light, they suggest all the pleasant associations of an English home.'[82] These qualities – the Englishness, the stylistic freedom, the suggestions of creative artisanship, and the old-fashioned domestic atmosphere – appealed to many of the period's architects and also to popular taste. A note in the *American Architect and*

Building News, based on observations in a British newspaper, states that the architectural fashion is part of a contemporary 'madness' for 'the manners' of Queen Anne:

At a noted crockery-shop in Piccadilly, the newest designs, I observe, are after patterns of a hundred and fifty years ago; and I am desired to admire the roughest and squattest mugs and pitchers, rather than the purest lines of Wedgwood or Greek work. As to the women who have been bitten, there is no end to their extravagances; and one lady, who looked as if she had just stepped out of one of Romney's pictures, gravely assured me this week, that she preferred a spinet to a piano.[83]

As Stevenson's analysis implies, new buildings in the Queen Anne style were of red brick with contrasting white window frames, and they featured many classical details, while retaining the high roofs, moulded chimneys, and often irregular plans of the medieval tradition. The red-brick architecture of the early seventeenth century had been strongly influenced by Dutch and Flemish classicism; the stepped or scrolled gables and the sculpted panels associated with the architecture of these countries were enthusiastically adopted as part of the new Queen Anne style.

Symbols of the contemporary spirit rather than the old classicism were often evident in the particular forms of Queen Anne decoration. Flowers, particularly the sunflower, were especially popular, appropriate in part because of their associations with cheery domesticity. The modestly formal gardens of the historical Queen Anne period (1702–14) came back into vogue and the flowers that came to be admired were the 'old-fashioned' ones, such as hollyhocks, day lilies, and single sunflowers. William Morris praised the sunflower as 'both interesting and beautiful, with its shapely chiselled yellow florets, relieved by the quaintly patterned sand-coloured centre clogged with honey and sweet with bees and butterflies.'[84] That the sunflower, because of either its sweet centre or its appearance of reflecting the sun, was interpreted as a symbol of happiness is indicated by a sunflower design embroidered on a piano cover around 1889: interwoven with the ray-like petals is the legend, 'Joy And Gladness Shall Be Found Herein, Thanskgiving & The Voice of Melody.'[85]

Stevenson and his contemporaries were attracted to what they called the Queen Anne style largely because it was transitional. Stevenson saw it as appropriate for his own age because, though classic forms proved more easily adaptable to 'domestic and civil architecture,' his contemporaries were trained in the 'principles and freedom of Gothic.'[86] Transitional phases in the architecture of other countries also had their attractions. The French chateau style, emerging from the period when Renaissance ideas first affected architecture in France, became especially influential. In 1878 a correspondent of the *American Architect and Building News*, searching London for information about 'this "pot-pourri" of architecture,' the Queen Anne style, 'went to Batsford's, the architectural book-sellers ... and there was told: "Oh, we have no books on that style. Our Queen Anne architects take their details from

Sauvageot's work on the French Chateaux!" '[87]

Many of Durand's and Tracy's buildings show Queen Anne influence. For example, both the 'Renaissance' and 'Gothic' houses described above are adorned with moulded stone and terra cotta panels. At Waverley sunflowers decorate the exterior frieze (fig. 114A) and interior woodwork such as the newel post (fig. 114B).

Most unfortunately, a modern remodelling of what was Mr Beattie's Queen Anne commercial store front makes it impossible to tell exactly what Tracy and Durand meant by the term 'Queen Anne' in 1880, though the fact that the store was to be 'of red brick and stone'[88] suggests that they had the English definitions of the style in mind. In many other respects, the firm's buildings show the influence of what came to be regarded as Queen Anne in America.

It is clear that during the 1870s and 1880s the firm increasingly looked to the United States for architectural ideas. The Italianate buildings designed in the 1870s followed an American trend. Both Tracy and Durand spent some time working as architects south of the border. As mentioned above, Tracy owned at least one American pattern book, and Durand subscribed to at least two American architectural journals. Durand's Federal Bank (1878) was said to be arranged according to 'the American plan,' and indeed may well have been based on William LeBaron Jenney's Portland Block in Chicago (1872).[89] In 1880 Durand and a delegation of Masons examined opera houses and Masonic halls in New York, Rochester, Albany, Troy, and Boston.

The firm was apparently typical in its orientation towards the United States. Whereas most architects of Robinson's generation had been raised or trained in Britain and brought with them their British ideas, many of the younger Canadian architects were native Canadians dependent for ideas on their North American experience. In 1889 the Canadian correspondent for the *American Architect and Building News* lamented Canada's position in a kind of architectural no-man's-land possessing neither British traditions nor American independence. The only feasible solution was to follow the American model:

An old-world country has been built up century after century, its builders and its artists have left the monuments of their genius to mark the progress of art, and the student of architecture has but to look around him for examples. America, though a new nation, *is* a nation in itself, capable of developing its national characteristics, its own art and its own science, but a colony of an old-world country is a people who possess, instinctively, all the national characteristics of the mother country, but, who are thrown on their beam-ends to live, to develop art and science for themselves without examples to instruct them, without, so far as art is concerned, the 'straw' to do the work with. Naturally, their examples are sought from the nearest country.[90]

Four years earlier the Montreal *Witness* had also noted the architectural progress of the United States. Its analysis is more whole-heartedly admiring and less tinged with self-pity: 'The United States is soon going to take the lead of other countries in the matter of modern architecture as it is natural that it should. A rapidly developing country, constantly requiring new conveniences, offers the most promising field for the ablest men of the age ... The young Western cities which have sprung up within the aesthetic era are fairy lands as compared with the new towns of thirty years ago.'[91]

Though heavily influenced by British movements, American architecture developed in somewhat different ways. Among the many causes for the growing architectural independence of the United States two stand out: the ready availability of wood as a building material, and the strong French influence.

The concept of constructional truth led to very different esthetic effects when applied to wood rather than to stone. Andrew Jackson Downing in 1847 recommended designs consistent with the intrinsic qualities of wood: 'When it is necessary to build of wood, our advice is always to choose a style which is rather light, than heavy – in other words one in which the style and material are in keeping with each other. It is in false taste to erect a wooden building in a massive and heavy style, which originated in the use of stone, as it would be senseless to build a mock fortification, intended to stand a real siege, whose walls and battlements are of thin pine boards.' Not only should wooden buildings be lighter in appearance, according to Downing, but their elements should be strongly vertical, in deference to the mode of their construction: 'We greatly prefer the vertical to the horizontal boarding, not only because it is more durable, but because it has an expression of strength and truthfulness which the other has not. The main timbers which enter into the frame of a wooden house and support the structure are vertical, and hence the vertical boarding properly signifies to the eye a wooden house.'[92]

As the concept of a true wooden architecture developed, the inner structural workings of a building came to be more thoroughly indicated on its exterior: the outline of the roof supports were repeated in gables and the pattern of major framing timbers came to be echoed on the outside walls. Thus there emerged in the United States what architectural historian Vincent J. Scully has defined as an independent style. He calls it the Stick style, the determining feature of which is a 'skeletonized' wooden wall that in later examples re-sembles an 'interwoven basketry of sticks.'[93] Whereas the Gothic movement in England led to an architecture with relatively simple outlines and flat wall surfaces, there developed in the United States an interest in busier surfaces, constantly interrupted not only by the skeletal elements themselves, but also by the bold and picturesque projections to which wood easily lent itself.

It is not surprising that these American tastes affected brick structures as well as wood, in Ontario as well as the United States. Although most of Durand's buildings were brick, and although he frequently takes advantage of his material to achieve interesting polychromatic effects, he rarely leaves broad expanses of wall uninterrupted, and the impulse behind his designs is almost always towards lightness and verticality. One could say of many of his designs what the *Advertiser* said of his Federal Bank: 'The style of archi-tecture is massive, without any appearance of heaviness.'[94]

Nor is it surprising that, when the Queen Anne rage hit America, its most influential characteristics were those that were consistent with building in wood rather than brick. The Queen Anne style gained popularity in the United States when the British government erected two half-timbered buildings at the Philadelphia Exposition in 1876, and it was the Old English phase that was most influential in the early stages of the American movement. Curiously, the term 'Queen Anne' came to be associated with Elizabethan half-timbering, hung tiles or shingles, elaborate gables and barge-boards, rows of small-paned windows, irregular plans with markedly projecting bays, jagged rooflines, and the conventional decorative motifs. In his influential book *Modern Dwellings* (New York 1878), H. Hudson Holly strongly recommends the 'Queen Anne' or 'free classic' style, but most of his illustrations show Stick-style buildings graced with Elizabethan features and sunflowers. The English red-brick buildings of the seventeenth and eighteenth centuries played a distinctly secondary role in the United States. When the style developed a pronounced classical character during the 1890s, it was more directly inspired by American Colonial architecture.[95]

While Endiang and Waverley could be called Queen Anne by American standards, the specifically Elizabethan character that especially marked the American version of the style is more evident in some of Durand's very last buildings – in the small-paned windows, shingles, and half-timbered gables of the LeBel and Mathewson houses (figs 164 and 167), for example. The Mathewson House is also among several buildings influenced by the Romanesque Revival, another strong American movement.

The Romanesque Revival dated from the 1850s in the United States. It gained a new impetus in the 1880s, however, from the work of H.H. Richardson, who developed an original and distinctive style in many ways opposite to the Stick style. In a sense, he took to an extreme the feelings about building with stone that had developed earlier in conjunction with English Gothicism. His buildings were often of roughly cut stone. Their heaviness was emphasized by very deeply set doors and windows and by massive forms. Though it had the solidity of Romanesque architecture and used a round-headed arch, Richardson's work was in fact highly eclectic. Among his borrowings were the use of polychromatic materials from the High Victorian Gothic tradition, the use of decorative panels and some Elizabethan details from the Queen Anne style, and Chateauesque wall dormers. Whatever his sources, he moulded diverse elements into unified sculptural masses that bore the mark of a highly personal style. His work was widely imitated, especially in the years immediately following his death in 1886.[96]

Only two of Durand's buildings were specifically Richardsonian in their approach: Upper Canada College (fig. 160) and the Canadian Savings and Loan Company (fig. 161). Durand may have been influenced by the Fuller designs for which he was supervising architect at that time; rather ironically, Fuller had taken to drawing plans very much in the style of the man who had replaced him in Albany. The Goderich Post Office, for example, was of rock-faced masonry, and the round-headed arches over the doors and windows are Richardsonian in both their broad span and their depth (fig. 93). Even the

93   Post Office, Customs, and Inland Revenue Offices, Goderich, 1888–91, designed by Thomas Fuller

smooth, wide brackets under the eaves project a sense of heaviness and solidity. While only two of Durand's buildings have a Richardsonian character, Durand made increasing use of the Romanesque arch after the middle 1880s, and several of his later churches have a distinctly Romanesque character.

Richardson had studied at the Ecole des Beaux-Arts in Paris. That institution exerted a strong influence on American architecture of the period, not only because eminent architects such as Richardson and R.M. Hunt were students there, but also because American architectural education tended to be modelled on the school. The Beaux-Arts approach was highly rationalistic, emphasizing functionalism and unity in all parts of a design: the floor plans, elevations, and massing of a building were all to be perfectly integrated. As one Beaux-Arts theorist argued in 1832, 'The walls of a monument are only its natural envelope; they are to the edifice they enclose what drapery is to the statue that it covers.'[97] It was expected, though, that the statue would be draped in a tasteful and elegant manner.

DURAND'S DEVELOPMENT

Although Durand did not have a formal Beaux-Arts training, it seems evident that he developed a considerable understanding of Beaux-Arts principles, probably during his years at Albany. An intelligent and rational approach to architectural design is always evident in his work. The exterior often mirrors the inner arrangements. Compared with English buildings of the period, a high percentage of Durand's designs are symmetrical; where less regular, the two halves of a façade are usually balanced overtly. His use of various styles and traditions is almost always analytical and self-conscious; he sometimes adopts a purposely playful or mannered attitude towards the forms he employs.

While Durand's general attitude towards design remains consistent, the specific forms of his work do change over the twelve years of his London career. His earlier buildings still have a strongly Italianate character, evident in the deep bracketed cornices and the window shapes. Interiors, too, often feature the deep mouldings, pronounced coves, and marble mantels used in houses of the 1870s.

The Queen Anne movement brought with it a new fashion in interiors which made an impact on Durand's work. The requisite qualities of this style are nicely summarized in the *Free Press*'s discussion of the Grand Opera House (fig. 101): 'To the visitor who enters the building during daylight, the general brightness of the interior and its compactness first call for attention. He admires the cosy appearance and rich beauty.'[98] Large windows made buildings bright; the plentiful use of wood, left in a natural finish, made them cosy; intricate carving and Eastlake mouldings (finer and shallower than the mouldings of the older style) made them rich. Durand used the newer style of interior in his early works, but usually only for the most substantial buildings, such as Oakwood (fig. 111) or Endiang (fig. 116). By the end of the 1880s the cosy Eastlake style is standard fare.

The window shapes in Durand's designs become more varied as the 1880s progress. He uses, and frequently combines, long, narrow Queen Anne windows, with small panes in their upper sections, and broad, round-arched Romanesque windows, often with an inventive arrangement of panes within the semi-circular frame. These designs take on a rather stark geometrical quality in buildings such as the Petrolia town hall (fig. 150); something of the sense of an abstract geometrical design is also created by the overall arrangement of the windows in the façade of the Canada Savings and Loan Company (fig. 161).

While he uses Romanesque elements, Durand's natural inclination seems to be towards the lightness and verticality usually found in the American Queen Anne style rather than towards the massiveness of Richardsonian Romanesque. Durand's work is often colourful and lively, and his imaginative and sometimes daring innovations, such as the polygonal stair towers of the Talbot Street Baptist Church (fig. 106) are generally very effective. For all their colour and boldness, however, Durand's buildings rarely possess the discordant quality that was common in his time, and his work is only occasionally restless. Even purposely distorted or exaggerated elements are generally subsumed within the prevailing orderliness of his designs. His feeling for balance and his sense of artistic control give his buildings a calm and stable quality that was not always evident in his life.

Charles Murray House, 1878

536 Queens Avenue, London

Charles Murray moved to London in 1874 as manager of the London branch of the new Federal Bank of Canada.[99] Three and a half years later, Durand received two commissions, an office for the bank (fig. 96) and a house for its manager.

Underlying the plan of the Murray house is a common Italianate arrangement, where two wings form an L, with a tower tucked in the inner corner. Durand's design introduced some typical High Victorian variations. He made the protruding section of the L a full three storeys high, terminating in a steep decorated gable that competes with the tower as a dominant feature of the design. The recessed wing also asserts itself, pushing forward to form a large two-storey polygonal bay. The new design declares a sort of architectural democracy, wherein each section claims the right to free expression and equal notice.

There are strong signs of American influence in the crossbracing of the gable and in the strong verticality of the building. The latter quality was not quite as pronounced as in the original design. According to the specification, the bay was to have a flat roof, surmounted by iron cresting painted in 'ultra marine blue' and accented with 'gold leaf.' A narrow verandah, reached through a side door from the vestibule, was to sit in front of the bay. It is not clear when either the polygonal roof or the very attractive Eastlake porch (fig. 94) were added; the latter is still absent on an 1888 insurance map.[100]

The interior has the same quality of modernized traditionalism that one finds outside. Despite the projecting bays of its façade, the house has a nearly rectangular floor plan with a centre hall, an arrangement like that found in many of Robinson's buildings. The dining room was moved to the back wing, however, leaving the entire ground floor of the main block to the hall, parlour, and library. The interior architraves have mouldings very similar to those found in Robinson's Italianate houses, but they are or appear to be natural rather than painted, thus imparting some of the warm and comfortable atmosphere admired by the proponents of the Queen Anne style. Homeyness did not mean modesty, however. The front entrance was especially impressive. One passed through a vestibule with a vaulted ceiling into a hall where a stairwell, open to the roof, admitted the diffused glow from a stained-glass skylight. Wide elliptical arches led to the rooms on either side. Throughout the house the tall windows were set in elegantly panelled embrasures designed to hold folding shutters.

Though Charles Murray apparently meant his house to be a showpiece,

94   Charles Murray House, London, front door

95   Charles Murray House

the specification reveals that he was well aware of the cost of luxury, and he quite frequently settled for a cheaper material – for grained pine rather than real chestnut trim, for example. Murray eventually was to let his ambition get the better of his financial prudence.

By 1886 Murray, no longer connected with the Federal Bank, was devoting his full-time attention to the Ontario Investment Association, with which he had been involved for several years. On 11 October 1887, at a general meeting of the shareholders, a detailed auditor's report was presented which, the *Advertiser* reported, 'showed the institution to be a total wreck,' with a mere $18,788 left after liabilities were met, of the '$724,247.96 paid in by the shareholders.' Charles Murray was discovered to have loaned himself $116,373 of which only about $30,000 could be recovered. He and his fellow conspirators had been masterminding fraudulent schemes for some time. In 1882 the Ontario Investment Association had loaned $332,929.08 to the non-existent London Stock, Debenture and Investment Company, of which Murray was the supposed president.[101] By the time these revelations became public, Murray was living in Omaha, Nebraska.[102] His London house still retains the traces of its meteoric first owner: Murray's initials are prominently incised in the keystone over the front door (fig. 94).

Federal Bank of Canada, 1878–9

North-east corner Dundas and Richmond streets, London (demolished)

The Federal Bank of Canada was incorporated in 1872 under management that an historian of Canadian banking has described as 'enterprising, ambitious and inclined somewhat to scoff at the policies pursued by other and older concerns.'[103] In September 1876, during its initial period of success, the bank opened a London branch at the north-east corner of Richmond and Dundas streets. Two years later the bank invested $35,000 in buying the site and immediately made plans to tear down the old structure in order to erect their own 'modern style of building.'[104] The *Advertiser* suggests a confluence of the architect's esthetic ambition and the bank's mercantile goals: 'Aside from the idea of the architect to erect a building that would be a credit to the city ... was that of giving the requisite accommodation for an institution doing such a rapidly increasing business as the Federal Bank.'[105]

Leaning against the modern building in the architectural drawing is a figure in distinctly old-fashioned dress. His measuring rod identifies him with the architect; his medieval garb links him with the traditional craftsman whose style of work meant so much to the contemporary Queen Anne movement. His presence in the drawing hints at Durand's perception of his own role, that of an artist craftsman, and at his concept of the building's style. The red-brick walls, 'free classic' details, and flowers in the lintels suggest that the building represents Durand's version of the English Queen Anne mode. If the measurer's jaunty air is a fair indication, he was well pleased with his achievement.

Though he may have been indebted to the English past for the general style of his building, Durand seems to have used a recent American building as a model for some of its particular features. The original design of William LeBaron Jenney's controversial Portland Block in Chicago had the same canted bay at the corner of the building, very similar dormers on the mansard roof, and an almost identical main door.[106] However, whereas the Chicago block is decisively High Victorian Gothic in style, with polychromy and pointed arches, in Durand's design the Gothic elements are clearly subordinated to classical details. Giant pilasters appear to support the stylized arches that wave above the top storey. The frieze is free Doric, though Gothic quatrefoils peer above the metopes. Palmettes adorn the cresting and the brackets.

The building's interior was at least as complex as its exterior, and its materials as elaborate. The *Advertiser* explained that the building was arranged 'on the American plan, the main flat raised, with stores and offices beneath'; one of these was to be occupied by the Canadian Savings and Loan Company. The third level was to be 'handsomely fitted up' for solicitor's offices.[107] The main floor constituted the lavish premises of the Federal Bank. Its floors

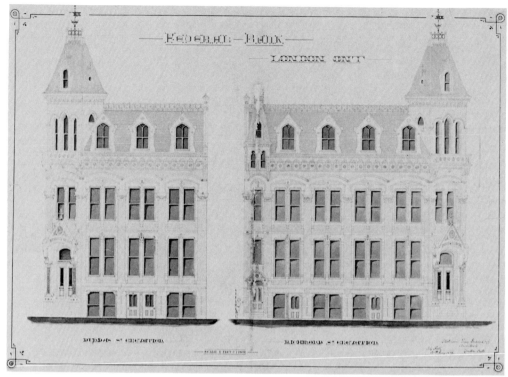

96   Federal Bank of Canada, London, architectural drawing showing Dundas Street and Richmond Street elevations

were of alternating black walnut and maple boards. The counters, tellers' boxes, and wainscotting combined cherry, ash, red oak, black walnut, and butternut, all given a natural finish. The architraves of the doors featured 'veneered french walnut columns.' The plaster ceiling was to be given a 'fresco decoration' throughout.[108]

The richness of its decor undoubtedly helped the Federal Bank to project a suitably prosperous image, but the image became increasingly deceptive in the following decade. It would be tempting to suspect that Charles Murray played some part in the bank's troubles, given his financial record elsewhere, were it not for the fact that these problems can be traced to political decisions taken at the head office. One of the bank's unorthodox practices was to inflate its stock's value through the manipulation of subsidiary companies. This device, combined with some risky speculations in commodities, brought the bank into serious difficulties in 1884 and again in 1887. On both occasions, it was bailed out by other banks, but the second rescue was limited to paying off debts, and was conditional on the bank's closing.[109] Thus the Federal Bank became one of several banks that failed during the last two decades of the century. Most collapsed, according to one authority, because of inadequate banking regulations rather than 'individual moral depravity' though 'there was certainly no lack of that.'[110]

In about 1888 the Federal Bank building was sold to a more successful competitor, the Canadian Bank of Commerce. That institution eventually followed the example of the Federal Bank in demolishing an inherited building to make way for its own architectural symbol.[111]

St George's Church (Anglican), 1879–81
Walton (demolished)

The village of Walton lies about forty-five miles north of London and twenty miles inland from Lake Huron, in the middle of the farmland of Huron County. When St George's Church was built, Walton also possessed a post office, a telegraph office, two hotels, two stores, a saw-mill, a Presbyterian church, and approximately 140 residents.[112] The building of the Anglican church was perceived as such an important regional project that the cornerstone-laying ceremony attracted flocks of speakers and spectators from miles around. Anglican ministers from Blyth, Clinton, and Brussels and the two Presbyterian ministers from Walton were among the speakers. The cornerstone, containing various church records and 'a number of the different coins then in use,' was laid with 'a very neat silver trowel' by the Orange Grand Master of Ontario. Following the ceremony about 600 people moved on to a dinner in John Hewitt's orchard, where tables were set 'with all the delicacies and substantials of the season.'[113] After this auspicious occasion, the community was greatly shocked two months later when the cornerstone was smashed and its contents stolen.[114] Despite the loss of its cornerstone, the church was completed by May 1881.

The very handsome perspective drawing of the church places it in a more urban environment, with wide sidewalks and elegantly dressed residents. It is an appropriate setting, for the design of St George's church is very sophisticated, involving a rather witty play on High Victorian conventions of Anglican parish church design. The western end is emphatically asymmetrical with one bay entirely missing. The idea that parishioners should enter through the porch is emphasized by a porch entranceway that is very large in proportion to the rest of the church and by the placement of the belfry over the porch instead of in its usual position at the east or west end of the nave. The very irregular plan, with its shifting wall planes and rooflines, takes the idea of convenience to an extreme. And the unusual brickwork elaborates on the concept of constructional truth, experimenting with the various designs that can result from different ways of arranging the bricks. The large pointed arch over the main door is relatively conventional, with wedge-shaped bricks positioned, like voussoirs, in a fan shape. Above that, however, the pointed gable is outlined by bichromatic courses that require trapezoidal bricks.

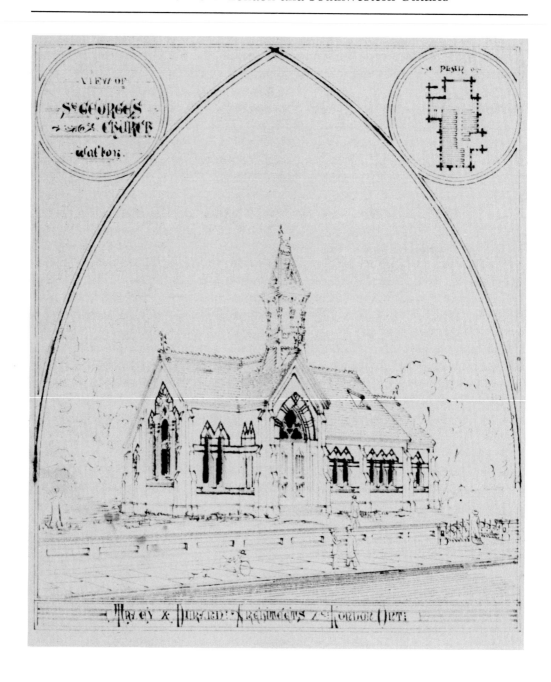

97   St George's Church, Walton, architectural perspective drawing

The standard rectangular bricks have been used around the other windows; their regular shapes form lines, not curves, so that the window openings are pointed rather than arched, and the upper line of the bichromatic brickwork seems to leap rather than glide around the church. Below the courses of red brick the windows are chamfered, appearing to open out into the less congested expanse of white brick.

For all its daring exaggeration the building possesses little of the tension often found in the period's buildings. Its exuberance is controlled by the evident concern with unity and balance. When seen directly from the west end, for example, the high porch and belfry on the south were perfectly countered by the northern bay of the nave and the nearly identical bay of the transept.

Although the perspective drawing is signed 'Tracy and Durand,' Tracy may well have been responsible for the original plans. They were accepted by the Synod in December of 1879,[115] at a time when there is no proof that Durand was working with Tracy.

Either the Anglican Synod failed to appreciate sufficiently its architectural gem, or the church authorities loved it too much. In the early 1960s, after the Anglican congregation in Walton dwindled away, the Synod refused to sell the building for less than $3,000, a price beyond the means of interested Mennonites. So, according to one Walton resident who remembers the scene, wreckers 'bulldozed under, glass and all,' possibly the most interesting parish church in south-western Ontario.[116]

Palmyra Baptist Church, 1880–1
Palmyra (dismantled)

The Baptist Church in Palmyra, a small village south-west of Chatham, could trace its history back to 1836, when meetings were held in the home of John Eberlee, one of the earliest settlers on the Talbot Road. As the congregation steadily expanded, it graduated to a schoolhouse and then, in 1881, to a surprisingly elaborate church (fig. 98). Local historians are rather vague as to the means and preparations for building the church. It seems that the Honourable David Mills, then minister of justice for Ontario and a native of Palmyra, was largely responsible for the idea and contributed generously towards the cost of the structure. It was probably through his influence that plans were procured from Tracy and Durand (fig. 99), or, as their names were mangled in church records, Racey and Durconal.[117]

   The terrain around Palmyra is relatively flat; the broad, low lines of the church harmonized with the surrounding landscape. It was a very dignified little church, with a rose window, tower, and dormers such as one might expect in a much larger edifice, though both the tower and porch in fact formed corners of the broad rectangular auditorium. It possessed several features typical of

98   Palmyra Baptist Church

99   Palmyra Baptist Church, detail of architectural drawing showing front elevation; drawing signed 'Tracy & Durand'

100   Palmyra Baptist Church, main entrance

High Victorian Gothic churches, such as the bichromatic effects, with white accents on the local red brickwork, and the gingerbread trim, but Tracy and Durand broke with tradition in substituting round-headed Norman or Romanesque windows for the pointed Gothic shape. Other aspects of the design for the church elaborate this round form. The round-headed apertures of the main façade and tower are extended into full circles, echoed in the bull's-eyes of the façade. The other main design elements are trefoils and quatrefoils, both composed of circles, found in the window tracery (fig. 100) and the barge-boards; even the blooms of the pierced flowers are quatrefoils.

    The church flourished for half a century, with capacity crowds attending services twice each Sunday, but 1937 church historian Joseph McDermott saw his community being eroded by 'the change in agricultural methods and the growth of cities': 'Though Kent County is the richest of farming communities and Palmyra lies in the county's most ideal spot, even here the population is not as numerous as in those good old days.'[118] Services in the church were discontinued in 1956. In 1985 the building was disassembled and transported to Whitby, where it is to be reconstructed and become part of a 'Christian heritage park of pioneer churches.'[119]

Masonic Temple and Grand Opera House, 1880–1

North-west corner Richmond and King streets, London (demolished)

The 1881 Masonic Temple represented the grand climax to a long series of Masonic meeting places, most of a much humbler character. Gatherings were held in London on a regular basis as early as 1829, and the Masons maintained a small but stable organization in the 1830s and 1840s. One 'most devoted Mason' provided his hotel's dining room as a makeshift meeting hall: 'with the Lodge furniture in his house, he felt as though he were living in a church.' This accommodation was probably superior to the garret of Robinson Hall, the 1847 gathering place: 'it was simply an attic with a floor ... [that] would sometimes wave up and down like a sheet of water.' During the 1850s there was what a *Free Press* report termed a 'boom in Masonry,' with the founding of three new lodges in the decade. Meeting spaces could now be rented in various commercial blocks. A significant advance was made in 1872 when the entire third floor of the new Huron and Erie building was especially outfitted as a meeting place for Masonic lodges. Very soon, the rapid growth of Freemasonry necessitated more ambitious plans.[120] The movement had come to play a very important social role in the London of the period. Most of the city's leading citizens were Masons, and virtually no public event – the opening of a church, a funeral, a cornerstone-laying ceremony – was complete without 'Masonic honours.'

Both its size and its dignity made the new Masonic Temple an appropriate home for such a prominent organization. The Second Empire style conveyed a feeling of impressiveness, and the building filled a large corner site (142 by 110 feet) on one of the city's main intersections. Most of the structure was not in fact devoted to providing Masonic quarters. There was space for several stores and offices, and the entire western portion of the building was given over to a three-storey opera house. The Masonic rooms occupied only the third and fourth storeys of the eastern end. That area was spacious enough, however, for a banqueting hall, a drill hall for the Knights Templar, and many meeting rooms, all decorated with 'carpeting and draperies ... purchased in foreign markets, and made up specially for the Temple.'[121]

The ten-foot wide main entrance on the Richmond Street side clearly demonstrated its purpose by the Masonic emblems carved on its pediment.[122] The original drawings show a relatively formal plan for the Richmond Street façade, with pilasters of various orders and elaborate lintels and pediments over the windows. As built, however, it more closely resembled the King Street façade, though its elements were more rigidly arranged and a large convex tower graced the central section. While the Richmond Street façade was

101   Masonic Temple and Grand Opera House, London, detail of architectural drawing showing King Street elevation; drawing signed 'Tracy & Durand'

meant to reflect the dignity of the Masons, the King Street façade belonged to the Grand Opera House. The architectural drawing (fig. 101) shows one of the Muses hovering lightly on the pommel of the central tower, while assorted musical nymphs add glamour to the iron railing of the balcony that leads off the theatre lobby. The Opera House has two entrances of its own, 'thoughtfully arranged,' according to the *Free Press*, so that 'those going to the galleries will not come in contact with the ladies and gentlemen who take seats on the lower floor.'[123] This side of the building possesses a movement and fluidity that contrasts with the more static regularity of the main façade. Instead of lining up in perfectly straight columns, the windows take on different configurations on different floors. The corner pavilion, for example, contains four windows on the third floor, three on the second, and two on the first. There is nothing random about the arrangement. The three-window pattern is echoed elsewhere in the façade, and the similar lines of the first and third storeys provide a sense of equilibrium. But there is a fascinating sense of shifting and rearranging patterns here that accords with the dramatic asymmetry of the balcony, balanced by the heavy first floor of the opposite wing. Like its guardian Muse, the whole façade seems delicately poised, caught for the instant in an admirably graceful posture.

Numerous other decorative elements added to the impression of liveliness. The building material was mainly Hamilton pressed red brick, with stone and iron trim; a course of tiles bearing various Masonic emblems was custom made in Stoke-on-Trent.[124] A more generally comprehensible kind of symbolism attached to the low-relief carvings spaced at intervals between the second and third storeys. These portray masters of all the 'arts,' so broadly defined as to include most areas of human achievement. Representing music were Rossini and Handel; Shakespeare and Molière stood for the literary arts; Wren for architecture; Columbus and Cartier for 'Discovery'; and George Stephenson, who designed the first steam locomotive, and Benjamin Franklin for 'Engineering and Invention.' Three London residents found their way into this gallery of notables: politicians David Mills and Colonel F.B. Leys, and Nicholas Wilson, one-time headmaster of the Union School. Queen Victoria and her son Edward, then Prince of Wales and Grand Master of the Masonic Order in England, completed the group.[125]

A great deal of money and attention also was lavished on the inside of the building. A *Free Press* reporter described the Opera House as a 'perfect little palace' with its gilt and scarlet railings, its frescoed walls and ceilings, its magnificent gaslight chandelier and electric sidelights along the wall. Durand appeared particularly proud of the folding wood and iron seats which had hooks underneath to hold hats. The theatre was designed to please actors as well as audiences. A Detroit firm was hired to paint numerous scenes so that the theatre could meet the requirements of any dramatic situation. There was, for example, a 'ship-deck scene,' deemed useful by the reporter 'in case of a "Pinafore" being perpetrated.' The painter consistently looks for praise from the interviewer and gets irony instead:

'I would like to show you a rocky pass I have here, and likewise a Gothic chamber. What do you think of them?'

'They are perfectly lovely. That is the most delightful rocky pass I ever saw. A fellow would hardly hesitate being shot in it. I suppose this is the point from which the maiden all forlorn ... casts herself into the bottomless abyss below, all because they want her to marry the aged marquis against her will?'[126]

The repertoire of the London Grand Opera House was discussed earlier in this chapter.

Aware that the threat of fire was especially severe in theatres, the architects went to considerable lengths to make the building fireproof.[127] But their efforts proved futile when fire broke out in the bill-posting room in 1900, completely gutting the interior. The structure was rebuilt with an extra storey and a new interior, but it suffered a second fire in later years, and the entire building was demolished in 1968.[128] The bas-relief portraits alone survive, as part of the Spencer Clark Collection of Historic Architecture at the Guild Inn in Toronto.

The London Club, 1881–2

177 Queens Avenue, London

Men's clubs, where gentlemen could eat, drink, read, play cards with friends, and make useful social and political contacts, formed an important part of eighteenth and nineteenth century British social life. Such institutions naturally arose in Canadian towns as well: the Toronto Club was established as early as 1835.[129] The gentlemen of the new London seem to have been curiously slow in following the international trend: the *Advertiser* observed in 1873 that an attempt to form a 'London Club,' under the leadership of Colonel John Walker, had not met with much success,[130] and the floundering club finally came to an end when the steward absconded with its funds.[131] Later efforts had more lasting results. The club became incorporated in 1880; its 1882 list of sixty-two members constituted the mercantile, professional, and political elite of the city. Capital was raised by selling shares, at $50 each, to members; using this method, $20,000 was raised within a year.[132] The club retains an influential place in London today.

Himself a member of the club, Durand appears to have been responsible for the design of its premises. It is hard to understand the *Free Press*'s description of the building as 'Gothic,'[133] except perhaps on the grounds of its polychromy: it was constructed of the local white brick with stone and red-brick trim. Otherwise, its details are mainly classical in character, very freely interpreted in the Queen Anne manner. The keystone of the arch over the main doorway (fig. 105), for example, takes the form of a giant bracket, supporting a pedestal that breaks the pediment above. The dentils, which appear on the dormers and the bay windows as well as the front entryway, are rather unexpectedly echoed in the design of the arch, by the chamfering of every other brick. As usual with Durand's façades, the imaginative parts are arranged into a carefully unified whole. Here, the pyramidal roofs over the end bays give the composition the character of a compressed pavilion plan and a certain French elegance as well.

Inside, the club had most of the comforts of a home away from home. Off the spacious ground floor hall (ten feet in width), large archways led to a smoking room on the left and a reading room on the right. The smoking room was evidently well used. A financial statement for May 1896 shows that members were paying more for the club's cigars ($389.18) than for its liquor ($244.15).[134] The reading room was evidently expected to receive as much attention, for it features an especially striking mantel (fig. 104). Instead of the marble or marble-like mantels found in the firm's earlier buildings, Durand has used the sort of elaborately carved wooden mantel that was thought to lend a 'cosy' touch to Queen Anne interiors. The dentils, volutes, and armorial shields all repeat prominent exterior details. Other equally interesting man-

102   The London Club, London, detail of architectural drawing showing front elevation

telpieces elsewhere in the building are less baronial in their imagery and
more typical of the period in their use of garden motifs.

   Behind the smoking and reading rooms on the first floor were a steward's
room, a reception room, and in the thirty-nine- by twenty-three foot rear
wing, a billiard room. The second storey contained sitting rooms, card rooms,
a small private dining room, and the main dining room. The kitchen,
servants' quarters, and six bedrooms for members were on the third floor.

   This impressive range of facilities initially cost the membership $9,204. It
took $30 more to provide a separate water closet for the servants, curiously
omitted the first time around. There were, however, more serious problems that
arose during the process of construction. George Elms, who had received
the contract for the brick and carpentry work, ran into various difficulties and
was eventually replaced by the firm of Wright and Durand, of which George's
brother Andrew was then a partner. Problems with the roof and with
drainage had to be solved after the building was ostensibly finished.[135]

103   The London Club

104   The London Club, reading room mantel and fender

105   The London Club, main entrance

It may have been the memory of these embarrassments that eventually led some members to take a seriously dim view of their club's architectural merits. 'Not even the most fanatically loyal member ... will claim for his clubhouse any degree of architectural beauty,' wrote historian Orlo Miller, in the club's 1954 official history. 'But the building is one of the Club's cherished traditions and the members love its ugly face.'[136] Possibly being cherished is better than being appreciated, for the London Club has very admirably preserved its underrated masterpiece. Except for the removal of some interior woodwork, the only significant change in the appearance of the original building is its colour. At some point in the club's history its vivid brickwork was painted a muted, monochromatic red.

Talbot Street Baptist Church, 1881–2
now First Christian Reformed Church, 513 Talbot Street, London

A Baptist congregation consisting of nine persons was formed in London in 1845. By 1850, when the membership had passed fifty, a chapel was built at the corner of York and Talbot streets. The late 1850s brought hard times to the young flock; 'a quarrelsome spirit was abroad in the church,' in the words of the Baptist *Reporter,* and a series of ill-suited pastors, given to drink or narcotics or eccentric views, created 'heavy troubles.'[137] The church managed to survive, and under the leadership of more constructive ministers after 1865 it grew to the point where a second congregation could be formed. Over time, the existing building still proved inadequate for an expanding congregation. The *Canadian Baptist* quoted a correspondent who had visited London in 1881: 'The Baptists are building a beautiful house of worship which will seat over 600 people. And they will fill it. God has blessed them with a continual revival for over two years ... And they are a live and aggressive people.'[138]

The new church was actually designed to hold 920 persons, 600 on the spacious main floor and 320 in the U-shaped gallery, supported by iron columns, that surrounded three sides of the hall.[139]

106   Talbot Street Baptist Church, London

107   Talbot Street Baptist Church, detail of architectural drawing showing front elevation

In keeping with evangelistic protestant tradition, the new church had a relatively broad hall. Durand has nevertheless followed his usual practice of dividing the façade into tall, narrow segments: the real width of the hall is disguised by the ambiguous relationship of the polygonal stair towers to the rest of the church. In fact, the side walls of the hall are approximately in line with the outer border of the side doors. The main part of the façade is, predictably, treated so as to emphasize its verticality: the slightly projecting central bay rises through a series of gradually narrowing steps from the broad central entranceway to the gabled bell-cote; the decorated windows are unusually lean. The buttressed pinnacles rise from the ground to terminate in spires. This verticality is effectively countered by the strong string courses and the horizontal rooflines of the polygonal side chambers.

The design of these stair towers make them an ingenious and remarkably

108   Talbot Street Baptist Church, upper part of main entrance

effective addition to the façade. Their shape is vaguely reminiscent of the chapels in the chevet of a French medieval cathedral, but here they have been moved from the apse to form side wings on the façade of a parish church. Their polygonal shape is echoed in the pinnacles; together, the pinnacles and towers give the church something of the massive, voluminous, satisfyingly solid quality associated with a Romanesque church, though none of the forms used here is specifically Romanesque in character.

Renovations around the turn of the century gave the interior an even more theatrical quality, with the addition of an elaborate iron railing around the gallery. Around the same time, the members of the congregation did their best to follow the developing fad for red brick by painting their bichromatic exterior in the single fashionable colour.[140] The Christian Reformed congregation that now owns the church has maintained it admirably. They have exposed the white brick with its red-brick accents. Unfortunately, they have also been forced to change the roofline. When the discovery of a problem with one of the main roof trusses resulted in the building of an entirely new roof, the original pinnacles and bell-cote were replaced by overhanging eaves.[141] Thus, the vertical elements of the façade now meet a rather abrupt termination.

Talbot Street Public School, 1881–2

South-east corner Talbot Street and Central Avenue, London (demolished)

St Peter's Roman Catholic Separate School, 1881–2

West side Clarence Street between Dufferin Avenue and Kent Street, London (demolished)

In 1865 London school principal J.B. Boyle worried that students were being pushed too hard, but he saw no way of correcting the problem because 'the voice of the parents is still in favour of more lessons.'[142] It is clear from his report and those of other officials that good educational programs were of great importance to the city and to many of its citizens. The Talbot Street School and St Peter's Separate School were both part of the substantial effort required to provide adequate facilities for the ever-growing numbers of London students.

One Peter Van Every had established a school near the London courthouse as early as 1827. His was the first of the many private schools that were to serve the city over the next forty years. By 1865, however, Superintendent Wilson could brag that 'there is scarcely a private school of any consequence to be found, all having been absorbed in the general [public] system.'[143]

That system had started in 1844, when the village had assumed control of one school in each of the four wards.[144] Five years later, however, the ward schools were abolished in favour of a central school, located on five landscaped acres between King, York, Colborne, and Burwell streets. The idea of the central school was gaining currency at the time; it allowed for graded classes, and could offer superior facilities and a broader curriculum.[145] However, the central school had a relatively short reign in London. Even before the Union School was built, ratepayers in St George's Ward, which stretched to the northern boundaries of the town, had complained that the Union School would be too far away, and in 1850 the town council voted money for St George's School. By 1855, boosted in part by a provincial ruling that allowed municipalities to levy school taxes and thereby provide free schools, the number of pupils rose to 1,823 from 600 five years before.[146] Numerous local schools sprang up to accommodate the extra numbers. A system evolved whereby students completed their early education at the ward schools and then attended more advanced classes at the Union School, as a bridge to the Grammar School or, later, the Collegiate Institute. A classical program, offering Latin, Greek, and French, was made available in the common schools after the mid-1850s. Though somewhat controversial, its existence was strongly defended by Superintendent Wilson in 1864: 'In a community like ours, where no advantage of birth or exclusive privilege obtains, and where

TALBOT STREET.

109   Talbot Street Public School, London, photograph, c. 1896

the way is open to the talented and aspiring, however humble their position, it becomes the duty of the patriot and the statesman to throw wide the portals of learning to all, and to give the means of making their talents available in the competition of life.'[147] The 1850s also marked the tentative beginnings of a separate school system in London, when the Religious of the Sacred Heart opened an Academy for girls, and the Dominican Father O'Brien established a school for Catholic boys.[148]

As city engineers, first Robinson and then Tracy had the responsibility for designing and overseeing the construction of the new schools. One of the first buildings for which Robinson is known to have been responsible was a frame schoolhouse on Talbot Street, built in 1858. Twenty-two years later, the *Free Press* felt no nostalgia when the building was razed to make way for the new brick school: 'the old chocolate coloured barn will not be missed by anyone.'[149]

Though the *Free Press* may not have noticed, there was likely a certain resemblance between the old and the new buildings, for Tracy and Durand were elaborating on what appears to have been the basic form of Robinson's schoolhouses: whether one or two storeys in height, they usually had symmetrical façades with a gable over a central projecting bay, and Gothic and Tudor details such as a finial and hood-moulds. Tracy and Durand built at least three other schools in the early 1880s that were almost identical to the Talbot Street School:[150] like Robinson's schoolhouses, all had a projecting

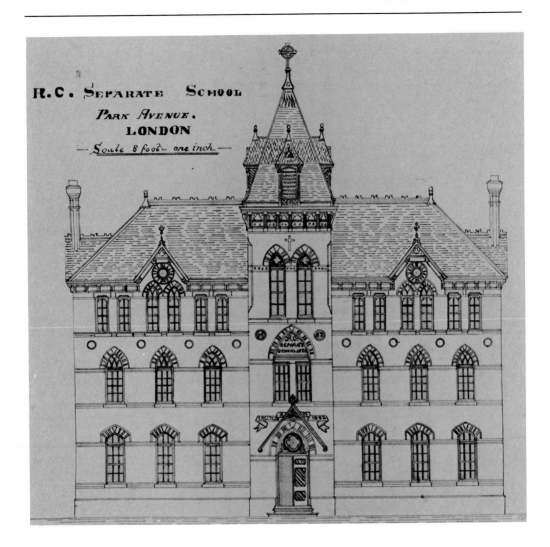

110   St Peter's Roman Catholic Separate School, London, detail of architectural drawing showing front elevation

central bay, and in each case, a basically classical plan was Gothicized, though the Gothic was now in the High Victorian mode. A variety of pointed and segmental arches crowned the windows; the frieze, window heads, and sill and lintel courses were bichromatic; the gable featured the decorative wood-work of the period. The most individualizing feature of these schools was their cupolas, each of an attractive and different pattern.

In 1892 the school was gutted by fire, and its 500 pupils were evacuated. When it was rebuilt, the original four rooms were increased to eight.[151] Classrooms – and classes – were large. Even the Simcoe Street School, built in 1889 as a model school, had classrooms designed to hold eighty students.[152]

Like the Talbot Street School, the new St Peter's School was replacing an old frame structure with the same name: the first St Peter's School had been established by Bishop Walsh soon after 1867.[153] The separate school was a more ambitious project than its secular counterparts. It was to be three storeys high, with a prominent tower instead of a mere gable, and with a wing at the back. Durand took advantage of these extra features to create a design that was more attractive than the firm's schoolhouse norm: its proportions seem less sprawling, and the busier third storey provides a pleasing crown for the rather ponderous levels below. Unfortunately, the Separate School Board decided not to erect the third storey, but the building's impressive tower, with its five-and-a-half-foot gilt cross at the top,[154] did provide an assertive symbol of the Separate School's role in London's educational system.

Oakwood, the Benjamin Cronyn Jr House, 1880–2

now part of Central Baptist Church, 602 Queens Avenue, London

As is often the case with home improvement plans, the additions Benjamin and Mary Cronyn contemplated for their North Street (now Queens Avenue) house became increasingly ambitious. The *Advertiser* reported on 10 November 1880 that Mr Benjamin Cronyn was erecting an addition and a stable for 'about $9,000.' On 3 August 1880 the *Free Press* described the new Cronyn residence as 'the most elaborate dwelling in the city,' finished at a cost of $25,000.

Both the timing and the lavishness of the new house suggest that it was financed by money that Mary Cronyn, born Goodhue, inherited from her father. Though George Goodhue's reputation as London's first millionaire exaggerates his wealth, he was London's richest citizen at the time of his death in 1870. Like each of her five siblings, Mary inherited approximately $130,000, but since Goodhue's will did not allow the children to claim their shares until after their mother's death, Mary took possession of her riches only in 1880.[155]

Benjamin Cronyn Jr brought a distinguished if less wealthy background to the marriage. His father, the first bishop of Huron, had placed his stamp on the Anglican church of south-western Ontario through his forceful personality and evangelical views. Benjamin Jr, a barrister like his brother Verschoyle, won early distinction himself in municipal politics. Elected an alderman in 1872 and 1873 (and chairman of the Finance Committee in the latter year), he then served two terms as mayor, in 1874 and 1875.[156]

The 1874 election campaign revealed the esteem in which he was held by his fellow-citizens. He was supported by the outgoing mayor, who criticized his opponent for having the effrontery to run against him: 'He ... thought it

111   Oakwood, the Benjamin Cronyn Jr House, London, photograph, c. 1896

was hardly becoming for Mr Campbell to enter the field when a man of Mr
Cronyn's position had been asked by representative men of both [political]
sides to fill the office.'[157] Cronyn's performance as mayor was so widely
approved that he gained a second term by acclamation. The *Advertiser*,
lukewarm towards Cronyn the previous year, was won over: 'It has
been admitted on all hands that he has fulfilled the duties of the position
admirably.'[158]

Oakwood, as the new Cronyn residence was named, was an ostentatious
but elegant structure, well suited to London's one-time head of state and
present social leader. The political context comes to mind because the Second
Empire style, as already noted, was often associated with political power,
and, though mansard roofs were placed on thousands of humbler structures,
the very size of Oakwood invites thoughts of officialdom. Nevertheless, there
is about the building a freedom and delicacy rarely found in government
buildings. The prominent garden façade almost seems to revel in its pronounced

irregularity. The strong sculptural effects and Baroque decoration usually featured in lavish Second Empire structures are here replaced by a consistently flat but varied surface: the stone course that runs above the windows is flush with the red-brick walls; the terra cotta panels are inset. The building gains its plasticity from the continual recession and advancement of the planes of the wall. This movement is emphasized by variations in the roofline, which, with its multiple chimney, dormers, heavy curb, and unusually high cresting, is markedly picturesque.

Oakwood is as interesting in its details as in its overall design. The interior panelling features exceptionally delicate moulding. On the outside, the Oakwood theme is developed in the intricately intertwined terra cotta oak leaves near the tower door, and in the branches that form Cronyn's initials on the front door. The naturalistic images are sometimes combined in rather unnatural ways. On the central terra cotta panel of the bay window, for example, fruits tumble out in profusion, not from the conventional cornucopias, but from the daffodil-like horns of two flowers. Despite its spaciousness (forty by sixty feet), Oakwood is so whimsical in its organization and decoration and its details are so finely wrought that the building has a somewhat fantastical, make-believe air, like a miniature palace, or a large dollhouse.

For Benjamin Cronyn Oakwood appears to have represented a taste for extravagance that was eventually to lead him into his own world of make-believe, and to cast a dark cloud over his reputation and his life. The auditor who in 1887 investigated Cronyn's neighbour, Charles Murray, for his fraudulent dealings in the Ontario Investment Association reported that the association's solicitors had also misused its funds. Cronyn and Greenlees had 'misapplied' $56,000 set aside to pay off certain loans, and, as the *Advertiser* summarized the matter, 'Mr B. Cronyn was personally lent $75,713.77 on security which will not realize the half.'[159] Like Murray, the Benjamin Cronyns took refuge from potential prosecution in the United States. Cronyn's relatives, particularly his brother Verschoyle, seem very honourably to have made restitution for his enormous debts. To the family's dismay, Benjamin eventually resumed his career of peculation in Burlington, Vermont, where he diverted an estimated $15,000 worth of insurance premiums and other funds entrusted to him.[160] Edward Cronyn, Verschoyle's son, observed, 'I think it must be in his [Benjamin's] case nothing short of a mania.' Benjamin himself, writing to thank his brother for his 'great kindness,' seemed sincerely distressed by the debacle: 'I am perfectly miserable and prostrate, and have not the least idea where to go to seek rest, which I feel cannot be found anywhere, for I am broken-hearted for all the trouble brought upon my dear wife, children, and relations.'[161] Benjamin returned to Toronto, but he never again resided in London.

Oakwood was purchased by manufacturer Frank Leonard, whose family lived there until about 1930, when it was bought by the Central Baptist Church.[162] Three sides of Oakwood are now hidden behind later additions, but the fourth side still provides a glimpse of the bishop's son's palace.

Waverley, the Charles Goodhue House, 1882–c. 1883

10 Grand Avenue, London

Waverley has always been something of a pastiche. Although Durand's imprint is stamped more clearly on its appearance than that of others who made contributions, the mansion is less a representative of one architect's skill than a symbol of the aspirations, or perhaps social ambitions, of several owners.

Like his sister Mary Cronyn, Charles Goodhue came into his inheritance in 1880, and, also like her, he immediately began to spend it on a transformation of his house. He had plans drawn in 1881 by Lieutenant Hamilton Tovey, the husband of another sister and a Royal Engineer in England. He then hired Tracy and Durand as local architects, and Durand gained Goodhue's approval for significant modifications.[163] Although Durand preserved the floor plans and the basic outlines of Tovey's design, he so thoroughly changed the detailing on the building that he gave it an entirely different quality. Thus, even in its 1882 form, Waverley combined two rather different architectural visions.

A comparison of Tovey's drawing (fig. 113) and the house as it was built in 1882 and 1883 pinpoints the exact nature of Durand's contribution to the design and indicates some of the differences between British and American esthetic principles. Tovey's design is in the British High Victorian tradition and emphasizes massiveness through simple, broad lines. His right bay, for example, shows a hipped roof and a pronounced string course between the two storeys; there is little other decoration. Durand replaced the hipped roof with a gable, complete with shingles, a decorative barge-board, and even turned posts. Below the gable there are bracketed eaves and decorative brickwork. Tovey's rows of three windows are replaced by pairs, the vertical lines of which emphasize the height of the bay. Similar developments occur elsewhere in the façade. The plain polygonal roof of Tovey's tower is broken into two flared tiers, with elaborately turned posts that form a balcony off the third-floor billiard room. Another balcony is placed over the vestibule, and Tovey's rather plain, cantilevered chimney is moulded and wedged into a second decorative gable. Whereas Tovey's design is relatively streamlined, with towers and chimneys reaching just to the roof ridge, Durand's roofline is purposely broken to create a picturesque composition. Where Tovey groups elements so as to leave free expanses of wall, Durand scatters details to fill in the unoccupied spaces. Tovey emphasizes breadth; Durand height. Tovey's building is solid and comfortable; Durand's is light and festive.

Since Tovey provided no sections, it is difficult to know just what he envisaged by way of interior fittings, but most of the lush original decoration – the drawing room fireplace, the architraves and spindlework of the main

112   Waverley, the Charles Goodhue House, London

113   Lieutenant Hamilton Tovey's design for Waverley, 1881

114   Waverley: LEFT, towers; RIGHT, cap of main staircase newel-post

doorways, much of the intricate panelling, the stairs with the beautifully carved newel post (fig. 114, RIGHT) that once held a lamp – seems of a piece with Durand's designs elsewhere. The use of the sunflower as a unifying motif throughout the house also seems to be his.

Charles Goodhue called his residence Waverley, after his father's house, Waverley Hall, in a less fashionable location on Bathurst Street. But he imitated his father in little else. George Goodhue, London's first merchant, had parlayed the art of bartering into a variety of substantial businesses. Later, he increased the fortune he had made as an entrepreneur by operating as a money-lender, often at exorbitant rates. A present-day historian has observed that the mourning for his death was 'muted.'[164]

His son seems to have been well liked. An obituary notice observes that 'he was universally respected and esteemed for his many excellent traits of character.'[165] But these do not seem to have included either ambition or drive. Although he trained as a barrister, there is little evidence that he often applied his skills. In an era when most of London's prominent citizens invested their money and hopes in numerous business enterprises, Charles Goodhue's contributions to London life seem to have been exclusively social. He was a Mason (Master of the Tuscan Lodge in 1879) and one of the nine founders of the London Club.[166] When he died in 1890, at the age of fifty-three, he had $64,500 left of his $130,000 inheritance to pass on to his wife and two children.

115   Waverley, dining room mantel

After Charles Goodhue's death, Waverley was purchased by Thomas Henry Smallman, a businessman whose talents had more in common with George Goodhue's. He prospered through investments in the rising oil industry of south-western Ontario, and when American oil began to threaten the market, he was instrumental in organizing a group of local refiners into the Imperial Oil Company. He was also an early director of the London Life Insurance Company.[167]

Waverley was plush, but not as large as some of the neighbouring houses. The Smallmans remedied this defect by adding a large wing at the rear of the house, designed by Moore and Henry. The additions and alterations involved a complete reorientation of the building, and the results merited an illustration in the *Canadian Architect and Builder* (June 1898; fig. 21). A picturesque bridge over the Traction Creek led to the new front of the house, formerly the side, where one entered a hall made by extending the old study. A huge mantel with classical details nearly filled one wall; the dining room mantel (fig. 115) also likely dates from this series of alterations. An enormous drawing room / ballroom then led off to the left, with an equally oversized master bedroom above. From outside, the new wing was integrated with the body of the house by the imaginative elaboration of Durand's motifs. Durand's double-tiered tower roof, for example, is echoed and enlarged in the massive turret over the new square bay, while two smaller attached turrets reconcile the square and polygonal forms (figs 21 and 114A). The porte-cochère was added at the same time – according to report, because Mr Smallman so admired the porte-cochère of John Labatt's house (fig. 116).[168]

The Smallmans' daughter and her husband, Eleanor and Claude Kyd Morgan, made their impact on the building by adding parquet floors and carved wooden ceilings.[169] The conservatory and the round porch are also twentieth-century additions.

The Shute Institute, which owned the mansion for nearly forty years, did an admirable job of preserving the traces of Waverley's affluent past. The house is now being changed again, in preparation for its use as a retirement home, and it is hoped that the new additions will not detract from the extraordinarily interesting historical montage.

Endiang, the John Labatt House, 1882–4

572 Queens Avenue, London (demolished)

John Labatt chose as the site for his new house grounds located adjacent to Oakwood. Unlike the Cronyn and Goodhue houses, however, John Labatt's $25,000 mansion[170] was financed by its owner's earnings.

John Labatt was the fourth son of John Kinder Labatt, who had founded the family brewery. After studying the art of brewing with an English master in West Virginia, John Jr brought his knowledge back to Ontario and worked at his brothers' brewery in Prescott until his father's death in 1866. J.K. Labatt's will stipulated that John be given the first chance to buy the London operation should his wife wish to sell. For two years John and his mother ran the brewery together; in 1868 John purchased it for himself. Though his enterprise suffered a substantial setback with the fire of 1874, and the factory was rebuilt (see fig. 59) only with the help of an uncle and a friend, the company flourished under John Labatt's leadership. By 1882 the business was valued at between $75,000 and $125,000, and he could afford to build Endiang.[171]

A reporter for the *Advertiser*, who visited the just completed house in April 1884 was particularly struck by its 'massiveness': 'Ascending the steps and entering the front door, the first thing that strikes any one is the massive elegance of the woodwork'; 'The visitor leaves with an indefinite idea of the massiveness of everything.'[172] The exterior view, preserved in Durand's exquisite watercolour, also makes one acutely aware of the building's massive dimensions. But the overall effect is lightened by the rather playful exaggeration of irregular elements (eg the bay window protruding from an already projecting bay) and by the delicacy and openness of some of the decoration. The front gable, for example, is recessed to form a balcony; the shapes of its posts and barge-board are repeated in the balcony of the corner gable, and, more surprisingly, in the dormer, equipped with its own miniature porch.

Fortunately, the reporter was not too awestruck to provide an admirably detailed account of the building's interior. Probably the most impressive area in the house was the twenty-foot-wide stair-hall, entered through the door from the porte-cochère. All the main downstairs rooms (entrance hall, stair-hall, reception room, drawing room, dining room, and library) had extensive wood panelling (mainly of oak and cherry), and most had frescoed ceilings. Much of the wood was elaborately carved with 'over 2,000 different designs,' appropriately placed. The carving above the dining room door represented 'flesh and fish': 'On the one side is a fish surrounded by water lilies, and on the other a hare among clover leaves.'

One of John Labatt's granddaughters still has fond memories of the house and gives an impression of what it was like to live in. French windows led

116   Endiang, the John Labatt House, London, architectural perspective drawing

from the drawing and dining rooms to a verandah on the east side from which one looked over the gardens to Oakwood. The third floor was mainly the domain of the men and the children. There was a billiard room and a den or smoking room, both with balconies, and it was understood that the men did their smoking up there. In general, she remembers the house as being wonderful for children, with the cow, sheep, and chickens in the coachhouse as added attractions. In fact, children must always have been strongly in evidence at Endiang, for John Labatt had three children by his first marriage and six by his second.[173]

John Labatt contributed to civic life by serving as an alderman in 1883 and sitting on the council of the London Board of Trade for several years. His business genius seems to have been focused on his brewery, since his ventures in other areas were mostly short-lived or unsuccessful. He left a personal estate of $289,606.96, most of which consisted of stock in the brewery, in addition to his house and land.[174] No remnant of the house now remains, massive and substantial though it seemed in its time.

Samuel Crawford House, 1882–3

514 Dundas Street, London

The house Durand designed for Samuel Crawford was considerably more modest, costing only $8,000,[175] than the Cronyn, Goodhue, and Labatt mansions, but it clearly represented a step upward for its owner. Until then Crawford had lived in a double house in the next block,[176] closer to the Globe Works, the foundry and agricultural implements factory that he had purchased around 1870. In 1881, however, he had sold the controlling interest in the company to his partners,[177] apparently with the intention of retiring. He was to return briefly to the plant, as manager, around 1883–4, after it became the North American Manufacturing Company under the leadership of Charles Deere, president of the John Deere Plow Company.[178] Otherwise, Crawford took advantage of his retirement to indulge other interests. He ran, successfully, for alderman in the 1882 election,[179] and in the same year he began making plans for a new and larger house.

His new house was in many ways conservative, with numerous typically Italianate features: the brackets under the eaves and the frieze with decorative mouldings; the simple sash windows, each with a separate stone lintel and keystone; the centre-hall plan; and even the rounded interior mouldings. But some of the Italianate features have been elaborated in a specifically High Victorian manner. There is a double system of bracketing, for example, with a row of small brackets running above the panelling, between the larger ones. The focal point of the house is the right bay, where the mansard roof tapers upwards to a pommelled dome, but this dramatic feature is effectively balanced by the intricate verandah and broad wing on the left. The Crawford house was quieter than, say, Oakwood, but it possessed a rather meditative dignity and grace of its own.

Crawford must have been impressed by George Durand, because he employed Durand in connection with various business enterprises before hiring him as the architect for his house. Durand's first job, on returning to London from the United States in 1877, had been at Crawford's Globe Works. In the following year Robinson, Tracy, and Durand designed Crawford's Block, located at the corner of Dundas and Adelaide streets, adjacent to the factory. In 1881 Tracy and Durand designed store fronts for buildings Crawford owned at 240 and 242 Dundas Street, and that same year Crawford hired his favourite architects to create a 'considerable addition' to the Globe Works. In 1885, after his own residence was completed, Crawford had Durand design two houses at the back of his property on North Street (fig. 131):[180] one was for Charles Crawford, presumably a relative.

Samuel Crawford did not have long to enjoy his expanding empire. After he died, in 1889 or 1890, his wife vacated the house, and it was purchased

117   Samuel Crawford House, London, photograph, c. 1896

by Thomas Beattie, a dry goods merchant who became president of the City Gas Company and served four terms as the Conservative MP for London. Much of the building's original elegance was lost when, in 1925, it was substantially altered in order to house several apartments, though its beautifully treed grounds, behind the original iron fence, still grant it an aura of graciousness.[181]

Stratford Pump House, 1882–3

now The Gallery Stratford, Stratford

'An eminent hydraulic engineer of London,' the Stratford *Beacon Weekly* told its readers on 25 August 1882, had devised an excellent plan for obtaining a reliable water supply from the river Avon.[182] Both local newspapers insisted that the town had long needed a public water system: it would lower insurance rates, attract industry, and diminish the threat of 'the typhoid and other fevers which have carried off so many valuable lives.' Because the town council had consistently blamed the tax burden for its lethargy in the matter, the newspapers were sympathetic when 'some of the heaviest ratepayers in Stratford' organized a private company to build a waterworks system and, as a first step, hired their own consultants.

The 'eminent hydraulic engineer' was John M. Moore. It is impressive that Moore, twenty-five years old and approximately four years beyond his apprenticeship, should have been so warmly endorsed. His 'clear and comprehensive' report proposed taking water from the drainage area of the Avon, filtering out impurities in settling basins, and then using duplicate steam engines to provide the necessary pressure. By October 1883 the *Beacon Weekly* was praising the 'splendid supply of pure, sparkling water [that] now courses through the pipes under the principal streets.'

Despite the newspapers' enthusiasm for the project, the Stratford Water Supply Company ran into some initial difficulties. Their records show that in May 1884 they were forced to have several signs erected along the Avon warning against washing sheep in the river. A more serious problem was the unexpected reluctance of the townspeople to subscribe to the new facility. An 1884 account lists only seventeen consumers in addition to the Grand Trunk Railway, which fortunately used prodigious amounts of water by itself. The council initially refused to pay for the use of the company's hydrants in case of fire. Things looked up in the second year, when there were fifty subscribers, and by 1903 the city was willing to pay $97,913.49 to make the water system a public utility.[183]

The Stratford Pump House would seem to be one of the architectural projects that Moore brought into Durand's office and carried out, at least in part, by himself. The building shows the influence of both of his masters. It uses the cottage model that Robinson had chosen for the London pump house and, more revealingly, it possesses the pilaster strips and corbelled cornice so characteristic of Robinson's work. These features are combined with the paired windows and polychromatic courses often employed by Durand. Although polychromatic effects were more frequently used on flat surfaces, the drawing showing the details of the brickwork (fig. 118) suggests that in this case the architect originally intended to exploit the various planes in

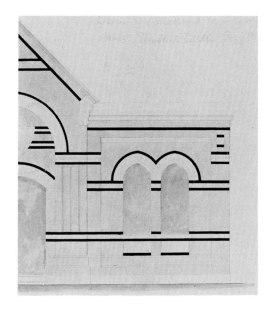

118   Stratford Pump House, detail of architectural drawing showing half of front elevation

119   Stratford Pump House, photograph, c. 1900

creating his distinctive polychromatic design. The drawing shows a more complicated brickwork pattern than the one actually implemented. The impost courses, for example, contain white bricks within the recessed panel and red bricks on the pilasters, and they come to an abrupt halt at the gable bay. As actually constructed, the building featured a bichromatic pattern (white with red trim rather than red with white and black accents) and more continuous lines that, though less ingenious, were also likely less cluttered in appearance.

The monumental entranceway also shows Durand's influence – in the wedge-shaped gable and the arch within an arch motif – and possibly his touch. The diagonal design of the brickwork between the arches echoes, in an interesting fashion, the diagonal boarding of the door. The vertical grooves to the side of the door effectively link the pump house to the smokestack, thus emphasizing the fact that this cottage was not designed for domesticity.

East London Town Hall, c. 1882–4

now Aeolian Hall, 795–7 Dundas Street, London

East London owed its beginnings in 1851 to one Murray Anderson, who built a house and a foundry, the latter subsequently purchased by Samuel Crawford, at the eastern city limits of London; these formed the nucleus of what became a highly industrialized suburb. During the oil boom of the 1860s numerous refineries sprang up along Adelaide Street, fuelling the town's growth. In 1874 East London was officially designated a village; seven years later it became a town[184] and began developing the facilities a town might be thought to require. Approximately $40,000 was spent on waterworks during 1882 and 1883. A site was purchased for the Town Hall,[185] and, as the datestones record, with an unusual concern for thoroughness, building was begun in September 1883 and finished in June 1884.

A year later Mayor Charles Lilley presented a bleak picture of the town's prospects: 'Refineries about all gone! Car Shops nearly all burned down! Free water and exemptions to other manufactories! Where will the revenue come from to keep up this independency?' The council was in serious financial straits. It could not complete the waterworks because the town could not sell the necessary debentures; it had borrowed money from other accounts to pay for the hall, which cost twice as much as its $7,000 estimate. Lilley strongly pushed amalgamation with London and he roundly criticized his predecessor for pursuing the more ambitious course: 'You do not want visionary men who build castles in the air,' he advised his constituents; 'they are generally very costly.'[186]

Lilley's advice apparently proved persuasive, for in 1885 the citizens of East London did vote for amalgamation, and its year-old Town Hall became redundant. It has nevertheless survived, serving a variety of functions ranging from firehall to cigar factory, and its upstairs auditorium has recently been refurbished as the Aeolian Hall, a well-equipped centre for musical performances.

The commission for the hall was probably obtained by Moore: it was he rather than Durand who signed the tender call.[187] As with the Stratford pump house, however, certain aspects of the design suggest that Durand participated to some extent in its creation, if only in an advisory capacity.

Like the Stratford building, the town hall relies on a familiar and conservative format: it has the central tower that was traditional for Canadian urban town halls,[188] the mansard roof thought essential for public buildings, and along the sides the alternating piers and Italianate windows that had constituted one of the firm's stock formulas in Robinson's time. The pattern is complicated on the sides, however, by the effective use of bichromatic brickwork, and it is very imaginatively elaborated on the façade. There, the segmental arches

120   East London Town Hall, London, architectural drawing showing half of front elevation and partial section

121   East London Town Hall

are expanded to encase large cast-iron and plate glass store windows, and the round-arched windows of the second floor become a unifying motif, appearing over the front door, in the dormers, in the top stage of the tower and in the second storey of each bay. Though the semi-circular window is used several times in the façade, there is interesting variety in both its tracery and its context. On the second floor, for example, a round-headed window featuring a common Italianate pattern of tracery is set between two rectangular windows to form a Palladian configuration.

With its intended spire, its tower, and the prominence given its long narrow windows, the East London Town Hall possessed the pronounced verticality typical of Durand's buildings of this period. This characteristic is ingeniously countered, in part, by the trapezoidal forms of the dormers, the datestones, and the ground-floor piers, which seem to anchor the structure to the ground. The resulting solidity of the building's appearance seems at odds with the ephemerality of its original purpose.

Guthrie Presbyterian Church, c. 1883–4

Melbourne

The first Presbyterian sermon preached in Melbourne, then Wendigo,[189] advised its listeners to 'Enlarge the place of thy tent' (Isaiah 5:42), but it took twelve years for the small group of Presbyterians in the town to get any kind of 'tent' at all. In 1870 they joined the Baptists and Methodists in erecting a 'Union Meeting House.' After another twelve years the Presbyterians could begin

122   Guthrie Presbyterian Church, Melbourne, detail of architectural drawing showing front elevation; drawing signed 'Geo. F. Durand'

123   Guthrie Presbyterian Church

considering a church of their own,[190] and in 1883 Durand reported that he was
working on plans for a Presbyterian church in Wendigo.[191]

Because the land around Melbourne, a village about twenty miles south-
west of London, is so flat, the town has no natural boundaries, and its
few streets seem to flow into the surrounding farmland. The setting proved
appropriate for Durand's most thorough development of the idea of the rustic
church. The overhanging eaves (of the porch, the main gable, and the bell-
cote) all have exposed purlins. The decorated barge-boards, whose pattern is
repeated in the bell-cote, dominate the façade, and the bell-cote has a purposely rough-hewn quality. Though the building is brick, it seems designed to
call attention to the technicalities of construction in wood: the purlins appear
to be extensions of the boards that carry the rafters; the decorative bracing
of the barge-boards hints at the system of beams and braces supporting
the roof; the bell-cote is a miniature timber frame structure on its own. The
wooden features are given especial emphasis by the relative plainness of the
brickwork. The only coloured accents in the built church were in the arches
over the windows, of a pale peach colour that just barely contrasts with the
white brick. The brick parts of the façade are enlivened not by surface decoration as much as by the use of interesting shapes: the centrepiece narrowing
in stages as it rises from the porch to the bell-cote, and the strikingly placed
oculi. The latter call attention to another wooden feature, the tracery, by

124   Guthrie Presbyterian Church, bell-cote

the use of a rather tantalizing pattern: the roundel contains a trefoil, which in turn contains a leaded quatrefoil.

It is perhaps rather disappointing to discover that the rustic theme is not carried into the church. There are some very interesting features there – the finely turned braces of the ceiling beams, the gilded iron ends of the pews – but they are striking partly for their very sophistication.

Melbourne has been particularly prone to fires over the course of its history,[192] and, for all its elaboration on the idea of wood, Guthrie Presbyterian Church has likely survived because it was brick. Except for the addition of a hall at the back, it still exists in very much its original form – even to the point of retaining its Presbyterian affiliation instead of joining the United Church.

Christ Church (Anglican), completed 1885
Delaware

Lieutenant-Governor Simcoe granted 2,000 acres in Delaware to one Ebenezer Allan in 1794, with the condition that Allan was to build saw- and grist-mills and a church. The mills were built promptly, but the church was still unfinished when the Reverend Richard Flood, a Church of Ireland priest, arrived around 1833. Under Flood's guidance, an Anglican church was finally erected in the village, though only seven people attended the first service. By 1844 the congregation had expanded to the extent that an addition was necessary. Interestingly, the addition included a very plain wooden crenellated tower, a Gothic frill on a simple classical structure.[193] The larger brick church that Durand designed in the early 1880s was arrayed in High Victorian Gothic dress, but it retained the conservative centre tower arrangement of its forebear, and, as in the case of the earlier church, its tower was its most prominent characteristic.

The new church possessed several of the rustic features found at Melbourne, such as overhanging eaves with exposed purlins and a decorated barge-board, but at Delaware they were given an entirely new context, as Durand developed various kinds of spatial effects. The roof is steeper and the eaves lower so that, seen from the side, the roof seems surprisingly massive. The top of the tower, from this view, appears correspondingly heavy. The tower looks quite different from the front, where one sees its narrow side and is mainly aware of its upward surge. The barge-board has an elastic appearance, as if it is being stretched by the aspiring tower. The interior benefits from the low walls in that the lower brackets and spandrels that support the roof beams create a more intimate air than exists in some of Durand's higher churches.

125 Christ Church, Delaware, detail of architectural drawing showing front elevation; drawing signed 'Geo. F. Durand'

126   Christ Church

127   Christ Church, window on south side

Durand's church was to seat 300 people and to cost $4,000, but the estimate proved over $1,000 too low and numerous sacred concerts and garden socials were staged over the following years to make up the difference.[194] Ironically, the larger membership that the church was built to accommodate soon dwindled; despite Delaware's early promise, the village watched nearby London flourish instead. The church now ministers to a congregation of about thirty-five families,[195] while the gravestones that surround it testify to its more populous past.

Moses Masuret House, c. 1883

East side Wellington Street between Dufferin Avenue and Wolfe Street, London (demolished)

John B. Laing House, c. 1884–5

East side Wellington Street between Dufferin Avenue and Wolfe Street, London (demolished)

Reviewing the 'great events' of the last decade, the *Free Press* gloated in 1882 about the development of the wholesale trade in London. There were now over thirty houses, the newspaper claimed, with travellers who 'send in orders from far away Winnipeg in the west and New Brunswick in the east.'[196] Prominent among the 'active, far-seeing men' who had given London an important place in Canadian commerce were John B. Laing and Moses Masuret. Laing was a pioneer in the wholesale trade, establishing his dry goods business in 1867. He also organized the London Chamber of Commerce, and served as its first president in 1875. Moses Masuret's wholesale grocery business was one of the many to get started in the 1870s. The *Advertiser* of 29 October 1888 was impressed with his comprehensive stock: 'teas, sugars, thousands of boxes of fruit, soap, starch and canned goods, hogsheads of syrups and vinegars, wooden ware such as matches, brooms and pails, spices, and, in fact, everything from everywhere which could properly come within the grocery line.' Masuret was the second vice-president of the Merchants' and Manufacturers' Exchange when it was organized in 1881, and in 1889 he was elected vice-president of the Board of Trade. He 'suitably replied,' as he accepted the latter post, joking about his ancestry in 'warning the members against French aggression.'[197]

The new houses that these men erected in the mid-1880s proved their prosperity: the cost of Laing's house escalated from $9,000 to $13,000 while in the course of construction.[198] The two buildings had much in common. Both were built on land across from Victoria Park that was just then being subdivided into fashionable building lots. Both used the same architect. Each had a traditional centre hall plan (fig. 130) that was unusual only in scale: the hall of the Laing house was ten feet four inches wide and thirteen feet six inches high. The formal make-up of the two façades is in many ways similar, showing that Victorian architects, like their descendants, were willing to build lavish houses on the same block that were almost identical. Each house features two gables with a dormer between; under each left gable is a two-storey square bay-window; under each right gable is a polygonal bay; over each centre door is a large window opening onto a balcony.

128 John B. Laing House, London, detail of architectural drawing showing front elevation; drawing signed 'Geo. F. Durand'

129 Moses Masuret House, London, detail of architectural drawing showing front elevation

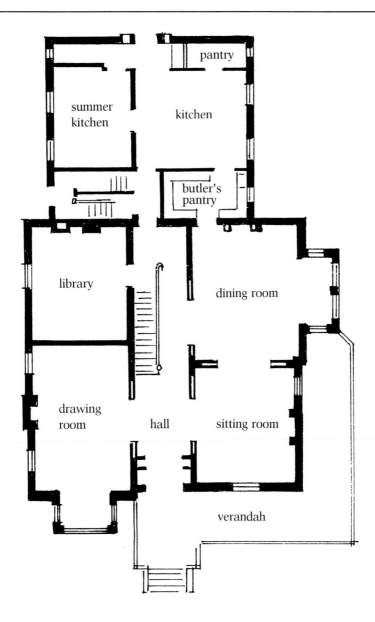

130   Moses Masuret House, ground floor plan adapted from original drawing

Despite their similarities, however, the houses make very different impressions. With its twin gables, the façade of the Laing house appears high and almost symmetrical. The more obvious asymmetry of the Masuret house makes it seem less austere, and its hooded dormer and balcony, along with the extended verandah, contribute to a false impression of greater breadth. Unlike some of their even wealthier contemporaries, both Laing and Masuret settled for local brick, but Masuret managed the rare feat of securing red brick from a North London brickyard.[199]

Laing lived in his mansion for only a year; it eventually became the YWCA. The Masuret family retained the house Moses built until the late 1940s when, like many other showpieces of the Victorian era, it was converted to apartments.[200] Both buildings were demolished in the late 1960s in order, ironically, to make way for a centennial project.

513 Queens Avenue, 1885–6
London

The house at 513 Queens Avenue was one of the two that Samuel Crawford had erected behind his house on Dundas Street (fig. 117). The other house, to the right, is a mirror image of its neighbour. With 'Gothic' features such as the decorated gable and the exceptionally bold bichromatic brickwork, they have little in common with Crawford's own dignified Second Empire residence.

Among the most interesting features of 513 Queens Avenue is the front gable, placed over a bay window in the currently fashionable manner. Here, the three divisions of the bay window are reflected in the design of the gable. The centre part seems to rise above the cornice and to terminate in a smaller decorated gable of its own. Where the bay slants back towards the wall, the sides of the larger gable appear to be supported by gracefully curved brackets; their incised woodwork is echoed in the panels directly above.

The purposeful irregularity of the gable is to some extent matched in the plan of the house. Except in his most elaborate mansions, Durand's previous houses, including those for Laing, Masuret, and Crawford, had projecting appendages or recessed bays that were too shallow to create more than a surface irregularity: behind the picturesque façade, one found the conventional centre- or side-hall plans that had descended from classical designs. The house at 513 Queens Avenue does not altogether conform to this tradition. One enters into a long stair-hall, with what were originally drawing and dining rooms to one's right and a kitchen wing to the rear of the latter. But behind the stairway, to the left in the photograph (fig. 131), is a small chamber that must have been designed as a study or a sitting room. This arrangement signals the advent in the firm's work of the more picturesque and irregular floor plans lauded in the Queen Anne house.

The house at 513 Queens Avenue was rented to Robert Larmour, his wife, and their five children.[201] Larmour was an assistant superintendent of the Grand Trunk Railroad who had been transferred to London after spending two decades in Stratford.[202] Samuel Crawford's just-completed house must have provided the Larmours with a cheerful welcome to their new city.

131   513 Queens Avenue, London

132   513 Queens Avenue, brackets above canted bay

Henry Dunn House, 1885

195 Elmwood Avenue, London

Henry Dunn immigrated from England in the late 1850s and, according to his obituary, became 'one of the earliest settlers in South London.' Though his employment, first as a labourer at Labatt's brewery and then as a teamster for Saunby's flour mill, would seem unlikely to make a man rich, he managed to purchase two acres of land on the south-west corner of Queen and James streets (now Ridout Street and Elmwood Avenue).[203] He lived on Queen Street, and in 1885 he built a $3,000 house around the corner on James Street for his daughter Elizabeth, a high-fashion seamstress.[204]

The basic design of the new house was descended from an Italianate form that had been popular in London for years. The older versions had a hipped roof, three front bays, and a side-hall plan. Later, it had become fashionable to add a small gable over the centre bay, and the firm was responsible for several houses of this type during the late 1870s and early 1880s. By 1885, however, Durand's stylistic predilections were clearly for more ornate and eclectic forms, and it seems probable that he designed the Dunn house as he did at his client's request. Henry Dunn's own residence at what is now 141 Ridout Street[205] was of the earlier type, without a gable, and either he or his daughter likely wanted the new house to be similar to the old.

The Dunn house on Elmwood Avenue is as refined as Durand's other versions of the type. The centre bay of the façade is characteristically built out into a projecting frontispiece, and the exterior details are pleasingly designed. The cross-patterned brickwork of the frieze, for example, imparts an interesting sense of texture to the otherwise smooth walls. On the side of the house the small window beneath the stairs (fig. 135) is given a corbelled round-headed arch to blend with the arch of the more elaborate window above. Some features, such as the front door that folds in to make a panelled wall in hot weather, link the house with Durand's more contemporary work.

There are more signs inside than out of the building's late date. Mixed with the many traditional Italianate features (such as the marble mantel, the deep cove and rounded mouldings of the cornice, and the hall arch) are various kinds of up-to-date woodwork. The mouldings of the inner doors (to the right in the drawing), the stair banisters, and the very elegant newel post all have a distinctly Eastlake character.

Houses as built often deviated in some respects from architects' drawings, but the changes here are rather curious. The frontispiece has been widened, and the correspondingly wider gable contains an elliptical rather than a semicircular arch. This is attractive enough, but the windows of the left-hand bay have not been moved accordingly; it was apparently decided to retain the symmetry of the drawing room while sacrificing the symmetry of the façade.

133   Henry Dunn House, London, detail of architectural drawing showing front
elevation

134   Henry Dunn House

135   Henry Dunn House, window on west side

One doubts that Durand supervised the construction.

Elizabeth Dunn eventually occupied the house her father had intended for her, but it took her thirty-five years to round the corner from what was by then Ridout Street. When her father died in 1898, 'Miss Lizzie' was residing 'at home,' and the Elmwood Street house was being rented. She went on living with her mother and brother until 1904 when, at nearly fifty years of age, she married Walter Orman and moved to his Byron farm. Five or six years later she was back at 141 Ridout, while her husband worked as a city carpenter. He died in 1920, the year that Lizzie finally became the mistress of 191 Elmwood, at the age of sixty-four. There she stayed, until her death in 1944.[206]

Perth County Buildings, 1885–7
Stratford

The substantial, exuberant, and expensive courthouse that Durand designed for Perth County in 1885 represented a dramatic turnabout in the county's attitude towards its official buildings. For the first thirty-five years of its existence the Perth County Council exhibited a remarkably mulish attitude towards providing adequate facilities for the enactment of the county's business. In 1850 the county council chose not to erect any buildings at all, only to discover that the county could not claim its official status or levy taxes until it had a courthouse and jail. The building then put up was meant to be cheap and utilitarian, but its usefulness was called into question as soon as it was opened.[207] County officials complained that their offices were more cramped than the jail cells; judges deplored the fact that the courtroom could not be properly ventilated.[208] The council ignored the provincial government's 1871 order to replace the jail, but when Chief Justice Adam Wilson refused to sit in the stuffy and odorous courtroom in 1884, council at last had to take notice. Even then, it petitioned the province for the right to use the old building for three more years. The request was denied.[209]

Once it was clear that new buildings were inevitable, however, the council determined not to repeat the former error of providing a poorly designed and makeshift building. The committee on county property promptly wrote Provincial Architect Kivas Tully and Prison Inspector Dr O'Reilly asking for recommended designs. The provincial authorities did not deal in ready-made plans, but suggestions were made as to appropriate models. By the end of January a substantial party of nine had visited the courthouse and jails of Dufferin and Peel counties. The delegation was composed of demanding if not discerning critics, as the committee's report on the Dufferin courthouse makes clear: 'the outside appearance is fairly good, but not commanding; the building is erected on low descending ground, and sunk too low in the ground; there seems too much ginger bread work upon it and its speckled appearance and short dumpy windows mar its effect; the roof is too much broken to be lasting.' The Peel County courtroom was 'gloomy and ill lighted.' The committee recommended 'that a competent and reliable architect be engaged to draw plans' for Perth County Buildings that could cost as much as $40,000.[210]

George Durand was appointed the architect in March, and by the middle of May he had completed plans for a new courthouse that was to take advantage of its commanding site, to have a relatively simple roofline, and to feature extraordinarily long and stately windows that would flood the cheerful courtroom with light. Though Durand's design clearly met many of the council's demands, the cost far exceeded their original guidelines, amounting eventually to $95,207.54.[211]

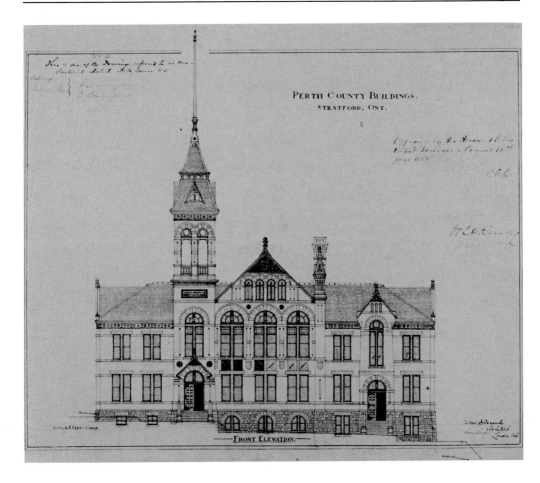

136   Perth County Building, Stratford, architectural drawing showing front elevation

The magnificent new structure was situated at the end of Ontario Street, where its striking façade would be seen by anyone approaching Stratford along the main road from the east; so carefully is the building sited in relation to Ontario Street that its two main entrances are directly aligned with the sidewalks. Seen from the front, the building's tall, bold windows, its tower, and its daring use of colour make it arrestingly dramatic. The building is of the local buff-coloured brick, accented by materials in various shades of reddish brown – plum-coloured Credit Valley stone, terra cotta, and wood painted now, as it was originally, in a vermilion red to which purple has been added[212] – that fall just short of clashing.

The courthouse stands on uneven ground, where the land slopes down to the river Avon, and Durand has effectively exploited its location in a second way by making a virtue out of the necessarily high foundation at the building's northern end. Of purplish brown, markedly rusticated stone, it has a massive, rugged Richardsonian character, intensified by the broad arches of the centre section. It is this heavy, prominent foundation that most effectively

137   Perth County Building

138   Perth County Building, centre section

139   Perth County Building, terra cotta head representing agriculture

140   Perth County Building, courtroom

balances the height and mass of the tower on the southern part of the building.

The principles of balance are easily detected in the Perth County Courthouse, owing to the fundamental regularity of its design. There is an underlying symmetry, despite the tower, pinnacle, and gable that interrupt it. The feeling of orderliness is further emphasized by the even rows of windows. The discipline, strength, and dignity of the courthouse make it a fitting symbol of the forces of law and justice.

One need not rely on the arcane symbolism of architectural form to recognize the building's function, however: the prominent terra cotta panels and medallions display more overt symbols. At the apex of the main gable, for example, the stern figure of justice stands between her sword and scales. Not far below, in the spandrels between the three great windows, are two amiable-looking ladies, conveniently labelled as manufacturing and agriculture (fig. 139), respectively. Six panels arranged along the courses between the first and second storeys depict symbols of justice in the centre two panels, with items representing art, science, agriculture, and architecture to the left and right. Other symbols of justice and Perth County appear elsewhere on the building.

Durand's part in designing these ornaments is difficult to define very precisely. They were apparently made by the Terra Cotta Company of Terra Cotta, Ontario, which did make designs to architects' specifications.[213] Durand habitually took considerable care over the particulars of his buildings' decorations: in this instance, his drawings for some of the courtroom furniture (fig. 140) still exist, as well as a detail of some of the interior woodwork.[214] As already indicated in chapter 2, the roundels above the doors seem to have been influenced by an illustration in Durand's possession. One H. Plaffehaeit has signed at least two of the terra cotta plaques,[215] however, thus asserting his claim for a part in their creation. Presumably he made the moulds in which they were cast and gave the two-dimensional sketches their sculptural forms. He may also have influenced their basic design.

Another artist whose memory should have been preserved is the wood carver. The mantels and especially the newel posts (fig. 141) display marvellous workmanship, mainly in creating impressively realistic depictions of various flowers, some of which are also symbolic. Despite its size and grandeur, the courthouse has a remarkably cheerful and comfortable atmosphere, attributable in large measure to the honey-coloured stain of the woodwork and the earthy colours of the encaustic tiles on the floors.

The front elevation of the jail (fig. 142) makes Perth County appear a pleasant place in which to be incarcerated as well as tried, but the domestic scale and design of its façade probably owes more to a consideration of its streetscape than to any thought of a group home for criminals. Behind the house-like front block of the jail stretches a large spartan wing that more clearly resembles a fortress.

In January 1887 the county council made plans to open the courthouse on the date of Queen Victoria's golden jubilee, 22 June, and it voted $500 to be spent on appropriate festivities. Apparently practical considerations

141   Perth County Building, newel-posts on landing of main staircase

142 Perth County Jail, Stratford, detail of architectural drawing showing front elevation; drawing signed 'George F. Durand'

triumphed over sentiment, since the formal opening was held with much less fanfare on 13 May at the beginning of the spring assizes, and on 22 June the council voted to put the $500 'in the general funds.'[216] It seems that the ceremony consisted mainly of opening the doors, but this apparently provided drama enough: 'When the doors were thrown open,' reported the *Beacon*, 'an admiring crowd took possession of its corridors, and expressions of surprise and delight were rife.'[217]

In December, when the final costs of the new building were settled, and even the reluctant towns of Stratford and St Marys had agreed to pay their share, the council expressed itself well satisfied with its choice of architect:

The committee in thus submitting our final report cannot close without conveying to Mr Geo. F. Durand, Architect, our appreciation of the very valuable services he has rendered to the County Council in not only designing but also in successfully carrying to completion the County buildings which, for beauty of design and a happy blending of chasteness of style, combined with all necessary conveniences in all the internal arrangements supplies ... all that the most cultivated taste would desire and all that the most rigid sanitary regulations could demand. And we would also express to Mr Durand our thanks for his courtesy and gentlemanly conduct that has always characterized his dealings with us.

Gratitude, however, had its limits. The following day, council had on its agenda the courteous architect's bill for $400 'in compensation for extra work,' and it decided that the request 'would not be entertained.'[218]

Carmel Presbyterian Church, 1886-7
now Hensall United Church, Hensall

Understandably reluctant to risk encountering wolves, bears, and wildcats in order to attend church in a nearby village, the Presbyterian families around what is now Hensall organized their own congregation and built their first church in 1848.[219] The enterprise was to produce great benefits for the young community, owing largely to the dedication of their first minister, the Reverend John Logie, who was fondly described in 1898 by one of his old parishioners: 'I remember him best as he was preaching, his long scant hair brushed back from the high forehead, the thin mobile lips quivering under the excitement of intense thought, the face turned slightly to the left and uplifted, the eyes, not looking at his congregation, but over and above them, to that particular left hand corner, and flashing back and forth, as the magnetic needle quivers under a strong current.'[220] Another source reports him to have been an enthusiastic scholar, capable of reading thirteen languages and speaking eleven. The second minister was more interested in 'fast horses' then learning, and one church history mildly comments that 'his was not the happiest ministry.' The scholarship and conscientiousness of his successor, the Reverend R.Y. Thomson, so enlarged his congregation that a bigger church was built, in 1886, on a new site. Hensall had turned into a flourishing village after the London, Huron, and Bruce railway located a station there in 1875, and the new edifice was located within the town.[221]

The Carmel Presbyterian Church was one of several designed by the firm between 1884 and 1889 that are based on the format favoured by William Robinson (see Christ Church, London, 1862–3; fig. 42),[222] a testimony to the versatility and sound composition of that pattern. All have a centre door, separated by a string course from a somewhat elaborate window grouping above, and by buttresses from the single bays to either side. These later versions often feature a tower, set completely to one side (though the tower of

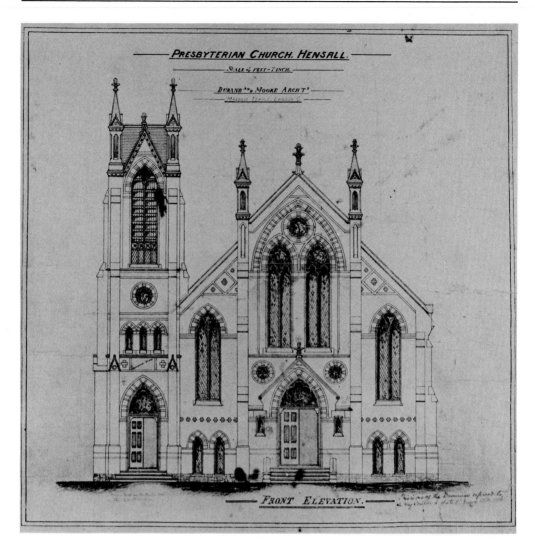

143   Carmel Presbyterian Church, Hensall, architectural drawing showing front elevation

the Hensall church seems never to have been built), bichromatic brickwork (here, red accents on buff brick), an arrangement of small windows around the entry, and, in the gable, an overriding arch that encompasses two arched windows and an oculus. Within this group of churches the Hensall church is especially striking in the extraordinary delicacy of its details. Mullions divide the windows into narrow units; the pinnacles have fine, sharp mouldings; and the slender lines of the bichromatic design form a filigree of brick.

144   Carmel Presbyterian Church

145   Carmel Presbyterian Church, front gable

Masonic Temple, 1887

Petrolia (demolished after a fire)

The vast swampland that lay about twenty miles east of the St Clair River remained sparsely settled until 1857, when an adventurer hoping to extract asphalt from the mysterious 'gum beds' dug for water and struck oil. The discoveries of the next few years created the boom towns of Oil Springs and then of Petrolia. Petrolia suffered a setback in the 1870s when the burgeoning Pennsylvania oil industry disrupted the Canadian export market,[223] but the creation of a more diversified economic base in the town contributed to a recovery during the 1880s. Its more stable prosperity was reflected in its appearance, as wooden buildings gave way to brick,[224] and imposing public buildings began to reflect a sense of civic pride. Durand's firm played an important role in this transformation, providing designs for the new town hall, two churches, a commercial block, a high school, and the Masonic Temple.[225]

The design for the Masonic Temple combines the dignity of a public building with the generous window space then fashionable for a commercial structure, thus reflecting the building's dual role. The Masonic rooms were located on the third floor, equipped with the most elegant windows. The rest of the building was designed as office and store space, though the post office ended up inhabiting the latter area. Durand elaborates on the conventional Italianate commercial block, with its bracketed cornice and round-arched windows, by arranging the arches in majestic arcading that encompasses all the windows on the two top storeys. As in the Perth County Courthouse, even the terra cotta panels are arranged to emphasize the building's vertical divisions. The centre bay projects to form a pedimented frontispiece, where the imposing entrance to the Masonic Hall is located. Durand provided two optional designs for the store and office fronts on the ground floor; one developed the Queen Anne theme of the second storey with its small-paned windows, the other elaborated on the heavier semi-circular arches of the third. Rather surprisingly, versions of both options were used. Thus the finished building had something of the tantalizing and experimental quality found in a child's flip-book, where one can discover a new picture by turning half a page.

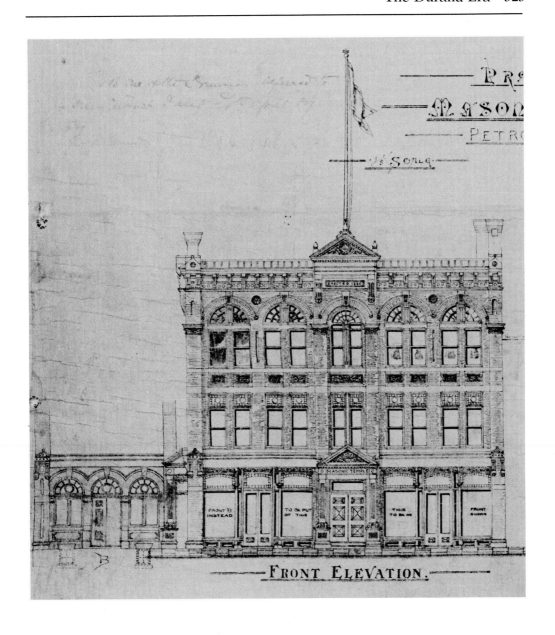

146   Masonic Temple, Petrolia, detail of architectural drawing showing front elevation; drawing signed 'Geo. F. Durand'

147   Masonic Temple, pediment above front entrance and terra cotta panel between second and third storeys

148   Masonic Temple

Victoria Hall, 1887–9
Petrolia

One by-product of Petrolia's revived prosperity during the 1880s was the feeling among some citizens that the town should have an imposing town hall.[226] The town council apparently had plans drawn up for a multi-purpose building as early as 1881, but the idea was voted down within council.[227] Three years later plans were again prepared and submitted to a referendum; the proposal was defeated for a variety of reasons. Some voters thought that projects such as a waterworks system should have priority; others felt that the public building should be more elaborate, incorporating an opera house. Vivid memories of Petrolia's boom and bust cycle had created optimism in some hearts and intense fearfulness in others. The issue became both more urgent and more contentious over the next few years. In 1886 the city clerk moved out of the old premises, complaining that the second storey rocked in the wind.[228] On two occasions, when first Sir John A. Macdonald and then Edward Blake came to speak, Petrolia displayed its impartiality by failing to provide a building capable of safely accommodating a large crowd.[229] In 1887 the council solicited new plans from Durand, and by January 1889 a capacity crowd was seated in the elegant 1,000 seat opera house of the new $35,000 town hall to witness the opening night festivities.[230] The mayor's speech that night betrayed his nervousness about the still vocal opposition: 'It is impossible for me to conjecture what your thoughts and feelings are as you sit here and view with complacency, perhaps, the commodiousness, the comfort, and the architectural beauties of this building, but I trust they are only those of contentment and gratification, and that nothing shall occur here this evening to mar the harmony that should reign within these walls.'[231] He was referring, in part, to the local Baptist minister's fulminations against the theatre on moral grounds, but other potential disrupters of the peace had objected to the hall, theatre included, for economic reasons. The critics were strong enough to warrant mention in the Petrolia *Advertiser*'s story on the opening: the 'grand success ... must have made those who have ... been croaking about the lavish expenditures feel like crawling into a hole and pulling the hole in after them.'[232]

Like the Strathroy Public Building designed many years before (fig. 46), and most urban town halls built during the intervening period,[233] Victoria Hall was designed to accommodate, together with an auditorium, most of the town's municipal services: fire station; jail; division court room; council chambers; and offices for the mayor, the town clerk, the chief of police, and the engineer. While the multiple functions of the Strathroy building were ingeniously fitted into a rectangular shape reminiscent of a Greek temple, Durand's design for Petrolia is an interesting exploration of the theory that 'form follows

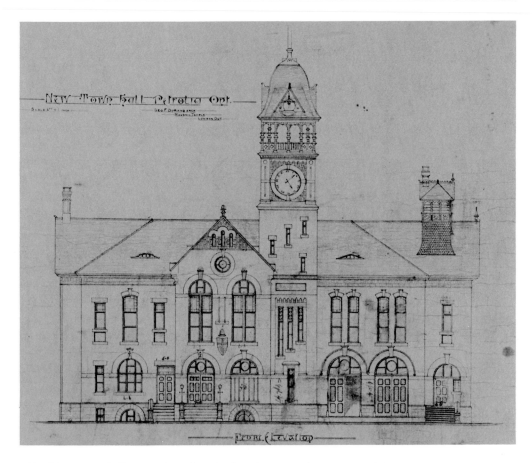

149   Victoria Hall, Petrolia, detail of architectural drawing of front elevation

function.' Victoria Hall gives the impression of being built around its various roles, as if the fire engines had been parked and the mayor seated before the walls began to rise. Durand is nowhere bound by considerations of symmetry or consistency: there is great variety in the size, shape, and grouping of the windows; the gable of the façade has a parapet while the other gables have decorated barge-boards. Each individual section of the façade has a character of its own, reflective of its use. Large double doors designate the fire station. The windows of the tower follow the line of the stairway it envelops. The entrance hall leading to the courtroom and the opera house is dignified by the parapeted gable bay.

In general, decoration is meted out as befits each section's role, so that the front gable wing and the towers are adorned with the most noteworthy features. The former boasts striking forms of ornamentation such as the decorated brickwork at the apex and the official plaques, with their representative oil scene and symbolic beehive (fig. 151), near the door. An almost blind window even makes this part of the façade symmetrical. But it is on the clock tower (fig. 152) that Durand lavishes most of the building's decorative detail, as

150   Victoria Hall

151   Victoria Hall, official plaques

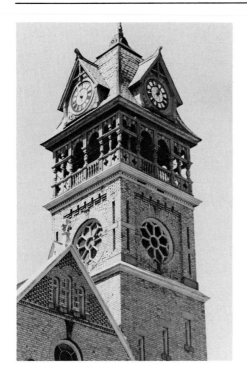

152 Victoria Hall, clock tower   153 Victoria Hall, opera box

if to stress the fact that towers exist mainly in order to look interesting.
At its top is a belvedere, with a bell-shaped roof and elaborately turned,
pierced, and reeded posts, railings, and spandrels. The stage below, originally
meant to hold the clock faces, matches the ornate woodwork above with equally
elaborate brickwork. The individuality of the building's various parts is aptly
epitomized by the hose-drying tower, a miniature house in itself, complete
with its own decorated gable, finial, and chimney.

To say that Durand has emphasized the parts of the Petrolia town hall
does not imply that he has forgotten the whole. The composition of the building
is carefully balanced, and the varying elements arranged with the overall effect
clearly in mind. For example, the broad arches that are strung along the ground
floor appear to provide a heavy base for the structure. These arched windows
are carefully integrated with the small-paned windows above by the use in
the semicircular portions of a design based on simple geometrical shapes. The
iron stair railing and balcony at the rear of the building (fig. 154) rely on the
same stark geometry and in fact use the motif of a circle held between two
vertical bars that is found in the round-headed windows. This interest in
basic geometrical shapes is also evident in interior features such as the
very dramatic opera box (fig. 153), rather blatantly placed to let its occupants
be seen rather than to allow them a view of the stage.

Possibly out of fear of the Baptist minister's admonitions, the opening night
program at Victoria Hall featured mainly local talent in a variety of innocent

154   Victoria Hall, rear double staircase

performances. The evening began with a 'double quartette' warbling 'Merrily, merrily goes the bark,' which, according to the Petrolia *Advertiser*, 'gave a foretaste of the intellectual feast in store for the audience.' The high point of the evening was Mr H. Corey's poetic account of local events:

> Out of the old town hall,
> Moved up into the new;
> All the spouting and the shouting
> Is just as good as through!
> ... Fare you well, old hall,
>   You ain't worth a cent,
> We're going to a better house,
>   Where we won't pay any rent.[234]

The better house had more glorious days ahead, when it would play host to operatic performances, grand balls, and some of the continent's best touring companies.[235] But the confidence in progress that had finally led to the erection of the town hall proved ill-founded. The departure of the Imperial Oil refineries in 1898 plunged the town into a second and more lasting economic depression,[236] and the building gradually fell into disrepair. In 1960 part of the first floor was renovated to accommodate the town offices once more.[237] The opera house was ultimately rescued by Victoria Playhouse Petrolia, an organization formed to restore the building and to revive the theatre. It has succeeded admirably on both counts, and Victoria Hall again serves as a multi-purpose building, though with some new purposes (convention centre, art gallery) replacing some of the old.[238]

Main Building, Western Fair, 1887
Queen's Park, London (destroyed by fire)

London's enthusiasm for a fair, which had been so strong in the 1860s, when the Crystal Palace (fig. 41) was built and the Western Fair established, faded surprisingly quickly. Part of the dissatisfaction during the 1870s concerned the fair's site. The northern part of the old Ordnance lands, which had been deeded to the East Middlesex Agricultural Society for exhibition purposes, were located close to the city centre, and it was felt by some that the land should not be closed off and remain idle most of the year when it could be developed as a source of tax revenue. By 1874 city council seriously considered turning the exhibition grounds into building lots.[239] Though nothing immediately came of these proposals, they were the first stage of a running debate that aroused political passions for the next thirteen years. Two referenda held in 1880 and 1881 on the sale of the exhibition grounds produced contradictory results.[240] Even when the decision to sell the old grounds was finally taken in 1885, the city fathers continued to vacillate as to where and whether new exhibition facilities would be built.[241]

The prime contenders for a new site were Graydon's Farm, Carling's Farm, and Salter's Grove (renamed Queen's Park in 1879). The choice was narrowed on 6 January 1886 when John Carling made an offer, good for one day, that council could not refuse. As a member of the federal cabinet, Carling was not in a position to sell property to the government. He agreed, however, when 'nailed' by Alderman Green, to sell Carling's Farm to the city for $40,000, on the understanding that it would be traded immediately to the government for the remaining militia grounds (figs 65 and 68).[242] The federal government built its military school on the Carling's Farm site, and the city turned a handsome profit on the militia and exhibition grounds, making expensive fair buildings more feasible.[243] With public opinion still divided, council did not decide upon the fair until 29 March 1887 when it voted nine to six in favour of spending $65,000 on exhibition buildings to be located at Queen's Park.[244]

George Durand, entering under the pseudonymn 'T Square,' won the competition for the design of the Main Building, in a contest that may have been decided in a somewhat frivolous spirit. The occasion of the judging was greatly enjoyed by the participants, including the *Free Press* reporter: 'the Committee were in a most jovial mood, and after almost tiring themselves out cracking "chestnuts" on each other, and "ringing church bells" at the competitors' sketches, they turned their attention to the *Advertiser* reporter, who was soundly snoring in his chair.'[245]

As noted before, London's first Crystal Palace (fig. 41) bore little resemblance to its namesake by Joseph Paxton, the influential iron and glass structure designed for the Great Exhibition of 1851. Durand's design for the second

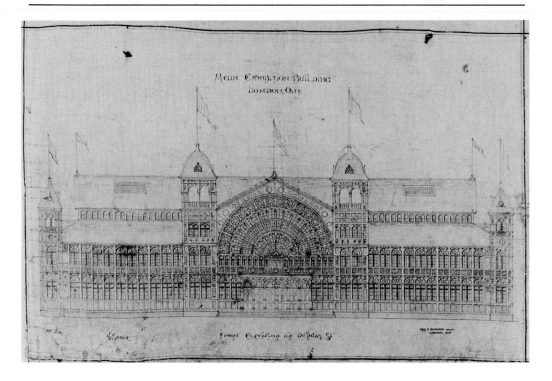

155   Main Building, Western Fair, London, architectural drawing showing front elevation

palace was strongly influenced by the prototype; even the great fan-shaped window over the entryway ultimately derives from the end wall of Paxton's round-arched roof, though by 1887 it had become the hallmark of an exhibition building. However, Durand chose to construct his building of glass and wood rather than glass and iron. Where Paxton's masterpiece was a demonstration of the structural possibilities of iron, Durand used various Stick-style techniques to call attention to the underlying wooden skeleton. From the outside the building as a whole seemed a remarkable structural accomplishment for the relatively thin boards appeared to support a great deal of weight, but the appearance was to some extent an illusion. Inside, the light, airy impression of the exterior was replaced by the 'very massive appearance' of the 'thirteen high circular arches' that form the building's main supports.

Painted in 'two delicate shades of terra cotta,' with trimmings 'in sage green, brown and Indian red,'[246] the new Crystal Palace looked appropriately festive on opening day, 19 September 1887. Though the fair was agricultural in emphasis, the Main Building was crowded with displays of arts and manufactured goods that ranged from organs and sewing machines to stuffed birds and examples of penmanship. One of the more striking displays, provided by the Morse Soap Company, was an elaborate model of a wedding breakfast, 'skilfully executed in soap ... so cunningly artistic as to be most deceptive': 'An elaborate bride's cake occupied the centre. At one end ... was a massive epergne laden with bananas, pomegranates and other choice fruits ... The city newspapers lay carelessly upon the table; on closer inspection they proved to be made of soap, like everything else.'[247]

The building's wooden structure was ultimately to prove its undoing. Early in the morning of 30 January 1927, Londoners were awakened by 'the most spectacular fire' the city had seen for some years. The whole city 'was illuminated by the reflection,' as, in minutes, the great Crystal Palace burned to the ground. 'The dry wood,' explained the *Advertiser*, 'offered no resistance.'[248]

Knox Presbyterian Church, 1887–8
Listowel

Colborne Street Methodist Church, 1888–9
now Colborne Street United Church, 711 Colborne Street, London

When the Presbyterians of Listowel, twenty-eight miles north-west of Stratford, built their first church in 1868, a talented church member named John Alexander played the roles of architect, building committee, and treasurer. Twenty years later the congregation was not only larger but also more ambitious, hiring the leading architect from the area's commercial metropolis to draft the plans.[249] The new church employed the round-headed arches that had figured prominently in several of Durand's most recent buildings; the use of two contrasting towers was also common on North American Romanesque churches. The higher tower on the Listowel church, a prominent landmark on its elevated site, alludes more to the Scottish background of the parishoners than to any Romanesque prototype, however, in that the corbelled turrets were a popular feature in Scottish baronial architecture. The old church was relegated to a back wing.[250]

The Listowel church was chosen as a model when the Wesleyan Methodist Church in London decided to erect a new building in 1888. The latter, however, was varied in some significant ways. Most obviously, both towers are symmetrical; the symmetrical design better suited the flat residential site of the London church, and it is also consistent with the broader proportions demanded by the semi-circular seating arrangement within. The design has been simplified: there are no oculi; only the rose window features complex tracery; instead of the terra cotta trim in the gable, there is brickwork identical with that in the courses above the doors. The breadth and simplicity of the London church, and the blunt proportions of its towers, all contribute to a sense of massiveness and heaviness that makes it seem Romanesque in spirit as well as in several of its details.

156   Knox Presbyterian Church, Listowel, architectural drawing showing front elevation

157   Colborne Street Methodist Church, London, detail of architectural drawing showing front elevation

The Colborne Street Methodists were a daughter church of the congregation established in London as early as 1833. They had expanded into the northern part of the city for exclusively evangelistic reasons, and the Sunday School was an important part of their mission. This church was one of the very few designed by the firm for which a Sunday School wing was part of the original design, and it was a very substantial part indeed. A main lecture hall was lined on two sides by classrooms, a vestry, and a library, most of which had glass walls that could be adjusted to increase the size of the auditorium. With the aid of the gallery above the classrooms, the complex could hold 600 people.[251] Interestingly, this wing bears a strong resemblance, both in its shape and its position, to John Alexander's old church in Listowel.

158   Colborne Street Methodist Church, detail of front

159   Colborne Street Methodist Church

Upper Canada College, 1887–91

Toronto (demolished)

'The new school is going to be awfully nice,' wrote London student Ronald Harris in October 1889, during his first term at Upper Canada College. In the following February he reported, 'They are getting it finished very quickly, and have all but a few of the windows in and some of the flooring done. The rooms will be very much nicer than they are here.' Harris had good reason to expect the new school to be 'nice.'[252] It was to cost approximately $270,000, not including the price of the spacious grounds and various 'extras.'[253] It had an imposing appearance that defiantly announced its triumphant emergence from a half-century-old debate about its right to exist.

In his official history of Upper Canada College, Richard Howard describes the school as 'springing like Athene out of the head of one decisive, strong-willed arrogant man.'[254] The man was Lieutenant-Governor Sir John Colborne, whose brain-child was influenced by his personal success in reviving a public school in Guernsey, and by the political argument that faced him on his arrival in Upper Canada. Anglican Archdeacon John Strachan, president of the provincial Board of Education, had developed a plan for a university (King's College), which had among its strong opponents those who thought it was deflecting funds from the province's four official grammar schools. Relying on his past success, Colborne decided to solve the educational dilemma in Upper Canada by creating another Guernsey-style college. It would replace the Royal Grammar School in Toronto and also serve as a preparatory school for the still dormant university; in its latter capacity the college would be subsidized by university funds.

Though the mostly Cambridge-trained masters Colborne imported established long-lasting standards of academic excellence at the school, its position within the province's increasingly ambitious educational system was always hard to define and harder to champion. As a result, Upper Canada College produced both a roster of well-educated and very influential Old Boys, who retained a fierce loyalty to their alma mater, and a long line of political opponents, who objected to the public subsidizing of what was regarded as an elitist institution. The conflict came to a head in 1887.

The King Street property occupied by the school had become extremely valuable, and the University, the endowments of which still supported the college, badly needed money. A Liberal MP gave notice of a motion that 'Upper Canada College be abolished ... as the instruction given in the College can be obtained in any well-conducted high school in the province.' The Old Boys rallied to the college's defence, and an ingenious compromise was reached: the college was to be preserved, but on a different site and with a reduced level of government support. It was to become entirely residential and therefore different in kind from the high schools with which it competed. Though in fact the school continued to accept day students, the principal, George Dickson, expanded on the virtues of its residential character when the new buildings opened in October 1891:

A boy can get as much mathematics and science in any good day school as he can get in Upper Canada College. It is something more than a teaching machine and differs from the day school in its functions ... here the boys meet each other under all the conditions of citizenship, not only in the school room, but on the play ground ... around the halls, in their rooms, over their meals – a little commonwealth in itself, governed to a large extent by a public sentiment. It is in such schools that pecularities of manner are toned down, and independent, self-reliant, strong character built up.[255]

In keeping with the idea of a residential school, a location north of the city was purchased. Durand's monumental, imposing design stresses the school's image as a public institution more than its function as a home away from home. It exudes authority and importance, dominating its scenic surroundings rather than blending with them. Its large central block was so situated as to face directly down Avenue Road, which was widened to 125 feet to make 'a fine driveway from the city.'

The account of the building in the London *Free Press* is so unusually detailed and technical as to suggest that Durand had issued his own description. It contains some useful guides to appreciating his design: 'while free from ornamental detail ... a picturesque effect is obtained by the division of the parts and grouping of the mass, the internal uses of the building ... being brought out and emphasized by the treatment of the exterior.'[256] The building is very restrained in its use of ornamentation, and the effect of what surface decoration there is was made more subtle by the similar colours of the major materials involved: the reddish brown Credit Valley sandstone, red brick, and terra cotta. The sparsity of distracting ornamentation does allow the basic shape of the building to stand out more clearly. The long façade, one side of a quadrangle, in fact relied on the traditional pavilion format, with a centre block divided by wings from two end pavilions. Though such formal lines make the exterior of Upper Canada College less revealing than that of Victoria Hall (fig. 150), Durand's design does provide symbolic hints as to the location of the most important parts of the building. The large, arched windows of the centre block lighted the assembly hall; the west tower indicated the entrance to the classroom wing; the more domestic bow-window in the east pavilion signalled the principal's twelve-room residence.

While the tower and bow window very slightly interrupt the college's symmetry, the façade's most striking deviation from the traditional pattern is in the size of the centre block. In creating its monumental effect, Durand has borrowed freely from the repertoire of forms employed by H.H. Richardson. The round corner pinnacles, the arcade, the pedimented wall dormer, and the pyramidal-roofed tower all feature prominently in Richardson's work and

160   Upper Canada College, Toronto, architectural perspective drawing

in that of his followers. Possibly Durand had been infected by the American
mania for the Richardsonian style during the tour he and Principal Dickson
made of 'the best schools in the Eastern States';[257] he was also familiar with
the Richardsonian Toronto City Hall designed by E.G. Lennox, which had
won over Durand's own design in the recent competition.

Despite these borrowings, Durand's block possesses neither a Richardsonian
sense of massiveness nor the sense of compression and exaggeration that
one finds in Richardson's work. The pinnacles are relatively small in diameter,
and the brick lacks the texture of Richardson's favoured rock-face stone. Indeed,
the block and tower between them have almost Georgian dimensions that
enable them to fit well into the pavilion organization, though both are oversized
in relation to the whole.

Durand's eagerness to exhibit his drawings of the college reveals his pride
in their design, but the finished buildings were to suffer a good deal of criticism. Because Durand died well before the college was finished, it is not entirely clear who was responsible for overseeing much of the new building's
construction. Kivas Tully was hired as a consulting engineer; he was acting in
that capacity by February 1890. Nevertheless, as late as June the board was
nagging Fred Henry to correct certain problems with the construction: 'the
flooring and plastering of the building have been proceeded with before the
lighting arrangements have been completed,' and the gas pipes were thought

insufficient. Meanwhile, the architects who were most frequently consulted, though in what capacity is not clear, were 'Messrs Strickland and Symons.'[258] Possibly too many architects spoiled the structure. Its poor construction was frequently noted. Principal Auden claimed in 1903 that 'the main building was only in tolerable condition; much bad work had been put into it.' When the building was condemned and, perhaps unnecessarily, entirely replaced in 1958, the *Globe and Mail* described the original edifice as 'jerry-built.'

For a time in the 1890s, it looked as if the college itself was also doomed to extinction yet again. Problems with morale and discipline in the new school led to the firing and replacement of the entire faculty and administration in 1895. The school revived under the principalship of the famous educator George Parkin, but the new building was to suffer another insult in the process. An impassioned imperialist, Parkin wished to emulate the British public schools in establishing small houses of boarders, each with a certain administrative independence. He held that a large building dictated a centralized system which worked against the opportunities for staff initiative and student character growth he was attempting to provide.[259] Parkin accepted a position elsewhere before he could put his reforms into effect, and Durand's building endured for a further fifty years, to be replaced by another centralized quadrangle.

Canadian Savings and Loan Company, 1889

420–2 Richmond Street, London (demolished)

The Canadian Savings and Loan Company was founded in 1875 and enjoyed what Goodspeed's *History of the County of Middlesex* later described as a 'more than usually prosperous career,' based on sound conservative practices: it 'places its funds in nothing but good Ontario real estate.' The company's president from 1884 until his death in 1890 was James Durand,[260] and he doubtless helped choose the architect for the firm's new building.

George Durand earned his father's trust. Portage red sandstone was imported from Michigan for the façade, and a Detroit sculptor, F.W. Peel,[261] was commissioned to execute the stone carvings for the building. The 'peculiar colour and quality of the stone' that occasioned 'considerable comment,' according to the *Advertiser*, was probably talked about because London architects rarely employed stone façades of any sort. In fact, the red-brown colour of the stone, its rock-face finish, the broad round-headed arches and the deep-set windows reflected the current Richardsonian fashion. The final character of the Savings and Loan façade was nevertheless very much Durand's own.

Even when working with rock-faced masonry, Durand managed to avoid creating the impression of weightiness that typified Richardson's work. In the Savings and Loan front, the natural heaviness of the material was counteracted in part by the large porportions of wall space devoted to windows, the shapes of which formed an interesting and extremely effective geometrical pattern against the monochromatic surface. Moreover, the upper two storeys seemed lighter in comparison with the main level. On the ground floor the stones were uniformly large (one stone was approximately as high as a man's head and derby hat combined). Their massiveness was complemented by the expansive windows; the unusual lack of mullions intensified the impression of the exaggerated size of the oculi. On the upper storeys the stonework was more refined: thin layers alternated with thick ones, and detailed, delicate designs were carved on the keystones, into the panels beneath the third-floor windows, along the cornice, and on the pediment. A final cause for the relative lightness of the façade lay in the strong vertical lines of the frontispiece and pediment, accentuated in the finished building by a most imperious lion perched on the pediment.

The paradox involved in a stone building with a light air is explored in Durand's façade by a mannered play on the principles of support. The pilasters that should hold up the door lintels, for example, extend only half-way down the abutment; the 'Scotch granite' pilasters that appear to support the heavy stone pediment rest somewhat precariously on the spandrels of the arches. Like Durand's exhibition building, the Savings and Loan façade has a somewhat

161   Canadian Savings and Loan Company, London, architectural drawing showing front elevation

illusionary quality, seemingly undercutting the prevalent principle of architectural Truth. In this instance, however, the play on images of support serves to reinforce the fact that the stone is after all a veneer: the real brick and iron supports are behind its imposing face.

The building was used by several important organizations. The Savings and Loan Company itself occupied the ground floor, with its impressive fifteen-foot ceilings. These rooms were finished in imported oak and divided into separate areas by wood and stained glass partitions; the dividers were only nine feet high, to allow the 'free circulation of atmosphere.' The floor above, finished in Canadian red pine, contained premises for the Board of Trade ('a neat meeting room ... a parlour, and a large library recess'), as well as room for two offices. The *Advertiser*'s enthusiastic account of the edifice may have expressed the view of a satisfied tenant: the newspaper had expanded from its own building next door into the basement and top floor of the new structure.[262] As far as we know, the *Free Press* across the street did not honour its neighbour with a full-fledged review.

The Canadian Savings and Loan Company occupied its grand quarters until 1906, when the firm merged with the Huron and Erie Savings and Loan Company.[263] Durand's building then served as the main branch in London of the Bank of Nova Scotia until the 1960s, when, like many monuments to London's past, it was demolished for the sake of a much inferior replacement.

Stratford General Hospital, 1889–93

now Rehabilitation and Extended Care Unit of Stratford General Hospital, Stratford

In his 1887 inaugural address Mayor J.C. MacGregor urged the establishment of a hospital in Stratford. He was concerned about the increased number of industrial accidents in the city since the injured could be treated only at home. He returned to the same theme at the hospital's opening in May 1891, recalling the time when he sent an injured man to the jail, 'as the only place then available for the purpose.'[264]

The mayor's inaugural address found a receptive audience in some determined and philanthropic ladies who subsequently organized a large public meeting in November 1888. From that time the hospital cause received remarkable public support. Within twenty-four hours the City of Stratford General Hospital Trust had been officially incorporated. Within a month $7,247.50 was pledged in subscriptions for the hospital.[265]

The trustees appointed Durand as the architect, apparently with the understanding that he would design an expandable building. The initial plan was for the tower and one wing to be built immediately, the other wing to be added when funds were available. It seems likely that the proportions of the various parts in Durand's design were chosen with an eye to its appearance as an asymmetrical structure, but such foresight proved unnecessary. It was decided to erect the whole building at once. So efficient were the money-raising efforts, complete with bazaars and amateur theatricals, that the $13,361 structure opened debt-free in 1891.[266]

In keeping with his work of this period, Durand combines Elizabethan and Romanesque qualities, though the gable wings give the building a predominantly Elizabethan quality. The façade might seem somewhat austere were it not for the very picturesque pinnacles, which echo the shape of the tower roof, and the extraordinarily generous wooden bays, which add a warm domestic quality.

The hospital's interior arrangements were said to be as commendable as its 'noble and imposing' exterior. There were four public wards containing eight beds each, to which a patient would be admitted for $2.80 a week, or less if he could not afford the payment. More affluent patients could get semi-private or private rooms for between $3 and $10 per week. Except for the lady superintendent's suite on the ground floor, the accommodations for the staff were all on the third floor, along with the dining room, laundry, and kitchen. The attic location of the latter two rooms was seen as 'a departure from the usual course,' designed 'to avoid unpleasant fumes from the nether-most regions.'[267] Provincial authorities later came to recommend the scheme.

When the hospital opened, flags were hoisted all over Stratford, and the

162   Stratford General Hospital, Stratford, detail of architectural drawing showing front elevation; drawing signed 'Geo. F. Durand'

building was so mobbed with well-wishers that the expected entertainers were unable to reach the platform. The Honourable J.M. Gibson did manage to deliver his dedicatory address, however, in which he praised the ladies who had so devotedly made the hospital possible: 'Women are taking a more prominent position in this country day by day ... We find them in the schools, seminaries of learning, and in other walks of life, discharging duties that for the most part used to be performed by the other sex ... But, if there is a special work for women, it is in connection with the charities, which all cities must necessarily promote.'[268]

John D. LeBel House, 1889–91

318 Wolfe Street, London

A native of Quebec, John LeBel arrived in London around 1878 and worked for a few years as a bookkeeper for lumber merchant Edward W. Hargreaves. By 1883 he had set himself up in business, still in the flourishing lumber trade. A promotional book on London's industries, published in 1887, claimed that he conducted 'a large business in the wholesale trade' and described him as 'a gentleman of experience, with ample capital.'[269] At about this time, he decided to spend some of his ample capital on a new house, to be built on the site of the old military grounds. He thus became one of the first home-owners to fulfil Alderman Toll's prediction that if those grounds were sold and subdivided, 'wealthy citizens ... would build their handsome residences in the centre of the city' instead of 'going out in the suburbs.'[270]

The house he built was large, though not on the scale of the Laing and Masuret houses (figs 128 and 129) that faced directly on the park. Its plan and façade more closely resembled those of the house at 513 Queens Avenue (fig. 131), but with some significant differences that point towards new directions in Durand's domestic architecture. The Gothic polychromy and Italianate brackets are gone. In their place are Elizabethan, or Old English, features such as small-paned windows; half-timbering; shingled surfaces; and lowered eaves, which extend nearly to the bottom of the frieze. The Wolfe Street house has more irregular contours, both inside and out. The roofline is complicated by the several dormers, the varying levels of the ridges, and the gable at the peak. A Romanesque arch leads into a porch within the verandah. The polygonal bay no longer has three equal sides. Inside, the broad bay window occupies one entire wall of the parlour; with the two corners at the other end canted to echo the bay, the parlour becomes an irregular octagon. The library behind the parlour features a similarly large bay, as do the bedrooms on the second floor and the playroom in the attic. The floor plan is innovative in some other ways as well. The hall, for example, has been divided into a spacious entrance hall and a broader staircase hall, an arrangement that was to be further developed in the Queen Anne houses designed by Moore and Henry: there the entrance hall sometimes becomes a separate room of its own, with Old English window seats and chimney corners to match the Elizabethan features without.

163   John D. LeBel House, London, detail of architectural drawing showing front elevation; drawing signed 'Geo. F. Durand'

164   John D. LeBel House

Henry Mathewson Double House, 1889–c. 1892

228–30 Central Avenue, London

Henry Mathewson's long and successful career testified to his versatility. Emigrating from Scotland in the early 1840s, he started life in London as a baker, then began manufacturing steam engines, and finally turned to journalism, first with the *Advertiser* and then with the *Free Press*. In 1889 he was a partner in the latter newspaper, and served as its secretary-treasurer.[271] When the old exhibition grounds were sold in 1888, he purchased a lot facing Victoria Park in order to dabble in real estate as well. He was eventually to build a double house on the site for use as an income property.

By the time that Mathewson started building in 1891 or 1892, some neighbouring houses had already gone up, and Mathewson was evidently much attracted by the double house erected for travel and insurance agent Thomas R. Parker. Durand had designed the Parker house in the fall of 1889, but the architect had died before seeing it through to completion. At some point, probably after Durand's death, Parker chose to substitute simple balconies with straight lines for those in Durand's drawing. It was in Mathewson's house, built according to the plans procured from Durand's successor, Fred Henry, that the original design for Parker was to be most closely realized.[272]

The design combines in a rather fascinating way the Elizabethan and Romanesque characteristics found in Durand's later work. The semi-circular arches unify all three levels of the porch; in the finished building they are also featured in the ground-floor windows. Most of the Old English details found in the LeBel house are also found here, but the double house has a more comprehensive Elizabethan air that derives less from individual details than from its overall organization. The façade suggests an H-plan though, instead of a centre recess, there are Durand's favoured large bay windows on each side. The contrast between the plain, massive Romanesque arches of the ground floor and the intricate, finer woodwork above creates an impression similar to that of the overhanging storey common in Elizabethan vernacular buildings.

Henry brought the porch complex forward to create a bolder and more dramatic effect than Durand intended. He also made some changes to the patterning of the upper storeys, though retaining Durand's concept of increasing delicacy. The finely pierced panels in the built gable have an almost papery appearance.

At about the same time as the Mathewson house was being built, Moore and Henry used its design as the basis for the Whiskard house (fig. 186). The existence of several other variations on this design reveals that Durand's influence upon his London colleagues extended beyond his death.

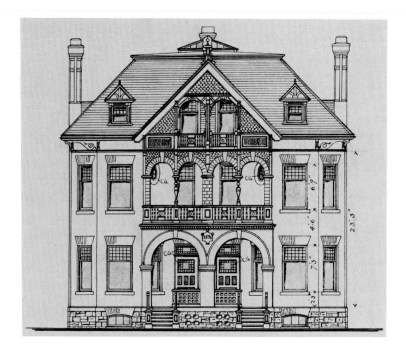

165 Thomas R. Parker Double House, London, detail of architectural drawing showing front elevation; drawing signed 'Geo. F. Durand'

166 Henry Mathewson Double House, London, balconies

167   Henry Mathewson Double House

CHAPTER FIVE

The Moore Era

JOHN MACKENZIE MOORE

WHEN JOHN M. MOORE left Durand's office in April 1888, he likely had strongly ambivalent feelings about his decision. The lawsuit that he subsequently brought against Durand displayed an intense bitterness towards his former employer that is easily understandable. Moore had achieved some recognition as a very competent engineer, yet his own cherished conception of himself as a partner had been slighted by the head of the firm. At the same time, the man who treated Moore's claims so lightly was widely recognized as one of the province's most distinguished architects, and the length of Moore's service with Durand's firm bespeaks the younger man's instincts of loyalty: he had apprenticed under Robinson and Tracy in the 1870s and had continued in the office after Robinson's retirement, working for Tracy and Durand and then for Durand alone. Thus when Moore established himself in business as a 'land surveyor, architect and engineer,'[1] he laboured under the double burden of a wounded spirit and an almost non-existent independent reputation as an architect. By the time of his death, forty-two years later, he had achieved national eminence in architectural circles. He had also gained a reputation as an honourable if demanding employer, a man who was consistently thoughtful in the treatment of his own subordinates.

168   John M. Moore (1857–1930), photograph, c. 1925

MOORE'S INDEPENDENT CAREER

Moore was certainly not without resources in 1888; among his advantages were well-established relatives, on both his side of the family and his wife's. His maternal grandfather, Duncan Mackenzie, was one of the first settlers in London Township. He had settled near what is now Hyde Park in 1818 and held several responsible positions in the developing settlement. He was also an active member of the Temperance League,[2] and one wonders how he felt when his daughter married a distiller. William Moore had learned the trade in his father's Peel County distillery. He was in Virginia, however, when he heard of a rebellion going on at home, and he quickly returned to Canada, walking all the way from Windsor to London in order to volunteer his loyal services. Six years later, in 1843, he was back in London, and operated both a distillery and a flour mill there until 1863. He disappears from view for five years, but by 1868 he had found employment with the Inland Revenue Department. He achieved the high rank of lieutenant-colonel in the East Middlesex Militia and also had time to father ten children of whom John Mackenzie Moore, born on 1 October 1857 was the fifth.[3] Another son, Percy, eventually became a member of the legislative assembly for North London and revealed his good taste by spending many years as the tenant in the Henry Dunn house (fig. 134).[4]

    John M. Moore married Louise Mary McClary on 27 April 1881. Her father, Oliver McClary, had established a foundry that got its start manufacturing tinware.[5] By the 1880s, still under the family's control, the firm had gained an

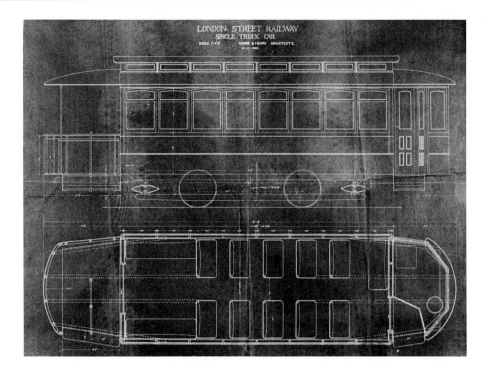

169   John M. Moore's design for a 'Single Truck Car' for the London Street Railway, 1905

international reputation as a manufacturer of stoves. The McClarys gave Moore's architectural venture a boost when they hired him to rebuild their factory after it was damaged by a fire on 30 November 1888. The *Advertiser* was rightly impressed by the speed of construction: 'There is probably no firm in Canada that has such a reputation for hustling as the McClary Manufacturing Company of this city. It is scarcely more than a month since a large portion of their shops on Wellington Street were burned to the ground, and already an immense block on King Street has been finished and is ready for occupation.'[6] Fifteen years later, the McClarys gave Moore an even more substantial commission, when they engaged him to design an entirely new plant, which was featured in the *Canadian Architect and Builder*. The in-laws gave Moore's work western exposure when he was selected to design their Vancouver storehouse (1897) and an addition to their Winnipeg offices (1899).[7]

While family connections helped create business opportunities for Moore, his own surveying and engineering knowledge ensured success in those fields. He was already recognized as an 'eminent hydraulic engineer' in the early 1880s, when he designed waterworks for Stratford (fig. 119) and East London.[8] One of his first commissions after he established his own firm was as a waterworks consultant for Walkerton (fig. 177). From 1894 to 1910 he was superintendent of the London waterworks.

Moore was appointed public engineer for at least five townships in the area: London, Westminster, Biddulph, Nissouri West, and Dorchester Station.[9] In this capacity he was very much involved in drainage problems, one of the major concerns of the period and a technical challenge dear to his own heart (one of his grandsons remembers him as 'a nut about drains').[10] A series of legislative acts passed during the 1860s and 1870s provided public funds for drainage projects to reclaim land and improve roads.[11] The township engineers responsible for overseeing these contracts needed tact – and courage – as well as a knowledge of the engineering requirements, because the installation of drains on one property inevitably had implications for the neighbours. Moore's correspondence suggests that bitter feeling often resulted from this situation. For example, Joseph Lockrey's letter to Moore describes hostilities in Belton from the point of view, one gathers, of the local inspectors: 'I went down to see Mr Bumbel's ditch but he refused to let me inspect the said ditch and when I turned my back he struck me with a club and you will have to look after the ditch as he refuses to have enny on elce to look at it and I wish you to look after it as soon as possible.'[12]

With his interests in engineering and architecture, Moore was naturally drawn to industrial design. His firm was responsible for a very large percentage of the factories that sprouted in London before the First World War, many of which provided new technology to the public. It designed the power station for the Canadian General Electric Company (1893), a boiler house for the London Electric Company (1899), and the four-storey exchange building for the Bell Telephone Company (1898). His company also undertook several projects for the London Street Railway Company, including a powerhouse (1895), car barns (1901), offices (1905), and a streetcar design (1905; fig. 169). Other commissions included work for several cigar factories and a headquarters building for the Empire Brass Manufacturing Company (1907; fig. 170) later to become EMCO), which made plumbers' and steamfitters' supplies. In terms of style, that building is typical of many of the firm's factories: blatantly utilitarian, with the size of the windows and their relationship to the piers the only major variables. The factories his firm designed just before the war, however, are more distinguished – in part, no doubt, because the architectural potential of functional structures was becoming more widely recognized and in part because some of these commissions represented extremely prestigious building projects. The large rectangular windows and tasteful proportions of the Battle Creek Toasted Corn Flake Company's London factory made a virtue of simplicity. The $250,000 biscuit factory the firm designed for D.S. Perrin & Company[14] was capped by a very striking modern Gothic cornice.

Moore knew when he started his own firm that he could count on his engineering skill as the foundation of an architectural business, but his experience in Durand's office suggests that his great talents as an organizer and businessman were then still untapped. Moore apparently learned from his distasteful experience as a junior partner not to risk within his own firm the sort of misunderstanding that had occurred between Durand and himself. The terms of Moore's partnerships were carefully defined in legal contracts. The

170   Perspective view of Empire Brass Manufacturing Company, London, designed in 1907 by Moore and Henry

articles of partnership drawn up between John Moore and Fred Henry in 1891 state that the firm will be called 'Moore and Henry,' that each partner will deduct $50 a month for living expenses, and that the profits will be shared at the end of each year, with Moore receiving a slightly larger percentage. The firm remained 'Moore and Henry' until 1908; then articles of partnership between Moore and J. Vicar Munro were drafted stating that the name would become 'Moore, Henry and Munro,' though only Moore and Munro were to divide the profits. Henry was in ill health by that time, and his name in the company's legal title seems to have been present merely as a gesture. It was dropped two years later. In 1912 Munro was placed on a salary of $100 a month in lieu of his share of the profits, although the firm still bore his name for one more year. In addition to spelling out the terms of the partnership, each document calls for adequate records to be maintained: 'Proper and correct books of account suitable for said business shall be kept in the office where said business is being carried on, and proper and correct entries made therein of all work or services performed ... of all moneys received, and of all expenditures in connection with said business.'[15]

Among the 'proper and correct books of account' were the journals recording each staff member's daily activities. Two of these daybooks from the years before the First World War still exist,[16] and they exhibit a considerably more painstaking attitude towards record-keeping than that which prevailed in Durand's office. Where Durand's daybook noted in general terms that 'JMM' was occupied with 'Petrolia Town Hall details' on 17 January 1888, Moore's daybook for 1899 states that on 12 June 'JAH' spent four hours 'drawing details of [the] skylight' for the London Printing and Lithography Company.

Sadly, the 1899 journal is more restrictive in its range as well as in its accounting than are Durand's daybooks: there is no intriguing chatter about the boss's whereabouts or the winners of the architects' and builders' baseball game to provide insights into other aspects of the firm's life. Since neither Moore nor Henry was paid according to tasks performed, neither's activities is recorded, and the daybook cannot be used to determine the exact division of their responsibilities. The 1912 journal is more revealing, because Vicar Munro was then salaried, and because the office had been organized along more efficient lines. In 1899 the staff was made up of somewhat itinerant architects and apprentices at varying stages in their development; by 1912 Moore's staff consisted of four permanent employees and additional temporary help when needed. Whereas the firm's earlier daybooks show all staff members working on each project, performing tasks appropriate to their skills, in 1912 a single staff member appears to have been responsible for seeing a project through all its stages. There is, nevertheless, a clearly discernible office hierarchy in 1912. O. Roy Moore (John M. Moore's son) and Donald Hennigar dealt mainly with industrial, engineering, and surveying projects, but the most important responsibilities, such as the Battle Creek Toasted Corn Flake Company and the Fireproof Warehousing Company, went to the junior Moore. Projects that required less engineering and more artistry – houses, churches, banks, schools, and a cottage for John McClary Moore, the partner's elder son – went to J. Vicar Munro and Courtney Reynolds. In this category, however, there seemed to be more shared buildings; Reynolds was clearly Munro's second-in-command. At the top of the tree, obviously very much in control of all the firm's productions, was John M. Moore.

As head of the firm, Moore would have handled the business and consulting aspects of the company's work. His outside roles and occasional references in the 1912 daybook (such as, under the initials 'CR,' 'measuring and surveying w/ JMM') make it clear that he also maintained his surveying and engineering interests. Just what he contributed to the artistic dimension of the firm is less certain, but the great variety in both the quality and the character of the firm's designs argues against any dominating artistic direction. On the contrary, the distinct change in style that occurred when J. Vicar Munro entered the business suggests that Moore left many of the esthetic decisions to his partners, an inference supported by the 1912 daybook.

In organizing his office around rather specialized functions, Moore was following the trend of his times. The 'day of the specialist,' predicted by architect W.E. Doran in 1889, had arrived. In the late nineteenth century the famous Chicago partnership Burnham and Root (1837–91), like that of Adler and Sullivan (1881–95), had already comprised one partner who was mainly a designer and one who was mainly a businessman.[17] And the businessman's talents were by no means regarded as inferior, even within the profession. An address by British architect Banister Fletcher, reported in a 1901 issue of the *Canadian Architect and Builder*, argued that architects must 'possess the business qualifications for guarding their [clients'] interests.' The theme was extended in 1902 by a New York architect named Julius Harder, in a spirited attack on the idea of the architect as artist: 'instead of our successful architects as a whole constituting a class of befogged dreamers, they are in reality fully as keen and of as large capacity in the business of money-getting as any other constituency in American affairs ... The architect must be a businessman first and an artist afterwards.'[18] John M. Moore filled that prescription.

There seems little doubt that it was in the area of industrial contracts that Moore's firm towered over the competition in the years before the war. His business was, however, active in other fields as well. Moore and Henry designed the YMCA in 1895. When a catastrophic fire gutted the Masonic Hall (fig. 101) in 1900, Moore and Henry created a new interior and added a fourth storey at the same time. The firm built several churches, including a great many country churches for the Roman Catholic diocese. It also designed a prodigious number of the new houses that were going up all over London.[19] Moore's personal stature within the profession was indicated by his election, as early as 1895, to the executive council of the Ontario Association of Architects.[20]

AFTER THE WAR

A study of Victorian architecture cannot reasonably extend beyond 1914. The altered economic conditions, tastes, and availability of materials made building after the First World War a different kind of art then it had been before. The story of Moore's life does not stop with the war, however: indeed, he achieved his greatest distinction in his later years.

Prior to the war, Moore had been involved in municipal affairs in his position as waterworks engineer; even earlier, while Tracy was on leave during the North West Rebellion in 1885, Moore had served as acting city engineer.[21] In 1916 he took a more direct part in city politics as a controller, and served two terms. In 1925 a petition was circulated asking him to run for mayor, and 1,500 signatures were collected. Moore mentioned this evidence of popular support frequently in his campaign, claiming that it constituted his main reason for seeking office.[22] He was probably conveying his true feelings to the voters, for he seems to have regarded so public a role as more a duty than a privilege: one obituary described him as 'a man of retiring nature, who shunned the limelight of public attention and approbation.'[23] His campaign platform was extremely vague ('Moore ... pledges himself to fight for the things of benefit to London and against those things which are not conducive to progress') compared with the twenty specific promises made by his colourful but less dignified opponent. He nevertheless won a substantial victory over his rival, who was both an incumbent and very popular.[24] Moore was such a popular mayor that he was elected to a second term by acclamation; unhappily, illness prevented him from serving more than half of his second year.[25]

Moore's performance as mayor revealed some of the qualities that made him a successful business man. In the interests of greater efficiency, he reorganized city council, city hall, and the fire department. Other major projects, such as the new Springbank Dam and a sanitary sewer system, reflected his concern with waterworks and sanitation; the former project represented a return to a previous interest in another way, since it had been Moore's idea to create Springbank Park. The *Advertiser* listed as one of Moore's major accomplishments as mayor 'a scheme for a new civic office building' which was 'later erected.'[26]

Much of Moore's success, as mayor and as architect, depended on his personal attributes, which are described with unusual thoroughness in his obituaries and are recalled vividly by two of his grandsons. While quiet, he was not 'low-key'; he chose his words carefully and expected his listeners to be attentive. He demanded a great deal, both of himself and of others: 'he wanted everyone to work twenty-four hours a day' and he worked hard himself; he had no hobbies and took few vacations. Though exacting, he was also scrupulously fair in his relations with other people. His self-discipline did not preclude humour (he had a 'dry wit') or sociability.[27] He dressed conservatively, always wearing a vest, tie, and watch fob. One grandson has particularly fond memories of Saturday mornings when he would ride in his grandfather's Model T Ford to visit the sites of projects under construction, go to the market, and return to his grandparents' house for lunch; John M. Moore would sometimes entertain the family with 'Indian stories – probably made up, but fascinating.'[28]

Moore seems to have possessed the rare ability to inspire in others the determination to live up to his high standards. An obituary explained part of the reason for his effectiveness: 'He had the reputation in the two years of his administration of knowing exactly when to leave an official alone to do his work. He knew what was to be done, and he never interfered unless he saw for himself that some other way of carrying out a project was a more efficient one.' City Clerk Samuel Baker asserted that the respect Moore showed his subordinates was more than reciprocated: 'Mr Moore was one of the most efficient mayors that the City of London ever had ... I don't know of anyone who won better service from the employees of this city than Mr Moore, because of his knowledge of the work and his readiness to understand everything that was going on. He had the happy faculty of demanding the very best from the staff, for they were anxious to please him, simply because he was what he was to them.'[29]

Undoubtedly, these qualities accounted in large measure for his firm's success as well. A partial list of the firm's undertakings during the 1920s shows that its dominance was no longer based exclusively on industrial projects. Between 1922 and 1924 J.M. Moore and Company, in association with F.H. Spier of Detroit, designed four structures for the new campus of the University of Western Ontario: the main arts and administration building, the natural sciences building, a boiler house, and a stately bridge over the Thames. Later commissions included a new Bell Telephone exchange (1929), the

171   London Life Insurance Company, London, designed in 1927; drawing signed 'John M. Moore & Co.'

$1 million Hotel London (1927), and the $750,000 head office of the London Life Insurance Company (1927). The latter, a monumental Neoclassical Revival structure (fig. 171) was hailed by the *Contract Record and Engineering Review* as 'one of the most handsome buildings erected in Canada in recent years.' The firm was also able to benefit from the expansion of local industries to other cities; it built branch plants in Hamilton and in St-Hyacinthe, Quebec.[30]

By the 1920s Moore's second son, O. Roy Moore, was taking a major part in the management of the business, but the senior partner remained actively involved in his profession throughout the decade, despite his duties as mayor, his advancing age, and the illnesses that plagued his final years. He also retained a prominent position in various professional organizations: for example, in 1927, he represented the Ontario Association of Architects on the Executive Council of the Royal Architectural Institute of Canada.[31]

The house Moore designed for himself in the mid-1920s is an interesting reflection of his architectural tastes and personal values. Until then he lived at 478 Waterloo Street in a large Italianate residence. In 1925 he decided to give up this house to his elder son, whose family could make good use of it, and to build a smaller house for himself and his wife at 1011 Wellington Street (fig. 172).[32] This house had only three bedrooms, including the maid's room, but it featured several amenities: a pantry, a den, a sunroom, and a billiard room. The correspondence shows that its materials, inside and out, were carefully chosen, and the exterior is striking, both for its material components and its unusual colour scheme – brownish grey stone and white stucco are surmounted by a green tile roof. Tile roofing was highly recommended but

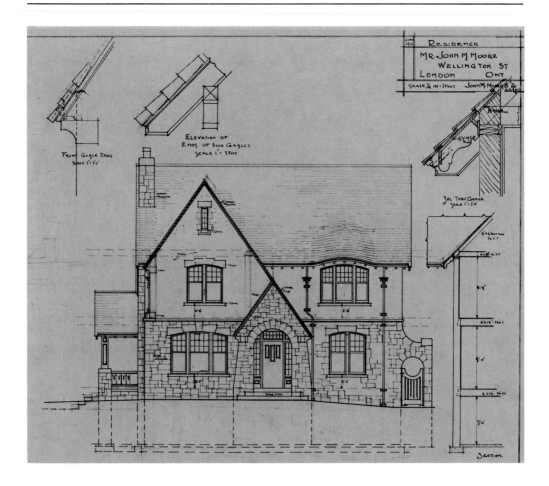

172   John M. Moore House, London

rarely used, owing to its expense. Moore's aim here was quality, not economy: the house cost $30,000 despite its relatively modest size and the absence of an architect's fee.[33]

It was in this house that John M. Moore died, on 19 June 1930. The London newspapers lamented the loss of an architect of 'exceptional ability' and one of the city's most public-spirited citizens. In addition to his more prominent roles, Moore's varied civic service included membership on university and hospital governing boards; like Tracy, he was an officer of the 7th Fusiliers.[34] Moore's business lived on, under the capable direction of his son O. Roy Moore. An era had ended with Moore's death, however; he was the last pupil of William Robinson, and a worthy inheritor of Robinson's tradition of practicality and engineering excellence.

STABILITY AND CHANGE IN THE MOORE ERA

In many ways, the London John M. Moore served as mayor in 1926 and 1927 had not changed from the London he knew as William Robinson's apprentice in the 1870s. For half a century the city seemed to value the same qualities in its mayor. Moore in 1925 and Benjamin Cronyn in 1874 fought successful election campaigns along the same lines: each presented himself as a candidate endorsed by prominent citizens and chose fiscal responsibility as his main campaign issue.[35]

Conservatism, an absorption in business, the cultivation of bourgeois virtues: the traits London looked for in its mayors often seemed to characterize the city itself. Fortunately for builders and architects, pride in home ownership was regarded as an outward and visible sign of the city's spiritual grace: 'A more elegant variety of residences have been erected,' the *Free Press* observed with satisfaction in early 1882, 'the rich and modestly circumstanced people alike have seen to the improvement of their homes.' More than thirty years later the *Free Press* equated social harmony with home ownership: 'Her people own their own homes to an extent that nowhere else obtains – it is estimated two-thirds of the population being in this fortunate position. One natural result of this is an intelligent, earnest working together of all classes for the advancement, the improvement, of the city as a whole.'[36]

London's religious and ethnic composition remained stable throughout the Moore years. The city was overwhelmingly Protestant, with 2,700 Catholics of a total population of 15,826 in 1871 and 5,262 out of 46,300 in 1911. The Methodists and Presbyterians together narrowly outnumbered the Anglicans in 1871 and widened their lead considerably by 1911. The number of Jews rose from 35 in 1871 to 569 in 1911, more than doubling in the last decade, but they still constituted less than 2 per cent of the population.

During the decade 1901–11 there was a flood of southern and eastern European immigration to the larger centres and the west of Canada, but these nationalities did not make their presence felt in London. Like the Jews, the Italians (103 in 1901; 224 in 1911) doubled their numbers, but remained a small minority. Only 946 people in 1911 had a 'European' (as opposed to British or Canadian) birthplace.

The immigrants chiefly responsible for London's growth between 1901 and 1911 were English. There were 2,489 people who claimed England as their birth-place in 1901; by 1911 the number was 6,206.[37] In 1910, the *Free Press* noted that 'a great number of English families' were creating a building boom 'all over West London.' A majority of these apparently modest houses were selling 'for a cost of about $1500.'[38]

In the first decade of the new century London's economic pattern confirmed the overall picture of stability. In Canada as a whole the years from 1900 to 1913 produced a frenetic boom. The value of London's goods went up an impressive 100.36 per cent, but Hamilton, in the same period, recorded a 221.95 per cent increase; the figures for Windsor, Brantford, and Stratford are 199.12 per cent, 185.12 per cent and 165.29 per cent. Within the London economy foundries were the largest single industry category in 1911, in terms of both capital ($3,529,228) and number of wage-earners (1,200). Bread and biscuit manufacture (McCormick's) was the second-leading employer, with a large increase from 1901, and cigar manufacturing, second in 1901, was still

173 'City of London, Canada,' 1893, lithograph printed by Toronto Lithographing Company

third in 1911.[39] 'The manager of one of the largest and most influential banks in the city' confided to the *Advertiser* in 1907 that London's prosperity was based on old companies rather than new-comers: 'He pointed out to the reporter that despite the fact that London is getting no industries to speak of, the city is growing at a tremendous rate ... Where is the work coming from? Not from new industries, but from the expansion of London's present factories.'[40]

London's population increase, from 37,981 in 1901 to 46,300 in 1911, was a respectable advance in a decade during which the movement was predominently to the largest cities. Yet it is interesting to observe that although London's rate of population growth was higher than those of its satellite centres (Woodstock, St Thomas, Chatham), it was lower than some smaller cities elsewhere in Ontario (Peterborough, Kitchener, Guelph).[41]

The statistics tend to confirm the claims London made for itself at this stage in its history. A promotional brochure issued by the city, *London The Forest City* (1906), states that 'There has been nothing of the leaps and bounds in the growth of London, the city never having experienced what in these days is termed a boom, but the progress has been steady, substantial, and of the come-to-stay kind.' While observing London's fiftieth birthday as a city, the *Free Press* congratulated the city in 1905 for being 'absolutely boomless.' The newspaper did have an explanation for its peculiar source of civic pride: 'London has never enjoyed a boom, and consequently has never suffered from one.'[42]

The reasons given for this steady prosperity are the same in 1905 as in 1875. The wholesale trade, just beginning to expand at the earlier date, continued to be a source of economic strength. London still defined itself as 'emphatically the railroad city of the Dominion': the city had landed the Grand

Trunk shops with a $100,000 bonus in 1895 and was looking eagerly to the CPR for dramatic expansion in 1910.[43] Above all, in these years before education and medicine became London's major businesses, the city saw itself as an industrial and manufacturing stronghold: 'one of the Greatest Commercial and Industrial Cities of the Dominion,' *London the Forest City* modestly claimed; the *Free Press* bragged, 'the tall chimneys are all smoking. There are no idle stacks.'[44]

Another element of continuity for more than a half-century was the blend of national patriotism and loyalty to England many Londoners seemed to feel. These sentiments emerged in the political campaigns and also in the military events that aroused in the citizens a passionate sense of duty. The participation of London volunteers in repelling the Fenian invasion and putting down the North West Rebellion has been mentioned in previous chapters. These episodes, for all their potential seriousness, did no harm to the London recruits, who found their reward in municipal banquets. The Boer War was another matter, since it brought suffering and death along with an outburst of patriotic enthusiasm. While determined London ladies were laying siege to Smallman and Ingram's store at its spring Millinery Opening ('for hours hundreds of ladies besieged the establishment unable to gain admission'),[45] Private George Taylor was discovering another side of life: 'On the next morning, I helped to bury the dead Canadians, 21 in all ... It was an awful sight ... We were all hungry for the want of grub. We marched 72 miles last week on half rations ... We have no tents here, and it rained all day yesterday and last night, and it was cold. A lot of the boys are laid up, but I don't feel bad, considering ... Well I guess I will say good-bye, and I hope it is not my last good-bye.'[46] Taylor did survive, but by October 1900 four London boys had died on the battlefield or of disease.[47]

Though Londoners could read about Taylor's and similar experiences in their newspaper, on the home front emotion continued to be optimistic and familiar in spirit. The British success in relieving the outpost town of Ladysmith produced a celebration comparable to the festivities arranged for the soldiers returning from the North-West Rebellion. For the *Free Press*, capturing the euphoria in its own prose, the Boer War parade had no rival in civic history: 'A day of wild rejoicing, of frenzied exultation, was climaxed at night with scenes such as [had] not before been witnessed. Literally, it might be said, the town was painted red. The streets were ablaze with red fire. Red bunting prevailed. Union Jacks with their wealth of red were everywhere.' The lesson of the day, the *Free Press* concluded, was 'London is loyal to the core.'[48]

That attachment to England, a powerful motive in any case, had been strengthened by the doctrines of imperialism that had emerged as a focus for political and economic debate in the years preceding the Boer War. Speaking at the 1896 annual meeting of the Board of Trade, the organization's president, John Bowman, linked economic prosperity with the national destiny and the bonds of empire: 'We have arrived at a position in the history of this Dominion when we must make advancement towards national greatness.

The doors of opportunity are opening ... With enlarged trade relations with the United Empire, this country should enter upon a period of great development and prosperity.'[49] In 1911 Prime Minister Laurier attempted to open another door of opportunity, the door marked free trade with the United States, but London, along with the rest of the country, refused to enter. The *Free Press*, backing the Conservative veteran Thomas Beattie in the 1911 campaign, certified him to be 'British to the backbone.' Beattie was not an inspiring candidate, and John McClary, the city's leading employer, felt obliged to intervene, as he did in the 1896 campaign, to bolster the Conservative cause. McClary's heavy-handed support itself became an issue, and the *Free Press* asserted that he was 'fighting the battle of Canadians against American aggression.' The newspaper's front-page headline proclaimed that the choice lay between 'Beattie or Buffalo.' When Beattie was elected, with a majority of 1,928, he said in his acceptance speech that he was 'thankful that the city had stood for this flag. Here the major waved a Union Jack.'[50]

Major Beattie was right. London had stood for the British flag, not only on this occasion, but on many occasions in the preceding fifty years. This political consistency was an important element among the factors that tended to promote stability in London's collective life.

Yet this principle of continuity is not the only pattern one can discern in London as a community. Viewed in other perspectives, London was a city that exhibited aspiration as well as placidity, social dynamism as well as stasis, becoming as well as being. This contrapuntal theme may be heard in the single word that appears so insistently in every contemporary account of the city: 'progress.' The article praising London as 'boomless' nevertheless maintains that 'Her story is a story of uninterrupted progress.' To progress is necessarily to change and, particularly in the Moore years, some fundamental changes took place.

Architects need change as a condition of employment – no doubt Moore, Henry, and Munro along with their colleagues rejoiced in the dramatic westward and southward expansion of the city in the 1900–14 period. According to the *Free Press* estimate, 'close to two hundred houses' were built in South London in 1905 and 1906: 'the passenger on a Ridout Street line car may not anywhere cast his eye without encountering evidence of growth.'[51]

The appearance of London was altered in a different way by the most powerful instrument of 'progress' in that day and ours: technology. Electric lighting of the streets began in 1886; a decade later residents of Wellington Street from Dufferin Avenue to Central Avenue 'had signed a petition for an asphalt pavement,' drawing the support of an alderman who argued that 'there are hundreds of bicycles and carriages going around there every night, and it is not safe.'[52] As early as 1883 the Forest City Bicycle Club had petitioned council for permission to use the exhibition grounds. In 1896 Moore's former client, T.G. Whiskard, became 'another prominent businessman to assume control of a bicycle.'[53] Less exalted travellers could make use of the London Street Railway Company, established in 1873, which was electrified in 1895. Verschoyle Cronyn, at one time president of the street railway, demonstrated flexibility of mind when approaching the age of seventy by becoming one of the first Londoners to own a motor car.[54]

London was a pioneer in the implementation of two technologies that transformed urban life – the telephone and hydro-electric power. London, Ontario had its first telephone exchange in 1879 – the same year service was initiated in London, England.[55] By 1900 the Ontario London had a 'splendid new exchange,' as the *Free Press* headlined its three-column story.[56] The newspaper's reporter was evidently dazzled by the mysteries of technology: 'A wonderful system, truly. Only the electrical expert, whose natural gifts have been trained to the fine point, may understand all that he sees in the new Exchange.' Credit was given where it was due: 'The new building has been completed at large cost. Not that waste occurred. Such careful architects as Moore and Henry had charge. But expense was not spared to secure a permanence perhaps equalled by no other building in London.' Technological advance created many new occupations in this period, particularly for women; among them was the job of the 'telephone girl.' The London exchange employed twenty-five of these paragons to serve its 1,350 customers. The *Free Press* launched into a lyrical portrait of this new breed:

The business man out of temper and the dyspeptic woman – they all come her way, and seem to think she was made to hear all the mean things that could not be said to anyone else ... In spite of all, the telephone girls of London – and it is so elsewhere – are as efficient, trust-worthy and well-behaved as the best young women of the land. They are bright and intelligent, of agreeable and courteous disposition and manner, and have a talent for attending to their own business.

Sir Adam Beck, London's apostle of publicly owned electric power, was not renowned for being agreeable or courteous, but he was chiefly responsible for bringing cheap electricity to his home city and to the entire province. In February of 1903, while he was mayor of London, Beck 'assumed the position of leadership' among municipal politicians just beginning to press for public ownership. After Beck turned to the legislature as the platform for his crusade, other London politicians remained loyal to his vision, and the city was one of a small number of Ontario municipalities that banded together to sign a first contract with Beck's Hydro Electric Power Commission.[57] Public power from Niagara Falls reached London on 30 November 1910, and Adam Beck was in the London transformer station to greet it: 'When the last volt had been thrown on to the wires at Niagara Falls the transformers in the power station here were singing merrily. "That is music, surely," said Hon. Adam Beck, chairman of the power commission, as he watched the volt-meter, and saw that the system was receiving the voltage of 140,000 without flinching.'[58]

Beck's career in its own way represented the principle of change as much as the technological processes and political strategies he championed. Of puritanical German Lutheran stock, he developed expensive habits and a taste for show horses; a hard-driving businessman (he had invented a new way of making cigar boxes), he became famous as a tireless advocate of public enterprise; a Conservative regional chief, in succession to John Carling, he eventually broke with his party and ran as an independent.[59]

The sounds of technology and change were not all as sweet as the polite chatter of the telephone girls or the music of the hydro wires. There were also the 'jeers and hisses and curses' that greeted Mayor Wilson in 1899 when he read the Riot Act and called in the militia after property of the London Street Railway Company had been 'wantonly destroyed' during the bitter strike of 1899.[60] The strike, launched against an absentee American owner, was not so much about wages as about recognition of the union, an issue that also surfaced in the cigar-makers' strike of 1910.[61] Rather surprisingly, the *Advertiser* chose to favour the cause of the streetcar employees; playing the old game of attacking its rival, the *Free Press* raised a new issue in a city the newspaper usually praised as a model of social harmony: 'A city journal, seemingly destitute … of a proper sense of its responsibility, has done its part every day in fomenting discontent and arousing class hatred.'[62] Whatever the cause, class division was certainly apparent in the subsequent mayoralty election. The Socialist Labour candidate, Fred Darch, lost by less than 300 votes to his opponent. David Ross, a Socialist Labour candidate for alderman, proclaimed, 'When the Maxim gun was trundled down the streets, the capitalists made a mistake in their excitement and panic.' Ross was elected.[63]

By July 1914 the *Free Press* had recovered its good temper and was praising London as 'one of the loveliest and smartest centers on the continent.'[64] With charming artlessness the editorial rediscovers the old talisman in professing to find 'the new spirit of progress that has seized upon the people of London.' The city's revitalization was aided by the fact that 'London went boldly and whole-heartedly into the hydro-electric project … and already the benefits are being reaped in a splendidly-lighted city, in cheap power for her manufacturers, in an abundance of current for the operation of her street railway and in many comforts and economies for the home.'

Just a month before, an Austrian archduke had been assassinated in a Serbian town. As the crisis leading to the First World War deepened with dizzying speed, the *Free Press* moved in its editorials from a detached and analytical 'Europe at War' (3 August) to a more emotional 'The Empire at War' only two days later. The former editorial asks: 'Can England continue neutral? There does not appear to be as yet anything that necessarily involves the motherland, save her understanding with France and Russia.' The latter editorial asserts: 'Inevitably England must have been drawn into the conflict of nations.' At the beginning of the crisis the newspaper could not even imagine that Canada might have a role to play in a European war; by 6 August Canada, like England, was perceived to have only one course of action: 'If need arises we will enlist not one but many divisions to maintain the flag and the empire.'

Along with the rest of the world London underestimated the profundity of the changes the war would bring. This was an understandable miscalculation. The new war seemed to be like all the others – an opportunity for the expression of patriotism and loyalty. The 7th Fusiliers gallantly volunteered to serve in Europe, just as the regiment had gone west during the North West Rebellion nearly thirty years before.[65] The Boer War was not only a more recent memory, but also a basis for confidence: 'the experience gained in South Africa and the lessons learned in mobilization and transport at that time will ... make Canada's part in the threatened conflict easier to prepare for.' This war would be an improvement on the South African model: 'There is every reason to believe that with the growth of imperial sentiment meanwhile the response would be even more general and enthusiastic than that which characterized the enlistment for the South African campaign.'[66]

There is interesting evidence that ordinary citizens felt more apprehension than bravado. The crisis coincided with an Old Boys' Reunion – a formal gathering of former Londoners, quite common at that time. The old boys were perhaps not as joyful as the *Free Press* wished to claim: 'The holiday spirit prevailed, in spite of the ominous rumours of war ... The consequences of so mighty a conflict filled each heart with horror. However, the old boys tried to forget the news of battle and they succeeded in doing so remarkably well.'[67] Sir Adam Beck was on hand to cure depression: 'He pointed out that London was coming into her own, that prosperity was her portion.' Beck's prophesy and the old boys' fears were both proved correct: London did prosper mightily in the ensuing years, while retaining some of its traditional character; at the same time, the war demonstrated that technology and change had its own evil momentum, that the dissolution of the more stable Victorian world had its cost.

THE IDEAL HOME

While Londoners welcomed 'progress' from the security of their own prosperous and stable world, accelerating technological development had its critics elsewhere. From the beginning of the nineteenth century the evils of the Industrial Revolution had not escaped attention in England, but it was the uncontrolled urbanization of the late Victorian period that aroused opposition in North America. Cities seemed to breed crime and hopelessness in the teeming slums and tension in the success-oriented affluent areas. The refuge in both instances was the well-run and tasteful home. An entry in an 1870 issue of *Appleton's Journal* idealized the home as 'a place of repose' after the trials of the marketplace, where a husband, back from the business wars, could 'take off his armor, relax his strained attention, and surrender himself to perfect rest.'[68] The curative powers of the home were increasingly regarded as a panacea. An illustration entitled 'As We Sow, We Shall Reap' in an American publication of 1884 showed that 'Pleasant, Beautiful' homes encouraged goodness and happiness; 'poverty' and 'squalor' bred 'brutal passion' and 'base desire.'[69] An early sociologist, writing in 1899, claimed:

'Every city, the majority of the citizens whereof are householders, is safe, not from riots, but from successful riots ... Building societies are the best form of special police and civic, unarmed militia. The dangerous classes are all nomadic.'[70] Presenting the positive side of this view, the *Free Press* gave a glowing account of virtuous, home-owning tradesmen listening eagerly to an election speech by Adam Beck: 'It was an audience largely composed of London East workingmen, and that means men who own their own comfortable, happy homes, and who are in consequence most deeply interested ... in the welfare of their city.'[71]

The increasing emphasis placed on the home as a promotor of psychological, moral, and civic health brought the field of domestic architecture into greater prominence. The *Canadian Architect and Builder* observed in 1895 that 'scientific house planning is a study of our own days.' Philadelphia architect William Price was applauded at the 1903 convention of the Ontario Association of Architects when he argued that the design of houses was more important than that of skyscrapers:

we have come to a time when neither the civic nor the religious is the ideal around which we build our civilization, but the individual, the domestic. Take all those high buildings with which you gentlemen are wrestling in pain and trouble ... what are they for? After all are they not merely the places that we go to (to get away from as soon as we can) that we may have enjoyable surroundings in our home life? That is the sole object, and while we should make them as little obnoxious as possible and keep them as quiet as possible, because they tend to ramp and rave ... our greatest effort should be put upon making the object of all this beautiful, and that is, after all, our homes. (Applause.)[72]

The growth of interest in house architecture and the emergence of the Queen Anne style were, to a large extent, interrelated phenomena, for the Queen Anne architects were mainly interested in domestic design, and the cheerful, cosy Queen Anne houses, self-consciously based on the common man's dwellings in the past, seemed perfectly to answer the needs of the present ideal home. Most crucially, their irregular contours allowed for great flexibility in the all-important plan of a house. In a paper on house planning read in 1898 before the Toronto Chapter of Architects Grant Helliwell argued that 'planning presents fully as wide a field as exterior design for the exercise of the imagination and the employment of those creative faculties which alone can produce the beautiful.'[73] The *Canadian Architect and Builder*, commenting in 1895 on the drawings displayed at the Royal Canadian Academy exhibition, complained that 'there is little satisfaction in either looking at or discussing a dwelling house without knowing its plan.'[74] The plan was to be carefully designed to accommodate the individual needs of the client's family, to allow for efficient movement from one place to another, to separate the public and private rooms, to make certain that, for example, the breakfast room got morning light while the drawing room faced west, and to see that the servants and the family were not constantly forced to cross paths.

Probably the most striking innovation of the period was the hall. The earliest Queen Anne, or Old English, country houses had incorporated in their plan a large communal room based on the all-purpose hall of the medieval dwelling, a large high-ceilinged room, usually dominated by a great fireplace, where the family and servants ate, lived, and sometimes slept. As the new style accommodated itself to the more humble demands of the middle-class dwelling, the idea of a welcoming, informal, but imposing hall-room remained. J.W.F. Newton's paper on 'The Planning of Small Houses,' delivered to the Birmingham Architectural Association in 1895, stated as an unequivocal requirement that even with a small house one should enter into a 'hall-sitting room' of 'about 9 ft. by 12,' instead of into the conventional long passageway. If possible, an 'inglenook' or a 'corner fireplace' should 'add to the picturesqueness of this cosy room.'[75] Grant Helliwell thought that the hall should form a 'beautiful,' 'imposing,' and 'useful' apartment, and advised 'specially' against a 'long, narrow effect.' Often the hall still contained the stairway, which angled up in the corner, but the stairway might be relegated to a separate stair-hall behind. The other rooms were to share the picturesque features of the hall. Newton suggested placing a 'long, low window, with a seat recessed, and a simple beamed ceiling' in the dining room. Helliwell prescribed that the walls of the drawing room 'be broken by bays, recesses or ingles.'[76] Intimate, quaint, crowded with potted plants and ladies' handiwork, filled with private nooks and corners, the ideal Queen Anne house created an inner world of its own. Though often located, thanks to the new streetcar lines, in a 'garden suburb,' the house tended to look inward, separated from the exterior world by high steps, vestibules, and art-glass windows.

The idea that every man should have his castle reigned without challenge in the Moore era and accounted, along with the growing population, for the large number of new houses built during that period. In the first nine months of 1894, a somewhat depressed year, 117 new dwellings were erected in London, and the *Canadian Architect and Builder* listed Moore and Henry first among those to whom credit was due for the fine character of these houses.[77] The early houses designed by Moore and Henry tended to be dependent on Durand's exterior designs, but where Durand usually relied on the conventional centre-hall and side-hall plans, Moore and Henry created plans that were original, varied, and irregular. There is usually a separate stair-hall that forms a room of its own, sometimes, as in the Sutherland house (fig. 209) with a fireplace and hall bench providing the requisite cosy atmosphere. The entrance hall was usually spacious; in the Leonard house (fig. 191) it comprised a very impressive room with a beamed ceiling and an alcove in the tower. Both plans show the characteristically irregular room shapes favoured by the times: the library of the Sutherland house features an alcove, a recessed window seat, and an angled corner fireplace; the drawing room of the Leonard house has an arch along one side leading to an alcove that was also accessible from the library.

In the 1890s the library was regarded as an almost essential room, but its use changed shortly after the turn of the century. Helliwell still assumed, in 1898, that the library would be used 'by a student,' or 'for a general family reading room.'[78] By 1906 conviviality had won out over intellectuality. An article in the *Canadian Architect and Builder* described the library as 'the most unconventional, free-and-easy room beneath the roof – the only one whose door is always open, and the one in which the family life is best developed.'[79] The change in function is indicated in Moore's and Henry's plans by a change in nomenclature: the 'library' has become the 'den.' There seems to have been a definite hierarchy of public rooms in that most of the firm's houses had both a 'drawing room' and a reception or sitting room, with the former generally retaining an elegant formality. As the hall became a more complete room, one of the other living rooms tended to disappear: the Leonard house has only a drawing room and the Sutherland house only a reception room. Just before the First World War, however, the halls, though still sizeable, reverted to being formal passageways, and it again became fashionable to have two living rooms, now called 'parlours,' 'sitting rooms,' or 'living rooms.' The new names apparently indicated a wish to turn away from the 'concentrated stiffness and glaring lack of welcome' that had been regarded as characteristic of the more formal drawing room.[80]

'A YEARNING FOR SIMPLICITY'

While the flexibility and cosiness of the Queen Anne style made it seem in some ways the perfect embodiment of the ideal home, other aspects – its eclecticism, its exuberant decoration and the very irregular lines of its wings and protruberances – eventually came in for criticism. A Toronto newspaper spoke of 'Queen Anne or Modern Bizarre'; an article in the *Canadian Architect and Builder* mocked 'Queen-in-Anne-ity.'[81] The idealization of the home was part of a broader movement that advocated greater simplicity in all areas of life; by that standard, Queen Anne houses were tastelessly showy and blatantly materialistic. One of the best-sellers of the Edwardian period was *The Simple Life*, written by a French clergyman named Charles Wagner, in which the 'man of modern times' is described as struggling in 'a maze of endless complication' from which he can escape only by developing 'simplicity' as a 'state of mind.' President Roosevelt invited Wagner to the United States in 1904, claiming that 'no other book ... contained so much that we of America ought to take to our hearts.'[82] Edward Bok, editor of the *Ladies Home Journal* after 1889, became a convert to Wagner's notions and constantly presented the ideal family as one which emphasized mental contentment over affluence, books and charities over elaborate toys and furniture, and 'simple lines and quiet detail' over 'useless turrets, filigree work or machine-made ornamentation.'[83]

The yearning for a simpler architecture was widespread, and took a variety of forms. Opponents of eclecticism designed in purer and more correct historical styles. For example, the prestigious firm of McKim, Mead and White gave impetus to the popular Neoclassical revival in the United States. Charles McKim explained to one client that he wanted to build like the Greeks, to the extent that he would not be able to insert a knife between fitted stones.[84] The 'English Wrenaissance,' as it has been playfully labelled, was a revival on patriotic grounds of the English Baroque style. Similar nationalistic motives resulted in a Colonial revival based on early American houses.[85]

The reaction against technology in favour of work done according to traditional methods found an important expression in the Arts and Crafts movement, begun by William Morris and his colleagues in the early 1860s. By 1904 twenty-five Arts and Crafts societies in the United States were producing quality hand-made goods, and attempting to educate the public about the virtues of their method. As in England by this date, Arts and Crafts enthusiasts had come to favour furniture and decoration with very simple lines, and the movement promoted an architectural style with the same qualities. Gustav Stickley's popular journal, *The Craftsman: An Illustrated Monthly Magazine for the Simplification of Life* (est. 1901), contained numerous plans suited to the movement's ideals.[86]

Simple lines characterized other stylistic developments as well. In the early 1880s there developed in New England a fashion based on using wood shingles as wall covering. Unlike the American Stick style, the new Shingle style concealed the wood frame of the house, replacing the busy, broken surface of the earlier buildings with long expanses of shingles. Its roofline was also quieter.[87] During the first decade of this century Frank Lloyd Wright, who claimed that his 'first feeling had been a yearning for simplicity,' developed a style of house with very pure, horizontal lines, to harmonize with the 'natural beauty' and 'quiet level' of the mid-western prairie.[88] Meanwhile, the Commercial style buildings of Chicago, with their unadorned piers and broad windows, were being widely imitated, and a kind of simplified Gothic, inspired largely by the work of the American architects Ralph Adams Cram and Bertram Grosvenor Goodhue, was being used for commercial buildings, schools, and churches.[89] Louis Sullivan, whose firm combined clear-cut forms with a distinctive sort of intricate ornamentation, was apparently right when he observed in 1906 that 'the intellectual trend of the hour is towards simplification.[90]

The *Canadian Architect and Builder* provides evidence that the case for simplicity was put forward in Canada. Grant Helliwell, for example, insists that 'simplicity and breadth of treatment are of the first importance in house design,' and goes on to describe several ways in which 'rest or repose in buildings may be obtained.' To build in the Queen Anne style is prohibited: 'It is impossible to give an air of quiet restfulness to a house whose façades are full of features – bays and turrets and balconies, windows large and small, square and round distract the eye and weary the brain in hopeless search for something on which to rest. A certain proportion of plain wall surface is an indispensible condition; without it repose is unattainable.'[91] An article in a

1901 issue argues against the use of contrived 'vagaries' intended to make buildings look 'picturesque': 'the picturesque, really and truly, will only come unsought' when an architect unifies his plan around a single 'leading idea,' 'whole and complete in itself.'[92] Architect William Price argued in 1903 for man-made rather than machine-made goods:

Now can we get the people we build for and the people we build with, to go with us, and return ... towards a more simple method of construction? ... I think that there is one way we can do it if no other ... instead of cluttering up the inside or the outside of our houses with numberless mouldings and brackets and 'the Lord knows what, of round and square, stuck here, there and everywhere,' without any special meaning except that our ancestors or forefathers did it in marble or some other material ... We can ... substitute for them extreme honest simplicity in construction, and a little bit of good carving.[93]

While there is some consensus about the desirability of greater simplicity in architecture and a good deal of discontent with existing stylistic practices, one senses in many articles of the *Canadian Architect and Builder* less certainty than Price expressed as to the specific direction a modern style should take. In a very comprehensive paper delivered at the 1896 convention of the Ontario Association of Architects, Toronto architect D.B. Dick discussed possible approaches to developing a new style and concluded that each had failed during the course of the century. He noted that in the past 'the change from one style to another was always the result of the introduction of new factors such as a change in structural methods caused by the attempt to solve new problems or supply new needs,' and that one might therefore expect 'modern opportunities' from 'the increase in knowledge of the properties and strength of materials and of the principles of framing, and the improvements in the manufacture of iron and steel and of glass.' Unfortunately, iron had been used mainly to make inferior copies of old forms; the skyscraper, 'the one great opportunity of modern times,' was also derivative and, moreover, impractical: 'A street of skyscrapers would defeat its own purposes, and a city of skyscrapers would be unfit to live in.' Neither the eclectic approach nor an attempt to capture 'some old style at an incomplete stage in its development' and 'carry it onward' had been any more successful. The best approach a young architect could take was to become a master of one historical style so that he could be creative within it. This option was questioned by none other than Moore's partner, Fred Henry, who asked 'how an architect who confined himself to one style, and practised in that style only, was to live.' Dick replied that 'it was not always possible to pursue the course that was theoretically the best.'[94]

Other articles also predicted little change in general stylistic practices. A paper copied from the *Builder* in 1899 foresaw only 'cycles of fashion in revivals of past styles,' since building symbolism was so firmly established: 'it is by association of ideas merely that certain styles are popularly apportioned to certain types of building.'[95] W.E. Doran argued that the development of a new style was impossible because of the 'high pressure' under which architects worked. Like many others, he was also concerned with the absence of any clearly Canadian style. He blames this deficiency on the many publications available; the effect of the glut was to make 'unconscious plagarism almost inevitable.'[96]

Another Montreal architect, Percy Nobbs, seems by 1913 to have become resigned to the non-existence of a specifically Canadian architecture: the United States, he maintained, had discovered new directions in design, and Canada was bound to be influenced by the 'highly developed and specialized architecture of the United States.' He doubted that Canadian architecture would ever develop a character of its own and warned that one should certainly not expect such a phenomenon soon:

there are many climates in Canada and the conditions of life vary greatly in the different provinces. The population is moreover very heterogeneous in character, and this polyglot people will probably evince a cosmopolitan eclecticism for a generation or two before any national expression of art can become possible! ... In the confusion of Babel the ultimate aspect of the tower must have been difficult to foresee – and so it is with Canadian architecture.[97]

Both the Canadian vacillation about new directions and the strong American influence were discernible in the buildings by Moore's firm. Indeed, the insecurity regarding stylistic questions that was found elsewhere in the province was heightened in the early work of Moore and Henry by their relative inexperience; both initially tended to be heavily dependent on Durand's designs. As in the rest of Ontario, there was a strongly conservative element in their work. Churches still employed the forms and motifs of the Victorian Gothic mode. Most houses were Queen Anne right up to 1913. The prevailing respect for simplicity and respose was nevertheless evident in a trend towards less complicated rooflines, less intricate ornament, and a greater emphasis on breadth. Richardson's influence was clearly apparent in much of the work of the 1890s; in the new century houses were more frequently influenced by the popular American revival styles.

It may have been the importance attached to early American architecture that led Moore to take an interest in his local architectural heritage. He bought and restored Dalmagary Cottage, the single-storey Georgian house near Hyde Park that had been built by his grandfather, Duncan Mackenzie, and used it as an occasional summer retreat.[98] He seems, however, never to have regarded it as a model for new designs of his own.

Before 1913 very clear-cut, uncomplicated designs seem to have been reserved for utilitarian structures such as factories, warehouses, and commercial buildings. After the war, the firm built houses in the Prairie style, as well as in a number of the modern period styles. Traces of the Victorian spirit never-theless remained in the firm's work, as is evident in one of its most important projects of the 1920s, the main building on the new campus of the University of Western Ontario.

THE NEW UNIVERSITY

Despite its rather shaky start in the old Collegiate Institute (fig. 43), the Western University had managed to survive. Its financial health improved considerably in 1908 when the city of London assumed primary responsibility for the institution, agreeing initially to pay $5,000 for five years.[99] With the burgeoning enrolment at the end of the war, the university felt that better facilities were required, to replace the rented space at Huron College and various sites around north London. The Board of Governors chose a location that, according to the *Journal* of the Royal Architectural Institute of Canada, was 'conceded by many as the finest University site in Canada.'[100] The project drew enthusiastic support from the area's citizens: the County of Middlesex contributed $100,000 to the university building project, as its memorial to the soldiers who had died in the war, and London voters approved the city's grant of $250,000. The provincial government assured the viability of the scheme by providing an initial capital grant of $800,000.[101]

After consulting John M. Moore about the new buildings, the board hired Detroit architect Frederick Spier, who had achieved recognition for his work at the University of Michigan, as an adviser. Spier and the university president, Sherwood Fox, made a tour of several American universities and recommended to the Board of Governors that buildings of stone, in a Collegiate Gothic style, be erected.[102] Spier provided tentative floor plans for the pro-posed buildings, and Moore's firm, hired as the main architects for the project, apparently drew elevations and oversaw their construction. Moore also served the university as a member of the Board of Governors; furnishings for the board's original meeting room, a richly panelled chamber in the tower of the Main Building, with a carved stone mantel and a beamed ceiling, were his own gift to the university.

The main building (fig. 174) still reflected some of the Victorian values outlined in chapter 1. A well-known Scottish planning expert, Thomas Adams,[103] assisted in the choice of an excellent site, at the end of the avenue leading to the university and at the top of a rise. With the benefit of this location, the irregular contours of the building's tower, hall, and battlements appear highly picturesque. Its Perpendicular Gothic style was ultimately based on a model drawn from the past, and it represented a continuation of the symbolic link between Gothicism and learning that had been established in the nineteenth century.

The meaning of the legacy from the previous centuries seems not to have been realized by the first commentators on the university's architectural style. Indeed, they seem to have taken pains to deny such an inheritance. Sherwood

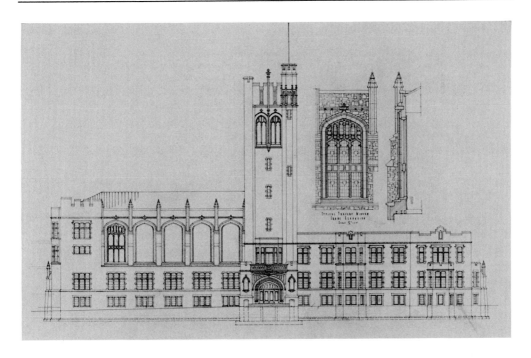

174   Main Arts and Administration Building, The University of Western Ontario, London, Ontario, 1922–4, designed by John M. Moore and Company in association with F.H. Spier (Detroit)

Fox advocated buildings like those at Princeton, not because of Princeton's academic tradition, but because London's university would occupy a similar terrain. Fred Landon, a Western graduate and professor, insisted that the style was chosen 'for the particular purpose of these buildings and for the setting in which they are placed ... There was no attempt made to reproduce any Oxford college or other model.'[104] Whereas a century before a building's style would have been praised on the grounds of its associations, by the 1920s even to admit those overtones was not fashionable. The new roles of architecture were purely functional and esthetic. The new university building was to be a reflection rather than a symbol of its builders' aspirations.

Dorchester Presbyterian Church, completed 1889
Dorchester

A Presbyterian congregation was organized in what was then Edwardsburgh in 1884. The following year, with the help of the Reverend Mr John Scott from St Andrew's Presbyterian Church in London, the congregation managed to build a simple, 'barely furnished' church on a country site some distance north of the village.[105] At about the same time the arrival of the railroad inaugurated a new name for the village, Dorchester Station (the 'station' was later dropped), and an assurance of prosperity. By 1888 Dorchester Station could claim a respectable number of industries – a flour mill, an agricultural implement factory, two pump works, a wagon shop, a mattress factory, and a planing mill – and 450 inhabitants.[106] The town's growth was mirrored in the expanded congregation of the Presbyterian church which, in 1889, built a larger and more substantial church, designed by the London architect who had provided plans for the new Methodist church nearby.[107]

John M. Moore's design for the Presbyterian church was very conservative. It used the same format, with a centre tower, that Robinson had employed over twenty years before. The tower design drew on various churches by Durand. The shape of the spire, for example, is like that of the Baptist Church in Palmyra (fig. 99); the three small windows over the door are also found in the design for St Philip's in Petrolia; the motif of an oculus cradled between the pointed arches was used by Durand in numerous contexts, including the tower of Christ Church, Delaware (fig. 125). Though derivative, the height and the lines of the Dorchester church make it a striking feature of the landscape. It now sits just at the village's edge, still serving a Presbyterian congregation. Seen from the highway or the train, across the flat surrounding fields, the church has the commanding and somewhat poignant quality of a tall ship sailing a calm sea.

175   Dorchester Presbyterian Church, detail of architectural drawing showing front elevation; drawing signed 'J.M. Moore'

176   Dorchester Presbyterian Church

Walkerton Pump House, c. 1890–2

Walkerton

In August 1890 the Town of Walkerton passed a by-law permitting the town to raise $25,000 for the construction of a waterworks system, having 'caused their Engineer John M. Moore, Esquire, to ascertain and report on the best source ... of supply.'[108] That Moore was town engineer for Walkerton attests to the wide range of his practice: the county seat of Bruce County, Walkerton is about ninety miles north of London. Histories of Walkerton display considerable pride in its progressiveness (which was customary) and beauty (which receives unusual emphasis). An 1867 directory says, for example, that 'it is beautifully situated on a plateau of slightly elevated ground forming the banks of the Saugeen river.' An 1880 atlas praises the town's 'literary and society organizations,' its communication and transportation facilities, its commercial enterprise ('Anything like a correct estimate of the number of business houses would require a regular census to compute'), and, especially, its architectural merit: the 'schools and churches ... would grace a city,' there were 'an unusually large number of exceptionally fine private residences,' and the prominent courthouse was 'a very fine white brick edifice.' Among the many complaints that were raised against the proposed waterworks was the *Bruce Herald*'s conviction that 'the works should be made an ornament to the town ... not behind the railway track through their yards.'[109]

Moore's design for the Pump House is hardly that of a civic monument, but it is in the firm's tradition of basing pump houses on popular domestic patterns (figs 74 and 119). In this case the model was not an Ontario Cottage but rather the one-and-a-half storey, gable-roofed dwelling that Douglas Richardson in *Ontario Towns* defines as 'the typical Ontario house.' Houses of this type had been built in rural areas for decades as a means of reducing taxes: storey-and-a-half houses paid less tax than two-storey houses, while containing the same amount of floor space.[110] The front gable that became an intrinsic part of the design served practical as well as esthetic purposes, allowing more light in the upper storey, providing ventilation in summer, and diverting the snow from over the door in winter. The basic design is dressed up here with horizontal lines of rough-textured brick, a simple verge-board, the round-arched window, and cresting along the roof ridge; nevertheless the building would not have been any fancier than many of its authentically domestic cousins. In fact, the Walkerton Pump House could claim a certain domesticity, for it contained a living room, a sitting room, and four bedrooms. There was no kitchen. Presumably the bedrooms were only meant to provide sleeping facilities for operators on the night shift.

One local historian believes that the system designed by Moore may not have been completed. Letters to the editor certainly indicate that the local

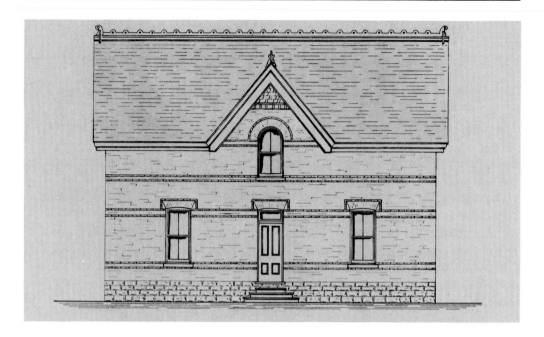

177   Walkerton Pump House, detail of architectural drawing showing front elevation; drawing signed 'J.M. Moore'

newspaper had a following in its opposition to the project. Nevertheless, one objection the *Herald* made does imply that some progress had been made: the newspaper claims in October of 1891 that the town council had already built the reservoir when it had as yet no title to the land.[111] Furthermore, an 1892 by-law 'to regulate the Working and Management of the Waterworks of the Town of Walkerton' contains a schedule of rates – $4.00 for a five-room house, $2.00 more for a bath-tub' to be paid 'in advance on the first days of April and October.'[112] Whether the citizens of Walkerton elected to choose thrift or cleanliness remains something of a mystery.

FRED HENRY

The young man who entered a partnership with John M. Moore in 1891 was well endowed with the gifts of nature and fortune. His father, Bernard Henry, is listed in a city directory shortly after Fred's birth as a dealer in books and stationery and the owner of a news depot; a brief biography of Fred Henry describes his father as 'one of the pioneer merchants of the City of London.'[113] The large house at 854 Richmond Street that Henry designed for himself in 1895[114] suggests that he must have had some source of independent means, possibly through his family. He was also handsome, popular, and off to a very promising start in his career. A niece recalls that when he married nine years later, in 1900, he was considered 'quite a catch.'[115]

Born on 8 August 1865, Henry reached the age of apprenticeship in the early 1880s, when he undertook a kind of double training: he simultaneously learned architecture from Durand and land surveying from Moore. He qualified as a land surveyor on 7 April 1887.[116] A month later he was appointed assistant city engineer under Thomas Tracy.[117] Possibly his experience in that position persuaded him against a career in engineering, for he resigned a year later, on 19 March 1888, apparently in order to seek broader experience elsewhere. The *City Council Proceedings* contain an acknowledgment of 'the efficient manner in which [Mr F. Henry] has discharged his duties in connection with this corporation,' and a wish for his 'every success in his profession wherever he may make his future home.' It is not certain where Henry did make his home during the following year, though the only surviving account of his life offers a clue that he might have been in New York.[118] By March 1889 he was back in Durand's office,[119] and on 27 June the *Free Press* reported that Henry was managing Durand's business during his illness. He carried on independently as Durand's successor for two years after his employer's death and then joined Moore in a partnership in which, as has already been mentioned, he apparently bore the major responsibility for the artistic side of the firm's work. Henry's taste for self-improvement and foreign travel seems to have persisted until 1891, for the Articles of Partnership drawn up with Moore specifically allow him 'the right to absent himself from the said business ... while on a visit which he now contemplates taking to the British Isles and Europe for the purpose of prosecuting his studies in the said profession.'[120]

Henry achieved several personal honours in the following years, while the firm of Moore and Henry was also gaining in prestige. Describing the Royal Canadian Academy exhibition in 1895, the *Canadian Architect and Builder* singled out Henry as the 'one exhibitor of original design' who was not from Toronto.[121] In 1899 he was elected to the executive council of the Ontario Association of Architects; in 1900 he became first vice president of that organization.[122] He was also granted the prestigious contract in December 1902 for a new drill hall and armoury in London, to replace what the *Free Press* had described a few months earlier as 'the old ramshackle shed built ... by the former Grit Government' (fig. 68).[123] The Grits were responsible for the new building, too, and Henry's commission testified to his standing as an

178   Fred Henry (1865–1929), from *Annual Report of the Association of Ontario Land Surveyors*, 1935

architect and as a Liberal. A few years earlier the newspaper had listed his name among the community leaders who had signed Liberal Charles S. Hyman's nomination papers in the 1896 federal election campaign.[124]

In keeping with prevailing practices, the basic design for the armoury was provided by the federal Department of Public Works. The chief architect was David Ewart, though T.E. Fuller, who was appointed architect in charge of military buildings in 1904, was probably involved in designing London's Drill Hall (fig. 179).[125] Based on the idea of a medieval castle, the red brick building develops the fortification theme with heavy detailing derived from the Richardsonian Romanesque style. Newspaper accounts of the building's double inauguration suggest a high level of interest in the new militia facilities. The Liberal *Advertiser* claimed that nearly 4,000 people crammed the 80-by-186-foot drill hall to hear Lord Aylmer officially open the building on 1 February 1905; 'very little promenading was done,' the *Advertiser* observed, 'because there was scarcely room to move.'[126] Two nights later, close to 1,000 privileged citizens attended the 7th Fusiliers' annual ball, described by the reporter as the 'social event of several seasons.' Ladies in 'mousseline silk' and 'lace entre deux' and men in uniform danced until 4:30 in the morning.[127]

Henry's own designs had been strongly influenced by the Romanesque style during the 1890s. The round arch is particulary prominent in the façades of the Saunders warehouse (fig. 185), the Struthers and Leonard houses (figs

179   London Armoury, London, completed in 1905, probably designed by T.W. Fuller, Department of Public Works

187 and 190), and the YMCA (fig. 192). The impression of massiveness that one associates with Richardson's work is created by several of Henry's early Queen Anne houses and in some of his Gothic churches; it derives from features such as the expanses of unadorned wall space, the towers and broad bays of the houses, and the thick prominent buttresses on churches. It is a sign of Henry's versatility that he could also achieve very delicate effects, as with the Pixley Mausoleum (fig. 197). The Romanesque influence is less evident in most of the later work; the houses rely more on classical details, such as Palladian windows, or, occasionally, the American Shingle style.

Sadly, like his teacher in architecture, Henry succumbed while still young to a serious illness, described by a neighbour as 'the palsy.'[128] By 1908 he was forced by his ill health into a premature retirement, though he retained a nominal partnership in the firm until 1910. He spent his last twenty years as an invalid. The same neighbour, the daughter of a close family friend, recalls turning the pages of the *Advertiser* for him when she was a child. She remembers him as a very intelligent man who retained his popularity and his good temper even though he 'shook all the time' and had trouble making himself understood. He and his wife, Teresa, seem to have created a model home, for she is reported to have raised their two children and cared for her helpless husband in an equally uncomplaining way. The sophisticated young traveller to the British Isles and Europe was now no longer able to leave the house, even to glimpse the houses he had built.

St George's Anglican Church, 1890

227 Wharncliffe Road North, London

The west façade of St George's is somewhat deceptive. Facing it directly, one has the illusion of looking at a relatively small church with porches on each side. In fact, what appear to be wings are not porches at all – they are entries at the back of the nave. The body of the church is as wide as the entire façade, and the building is by no means small, seating 400 people.[129] The small scale of the façade gives the building the air of a rural village church, and this is enhanced by such rustic features as the verge-board, the purlins, and the bell-cote with its exquisite weathervane (fig. 180). The latter features, not present in the original design (fig. 181), were evidently a happy afterthought. The rustic elements and even the idea of the pretend-porch were borrowed from Durand, whose design for the Palmyra Baptist Church (fig. 99) was very similar. Where Durand placed a tower, however, Henry has introduced a second porch, and the resulting near-symmetry gives St George's a distinctive quality of its own.

Inside, the church has the friendly, light atmosphere that architects tried to achieve in houses of the period. Chiefly responsible for the cheerful effect are the steep wooden ceiling and the large stained glass windows, in the appealing Easter colours that were fashionable at the time – fresh spring green, baby blue, gold, primrose, orange, and the wide range of pinks and purples beloved in 'the mauve decade.'

The rural air of the church was appropriate. People still thought of London West as a village rather than a suburb in 1890, though its old name of Petersburgh had been formally dropped ten years before. The unassuming scale of the church was also fitting, for it was situated in a mainly working-class area. As Goodspeed's *History of the County of Middlesex* explained, 'While London West is a pretty place throughout, there are not many residences of a palatial description within its borders.'[130]

When the cornerstone of St George's was laid on 25 June 1890, the Bishop concluded his message with a prayer for the 'dear young rector' who had recently assumed responsibility for the parish. George B. Sage stayed for fifty years, and became greatly beloved as a 'devout Parish Priest' and greatly admired as a 'prominent scholar.' He taught mathematics, philosophy, and literature at the Western University. According to an obituary, he was 'one of the most widely read men in Canada in Christian apologetics and philosophy.'[131] A parish ministry in a university city was ideally suited to his multiple talents.

180   St George's Anglican Church, London, bell-cote

181   St George's Anglican Church, detail of architectural drawing showing front elevation; drawing signed 'Fred Henry'

182   St George's Anglican Church

Burns' Presbyterian Church, 1891
Mosa

On 17 September 1891, the Glencoe *Transcript* published a column from their very excited correspondent in Kilmartin: 'Our heretofore insignificant little burgh was the scene of one of the most interesting events which shall be recorded in history for coming generations of this locality.' The fascinating occasion was the laying of the cornerstone for the new Presbyterian church, a ceremony 'attended by over a thousand people.' The reporter's own absorption in the service shines through his eloquent account:

Psalm 100 was sung by the congregation, seemingly with more depth of feeling than ever before ... Mr Gow read an historical sketch of the progress of the congregation. Not a person moved, showing how deeply impressed they were with that gentleman's elocutionary talent ... Disregarding the heat, to add to the solemnity of the occasion, every umbrella was lowered and the men stood with uncovered heads just as the cornerstone was being laid.[132]

The church had long been central to the lives of the Highland Scots in the area. Church histories point out that the Argyllshire immigrants (c. 1830) 'were not long settled in their new homes when they longed for and prayed that the ordinances of the Gospel might be dispensed among them'; when a minister paid an 'occasional visit,' they 'trudged through miles of unbroken forest and swampy ground to join in the singing of good old Gaelic Psalms and Paraphrases ... and to listen to the exposition of God's Holy Word.' It was from such a 'parentage of perfect healthiness' that the 'infant' church grew by 'proper nourishment' to 'the stature of manhood,' represented by the new church of 1890, the congregation's fourth building. The parish had outgrown two earlier log structures, and a third church, constructed of brick, had proved unable to bear the slate roof the parishioners had conscientiously added in 1885.[133]

Its replacement (fig. 184), designed by Henry, had a properly supported slate roof and a polygonal core designed to allow more pews close to the pulpit. The polygonal plan had a venerable history among the Scots (see fig. 40), and it had recently become popular with other Protestant congregations in the London region. While Henry chose to make St George's look narrower than it was, probably out of respect for its site, he had taken advantage of the open country setting and the broad wings of the Mosa church to give the façade an appearance of breadth. The positioning of the doors draws the eye towards the sides of the façade, an attraction that is unwittingly furthered by the lack of a focal point in the centre bay. The row of arched windows near the bottom

183 Burns' Presbyterian Church, Mosa, detail of architectural drawing showing front elevation; drawing signed 'Fred Henry'

of this bay and the corbelling that cuts across the gable create strong horizontal lines. Other elements in the original design (fig. 183) – the stocky bellcote and the short chimneys placed broadside to the front – would have echoed the building's wide proportions. Looking expansive and friendly in its picturesque location, on a small ridge set in gently rolling hills, the church still invites its devout community to the 'exposition of God's Holy Word.'

184   Burns' Presbyterian Church

W.E. Saunders and Company, c. 1892

East side Clarence Street between King and York streets, London (demolished)

William Edward Saunders was the eldest son in a genuinely remarkable family. His father, William Saunders, was both a druggist and a pioneering manufacturer of drugs; in 1877 he became president of the American Pharmaceutical Association.[184] William Saunders the elder was also a gifted amateur scientist in the fields of ornithology and entomology. In 1886, he reported to the federal government on the possibility of establishing a network of experimental farms, and was himself appointed director of the system he recommended. While he held that position, he and his sons developed the famous Marquis strain of wheat, a variety hardy enough to survive the Canadian climate. Of William Saunders's five sons, Charles was his father's main collaborator on the wheat project, but all were reported to have participated in the work.[135] 'It has been said,' the *Free Press* stated, that 'the Saunders gave more wealth to the world than any other family in history – for they made possible the opening up of the great wheat land of the western part of the continent.'[136] Their achievements spanned many fields: Henry became a well-known cellist and botanist; Arthur, a college dean, was very much involved in the Marquis project; Frederick was a physics professor, ornithologist, and musician; Charles, a one-time chemistry professor, then a music teacher and critic, eventually joined his father in the work at the Dominion Experimental Farm.[137]

William Edwin Saunders's main professional role was as a legatee of his father's pharmaceutical firm. William and his brother Henry had assumed joint control of the company in 1885; in 1892, William took over the expanding manufacturing and wholesale part of the business.[138] His major scientific contributions, however, were in ornithology. The *Free Press* recalled that 'he would lie for hours in the long grass or stand motionless in marshland, eyes and ears strained for the song and sight of his beloved friends.'[139] He was also a keen entomologist. His collection of insects was displayed at the Philadelphia Centennial Exhibition (1876) when he was fifteen years old; he later donated 4,000 specimens to the University of Western Ontario. He was a founder of the Ontario Entomological Society, and the first president of the Federation of Ontario Naturalists.[140]

W.E. Saunders was also a success in managing his business. He controlled the flourishing wholesale company until 1929. The greatest challenge to his organizational skills may have occurred during the influenza epidemic of 1890, when day and night shifts were required for several months to meet the

185   W.E. Saunders and Company, London (building on left), detail of architectural drawing showing front elevation; drawing signed 'Moore & Henry'

demand for the firm's products.[141] It was probably the company's expansion during this period that made a new building for the wholesale trade desirable in 1892.

It seems appropriate that a building for a family that had contributed so much to society's well-being should make a point of good neighbourliness. The Saunders warehouse is most carefully integrated with the Lawson and Jones building beside it: it is of the same height; divisions between storeys and even window panes are usually at the same level; the far side of the building is adorned with an end block identical to those next door. Despite the strong similarities, however, there is little comparison between the two structures. Such features as the heavily textured, battered foundations of the piers and the two-storey arcading above give the building for W.E. Saunders and Company a monumental quality that the family-based business well deserved.

Thomas G. Whiskard House, c. 1892–3
South-east corner Wellington and Wolfe streets, London (demolished)

'In the business world,' the *Free Press* reported in 1919, 'Mr Whiskard was known as one of the fairest and squarest to deal with.'[142] Advertisements for 'Whiskard's Three Busy Stores' show that the establishment prided itself on fair prices. Underneath the appeal to the imagination in such slogans as 'A Store of Ideas and Uncommon Resources' and 'Cultivate a Greater Intimacy with This Store' there was the constant appeal to the frugal purse: 'This store is a money saving store.'[143] The earnestness of the store's advertisement about its spring Millinery Opening, an 'annual event ... of no little importance to the women of the city and vicinity' is echoed in the *Free Press*'s news report several days later: 'A visit to Mr Whiskard's busy stores this week is time most interestingly and profitably spent.' Much profit could no doubt be gained from the contemplation of 'a beautiful nile green turban, trimmed with white chiffon, wings and green poppies.' Turbans in general were 'very popular this year' (1900), and 'exhibited in many beautiful colours and trimmings.'[144]

Thomas Whiskard appears to have lived quite modestly until 1892, occupying the same Dundas Street premises as his stores. Then, at about fifty years of age,[145] he apparently decided to reap the fruits of his labour by building an elaborate and substantial house for himself and his wife (he had no children) facing Victoria Park. The design of the Whiskard house was clearly influenced by that of the Mathewson house (fig. 167) just around the corner: it has the same combination of massive brick arches on the ground floor and delicate woodwork above, and a very similar roofline, with a centre gable and symmetrically placed half-timbered dormers. In the Mathewson house, however, the symmetry of the roofline was part of the overall symmetry of the façade; in the Whiskard house, even the apparent rectangular shape of the façade is deceptive, for behind the porch-balcony complex that extends around one corner is a large polygonal bay window, like the base of a corner tower. The plan of the entire house exhibits typical Queen Anne intricacy, and the exterior decoration also seems to insist on a considerable freedom of form. Where the Mathewson house, for example, has only round arches, the arches of the Whiskard house are round, pointed, straight-topped, and even Tudor in shape. The design attempts to contain a variety of dynamic elements within an orderly, controlling framework, but it seems an open question as to which side wins. The house's greatest charms are those associated with its almost infinite variety.

After Whiskard's death in 1919, his house was bought by the Ursuline nuns of Chatham. They had just completed an arrangement for establishing a Catholic women's college as an affiliate of the University of Western Ontario,

186   Thomas G. Whiskard House, London, detail of architectural drawing showing front elevation

and had purchased land immediately west of the main campus, for the erection of their own college building. The Whiskard house served as an immediate but temporary home for Brescia College. Preparing the house to accommodate classrooms and living space for twenty people turned out to be a challenging task, especially since the sisters did not share the Whiskards' taste. 'The former owners had been "brave in colours," ' wrote Sister St Michael Major, and, in her opinion, 'the reds, blues and greens of the mural decoration needed toning down.'[146] The 'Ideas and Uncommon Resources' Mr Whiskard claimed to have possessed were evidently more appealing to his customers than to the Ursuline sisters.

Robert C. Struthers House, c. 1894

East Side Wellington Street between Dufferin Avenue and Wolfe Street, London (demolished)

Like his new neighbour Thomas Whiskard, Robert C. Struthers had prospered in the dry goods business. Struthers, however, was in the wholesale end of the trade. He had begun his career as a schoolteacher, a profession which he very quickly discarded in favour of life as a commercial traveller. After several years as an agent for another dry goods firm, he went into business for himself around 1881.[147] By 1905 he had travelled a good deal for his own firm, 'having crossed the ocean ninety times on purchasing trips' according to the *Free Press,* and he employed six other travellers. The newspaper's account of the city's exuberant celebrations following a British victory in the Boer War show that Struthers was well-liked by those who worked for him: 'A gaily decorated Tally-Ho, drawn by four cream horses, was engaged [by the employees of R.C. Struthers and Company] and securing a bass drum and several brass instruments, an impromptu band was organized. During the drive the "boys" serenaded Mr R.C. Struthers at his warehouse, and also at his residence on Wellington street. They heartily sang "For He's a Jolly Good Fellow" and gave three cheers and a tiger for their employer.'[148]

The Wellington Street house where this concert was given was an imposing edifice which, with its two corner towers, was vaguely reminiscent of a French chateau. The way in which the towers curve back from the plane of the front wall points to the work of H.H. Richardson as a more immediate influence.[149] The house has a sculptural quality similar to that often found in Richardson's work: the idea of roundness is echoed in the actual shape of the building – in the corner towers, their conical roofs, the flared eaves and foundation, and the arcade – rather than in surface ornamentation. There is also a Richardsonian sense of massiveness, created mainly by the smooth, relatively unbroken areas of wall surface, the thick foundation, and the strong horizontal lines of the building.

The chateauesque profile of the Struthers house has been adapted to accommodate a typically imaginative Queen Anne floor plan. On the main floor the right tower contains an alcove off the sitting room; the tower on the left forms one of the four rounded corners of the drawing room. The large polygonal bay projecting at the south side of the building constitutes one wall of the dining room. In the Queen Anne manner, considerations of symmetry have been sacrificed to functional requirements. The chateau-like façade is slightly off-centre, as if the building as a whole shifted to the north while the centre section remained in place. As with the Whiskard house, Henry seems to be experimenting with the confrontation of two antithetical principles of

187   Robert C. Struthers House, London, detail of architectural drawing showing front elevation; drawing signed 'Moore & Henry'

esthetic compositon, one symmetrical and contained, the other functional and restless. The result is that, despite its strong, simple lines, the Struthers house has little of the repose then coming to be greatly admired, and the massive chateau seems tantalizingly unstable.

Charles W. Leonard House, c. 1893–4

360 Queens Avenue, London

Charles Leonard was the third son of Elijah Leonard, who had built a foundry in London in 1838; Charles and his brother Frank became co-owners of the prospering business in 1875. The firm's line of products changed over the years to take advantage of market conditions. In the late 1850s the company made railroad cars; before and after that period it specialized in agricultural implements. By the 1890s it was best known for its boilers and steam engines.[150]

Leonard engines were effusively praised throughout eastern Canada. An 1879 issue of the Cornwall *Reporter* commented on one 'perfect gem' of an engine: 'We only wish that Messrs Leonard of London, whose handiwork it is, could hear one half of the encomiums called forth by the appearance and working of the Little Giant.'[151] In 1901, the Acadia Electric Company of Wolfville, Nova Scotia wrote to praise the 'little 45 H.P. Leonard Boiler' which furnished enough steam to keep '900 lights on at one time': 'Allow us to congratulate you on turning out such an elegant engine.'[152] Charles's technological interests were no doubt at least partly responsible for the fact that his $12,000 house, built around 1893, was apparently the first designed by the firm to have electric lighting.

Moore and Henry produced alternate elevations for the Leonard house, both based on essentially the same floor plan. One uses rounded forms reminiscent of the Struthers house (fig. 187); the other, which was chosen, has a crisp, angular quality. There is no attempt here, as in earlier houses, to hide the real outline of the rooms behind veiling porches and verandahs: the interior volumes are directly related to the exterior masses. Indeed, all aspects of the built house seem directly and emphatically stated. The broad gable bay projects forward decisively; its eaves have a wide overhang; the tower has a distinctive presence of its own; even the Credit Valley brownstone foundation seems inclined to climb above its boundaries.[153] Though somewhat outspoken, the building illustrates the trend towards simplification in the firm's work: the ornamental woodwork, for example, is both less in evidence and less elaborate than the verandah of the Mathewson house (fig. 167). The Eastlake turnings have given way to classical columns, and the main cornice decoration is a fine row of dentils. The classical bias evident in these details also accounts for the Palladian window in the gable.

A similar classical emphasis is also observable inside. As in the grander houses of the previous decade, natural woods are still given prominence (the hall and dining room have panelled ceilings), but the detailing differs from what one finds in the earlier houses. The door lintels, for example, resemble classical entablatures.

Charles was the more retiring of the two brothers. While Frank gained

188   Charles W. Leonard House, London, upper part of tower.

189   Charles W. Leonard House, detail of architectural drawing showing front elevation; drawing signed 'Moore & Henry'

190   Charles W. Leonard House

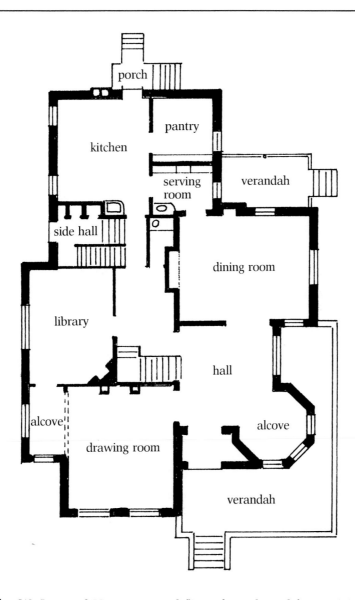

191   Charles W. Leonard House, ground floor plan adapted from original drawing

civic prominence in capacities such as alderman and president of the Chamber of Commerce, Charles limited himself to social roles such as membership in the London Club and the London Hunt and Country Club.[154] He also seems to have possessed a kind of wanderlust in relation to residences. He had lived in several different dwellings prior to 1894, and around 1902 he deserted the Queens Avenue house for another, not dissimilar, dwelling (fig. 208), also designed by Moore and Henry, situated close to Victoria Park.[155]

Young Men's Christian Association, 1895–7

West side Wellington Street between Dundas Street and Queens Avenue, London (destroyed by fire)

The Young Men's Christian Association was founded in London, England, in 1844, and by 1856, according to one local history, its 'organization was perfected' in London, Canada West.[156] The association nevertheless fell into a decline, probably because it came to be linked to one church (it is identified as the Church of England YMCA in the 1868–69 city directory). In 1873, it was reorganized on a broader basis.[157] After twenty years of growth, both in size and in range of activities, the YMCA was thought by some members to require its own building with appropriate facilities: according to the minute book, 'the whole discussion [at a February 1895 meeting of the board of trustees] might be summed up in the expressive words of one of the number who said we had to "Build or Bust."'[158]

A competition for the design of the building, in which competitors had to use pseudonyms, attracted twelve entries, of which 'Simplicity' took the prize. 'Simplicity' turned out to be the submission of Moore and Henry, though Henry's steady attendance at subsequent board meetings suggests that he was its author.[159] Henry apparently became quite involved in the project: when

193   YMCA, detail of architectural drawing showing front elevation; drawing is signed 'Moore & Henry'

it was decided to use 'Buff pressed brick' for the front of the building, he volunteered 'to secure a $500 subscription to pay for the same.'[160]

The name Henry chose for his plans attests to the period's taste, but it is hard to see just how it applies to his design. The large, off-centre entrance arch and the general outlines of the front elevation were almost certainly inspired by H.H. Richardson's Trinity Church Rectory (1879–80) in Boston,[161] and a comparison of the rectory and the YMCA shows just how complicated Henry's design is. Richardson's façade is flat; Henry's has projecting gable bays and a bay window. Intricate ornamentation in the rectory is mainly confined to carefully placed panels; in its original state, the third storey of the YMCA was riddled with elaborate corbelling, textured brickwork, and intricately carved dormers and window surrounds, all of which blended perfectly with the raised cut-work of the wooden cupola. Richardson's windows generally have straight lintels; Henry has used ogee arches to give straight and round-headed windows alike a pointed shape, which is echoed in the dormers, the gables, and the cupola's spire. For the quiet, meditative character of the rectory, Henry has substituted a spirited, rather nervous quality. Its liveliness was undoubtedly a more accurate reflection of the activities within the new building's walls.

Much of the interior was devoted to athletic facilities: bowling alleys, a 'swimming tank,' and a gymnasium. There were also several reception and sitting rooms, an auditorium (which the trustees were willing to name 'Jubilee Hall' in honor of Queen Victoria if the gesture added enough money to the building fund), and several classrooms, designed to accommodate a variety of educational programs.[162] In October 1897 the educational committee arranged classes in the Bible, 'Woodworking, Mechanical Drawing, Greek Music and Photography.' Some parts of the building were leased to other organizations. After considerable bargaining, W.E. Saunders obtained a second-floor room at the front for the Entomology Society. Trustee J.W. Westervelt used most of the third floor for his Forest City Business and Shorthand College.[163]

Pixley Mausoleum, 1895–7
Woodland Cemetery, London

'ANNIE PIXLEY DEAD,' lamented the headline in the first section of the New York *Times* of 10 November 1893; 'The Popular Actress Breathes Her Last in a Foreign Land.' She died in London, England, partly, in the *Times*'s view, as the result of a tragedy that had occurred five years before near London, Ontario. She was buried in the latter city, where her husband, Robert Fulford, erected a magnificent mausoleum, designed by Moore and Henry, in her honour.

The New York *Times* obituary proved that the reporter was a great fan of Annie Pixley's: she 'was an attractive and charming woman, combining with a most piquant and agreeable brusquerie all the bewitching softness and charm of an Irish girl ... In appearance, she was easily the prettiest of all the soubrettes upon the stage.' Born with the maiden name of Shea in Brooklyn,[164] Annie Pixley played in a variety of musical comedies, but the part for which she was best known was the starring role in *M'liss, Child of the Plains*, based on a story by Bret Harte, though he would not have approved the stage version. He felt that 'the charm of M'liss is that she is a mere *child*, and it is very difficult for a grown actress to represent such a character – in love!'[165] Annie Pixley evidently succeeded. A *Free Press* review of her debut at London's Grand Opera House (fig. 101) on 20 February 1882 shows what

194   Pixley Mausoleum, London, from *Canadian Architect and Builder*, July 1897

the role demanded: 'Annie Pixley appears as a young girl who is the life of the camp, impulsive, high spirited, clever and dashing, the favourite of all the boys and as pure as the gold in her drunken father's mine. She becomes the heroine of many rough scenes in which she displays strong emotional power as well as a graceful and nimble manner that is charming.' Annie Pixley played *M'liss* in London on at least two other dates, 19 December 1882 and 14 May 1886.[166]

Less than two months after the latter performance, while Annie and her manager-husband were on tour, their twelve-year-old son Tommy died in Port Stanley, Ontario, where he was staying with relatives. The reputed cause of death was drowning though an official report blamed 'congestion of the brain.' He was buried at Woodland cemetery on 6 July 1886.[167]

The New York *Times* reported that Annie Pixley 'never recovered from the terrible blow inflicted on her by the death of her only child.' By the time of her own premature death, at the age of thirty-eight, 'she had grown weak and depressed, as she had grown stout to an unwholesome and unbeautiful degree, and she subsided into a hopeless melancholia.' Her ashes were eventually placed with her son's body in the mausoleum commissioned by her husband. His ashes now reside there as well.

Set on the 50 by 100 foot plot purchased by Robert Fulford,[168] the mausoleum is both picturesque and surprisingly monumental for a small structure. The three steps that lead up a small incline some distance in front of the building

195   Pixley Mausoleum, statue representing drama

196   Pixley Mausoleum, one of the lions flanking the entrance gates

encourage one to make a ceremonial approach. Massive forms, such as the pilasters holding the statues, the marble slabs that comprise the roof, and the thick wall indicated by the deep-set entrance, combine with rich materials to make the memorial imposing. It is built mainly of granite from Stanstead, Quebec, though polished Swedish granite is used for the columns beside the entrance.[169] The gates, modelled according to the design provided by Moore and Henry, are of solid bronze. Inside, the sandstone wall has marble wainscotting, the granite floor is covered with encaustic tiles, and stained glass windows illustrate appropriate texts. Directly in front of the window, and between the reliquaries holding his parents' ashes, is a marble bust of Tommy.

Possibly the most moving aspect of the impressive mausoleum is its sculpture, the work of 'Messrs Allward and Sturgeon, of Toronto.' The general scheme – for the guardian lions at the door, and the three figures representing Drama, Victory, and Music above – was part of the firm's plans, but the sculptors have done a magnificent job of giving it realistic and riveting forms. Most striking of all are the wistful faces of ladies and lions alike: all wear an expression similar to that on the mask of tragedy (fig. 195). It reflects, not the anguish of a torturing moment, but the quiet recognition of an infinite sorrow.

197   Pixley Mausoleum

St Matthew's Anglican Church, 1895
940 Dundas Street, London

St John's-in-the-Woods (Anglican) Church, c. 1898
Aughrim

In the latter part of the 1890s, Moore and Henry used virtually the same design for Anglican churches in two very different settings, one in industrial East London, the other, St John's-in-the-Woods, located in the country about thirty-five miles south-east of Sarnia. The low eaves and the high peak of the basic design would make the façade almost A-shaped, were it not for the bell-cote and its base. The result is emphatically asymmetric, with the bell-cote on one side countered only by an expanse of unadorned wall on the other. Both the streamlined profile and the areas of uninterrupted wall space illustrate the prevailing trend towards simplicity, a quality no doubt appreciated in both churches, since simplicity could also be economical.

St Matthew's Church began life as St Luke's Mission Church in what proved to be an unproductive location on Hamilton Road. In 1881 the vestry concluded, 'with deep regret, that after an existence of six years, St Luke's Church has not flourished or grown in the situation where it at present stands,' and decided to buy the mortuary chapel of what had been St Paul's Cemetery, on Dundas Street.[170] There the church grew until, in 1895, it needed a larger building, though it was hardly prosperous in a material sense. The new $8,000 church opened with a debt of $3,500 in December 1895, and it was not consecrated until 1912, when the debt was finally paid off.[171] Despite its concern for economy, the St Matthew's congregation opted for the full tower, shown on the perspective drawing of the church featured in the *Canadian Architect and Builder*, instead of the more rustic bell-cote.[172]

In deference to its smaller size (St John's seated 165, St Matthew's 350),[173] the narthex has been omitted at St John's, though its horizontal line is maintained to some extent in the row of three arched windows. Inside, the church's modest size becomes a virtue in achieving an almost domestic sense of cosiness, to which the expansive wooden ceiling makes a significant contribution. Even more crucial to the impression of interior richness are the stained glass windows. Produced by Hobbs Manufacturing Company in London,[174] they exhibit a striking palette of often pale colours, arranged in various imaginative abstract patterns, making the church glorious as well as comfortable.

St John's seems little changed since 1899. It still occupies a charming rural site, above the Sydenham River, at a curve in the road, with its woods on one side and open fields on the other. A one-room schoolhouse still sits across

198 St Matthew's Anglican Church, London, detail of architectural drawing showing front elevation

the road, complete with its original verandah, and the church still uses the outhouse in its backyard. The small group of parishioners who now support the church are, however, more dependent on technology than might at first appear: they earn the money for the building's maintenance by selling concessions at the local tractor pulls.

199 St John's-in-the-Woods Church, Aughrim

Arva Methodist Church, 1898

now Arva United Church, Arva

Arva, a village about five miles north of London, is now mainly a commuter town, but it had an active industrial and commercial life of its own a century ago. In 1880 it claimed 260 inhabitants, two hotels, a flour mill (which is still there), a wagon factory, two blacksmiths, a harness maker, a shoemaker, and a few shops.[175] An Anglican church had been established there before 1845, and probably gave the village its first name, St John's. Because postmasters of the period had the right to name their own stations, many villages, including Arva, ended up with two names. The first postmaster in St John's, Joseph Sifton, called his station Arva after a town in Ireland, and, as was often the case, it was his choice that eventually became official.[176] It seems likely that Sifton was a Methodist, and thus little inclined to promote the old nomenclature: a Joseph Sifton and a Charles W. Sifton were on the building committee of the new Methodist church erected in 1898 to replace an older frame structure.[177]

The minutes of the building committee refer to Moore as the architect, thus providing evidence that Moore retained some interest in creating designs. The church is a striking example of the Protestant trend towards broader churches. While described in the minutes as 'square,'[178] its corners are in fact canted to form a polygonal core, with short extensions to the front and back. The building has little external ornamentation, though the original architectural drawings show shallow decorative barge-boards on the gables. Its esthetic impact relies mainly on the interplay of shapes: the varied angles of the walls, the gabled and hipped parts of the roof, the prominent buttresses that even climb almost to the top of the side and back gables. The arrangement of spaces, dictated by the building's overall shape, is largely responsible for one's impressions of the interior as well: the steep ascent to the sanctuary lends a dramatic quality to the entrance (fig. 204), moulded beams outline the various planes of the roof, the breadth of the church allows the curved pews (fig. 201) to form a semi-circle around the pulpit. The interior decoration is also simple, but individual examples are often striking. At the front of the church, for example, is a rose window that looks like a kaleidoscope stopped forever at a particular juncture of varicoloured geometric shapes. With applied mouldings that imitate a fluted shaft and a capital boasting finely carved acanthus leaves, the post supporting the chancel arch (fig. 203) shows the same interest in classical forms that was evident in the firm's houses at the time.

Despite such elegant surroundings, the minister whose preaching provided the focal point of the broad sanctuary must have needed considerable dedication. In 1899, Arva shared a three-point charge with Hyde Park and Melrose.

200   Arva Methodist Church,
front and side buttresses

201   Arva Methodist Church,
pew end

202   Arva Methodist Church

203   Arva Methodist Church, chancel arch pier

204   Arva Methodist Church, entrance hall staircase

The minister theoretically received an annual salary of $650 plus '$50 for horse keep,' but he may have had trouble collecting it. In 1902, the Reverend Mr W.J. Waddell, the third incumbent since the church was built three years before, announced that he had received a call to a Michigan congregation. In an effort to keep him, 'the official board, knowing the pastor's salary to be in considerable arrears ... voted to pay the deficiency in a short time.' Only in 1918 was the minister granted a holiday.[179] With such working conditions, it is not surprising that the attraction of church architecture did not prevent a rapid turnover behind the pulpit.

Cy Warman House, c. 1898

100 Cheapside Street, London

Cy Warman was born in Illinois, and had a varied career – as farmer, wheat broker, railwayman, and journalist – before gaining the sobriquet of 'Poet of the Rockies' for his poems and stories of a railroader's life. While visiting London in the early 1890s, he fell in love with a Kansas girl, Myrtle Marie Jones, who was then a student at the Academy of the Sacred Heart in the city. According to legend, he wrote a proposal of marriage while sitting in Victoria Park one evening, though only the last lines of his poem could possibly be construed as a proposal:

> ... your soul so pure and sweet
> Makes my happiness complete.
> Makes me falter at your feet, sweet Marie.[180]

However subtle, the proposal was accepted, and 'Sweet Marie,' set to music by Raymond Moore, established Cy Warman's fame and wealth. In the late 1890s, the Warmans returned to live in the city of their courtship, in order to provide the increasingly popular author with 'the seclusion his literary work demanded.'[181] They commissioned Moore and Henry to design a house, and took up residence in a part of North London that was then becoming fashionable.[182]

Probably the Warmans made some suggestions regarding the style of their new house, for it is rather different from anything else the firm produced at that time. The strong influence of the American Shingle style is evident in the expanses of shingles – in the gables and even extending below the eaves to cover the upper part of the first storey – and in the house's open and informal floor plan. The Shingle style was especially popular for summer homes,[183]

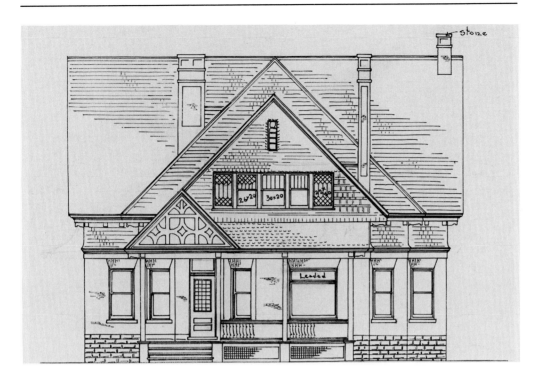

205   Cy Warman House, London, detail of architectural drawing showing front elevation; drawing signed 'Moore & Henry'

206   Cy Warman House

207   Cy Warman House, gable on west side

and its broad expansive proportions often lent themselves to a floor plan designed for relatively casual living. Here, both the parlour and study seem to flow into the large reception hall; some bedrooms, as well as the public rooms, are located on the first floor. The Queen Anne origins of the Shingle style are evident in the hints of both Old English and classical trim. The row of small paned windows in the front gable and the proposed half-timbering above the porch (fig. 205) are Elizabethan in character. The stylized shell motif on the side gable gives the window complex Palladian contours (fig. 207).

The Warmans may have thought the Shingle style especially appropriate for what they envisaged as a full-time retreat, but the secluded life apparently palled. Cy Warman returned to railway work in London as an executive for the Grand Trunk Railway. On one of the many trips that formed part of his job, he fell seriously ill in Chicago, and he died a few days later.[184] He had suffered other illnesses in his last years,[185] and his final poems often had the subject of approaching death as their central theme:

> Oft, when I feel my engine swerve,
> As o'er strange rails we fare,
> I strain my eye around the curve
> For what awaits us there ...
> Swift towards life's terminal I trend.
> The run seems short tonight.
> God only knows what's at the end –
> I hope the lamps are white.[186]

D. Warden Sutherland House, c. 1900–1

284 Central Avenue, London

D.W. Sutherland appears to have had a meteoric career in London, where he shone brightly for a while, and then disappeared from view. When first listed in a city directory, in 1894, he was working as a clerk for a druggist named William T. Strong. By 1897 he was Strong's partner, and their firm was involved in the wholesale as well as the retail side of the business. Around 1900, presumably bouyed up by his commercial successes, he commissioned an extremely luxurious Queen Anne house, which he occupied for one year. In 1903 he was boarding in a more modest house on Albert Street, and by 1904 he was no longer in town.[186]

The format of the Sutherland house resembles that of the Leonard house (fig. 190), but its features are even more pronounced. The tower is proportionately broader, the eaves wider, and the materials more various. The basic facing material is pressed red brick. Roughly textured stone is used for the foundation, and smooth-faced stone, cut in a variety of patterns, adorns the centre bay: alternating narrow and broad voussoirs create a sun-burst effect around the front door; on the second storey, a rectangular arch, supported by triangular brackets, reverses the usual order in that the arch is of windows, and it surrounds a brick panel. The plans show shingling and half-timbering in the gables, and diagonal boarding on the bay windows along one side. As with the Leonard house, the detailing – swags, balustrades, and urns – is largely classical, though there is more of this as well. The combination of brick, cut stone, and classicizing trim gives the house a somewhat English air, though the exuberance of its treatment probably owes more to North American influences.

While lavish in its use and treatment of rich materials, the house has a somewhat simpler plan than that of the Leonard house (fig. 191). Its general outlines, with a kitchen behind a stairway-reception area on one side, and a dining room and a living room of some description on the other, was to be used in dozens of smaller houses during the next decade.

It seems likely that the house represented an over-indulgence on Sutherland's part. In the following years, the edifice was owned by a succession of London's leading industrialists who were better able to afford it. Appropriately enough, its second owner was Charles Leonard, who stayed there for two years. Lumberman George H. Belton also had a relatively short occupancy, of six years. It was the fourth owner, Frank McCormick, of McCormick's Biscuit Company, who finally adopted the building as his permanent home. He moved into the house around 1913, and remained for fifty years.[187]

208   D. Warden Sutherland House, London, architectural drawing showing front elevation; drawing signed 'Moore & Henry'

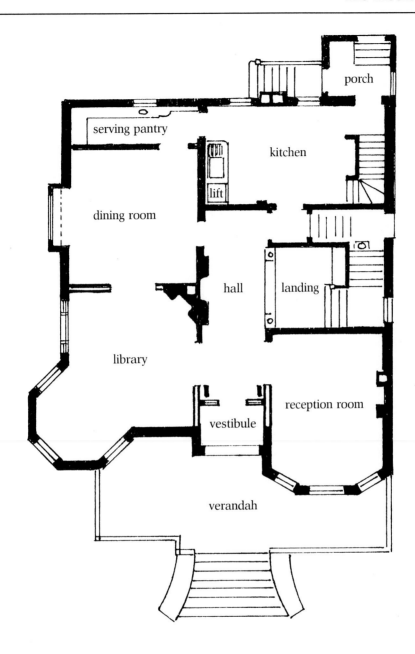

209   D. Warden Sutherland House, ground floor plan adapted from original drawing

Mrs O'Donnell's Store and Dwelling, 1902–6

623 Richmond Street, London

Bridget O'Donnell, a widow, operated one of 178 neighbourhood grocery stores in London in 1906, when she moved down the street to her new premises.[188] They were in many ways typical of these neighbourhood stores – in providing a house and shop in the same building, in being unpretentious in design, and in using very large plate glass windows to display their owner's wares. Particularly attractive features of Mrs O'Donnell's building are the unusually generous segmented arches over the house windows. Placing display windows on both the front and sides of the building created an inviting corner entrance, but at the expense of a perfectly balanced front façade. As often happened during the period, consideration of interior function took precedence over exterior esthetics.

The front half of the ground floor held Mrs O'Donnell's store; at the back were a kitchen, pantry, and dining room. Upstairs were a sitting room, four bedrooms, and a bathroom. A full basement allowed room for storage.[189]

In 1907 or 1908 the business was taken over by a James O'Donnell, probably Bridget's son, who operated it as a neighbourhood grocery store until 1957. In 1923, he added to his income by reducing his living space and converting the upstairs rooms into apartments.[190] The building is now one of several small shops which still retain an appealing neighbourhood atmosphere, though their specialized merchandise appeals to a city-wide clientele.

210   Mrs O'Donnell's Store and Dwelling, London

211   Mrs O'Donnell's Store and Dwelling, side display window

Power House, McClary Manufacturing Company, completed 1904

West side Adelaide Street between Nelson and Trafalgar streets, London

McClary's, the tin and iron works business established in the late 1840s by Moore's father-in-law Oliver McClary and Oliver's brother John, became one of London's, and indeed Canada's, leading industries. The *Advertiser* bragged in 1882 that McClary's 'well-known wares, especially in the line of stoves, pressed tin ware, japanned and other fancy goods, now find their way into every town, village, hamlet, nook and corner of not only the Dominion of Canada, but likewise across the briny deep, having even obtained orders for the Australian market.'[191] At that date, the company employed 250 men in London, and had branch warehouses in Toronto and Winnipeg. Two years later, the firm was reported to export goods to England, Scotland, and the West Indies, as well as Australia.[192] By the early 1900s, the firm had 700 London employees, and four more branch warehouses, in Vancouver, Hamilton, Montreal, and Saint John.[193] Describing London's manufacturing growth, the *Free Press* announced in 1905 that 'the other day a McClary stove was shipped to the very heart of darkest Africa, carried inland hundreds of miles upon the backs of natives.'[194]

To meet the expanding demand for its products, the firm decided shortly after the turn of the century to relegate its old Wellington Street plant to the manufacture of tin and enamel ware, and to build a new factory, to be designed by Moore, that would handle the foundry work.[195] The *Canadian Architect and Builder* was so impressed with the facilities finished in 1904 that it devoted four pages to descriptions and illustrations of the new factory, which it obviously considered a masterpiece of industrial design.[196] The project seems to have been brilliantly planned. Among the many features praised were the efficient layout that avoided 'the necessity of any piece in process of manufacture being carried back to any point it has once passed'; the arrangement of the electrical equipment so as to make the plant 'one of the cleanest, best lighted, and best ventilated ... to be found anywhere'; and the 'absolutely fireproof' steel and concrete construction of the mounting shop. The power house contained 'three 100 h.p. standard internal fired Scotch boilers, manufactured by E. Leonard & Sons.' Probably the most distinctive aspect of that building's external appearance was the absence of a tall stack, the result of a special induced-draft apparatus requiring only a forty-foot chimney.

The design of the power house, like that of the other buildings, was much less innovative in esthetic terms. It employed the basically Italianate format used by Robinson thirty years before, though the oversized oculus was an attractive – and useful – variation on the old theme.

SCALE 4 FT - 1 IN.

EAST   ELEVATION

212   Power House, McClary Manufacturing Company, London, detail of architectural drawing showing east elevation; drawing signed 'Moore & Henry'

The big products of the new factory were the 'sunshine' furnace (so clean and efficient, according to the advertisement, that a man could shovel in the coal while immaculately dressed in his best suit),[197] the 'Cornwall' steel range, and the 'Pandora' iron range, which, in a curious reversal of the Greek myth, was designed to do away with trouble: 'it saves you worry; it saves you time and money; it saves you backaches and headaches, because it is so easy to manage and so reliable.'[198]

The *Free Press* stated in 1905 that McClary's employed nearly 1,200 people in London alone.[199] Over 4,000 people (including employees and their families) turned out on 14 July 1914 for the company's annual picnic in Port Stanley. The employees played baseball (the foundrymen won), had a tug-of-war (the foundrymen won), and watched a baby contest (the winner was not announced).[200]

The days of Moore's wonderfully efficient factory, now manufacturing refrigerators, are numbered. In 1927, McClary's was bought by General Steel Wares, which fifty years later merged with Canadian General Electric to become CAMCO.[201] CAMCO has just announced the closing of the London plant by September 1987 because of 'a developing ... obsolescence.'[202]

JOHN VICAR MUNRO

Though the most contemporary of the architects discussed in this study, J. Vicar Munro is the most elusive. Very few facts concerning his life are available, and some of those are open to question.

He was born in Westminster township on 7 April 1872, the son of John and Christina Munro. He attended Public School No. 10 in Westminster township and London Collegiate Institute (fig. 82), and then sought professional training as an architect. His obituaries claim that 'he completed a course of surveying and architecture in the School of Science at Toronto.'[203] Some support for this assertion would seem to lie in the fact that he subsequently fulfilled only a three-year apprenticeship under Fred Henry, whereas the Ontario Association of Architects at that time was insisting on a five-year apprenticeship for students who did not take a university course.[204] The complete matriculation records for the School of Science do not contain Munro's name, however; it would seem that, at best, he can only have attended classes at the school on an informal basis. When he filled out an application for membership in the OAA in 1931, he claimed to have served a five-year apprenticeship.[205]

Munro did please his master. Fred Henry's formal statement of 30 March 1894 states that Munro 'served faithfully and regularly for three years ... as my apprentice,' and goes on to recommend Munro's character in most complimentary terms: 'I have always found him to be studious, honest, industrious, sober and trustworthy in every respect.'[206] Moore and Henry employed Munro for two more years (1894–6) as a draughtsman,[207] and when Henry's health failed Munro returned as a partner.

Twelve years elapsed between the two stages in Munro's connection with the firm. According to Munro's OAA application, he worked in the intervening period for well-known architects in New York and Baltimore. He claims to have spent eight years with H. Gilbert in New York City, and then four years with the firm of Baldwin and Pennington in Baltimore. That firm then had as a major commission the west annex to the Maryland State House at Annapolis.[208]

When he returned to Canada, and Moore's firm, in 1908, Munro brought with him an enthusiasm for the Revival styles then popular in the United States. St Peter's Parish Hall (fig. 213), for example, and the elaborate porticoes of the McDonald house (fig. 220) and Blackfriars (fig. 222) all show the influence of the American Colonial Revival. The cottage he designed for his partner's son, John McClary Moore, relies on the Shingle style. The Keene House (fig. 224) is an early example of the Tudor Revival style that was to flourish after the war. Munro seems to have adopted a very conscientious and careful approach to his work, in that his buildings are always well planned and well finished, inside and out.

Despite the generally high quality of his work, Munro appears to have suffered a demotion within the firm's hierarchy. When he first entered a partnership with Moore in 1908, it was agreed that both men would take $60 a month on a regular basis, and divide the profits at the end of the year, with

Moore getting a somewhat larger share. In 1910, a clause was added assuring Munro of at least $1200 a year, and he was still to receive his portion of the profits. In 1912, significant changes were made. The contract was renewed for only six months, and though the firm was still to be called Moore and Munro, the latter was to receive only a salary of $1200 a year.[209] No reasons are given for this new arrangement, but two probable explanations present themselves. John M. Moore's son, O. Roy, was by then actively involved in the firm's work. A more important consideration may have been the fact that most of the firm's profits at the time came from the large industrial projects on which it was engaged. As mentioned earlier in this chapter, Munro's domain seems to have comprised the more artistic but less lucrative smaller commissions. The partnership between Moore and Munro was dissolved on 22 February 1913,[210] and Munro set up business for himself. He worked again for Moore's firm during the 1920s when the large number of important projects with which it was involved necessitated extra help.[211]

Munro's non-professional interests included St Andrew's Presbyterian church, where he was a member of the Board of Management, and the Masons. He and his wife, Addah Agnes Paul Munro, who was from Maryland, lived at 367 Maitland Street and then at 419 William Street until his death on 28 December 1936.[212] A woman who was a stenographer in Moore's office during the 1920s remembers Munro as a modest, self-effacing man, who always hesitated to present his ideas, fearing they were rather old-fashioned.[213]

St Peter's Parish Hall, 1908

East side Richmond Street between Dufferin Avenue and Kent Street, London
(demolished)

Like most other Georgian Revival buildings of the early twentieth century, St
Peter's Parish Hall could hardly be mistaken for an actual Georgian building.
Most revealing is the fact that its quoins, the string course below the cornice,
and the impressive window trim over the front door were all of terra cotta
rather than stone or wood. Moreover, while the eighteenth-century paradigm
on which the hall is based had a projecting frontispiece with corner quoins,
the centre bay here is flush with the rest of the façade, and the prominent
centre quoins are purely decorative. Indeed, the decorative value of most of
the classical features is emphasized by their exaggerated size. The quoins
are especially large; the porch, with its coupled piers and columns, is monumental; the cornice is decorated by prominent dentils and block modillions.

The over-statement was appropriate for the parish hall, since it was
obviously meant to have a certain grandeur. Sheets and sheets of drawings
devoted to designs for the hall's interior details – for the chapel, the hall's
auditorium, the wood trim – indicate the importance initially attached to the
structure. It is therefore rather surprising that the church has preserved no
records indicating its original uses. The probable functions of a church hall were
extended in the 1930s when high school classes began to be taught there;
they continued, under the name of De La Salle High School, until 1951. A
school still occupies the site, but the old St Peter's Hall was demolished,
around 1970, to make room for the new St Peter's School.[214]

213 St Peter's Parish Hall, London, detail of architectural drawing showing front elevation; drawing signed 'Moore, Henry and Munro'

Ontario Furniture Company, 1909
228–30 Dundas Street, London

A few years after the Ontario Furniture Company moved into the premises previously occupied by Whiskard's dry goods store, its owners celebrated the building's new use with a new store front. The design produced by Moore, Henry, and Munro shows the influences of the Commercial style – in the large amounts of window space, in the tiers of bay windows, and in the façade's skeletal appearance.[215] Often Commercial style buildings were quite plain, but there is a significant amount of decoration here. The cornice, the brackets, the mullions, and the centre panels are all made of metal.

The Ontario Furniture Company seems to have been much like Whiskard's in spirit if not in appearance. 'No one can doubt,' read a 1907 advertisement, 'that the keynote appealing to each individual purse is "Best quality at the very lowest prices." '[216] Purses must have been greatly attracted by some of the merchandise at least. The same advertisement went on to announce, 'We carry over forty different styles of sideboards. From $7.50 up to $150.' Their 1915 catalogue shows that the store dealt in a large range of items as well as a large range of prices. It included a great deal of oak furniture (plain, pressed, or with applied mouldings), some wicker, brass, and iron beds, lace curtains, carpets, baby and doll carriages, and even 'Happy Thought' stoves and ranges. One could buy a sofa bed for $27.50, or a solid oak extension table for $11.50. A pressed back oak dining room chair could be had for 90¢.[217] The Furniture Company was obviously able to put its generous bay windows to excellent use, both in displaying its wares and in advertising its 'very lowest prices.'

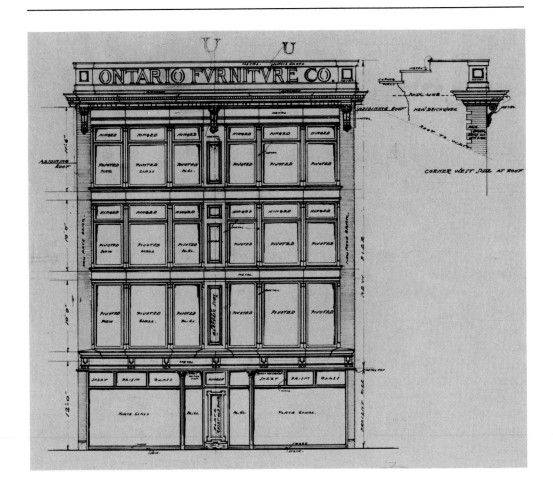

214   Ontario Furniture Company, London, detail of architectural drawing showing front elevation; drawing signed 'Moore Henry & Munro'

Arthur E. McClary House, c. 1909

400 Queens Avenue, London

Arthur Edward McClary was Oliver McClary's son (and John M. Moore's brother-in-law). Although he held a financial interest in the family firm, he was prevented by ill health from taking an active part in its management. The fields in which he was most busily engaged, according to his obituary, were equestrian and domestic. He was 'a great lover of the outdoors,' who 'at one time maintained a stable of high class horses.'[218] His domestic interests appear to have been two-sided. 'His deepest delight,' wrote an early biographer, 'was found in the family circle,' consisting of his wife and two children. He is also said to have been 'a realtor' for some time, and to have 'erected a number of homes.'[219] Three of these homes, all designed by Moore, Henry, and Munro, can be seen in figure 216: A.E. McClary built the corner house as his own residence, and the double house beyond, probably as a rental property.

The house that was his own is a simplified version of the Queen Anne style. There is no tower; the single gables at the front and side preside over bays that project only slightly from the rectangular body of the edifice. The prominent porch that extends across the front of the house is symmetrical. The interior plan also represents a turn away from the more fanciful eccentricities of earlier Queen Anne houses. The sitting room, parlour, and dining room are all perfectly rectangular, with fireplaces centred on one wall; only the den behind the stairs, with its corner fireplace and bow window, partakes of the old whimsicality. There is a separate stair-hall beyond the entrance hall, but together they form a long central passageway highly reminiscent of the traditional centre-hall plan.[220]

The building's classicizing details seem very much at home on this decorously restrained edifice, with its hints of symmetry. The porch features Ionic columns and a pediment; the front door has oversized fanlights and sidelights of bevelled glass; the usual Palladian windows adorn the gables. The modillions add a lively rhythm, which is echoed in the constructed building by the roof cresting. The interior trim also has a definitely classical character. Ionic pillars mark the boundary between the entrance and stair halls (fig. 218), for example, and the sitting room features a Baroque mantel (fig. 217); the Art Nouveau design in the tiles is a rather curious complement.

Though restrained in its contours, the house is lavish in its interior decoration. A stained glass skylight over the stairwell diffuses a warm glow over the central part of the house. The liberal use of natural hardwoods – for mantels, wainscotting, columns, beams, architraves, and the stairway – gives the rooms the rich, cosy quality still sought at the time by dedicated homemakers.

215   Arthur E. McClary House, London, detail of architectural drawing showing
front elevation; drawing signed 'Moore, Henry & Munro'

216   Arthur E. McClary House

217   Arthur E. McClary House, mantel in sitting room

218   Arthur E. McClary House, upper part of Composite columns in main hallway

Robert D. McDonald House, 1910–11
471 Waterloo Street, London

Addition to Blackfriars, c. 1912
90 Central Avenue, London

Everything about the Robert D. McDonald house seems governed by a spirit of bountifulness. Like Arthur McClary's house, it exhibits classical trim on a Queen Anne edifice, but the McDonald house has little of the earlier building's restraint or simplicity. In addition to the balustraded verandah, the later house has a giant Corinthian portico (fig. 25). Porticoes are generally to be found on symmetrical Georgian buildings; here, the portico is bestowed upon a typically asymmetrical Queen Anne façade, complete with a tower, a dormer, and a multi-level roofline. The composition is remarkably successful, partly because the design is well balanced, and partly because all of the building's features are on such a monumental scale. The tower forms a very generous bay window; the hung tiles on the gables and overhanging storey (fig. 221) are heavier and larger than the more common shingle.

There is no mean-spiritedness inside, either. The rooms are spacious; wainscotting in the dining room is approximately five feet high; the wainscotting of the hall is of mahogany. Everything is very finely finished: the entablatures over the doors; the dentils and the egg-and-dart design of the cornices; the surround of the landing window, with capitals matching those of the full-length columns between the two halls. The landing window contains what is reputedly Tiffany glass. The only possible sign of skimpiness is on the second floor, where wood grained to look like mahogany is used in place of the real thing.

R.D. McDonald earned the money to pay for this imposing structure in one of London's foremost industries of the time, cigar-making. The local industry developed after the federal government, as part of the National Policy, placed a tariff on German cigars in 1879.[221] An early historian, who seems to have received much of his information directly from R.D. McDonald, explains that a great stimulus to the cigar trade was the 'treating system': it was customary bar-room etiquette to take turns buying a round, and the courtesy could be repeated several times during a night. The way to avoid complete intoxication, if that were one's aim, was to accept cigars instead of drinks, though many of the cigars so procured served only to make pockets bulge and cigar manufacturers' profits soar. McDonald estimated that approximately 50 to 65 per cent of his sales depended upon the treating ritual. By 1912, there were twenty-one cigar manufacturers in London. The city produced more

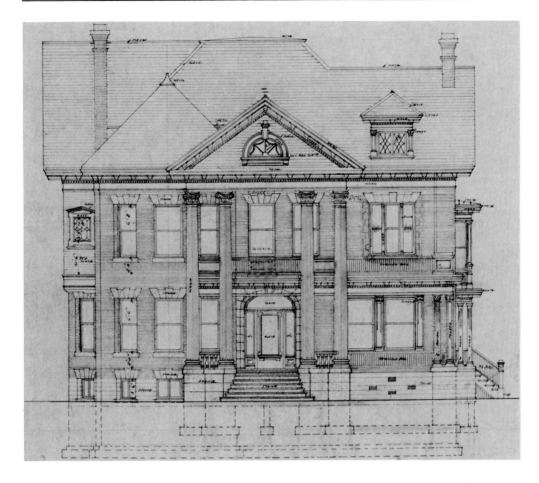

219   Robert D. McDonald House, London, detail of architectural drawing showing front elevation; drawing signed 'Moore, Henry & Munro'

cigars than any other in the Dominion, with the exception of Montreal. A newspaper report of 1905 had claimed that 'London-made cigars were the first to penetrate in dog teams the wilds of the Yukon, that they might bring solace to the lonely miners of Dawson City.'[222]

Robert D. McDonald joined cigar manufacturer H. McKay & Company around 1888, as a clerk. He rose to the position of bookkeeper the following year, and in 1891 he and another McKay employee, Harry Line, established their own business, with twenty employees. By 1910 they had 200 people working for them,[223] and McDonald's fortune must have seemed sufficiently assured to make his mansion appear a safe venture.

The enthusiam for cigars diminished greatly over the next decade, for reasons McDonald could hardly have foreseen: the Ontario Local Option act put an end to bar-rooms in many municipalities; tariffs were increased during the First World War; and, the most damaging blow, cigarettes became a war-time fad that continued to grow in popularity afterwards. In 1930, only ten cigar

220   Robert D. McDonald House

factories were still operating in London, with greatly reduced output.[224]
McDonald withdrew from the business around 1918.[225]

Compelled to leave a business in which he had prospered for twenty years,
McDonald seems not to have found significant employment afterwards. In
1930, he sold his grand Waterloo Street residence, and retreated to more
modest accommodations, first on Princess Avenue and then on Kent Street.[226]
The house of his days of glory itself suffered a decline, but in recent years it
has been carefully and tastefully restored by a group of local barristers.[227]

The McDonald house was one of the few in its time to warrant a newspaper
notice,[228] and its central location and striking appearance must in any event
have ensured a good deal of attention. It seems to have been directly copied
in another of the firm's buildings, Blackfriars.

When a seminary was established in the Roman Catholic bishop's palace
(fig. 53), Bishop Michael Fallon found himself in need of a new residence.
With money given him by friends in Buffalo,[229] he bought the graceful Italianate
house that had been designed by William Robinson in 1875 for Thomas Kent,
a prominent financier. Kent had called the house 'Firbrae,' but Fallon re-named
it 'Blackfriars.' As was typical of Robinson's houses, it had graceful proportions, carefully selected ornamental details (such as brick quoins, textured
keystones and a decorative brick cornice), and an overall air of quiet reserve.
In a memorandum dated 16 November 1928, Bishop Fallon explained that,
owing to the building's 'rather dilapidated condition,' he had spent his own
money on certain improvements, including a 'verandah.' The 'verandah' was

221   Robert D. McDonald House, gable and second-storey overhang with hung tiles

222   Blackfriars, London

in fact a combination porch-portico almost identical to that of the McDonald house; the only significant differences are that, for Bishop Fallon, Moore and Munro extended the porch across the entire façade, and placed freely interpreted Ionic capitals on the columns (the enclosed second-storey porch was a later addition).

The addition probably did create an imposing entrance for the bishop's residence, but it tended to overpower the house behind. The Kent house is neither outspoken nor monumental enough to bear such grandeur, and the addition ends up looking unnatural, like a sunflower grafted on a rosebush.

Charles E. Keene House, 1912–13

553 Dufferin Avenue, London

One of the last buildings J. Vicar Munro designed while working as Moore's partner was a Tudor Revival house for Charles Keene. The Tudor Revival style represents a return by the firm to a pure historicism. Half-timbering appeared earlier in their work, usually as decoration on a Queen Anne gable or dormer, while the rest of the building combined classical, Romanesque, Italianate, Elizabethan, and Stick style motifs. The style used for the Keene House attempts actually to imitate vernacular Tudor buildings, instead of creating a vaguely old-fashioned impression.

The Tudor cottage took on a special symbolic meaning in the early twentieth century through its associations with the era of the home artisan and the pre-technological processes of manufacturing. Houses in the Tudor Revival style were frequently illustrated in Gustav Stickley's *The Craftsman*. The Arts and Crafts movement also promoted simplicity in home decoration and, predictably, a generous use of built-in furnishings.[231]

Both simplicity and craftsmanship are greatly, though not exclusively, in evidence in the Keene house. The high baseboards feature a chamfered edge and a single groove, instead of the elaborate series of mouldings previously in vogue. Instead of marble or carved wood, the mantels are of rug brick with a thick wooden slab as a mantel shelf; often bricks along the outer perimeters of the mantels are piled to the ceiling, thus creating an attractive embrasure above the fireplace. Built-in cupboards abound (fig. 225); all are free of mouldings. The cupboards in the bedrooms are very carefully modelled, in the artisan tradition, for particular uses. The man's closet has many shelves, and low bars for hangers; the woman's closet is larger, and it features high bars and fewer shelves. The present owners speculate that a curious cupboard over the mantel in what was clearly Mr Keene's bedroom must have been designed to hold his brandy.[232]

223   Charles E. Keene House, London, detail of blueprint showing front elevation; drawing signed 'Moore & Munro'

The *Craftsman*-inspired character of the house was in one sense most appropriate for its owner. Charles Keene had worked for many years as a professional cabinetmaker before he began his career in selling furniture. Moreover, he clearly accepted the Arts and Crafts ideal of integrated furnishings and architecture. In addition to the many built-in cupboards, some free-standing pieces, such as the dining room sideboard (fig. 225), were custom-made to fit the house.[233] Elsewhere the house was modelled to fit the furniture: the original plans show, next to the living room fireplace, a bay window made to measure for the 'owner's davenport.'

Both the Baroque style of the sideboard, however, and the wide range of furniture styles carried by Keene's stores prove that his identification with the Arts and Crafts movement had its limits. Charles and Arthur Keene held a partnership in the Keene Brothers furniture store from 1892 until the end of 1914, when Arthur staged a coup of some sort and took full control of the company.[234] By 1919, Charles had joined other Keene relatives at the Ontario Furniture Company (fig. 214); from 1926 to 1945 he was president of that firm (the Keene family continued its association with Ontario Furniture until 1965, recording sixty years of business at the same location).[235] Both furniture stores carried a bargain-basement line (eg, the 'massive dressers' at Keene Brothers were $11.95 each, and the 'metal beds' could be had for $2.25), and it is clear that both carried a vast stock of factory-made items.[236] Keene evidently did not see his own largely hand-crafted house as a model for his customers to emulate.

224 Charles E. Keene House

225   Charles E. Keene House, built-in cupboards, drawers, and glazed cabinet in dining room

Keene's house was most progressive for 1913 London. It seems vastly different from the McDonald house, and it anticipates the firm's work after the First World War, both in its Tudor Revival style and in its simpler interior and exterior lines. The roofline over the body of the house, for example, is formed by a single straight ridge, broken only by two chimneys, and the exposed timbers in the half-timbered sections are all vertical.

The variousness that helped to make earlier buildings picturesque is still in evidence, despite the Keene house's smoother profile. The architectural drawings of the proposed house especially display this quality. In the drawings, a large bow window fronts the dining room; an oriel window and the davenport bay adorn the west side; and, on the east, an extension off the kitchen holds a built-in ironing board and the sewing machine. The plan was simplified in the finished house, but it still features a projecting gable wing, a bay window at the front of the living room, and some interestingly canted windows at the side.

For all that in some respects it represents a turn to the future, the Keene house has by no means abandoned either the nineteenth-century architectural tradition, or the London tradition of William Robinson's firm. Its use of picturesque elements, its historicism, and its recognized symbolic value still draw on the Victorian inheritance.

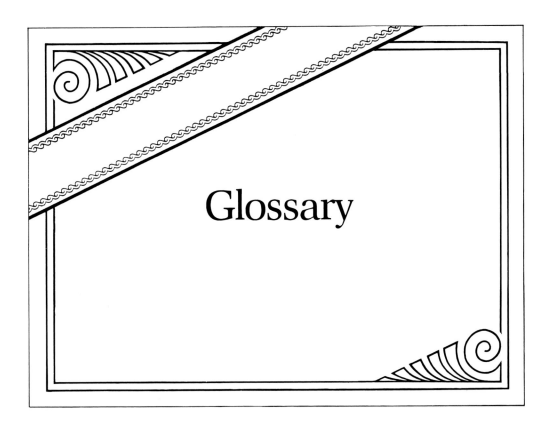

Glossary

ARCADE: a series of arches raised on columns

ARCHITRAVE: 1/ lowest section of an entablature; 2/ door or window surround

BALUSTER: one of a series of small upright members that support a handrail

BANISTER: see BALUSTER

BARGE-BOARD: decorative board that hangs from the edge of a gable, also called verge-board

BATTLEMENT: reinforced parapet composed of regularly spaced vertical projections (merlons) and openings (crenels)

BAY: structural division in the elevation of a building; usually corresponds to a door or window opening

BAY WINDOW: window in a projecting bay

BELL-COTE: small belfry

BELVEDERE: roof-top structure with a vista

BLIND ARCADE: decorative series of arches applied to a wall

BLOCK MODILLION: see MODILLION

BOW-WINDOW: rounded bay window

BRACKET: projecting wall member that supports

elements which are independent of the wall

BULL'S-EYE: circular opening; can be open or glazed

CANTED: angled or slanted

CAPITAL: upper part of a column, generally decorated

CHAMFERED: bevelled or canted corner

COLUMN: vertical cylindrical unit, generally composed of a base, shaft, and capital

COMPOSITE ORDER: Roman interpretation of the Corinthian order, distinguished by a capital decorated with both acanthus leaves and large volutes

CORBEL: projection, gradually stepped forward from bottom to top, that supports (or helps support) a projecting element above

CORBEL TABLE: projecting masonry course supported by a series of corbels

CORINTHIAN ORDER: most ornate Greek column and entablature, distinguished by a capital decorated with acanthus leaves

CORNICE: upper section of an entablature

COURSE: continuous row of masonry units

COVE: concave moulding that frequently provides a transition from the wall to the ceiling or floor

CRENEL: one of the regularly spaced openings between merlons in a battlement

CRENELLATED: distinct pattern of alternating crenels (openings) and merlins (projections)

CRESTING: decorative roof element, frequently pierced

CROSS GABLE: gable placed parallel to the ridge of a roof

CUPOLA: roof structure composed of a dome-shaped roof set on a circular or polygonal base

DECORATED STYLE: middle phase of English Gothic, distinguished by elaborate window tracery

DENTIL: square, block-like shape that is repeated as a band in a classical cornice

DORIC ORDER: simplest Greek column and entablature, distinguished by a plain, cushion capital and frieze composed of triglyphs and metopes

DRIP MOULDING: moulding placed over the top of a door or window to help divert rainwater to the sides

EARLY ENGLISH STYLE: first phase of English Gothic, generally distinguished by lancet windows without tracery

ELEVATION: two-dimensional drawing of the front, side, or back of a building

EMBRASURE: side walls of a door or window opening

ENGAGED COLUMN: column embedded in a wall

ENTABLATURE: beam supported by columns, divided horizontally into a cornice (upper section), frieze (middle section), and architrave (lower section)

FAÇADE: architectural front or the main elevation

FINIAL: ornament terminating the apex of a gable, pinnacle, spire, etc

FRIEZE: middle section of an entablature; may be plain or decorated

FRONTISPIECE: emphasized central bay or section of a main elevation

GABLE: triangular area created by the sloping planes of a roof

HALF-TIMBERED: timber framing with plaster or masonry infill

HEAD: upper member at the top of a door or window

HIPPED ROOF: roof with four sloping sides

HOOD-MOULD: see DRIP MOULD

IMPOST: point from which an arch springs

IN ANTIS: portico columns set between projecting side walls that are finished with pilasters

IONIC ORDER: an elegant Greek column and entablature, distinguished by a capital decorated with prominent volutes

KEYSTONE: centrally placed stone in an arch

LABEL STOP: decorative termination of a drip mould or hood-mould

LANCET: narrow window with a pointed arch and no tracery

LANTERN: roof structure with windows

LINTEL: horizontal structural member at the top of a door or window

LOGGIA: arcaded or columnaded porch or structure

MANSARD (ROOF): roof with double sloping sides, lower slope steeper

MANTEL: decorative work around a fireplace

MERLON: one of the regularly spaced projections between crenels in a battlement

METOPE: square space between the triglyphs of a Doric frieze, frequently decorated

MODILLION: horizontal bracket, either scrolled or block-shape, that helps to support a cornice

MULLIONS: vertical separations between windows in a series

NEWEL-POST: decorative post, at the stair foot, head, or landing corner, that helps to support a handrail

OCULUS: see ROUNDEL

OGEE ARCH: pointed arch with sides of reverse curves, the upper part convex, the lower part concave

ORDER: grouping of columns with an entablature

ORIEL WINDOW: bay window projecting from a wall, generally supported by a corbel

PALLADIAN WINDOW: large window divided vertically into three sections, with the central section higher and arched

PARAPET: 1/ wall for defence; 2/ part of the wall above the roof

PAVILION: projecting central or end section of a building

PEDIMENT: 1/ triangular area formed by the gable end of a Greek temple; 2/ decorative triangular element placed over a door or window

PERPENDICULAR STYLE: last phase of English Gothic, generally distinguished by broad windows with prominent vertical divisions

PIANO NOBILE: main storey, above the ground storey

PIER: 1/ thickened column; 2/ structural member partially embedded in a wall and revealed as a thickened section, usually positioned at regular intervals

PILASTER: column or pier of rectangular section that is engaged in a wall

PILASTER STRIP: pilaster of minimal projection without a base or capital

PINNACLE: 1/ turret; 2/ small-scale decorative shaft or member with a spire or pyramidal-shaped termination

POMMEL: globular finial

PORTICO: porch composed of columns supporting a roof

PURLIN: horizontal timber laid over principal rafters and under secondary rafters that helps carry the roof sheathing; sometimes exposed at the gable ends

QUATREFOIL: pattern composed of four lobes

QUOIN: stone or brick used to reinforce a corner, usually distinguished from surrounding masonry

RAKING CORNICE: cornice repeating the angle of a sloping gable, pediment, etc

ROUNDEL: round panel or window, also called oculus

RUSTICATED: rough or smoothly textured masonry with pronounced recessed joints

SADDLEBACK ROOF: wedge-shaped roof

SECTION: drawing of a vertical slice through a building

SEGMENTAL ARCH: round arch with an inner face less than a semicircle

SILL (WINDOW): horizontal element at the bottom of a window frame

SPANDREL: triangular area between arches in a series

SPIRE: pointed polygonal structure placed on a tower

STRING COURSE: band of masonry, usually narrow, that extends across a façade

SURROUND: decoration around a door or window opening

TRACERY: ornamental open-work in the upper part of a window; pattern can be applied to other surfaces

TREFOIL: pattern composed of three lobes

TRIGLYPH: block between the metopes of a Doric frieze; composed of three vertical bands separated by grooves

TUDOR ARCH: shallow pointed arch with curves determined by four centres

TURRET: small tower, frequently corbelled from the corner of a building

VERGE-BOARD: see BARGE-BOARD

VERNACULAR ARCHITECTURE: buildings that employ commonly used forms and materials

VOLUTE: scroll-like ornamentation used in Ionic and Composite capitals

VOUSSOIR: one of a series of wedge-shaped stones or bricks used to form an arch

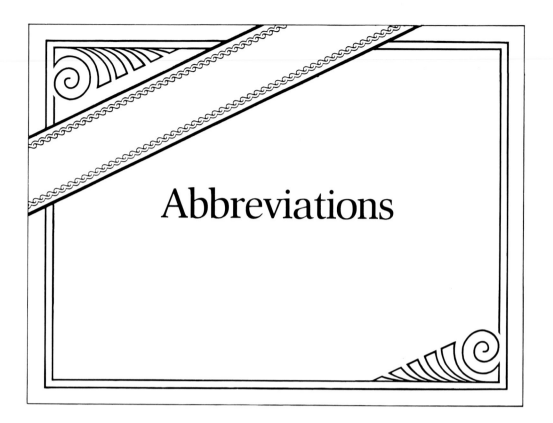

Abbreviations

AABN
American Architect and Building News

CAB
Canadian Architect and Builder

Directories
London City Directories, Regional Collection

Goodspeed
History of the County of Middlesex, Canada.
Toronto and London: W.A. & C.L. Good-
speed, 1889

Huron Archives
Diocese of Huron Archives, Huron College

Journal
Royal Architectural Institute of Canada
Journal

London Room
London Room, London Public Library

Murphy-Moore Collection
The Murphy-Moore Collection, Regional
Collection

OLS
*Annual Report of the Association of Ontario
Land Surveyors*

Proceedings
London City Council Proceedings, Regional
Collection

Province
Jesse Edgar Middleton and Fred Landon, *The
Province of Ontario: A History 1615–1927.*
5 vols. Toronto: Dominion Publishing, 1927

Regional Collection
Regional Collection, D.B. Weldon Library,
University of Western Ontario

Scott
Benjamin Samuel Scott, 'The Economic and
Industrial History of the city of London,
Canada, from the beginning of the first rail-
way, 1855, to the present, 1930.' MA Diss.
Western Ontario, 1930

United Church Archives
United Church of Canada, Central Archives,
Victoria College

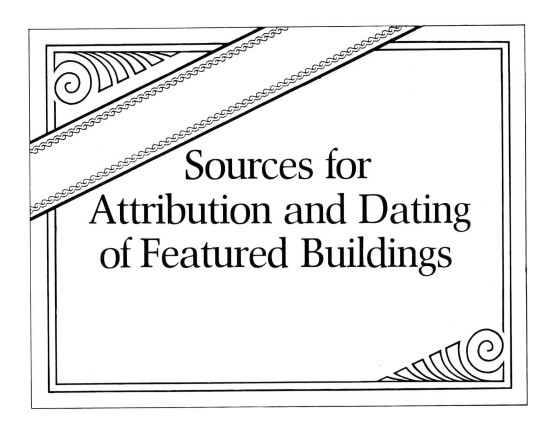

Sources for Attribution and Dating of Featured Buildings

The architectural drawings, specification book, and daybooks listed here are in the Murphy-Moore Collection unless otherwise noted.

Provincial Exhibition Building, London: *Free Press*, 18 April 1861

Christ Church (Anglican), London: Architectural drawing; *Free Press*, 10 Sept. 1862

The Collegiate Institute, London: *Free Press*, 26 Sept. 1864

The Crystal Block, London: *Free Press*, 3 June 1865

Strathroy Public Building, Strathroy: Architectural drawing

Christ Church (Anglican), Dresden: Frances E.J. Rogers, *The History of the Parish of Christ Church, Dresden*

St Andrew's Presbyterian Church and Manse, London: *Free Press*, 25 May 1868 and 11 July 1871

Custom House, London: *Advertiser*, 22 Aug. 1870

Bishop's Palace, London: *Advertiser*, 7 April 1870

Huron and Erie Savings and Loan Society, London: *Free Press*, 27 June 1870

Reid's "Crystal Hall," London: *Free Press*, 22 Sept. 1873

Labatt's Brewery, London: *Advertiser*, 25 April 1874

City Hospital, London: *Free Press*, 12 Aug. 1874

Cottage for Alexander Johnston, London: *Advertiser*, 9 Sept. 1874

David C. Hannah Double House, London: *Advertiser*, 22 Aug. 1874

Militia Buildings: Office and Drill Shed, London: *Advertiser*, 17 May 1876

St Andrew's Presbyterian Church, Strathroy: Architectural drawing; Strathroy *Age*, 14 Dec. 1877

Nathaniel Reid Cottage, London: Directories

Pump House, London: *Proceedings*,
16 July 1877

First Congregational Church, London:
Advertiser, 10 April 1875

London Mechanics' Institute, London:
Specification Book; *Advertiser*, 11 Sept. 1876

High School, London: *Advertiser*,
9 Aug. 1877

The Grigg House, London: Specification Book;
Advertiser, 24 April 1879

Trinity Anglican Church, Birr: Specification
Book; *Advertiser*, 19 Jan. 1880

Charles Murray House, London: Specification
Book; *Advertiser*, 5 March 1878

Federal Bank of Canada, London: Architectural
drawing; Specification Book

St George's Church (Anglican), Walton:
Architectural drawing; *Huron Expositor*,
11 June 1880

Palmyra Baptist Church, Palmyra: Architectural
drawing

Masonic Temple and Grand Opera House,
London: Architectural drawing; Specification
Book; *Advertiser*, 17 May 1880

The London Club, London: Architectural
drawing; Specification Book; *Free Press*,
6 May 1881

Talbot Street Baptist Church, London:
Architectural drawing; Specification Book;
Free Press, 9 April 1881

Talbot Street Public School, London: *Free
Press*, 14 June 1881

St Peter's Roman Catholic Separate School,
London: Architectural drawing; Specification
Book; *Advertiser*, 17 Sept. 1881

Oakwood, the Benjamin Cronyn Jr House,
London: Specification Book; *Advertiser*,
18 March 1881

Waverley, the Charles Goodhue House,
London: Architectural drawing; *Advertiser*,
12 July 1882

Endiang, the John Labatt House, London:
Architectural drawing; Specification Book;
Advertiser, 16 July 1882

Samuel Crawford House, London: Specification
Book; *Free Press*, 10 May 1883

Stratford Pump House, Stratford: Architectural
drawing; *Stratford Times*, 20 Sept. 1882 and
12 Sept. 1883

East London Town Hall, London: Architectural
drawing; *Advertiser*, 25 Aug. 1883

Guthrie Presbyterian Church, Melbourne:
Architectural drawing; *Free Press*, 10 May 1883

Christ Church (Anglican), Delaware:
Architectural drawing; *Advertiser*,
21 Jan. 1884

Moses Masuret House, London: Architectural
drawing; *Free Press*, 10 May 1883

John B. Laing House, London: Architectural
drawing; *Advertiser*, 24 March 1884

513 Queens Avenue, London: *Advertiser*,
5 Sept. 1885

Henry Dunn House, London: Architectural drawing; *Free Press*, 29 March 1886

Perth County Buildings, Stratford:
Architectural drawing; Perth County Council
Minutes

Carmel Presbyterian Church, Hensall:
Architecural drawing; Reverend Percy A.
Ferguson, *Witnessing Through a Century*

Masonic Temple, Petrolia: Architectural
drawing; *Advertiser*, 24 March 1887

Victoria Hall, Petrolia: Architectural drawing;
Petrolia Council Minutes

Main Building, Western Fair, London:
Architectural drawing; *Advertiser*,
6 June 1887

Knox Presbyterian Church, Listowel:
Architectural drawing; 1888 Daybook; Thomas
Hardie, compiler, *Knox Presbyterian Church*

Colborne Street Methodist Church, London:
Architectural drawing; 1888 Daybook;
Advertiser, 15 Dec. 1888

Upper Canada College, Toronto: Architectural drawing, Archives of Ontario, Toronto; 1888 Daybook; *Free Press*, 19 Dec. 1887

Canadian Savings and Loan Company, London: Architecural drawing; 1889 Daybook; *Advertiser*, 4 April 1889

Stratford General Hospital, Stratford: Architectural drawing; 1889 Daybook; *Advertiser*, 27 May 1889

John D. LeBel House, London: Architectural drawing; 1889 Daybook; *Advertiser*, 16 Sept. 1889

Henry Mathewson Double House, London: Architectural drawing; 1889 Daybook; *Advertiser*, 22 Oct. 1889

Dorchester Presbyterian Church, Dorchester: Architectural drawing; *Advertiser*, 11 April 1889

Walkerton Pump House, Walkerton: Architectural drawing; By-Law No. 375, Town of Walkerton, 26 Aug. 1890

St George's Anglican Church, London: Architectural drawing; *Advertiser*, 22 March 1890

Burns' Presbyterian Church, Mosa: Architectural drawing; *Glencoe Transcript*, 3 Sept. 1891

W.E. Saunders and Company, London: Architectural drawing; *Contract Record*, 26 March 1892

Thomas G. Whiskard House, London: Architectural drawing; Directories

Robert C. Struthers House, London: Architectural drawing; *Contract Record*, 4 May 1893 and 5 April 1894

Charles W. Leonard House, London: Architectural drawing; CAB, VI (1893); *Contract Record*, 1 June 1893

Young Men's Christian Association, London:

Architectural drawing; CAB, IX (1896); *Contract Record*, 15 Aug. 1895, 21 May 1896, and 26 Nov. 1896

Pixley Mausoleum, London: Architectural drawing; CAB, X (1897); *Contract Record*, 16 May 1895

St Matthew's Anglican Church, London: Architectural drawing; *Contract Record*, 30 May 1895

St John's-in-the-Woods (Anglican) Church, Aughrim: *Canadian Churchman*, 26 Jan. 1899

Arva Methodist Church, Arva: Architectural drawing; Minutes of Building Committee

Cy Warman House, London: Architectural drawing; 1899 Daybook

D. Warden Sutherland House, London: Architectural drawing; *Contract Record*, 26 Dec. 1900 and 13 March 1901

Mrs O'Donnell's Store and Dwelling, London: Architectural drawing; *Contract Record*, 16 Sept. 1902

Power House, McClary Manufacturing Company, London: Architectural drawing; CAB, XVII (1904)

St Peter's Parish Hall, London: Architectural drawing; *Contract Record*, 10 June 1908 and 22 July 1908

Ontario Furniture Company, London: Architectural drawing

Arthur E. McClary House, London: Architectural drawing; Directories

Robert D. McDonald House, London: Architectural drawing; *Free Press*, 23 March 1910

Addition to Blackfriars, London: Architectural drawing; Directories

Charles E. Keene House, London: Architectural drawing; 1912 Daybook

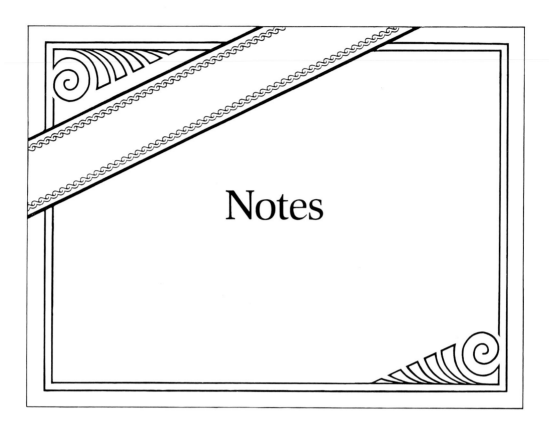

Notes

1 *Free Press*, 9 Nov. 1878.
2 Information about Simcoe and his
ambitions for the London area can be
found in the following works: Clarence
T. Campbell, 'The Beginning of London,' *Ontario Historical Society Papers
and Records*, 9 (1910), 61–67; Gerald
M. Craig, *Upper Canada: The Formative
Years, 1784–1841* (Toronto: McClelland
and Stewart, 1963), pp. 20–41; Fred
Landon, *Western Ontario and the
American Frontier* (Toronto: McClelland
and Stewart, 1967), pp. 3–7; S.R.
Mealing, 'The Enthusiasms of John
Graves Simcoe,' *Annual Report of the
Canadian Historical Association* (1958),
pp. 50–62.
3 The relevant excerpts from E.B. Littlehales's diary are included in 'Governor
Simcoe's Tour through Southern On-
tario,' *London and Middlesex Historical
Society Transactions*, Part 8 (1917), pp.
13, 14.

4 *Mrs Simcoe's Diary*, ed. Mary Quayle
Innis (Toronto: Macmillan, 1965), pp.
88–89.
5 Frederick H. Armstrong and Daniel
J. Brock, 'The Rise of London: A Study
of Urban Evolution in Nineteenth-
Century Southwestern Ontario,' *Aspects
of Nineteenth-Century Ontario: Essays
Presented to James J. Talman*, eds.
F.H. Armstrong, H.A. Stevenson, and
J.D. Wilson (Toronto: Univ. of Toronto
Press, 1974), p. 86.
6 Duke of Portland, quoted in Campbell,
p. 67.
7 *Lord Selkirk's Diary, 1803–1804*, ed.
Patrick C.T. White (Toronto: Champlain
Society, 1958), p. 306. On the formation of the London District and Middle-
sex County, see George W. Spragge,
'The Districts of Upper Canada, 1788–
1849,' *Ontario History* 39 (1947), pp.
97–100.
8 Colonel Thomas Talbot to George
Hillier, Secretary to Lieutenant-Governor
Maitland, April 24, 1827, quoted in

Fred Coyne Hamil, 'Colonel Talbot and the Early History of London,' *Ontario History*, 43 (1951), 162. Hamil identifies the accommodations offered by 'Mrs Swartz,' mentioned in the letter, with the tavern on Commissioners Road that was owned by Bartholomew Swartz.

9 Sources of information about Talbot are as follows: E.A. Cruickshank, 'The Early History of the London District,' OHS *Papers and Records*, 24 (1927), 3–138; C.O. Ermatinger, *The Talbot Regime, or the First Half Century of the Talbot Settlement* (St Thomas, Ont.: The Municipal World, 1904); Edward Ermatinger, *Life of Colonel Talbot and the Talbot Settlement*, intro. James J. Talman (1859; rpt. Belleville, Ont.: Mika, 1972); Fred Coyne Hamil, *Lake Erie Baron: The Story of Colonel Thomas Talbot* (Toronto: Macmillan, 1955); Fred Landon, 'The Talbot Settlement' and 'Talbot Lands after the War,' *Province* I, 113–135, 288–306.

10 *Mrs Simcoe's Diary*, p. 52.

11 E. Ermatinger, p. 15.

12 Letter of May 16, 1801, *The Talbot Papers*, ed. James H. Coyne, Transactions of the Royal Society of Canada (1908), I, 76, 77.

13 Anna Jameson, *Winter Studies and Summer Rambles in Canada* (London: Saunders and Otley, 1838; rpt. Toronto: Coles, 1970), II, 182, 195–196.

14 Hamil, *Lake Erie Baron*, pp. 49, 54.

15 See Hamil, pp. 46, 47, 104. Lord Durham's report claimed that Talbot had been granted 48,500 acres (Campbell, p. 66).

16 John S. Brock to Daniel D. Brock, 22 September 1817, quoted in Hamil, p. 90.

17 E. Ermatinger, p. 65. Simcoe's comments to Hobart, as paraphrased by Hamil, p. 43.

18 Hamil, summarizing Colborne's conclusions, p. 121.

19 James B. Brown, *Views of Canada and the Colonists: by a Four Years Resident*, 2nd ed., (Edinburgh: Adam and Charles Black, 1851 [1st ed., 1844]), p. 270.

20 'Talbot Road: A Poem,' *The Poems of Adam Hood Burwell, Pioneer Poet of Upper Canada*, ed. Carl F. Klinck, Western Ontario History Nuggets, No. 31 (London, Ont.: Lawson Library, Univ. of Western Ontario, May 1963), lines 11–16.

21 The observations by Sir Francis Bond Head and Lewis McGillivray are quoted in Hamil, pp. 116, 157, 285. Anna Jameson's comment is in *Winter Studies and Summer Rambles*, II, 201.

22 Quoted in Hamil, p. 271.

23 Information on the early settlement of Westminster Township can be found in Hamil, *Lake Erie Baron*, ch. 5, and Guy St-Denis, *Byron: Pioneer Days in Westminster Township*, ed. Frederick H. Armstrong, Vol. I (Lambeth, Ontario: Crinklaw Press, 1985). The early settlement in London Township and the official preparations for establishing London as the administrative seat of the London District are discussed in Archie Bremner, *City of London, Ontario, Canada: The Pioneer Period and The London of To-Day*, 2nd ed. (London, Ont.: London Printing and Lithographing, 1900); Daniel James Brock, *Richard Talbot, The Tipperary Irish and the Formative Years of London Township: 1818–1826*, M.A. Diss. Western Ontario, 1969; Campbell, 'The Beginning of London'; Goodspeed, chapters 3 and 13; and Fred Coyne Hamil, 'Colonel Talbot and the Early History of London,' *Ontario History*, 43 (1951), 159–75. 'The Rise of London,' by Armstrong and Brock, contains a comprehensive account of the reasons for locating the District Town at London.

24 Minutes of meetings held by the London Court House commissioners, Regional Collection.

25 Talbot to Hillier, 7 March 1826, Upper Canada Sundries, Public Archives of Canada.

26 Talbot to Hillier, 24 April 1827 and 28 June 1827, quoted in Hamil, 'Talbot and the Early History of London,' 162, 164.

27 *The Canadian Journal of Alfred Domett*, ed. E.A. Horsman and Lillian Rea Benson (London, Ont.: Univ. of Western Ontario, 1955) p. 49. A wide-ranging description of London's first decade and a half is given in Clarence T. Campbell, 'The Settlement of London,' London and Middlesex Historical Society *Transactions*, III (1911), 8–51.

28 Hamil, 'Colonel Talbot,' 165n. That the building was to house the mechanics was mentioned in the London (U.C.) *Sun*, 29 March 1832, and reported in the *Courier of Upper Canada*, (Toronto), 28 April 1832.

29 John Richards, in Andrew Picken, *The Canadas* (London: Effingham Wilson, 1832), p. 302. Talbot, quoted in Orlo Miller, *A Century of Western Ontario: The Story of London, 'The Free Press,' and Western Ontario, 1849–1949* (Toronto: Ryerson Press, 1949), pp. 28, 29.

30 Domett, p. 49; Campbell, 'The Settlement of London,' 20; Marion MacRae and Anthony Adamson, *Cornerstones of Order: Courthouse and Town Halls of Ontario, 1784–1914* (Toronto: Clarke Irwin, 1983), p. 96; Macdonald's Journal, quoted in Hamil, 'Colonel Talbot,' 174.

31 Talbot, The *Sun*, 7 July 1831, quoted in Daniel J. Brock, 'A Brief Sketch of the Early History of London's Court House and Jail,' *A Miscellany of London – Part I*, ed. Elizabeth Spicer, Occasional Paper #22 (London, Ont.: London Public Library and Art Museum, 1976), p. 33. Jameson, II, 145; Proudfoot, 'The Proudfoot Papers,' ed. Harriet Priddis, London and Middlesex Historical Society *Transactions*, VI (1915), pp. 57, 58. Contemporary comments on Ewart's courthouse can be found in MacRae and Adamson, pp. 92–99, and

in Mathilde Brosseau, *Gothic Revival in Canadian Architecture*, Canadian Historic Sites: Occasional Papers in Archaeology and History, No. 25 (Ottawa: Parks Canada, 1980), pp. 66, 67.

32 Marion MacRae, manuscript of entry on John Ewart for the *Dictionary of Canadian Biography*, in process of publication by Univ. of Toronto Press.

33 Statistics regarding book sales: Richard D. Altick, *The English Common Reader: A Social History of the Mass Reading Public, 1800–1900* (Chicago: Univ. of Chicago Press, 1967), pp. 383, 388. Pompeii: J. Mordaunt Crook, *The Greek Revival: Neo-Classical Attitudes in British Architecture, 1760–1870* (London: John Murray, 1972), p. 36. Macauley, 'Essay on Hallam,' quoted in G.P. Gooch, *History and Historians in the Nineteenth Century* (1913; rpt. Boston: Beacon Press, 1959), p. 292. Sartorial fashions: Vanda Foster, *A Visual History of Costume: The Nineteenth Century* (London: BT Batsford, 1984), p. 12; Iris Brooke and James Laver, *English Costume of the Nineteenth Century* (London: A & C Black, 1929), p. 10.

34 Thomas Love Peacock, 'Nightmare Abbey,' *The Complete Novels*, ed. David Garnett (1948; rpt. London: Rupert Hart-Davis, 1963), I, 362; Pope, *An Essay on Man* (1733); Mallet, quoted in Kenneth Clark, *The Gothic Revival: An Essay in the History of Taste*, 3rd ed. (Harmondsworth: Penguin Books, 1964), p. 19.

35 Horace Walpole, *The Castle of Otranto* (1764), in *Three Eighteenth-Century Romances*, intro. Harrison R. Steeves (New York: Scribner's, 1959), pp. 9, 19; Thomas Whately, *Poems Chiefly Pastoral* (1766), quoted in Terence Davis, *The Gothick Taste* (Rutherford: Fairleigh Dickinson University Press, 1975), p. 18. On Strawberry Hill: Walpole, *A Description of the Villa ... at Strawberry-Hill* (1784; rpt. London, Gregg Press, 1964), p. iii; Davis, p. 69.

36 Seymour: Horace Walpole to G. Montagu, 23 Dec. 1759, quoted in Davis, p. 88. William Wordsworth: 'Preface to *Lyrical Ballads*' (1802). Percy Bysshe Shelley: 'Ode to the West Wind' (1819).

37 Wordsworth: *Prelude*, Book II (1850). George Gordon, Lord Byron: *Childe Harold's Pilgrimmage*, Canto IV (1818). John Keats: 'On Seeing the Elgin Marbles for the First Time' (1817). Samuel Taylor Coleridge: 'Kubla Khan' (1797).

38 Stuart and Revett, quoted in Crook, p. 16.

39 Accounts of the explorations in Greece and Italy and of the resulting publications can be found in Crook, pp. 1–62, and in John Summerson, *Architecture in Britain 1530 to 1830*, 4th ed. (Baltimore: Penguin Books, 1969), pp. 249– 252. Adam, quoted in Crook, p. 16. Gourbillon, quoted in Crook, pp. 23, 24.

40 See the discussions of English antiquarians in Clark, pp. 13–16, and Davis, pp. 18–21. On drawings in the *Gentleman's Magazine*: James Macaulay, *The Gothic Revival 1745–1845* (Glasgow: Blackie, 1975), p. 30. On Britton: Paul Frankl, *The Gothic* (Princeton: Princeton Univ. Press, 1960), p. 498.

41 John Claudius Loudon, *An Encyclopaedia of Cottage, Farm and Villa Architecture*, 2nd ed., ed. Mrs Loudon (London: Longman, Brown, Green, 1853), Table of Contents; John Plaw, *Ferme Ornée* (London: I. and J. Taylor, 1795), p. 10; Alan Gowans, *Images of American Living: Four Centuries of Architecture and Furniture as Cultural Expression* (1964; rpt. New York: Harper & Row, 1976), p. 247.

42 'Norman,' 'Early English,' 'Decorated,' and 'Perpendicular': terms used by Thomas Rickman in *Attempt to Discriminate the Styles of English Architecture* (1817).

43 Especially useful histories of western architecture are: R. Furneaux Jordan, *Western Architecture* (1969; rpt. London: Thames and Hudson, 1983); Spiro Kostof, *A History of Architecture: Settings and Rituals* (Oxford: Oxford Univ. Press, 1985); Nikolaus Pevsner, *An Outline of European Architecture*, 7th ed. (Harmondsworth: Penguin, 1963); John Summerson, *The Classical Language of Architecture*, 2nd ed. (1963; rpt. London: Thames and Hudson, 1980).

44 Summerson, *Classical Language*, pp. 14, 15.

45 Andrea Palladio, *The Four Books of Architecture* (1570; rpt. of Isaac Ware's 1878 ed., New York: Dover, 1965), Preface, pp. 1, 25, 38.

46 Lionello Puppi, *Andrea Palladio*, trans. Pearl Sanders (London: Phaidon, 1975), pp. 276–81.

47 Summerson, *Classical Language*, pp. 64, 67.

48 Colin Campbell, 'The Introduction,' *Vitruvius Britannicus* (1715–25; rpt. New York: Benjamin Blom, 1967), n. pag.

49 Alexander Pope, *Moral Essays*: 'Epistle IV: To Richard Boyle, Earl of Burlington' (1730–1).

50 Campbell, 'Introduction,' III, 9, plate 48.

51 See Nathalie Clerk, *Palladian Style in Canadian Architecture* (Ottawa: Parks Canada, 1984).

52 Quoted in Summerson, *Architecture in Britain*, p. 261.

53 Goethe: quoted in Crook, p. 22. Chambers: quoted in Crook, pp. 87, 88.

54 Laugier, quoted in Summerson, *Architecture in Britain*, p. 247.

55 Leslie Maitland, *Neoclassical Architecture in Canada* (Ottawa: Parks Canada, 1984), pp. 25–30; Gowans, pp. 267–274; Summerson, *Classical Language*, p. 96.

56 Civil Secretary's Correspondence, 19 Dec. 1839, Upper Canada Sundries, items 128741, 128742, Public Archives of Canada. Information supplied by Guy St-Denis.

57 Edward Allen Talbot, *Sun*, 7 July 1831, quoted in Brock, 'Brief Sketch,' p. 33.

58 On Romanesque architecture, see K.J. Conant, *Carolingian and Romanesque Architecture 800–1200*, 2nd ed. (Harmondsworth: Penguin, 1966); Jordan, pp. 95–123; Hans Erich Kubach, *Romanesque Architecture* (New York: Harry N. Abrams, 1972); Raymond Oursel, *Living Architecture: Romanesque* (London: Oldbourne, 1967).

59 On Gothic architecture, see James H. Acland, *Medieval Structure: The Gothic Vault* (Toronto: Univ. of Toronto Press, 1972); Georges Duby, *The Age of the Cathedrals*, trans. Eleanor Levieux and Barbara Thompson (Chicago: Univ. of Chicago Press, 1981); Paul Frankl, *Gothic Architecture* (Harmondsworth: Penguin, 1962); Jordan, pp. 124–165; Otto von Simson, *The Gothic Cathedral* (New York: Harper & Row, 1956).

60 Abbé Suger: quoted in von Simson, p. 100. Lyric: 'Of oon that is so faire and bright'; can be found in *One Hundred Middle English Lyrics*, ed. Robert D. Stevick (Indianapolis: Bobbs-Merrill, 1964), no. 11.

61 See G.H. Cook, *The English Mediaeval Parish Church* (London: J.M. Dent & Sons, 1970), chapter 9, passim; Geoffrey Webb, *Architecture in Britain: The Middle Ages*, 2nd ed. (Harmondsworth: Penguin, 1965), pp. 185–92.

62 See Hugh Braun, *The English Castle* (London: B.T. Batsford, 1936).

63 'There is no 'Elizabethan Style.' Elizabethan architecture consists of the Tudor-Gothic tradition ...' (Summerson, *Architecture in Britain*, p. 20). (See also Webb, chap. 11.) On Tudor-Gothic houses, see Margaret Wood, *The English Mediaeval House* (1965; rpt. London: Ferndale Editions, 1981), passim. On Hampton Court, see Mark Girouard, *Historic Houses of Britain* (London: Artus, 1979), pp. 16–23. On the love of intricacy, see Mark Girouard, *Robert Smythson & The Elizabethan Country House* (New Haven: Yale Univ. Press, 1983), pp. 18–28.

64 Vasari: quoted in Georg Germann, *Gothic Revival*, trans. Gerald Onn (London: Lund Humphries with the Architectural Association, 1972), p. 38. Warton: Germann, p. 40. Gothic orders: Batty Langley and Thomas Langley, *Gothic Architecture, Improved by Rules and Proportions* (1742; rpt. New York: Benjamin Blom, 1972, from the 1747 edition).

65 Scholarly treatises: see Frankl, *The Gothic*, pp. 525–39; Germann, pp. 41–45; H.R. Hitchcock, introduction to A.W.N. Pugin, *Contrasts* (2nd ed. 1841; rpt. Leicester: Leicester Univ. Press, 1969), pp. 9–11. Quotation: Rickman, quoted in Germann, p. 44.

66 A. Welby Pugin, *The True Principles of Pointed or Christian Architecture* (1841; rpt. Oxford: St Barnabas Press, 1969), pp. 48, 49.

67 Talbot, quoted in Brock, 'Brief Sketch,' p. 33; Repton, quoted in Macaulay, p. 203.

68 See Walter John Hipple Jr, *The Beautiful, The Sublime, & The Picturesque in Eighteenth-Century British Aesthetic Theory* (Carbondale: Southern Illinois Univ. Press, 1957).

69 Hipple, pp. 16–19. Quotation: Addison, quoted in Hipple, p. 19.

70 Edmund Burke, *A Philosophical Enquiry into the Origin of Our Ideas of the Sublime and Beautiful* (1759; rpt. New York: Garland Publishing, Inc., 1971), pp. 58, 59, 161–63.

71 On the Picturesque and Gilpin, see Hipple, pp. 185–201. On hedge-rows: Gilpin, quoted in Macaulay, p. 176.

72 *Sir Uvedale Price on the Picturesque*, edited and expanded by Sir Thomas Dick Lauder (Edinburgh: Caldwell, Lloyd, 1842), p. 84. On Price's definitions, see Hipple, pp. 210, 211.

73 Price, p. 330.

74 Quoted in Peter Kidson, Peter Murray, and Paul Thompson, *A History of English Architecture*, 2nd ed. (Harmondsworth: Penguin, 1979), p. 239.

75 Price, pp. 364, 367.
76 Price, quoted in Hipple, p. 215. *The Landscape Gardening and Landscape Architecture of the Late Humphrey Repton, Esq.*, ed. J.C. Loudon (London: Longman, 1840), p. 374, fig. 124.
77 Jameson, I, 96. *Ancaster Gazette*, in Elizabeth Spicer, ed., *Descriptions of London and its Environs, 1793–1847*, Western Ontario History Nuggets, No. 31 (London, Ont.: Lawson Library, Univ. of Western Ontario, June 1964), p. 18. Catharine Parr Traill, *The Backwoods of Canada* (1836; rpt. Toronto: Coles, 1971), p. 199.
78 Price, p. 367; William Lyon Mackenzie, *Sketches of Canada and the United States* (London: Effingham Wilson, 1833), p. 230. The influence of the Picturesque on Canadian architecture is discussed in Janet Wright, *Architecture of the Picturesque in Canada* (Ottawa: Parks Canada, 1984).
79 Church Building Act: see Clark, pp. 81, 82. Carter: quoted in Germann, p. 56. Goodwin: quoted in Clark, p. 98. Home District Court House: MacRae and Adamson, *Cornerstones of Order*, pp. 39–44.
80 Criticism: see Clark, pp. 99–103. Commissioners' defense: quoted in Germann, p. 67.
81 Jefferson: Gilbert Chinard, *Thomas Jefferson* (1929; rpt. Ann Arbor: Univ. of Michigan Press, 1957), p. 170; Gowans, pp. 246–47. Latrobe: quoted in Gowans, p. 261. Pugin: *True Principles*, p. 47.
82 Eg. Cl. T. Campbell's claim, in 'The Settlement of London,' that 'out of compliment to Col. Talbot, [the courthouse's] exterior was designed in imitation of Malahide Castle' (p. 13).
83 Edward Allen Talbot: London *Sun*, 7 July 1831, quoted in Brock, 'Brief Sketch,' p. 33. Ewart: Talbot to Hillier, 24 April 1827, quoted in Hamil, 'Colonel Talbot and London,' 162.
84 Macaulay, p. 46; Hamil, *Lake Erie Baron*, p. 3.
85 Quoted in Hamil, *Lake Erie Baron*, p. 188.
86 Woodman, quoted in Fred Landon, 'London and its Vicinity 1837–38,' *Ontario Historical Society Papers and Records*, XXIV (1927), 414. Rebellion: Craig, pp. 247–49; Landon, *Western Ontario*, pp. 161–65; Colin Read, *The Rising in Western Upper Canada, 1837–8* (Toronto: Univ. of Toronto Press, 1982).
87 Fred Landon, *Western Ontario*, pp. 166, 181.
88 *Life and Adventures of Col. L.A. Norton*, quoted in Spicer, *Miscellany*, pp. 24, 25; Theller, *Canada in 1837–38, showing ... the causes of the late attempted revolution, and of its failure*, I, (Philadelphia: Henry F. Anners, 1841), p. 147.
89 'As early as 1836 the Chairman of the Quarter Sessions petitioned the Legislative Assembly of Upper Canada for authority to effect a loan of £5,000 to build a new gaol and court house at London.' (Christina Southam and C.J. Taylor, 'Middlesex Court Centre, London, Ontario,' Staff Report, Canadian Inventory of Historic Building, National Historic Parks and Sites Branch, Parks Canada, p. 4.)
90 Orlo Miller, 'The Fat Years and the Lean: London (Canada) in Boom and Depression, 1851–61,' *Ontario History* LIII (1961), 74.
91 On London's development during the 1840s and 1850s, see Armstrong and Brock, 'The Rise of London,' pp. 91–93.
92 Population: *Free Press*, 11 June 1856. A 'wild wooden place': Brown, pp. 97, 99. By-laws passed in 1850 and 1855 'Preventing the Erection of Wooden Buildings': *1856–57 City Directory*, pp. 41, 42, 48–50. 'Like the phoenix': *Free Press*, 29 May 1865.
93 Garrison: Sir James E. Alexander, *L'Acadie; or, seven years' exploration in British America* (London: Henry Colburn, 1849), pp. 152, 183. Literary

culture: *Free Press*, 15 Feb. 1856.

94 Talbot, quoted in Hamil, *Lake Erie Baron*, pp. 272, 273.

95 Jurisdiction: Armstrong and Brock, 'The Rise of London,' p. 89. Population: *Census of Canada*, 1871, 1881. Chief Justice Harrison: *Free Press*, 23 Nov. 1877.

96 *Free Press*, 23 Nov. 1877; Specification Book, p. 159, Murphy-Moore Collection.

97 *Free Press*, 9 Nov. 1878.

98 On locating the capital: W.L. Morton, *The Critical Years, 1857–1873* (Toronto: McClelland and Stewart, 1964), pp. 13, 14. Governor Monck: *Stones of History: Canada's Houses of Parliament*, produced by the National Film Board of Canada (Ottawa: The Queen's Printer, 1967), n.p.

99 *Stones of History*, n.p.

100 Eve Blau, *Ruskinian Gothic, The Architecture of Deane and Woodward, 1845–1861* (Princeton: Princeton Univ. Press, 1982), pp. 48, 49; Roger Dixon and Stefan Muthesius, *Victorian Architecture*, 2nd ed. (London: Thames and Hudson, 1985), pp. 158 ff.

101 Charles Trick Currelly, *I Brought the Ages Home* (Toronto: Ryerson, 1956), p. 38, passim.

102 Ruskin, *Seven Lamps*, 5n.

103 Price and Knight: quoted in Martin Price, 'The Picturesque Moment,' *From Sensibility to Romanticism: Essays Presented to Frederick A. Pottle*, ed. Frederick W. Hilles and Harold Bloom (London: Oxford Univ. Press, 1965), pp. 275, 276.

104 Matthew Arnold, 'The Scholar Gypsy,' (1853).

CHAPTER TWO

1 Charles Dickens, *The Life and Adventures of Martin Chuzzlewit*, ed. P.N. Furbank (Harmondsworth: Penguin, 1968), pp. 419–20.

2 Both Peters and architect W.B. Leather were appointed to the building committee that was to oversee the construction of the market and the city hall (Goodspeed, p. 283). Peters credits himself with the market, however, on his 1855 map of London (Regional Collection), and one of his obituaries (*Free Press*, 3 Feb. 1882) claims that he designed the City Hall.

3 6 of 9: Directories, *Free Press*, 26 March 1856. Best's appointment: *Free Press*, 26 March 1856; Robinson's appointment: City Council Minutes, 18 May 1857.

4 'Some of London's Earliest Builders and Architects,' *London and Its Men of Affairs* (1915), p. 114, Regional Collection.

5 Goodspeed, pp. 980–81.

6 See Martin S. Briggs, *The Architect in History* (New York: DaCapo Press, 1974) and Spiro Kostof, ed., *The Architect* (New York: Oxford Univ. Press, 1977).

7 Andrew Saint, *The Image of the Architect* (New Haven: Yale Univ. Press, 1983), p. 58.

8 Shirley Morriss, 'John G. Howard: Work in Progress,' paper delivered at *Recent Research in Canadian Architectural History* conference, York University, 9 Feb. 1985.

9 *1856–57 City Directory*, Regional Collection.

10 Saint, pp. 64–66, 87–90.

11 Frank Jenkins, *Architect and Patron: A study of professional relations and practice in England from the sixteenth century to the present day* (London: Oxford Univ. Press, 1961), p. 211.

12 Howard Colvin, *A Biographical Dictionary of British Architects 1600–1840* (London: Murray, 1978), p. 39.

13 Jenkins, pp. 31–39, 111, 107–08.

14 Jenkins, p. 108.

15 Jenkins, p. 111.

16 Jenkins, pp. 109, 110.

17 Jenkins, pp. 113–115; Saint pp. 61, 66.

18 Jenkins, p. 204.
19 A.W.N. Pugin, *Contrasts* (1836; rpt. Leicester: Leicester Univ. Press, 1969), p. vii.
20 Surveyors' Club: F.M.L. Thompson, *Chartered Surveyors* (London: Routledge & Kegan Paul, 1968), pp. 71–72. Society of Architects and Surveyors: Jenkins, p. 118. Institution of Surveyors: Thompson, pp. 128–31.
21 Eric Arthur, *Toronto: No Mean City*, 2nd ed. (Toronto: Univ. of Toronto Press, 1974), p. 243. Stephen A. Otto to Nancy Tausky and Lynne DiStefano, 18 Dec. 1985 (draft of revised appendix for *No Mean City*).
22 *Canadian Journal*, N.S.: I (1856), 571–580. Canadian Institute: L.J. Burpee, Sandford Fleming, *Empire Builder* (Toronto: Oxford Univ. Press, 1915), pp. 37–46; D.R. Keys, 'The Royal Canadian Institute in its Relations with the University of Toronto,' *University of Toronto Monthly* (June 1922), Canadian Institute Archives; *The Canadian Journal* (Sept. 1852), p. 50; Stephen A. Otto, 'Architectural Profession in the Nineteenth Century,' to be published as an appendix in the revised edition of Eric Arthur's *No Mean City* (Toronto: Univ. of Toronto Press, 1986). Atheneum merger: Samuel Thompson, *Reminiscences of a Canadian Pioneer* (Toronto: Hunter, Rose, 1884), pp. 342–44.
23 Association of Architects: Stephen A. Otto, 'A Note on the Association of Architects, Civil Engineers and Public Land Surveyors of the Province of Canada,' 27 June 1983, unpublished manuscript. Association of Provincial Land Surveyors: 'An Act to incorporate the Association of Provincial Land Surveyors, and Institute of Civil Engineers,' *Statutes of the Province of Canada*, 1859, 641. Merger: Toronto *Globe*, 25 Jan. 1862.
24 Stephen A. Otto to Nancy Tausky and Lynne DiStefano, 18 Dec. 1985.
25 Dominion Land Surveyors: Don W. Thomson, *Men and Meridians: The History of Surveying and Mapping in Canada* (Ottawa: Dept. of Energy, Mines and Resources, 1967), II, 63. Engineering Institute: 'An Engineering Perspective: A Brief to the Professional Organizations Committee,' Association of Professional Engineers of Ontario, n.d., p. 4. Architectural Guild: Arthur, p. 243. OAA founding, Durand chairman: *CAB*, II (1889), p. 40. Ontario Land Surveyors: OLS, I (1886), 20.
26 Willis Chipman, 'Report of the Provisional Executive Committee,' OLS, I (1886), 20.
27 *CAB*, II (1889), 40–41.
28 William H. Wisely, *The American Civil Engineer 1852–1974* (New York: American Society of Civil Engineers, 1974), pp. 5–15; Saint, p. 80.
29 Upjohn, Hunt: Saint, pp. 79–80. Galbraith: *CAB*, II (1889), 42.
30 *CAB*, VII (1894), 157.
31 *Statutes of Upper Canada*, 1798, Chap. I, 110.
32 *Statutes of Upper Canada*, 1818, Chap. XIV, 263; *Provincial Statutes of Canada*, 1849, III, Cap. XXXV, 228; *Statutes of the Province of Canada*, 1856, Cap. XIII, 22; *Statutes of the Province of Canada*, 1857, Cap. XXXVII, 145. A discussion of several relevant statutes is in Villiers Sankey, 'The Surveyor's Act,' OLS, I (1886), 24–29.
33 Surveyors: Thompson, p. 193; RIBA: Jenkins, p. 173; Western Association: Saint, pp. 89–90.
34 'An Engineering Perspective,' Association of Professional Engineers of Ontario, p. 5.
35 *CAB*, II (1889), 137.
36 *CAB*, II (1889), 137.
37 Jenkins, p. 160.
38 John Howard Diary, 3 May 1841, 25 June 1841, 5 Feb. 1842, 12 Nov. 1842, 2 Nov. 1846, 1 Oct. 1847, 15 Oct. 1847, Baldwin Room, Metropolitan Toronto Library.

39 W.B. Leather to 'the Revd H.I. Grasett and the members of the Church building Committee,' 25 July 1850, St James Cathedral Archives, Toronto.

40 Dickens, p. 64.

41 Jenkins, p. 163.

42 Saint, p. 54.

43 Robert C. Tuck, *Gothic Dreams: the Life and Times of a Canadian Architect, William Critchlow Harris 1854–1913* (Toronto: Dundurn, 1978), p. 28.

44 Saint, p. 54.

45 Jenkins, pp. 163–64.

46 Tuck, p. 27.

47 Goodspeed, p. 981.

48 For builders' guides and pattern books, see Henry-Russell Hitchcock, *American Architectural Books* (1946; rpt. Minneapolis: Univ. of Minnesota Press, 1962), pp. iii, iv. Quotation: Loudon, *Encyclopaedia* pp. 1, 48, 821 (see note 41, chap. 1).

49 Andrew Jackson Downing, *Victorian Cottage Residences* (orig. *Cottage Residences*, 1873; rpt. New York: Dover, 1981), pp. 40, 50, 52.

50 William Wilds, *Elementary and practical instructions on the art of building cottages and houses for the humbler classes* (London: John Weale, 1835).

51 *Patriot*, 4 Nov. 1848.

52 Wetherall library: *British Colonist*, 20 March 1846. Cumberland library: Thomas Fisher Rare Books Library, University of Toronto. Burke, Storm, and Rastrick libraries: information supplied by Stephen A. Otto. The list of books offered for sale by Rastrick in the 1860s is in the Public Archives of Canada (RG 11, B1 (a) v. 372, subj. 995, item 00375). Howard's gift: *Incidents in the Life of John G. Howard, Esq.* (Toronto: Copp Clark: 1885), p. 15. Toronto Public Library holdings: CAB, I, No. 6 (1888), 6–7.

53 Robinson's copy of *Tubular and other Iron Girder Bridges* is part of the library handed down by Robinson's firm, and now in the office of Ronald E. Murphy,

Architect. A copy of *Villas and Cottages* bearing Tracy's signature is in the Stratford-Perth Archives.

54 Durand's library: A catalogue of all books inherited from Durand, his wife, and his descendants, prepared by Katherine D. Holth. American journals: 1889 Daybook used in Durand's office. *Materiaux et Documents*: Office of Ronald E. Murphy, Architect.

55 Crypt gate: Peter Ramm, *Der Merseburger Dom* (Weimar: Hermann Böhlaus Nachfolger, 1977), pp. 52–55, 73. Terra Cotta Company: Perth County Council *Minutes*, 31 Dec. 1887.

56 J. George Hodgins, *The School House: Its Architecture* (Toronto: Copp, Clark, 1876), p. iii, iv. On the earlier publications by Ryerson and Hodgson, see Ralph Greenhill, Ken MacPherson, Douglas Richardson, 'Public Buildings and Schools,' *Ontario Towns* (Ottawa: Oberon, 1974), n. pag.

57 'Prefatory Notes,' *Designs for Village, Town and City Churches*, published by the Committee on Church Architecture of the General Assembly of the Presbyterian Church in Canada (Toronto: 1893).

58 CAB, IV (1891), 103; CAB, V (1892), 3.

59 CAB, V (1892), 71.

60 CAB, VI (1893), 73.

61 *Canada Farmer*, I (1864), 20.

62 *Canada Farmer*, II (1865), 116.

63 *Canadian Builder: Advertiser*, 13 Oct. 1869; *Free Press*, 1 March 1870; Stephen A. Otto, 'The (Canadian) Builder (and Mechanics' Magazine),' unpublished manuscript, 18 June 1980, rev. 4 Oct. 1981. *Architectural Review:* I (March 1869), 608 (noting existence of the *Canadian Builder*); II (Feb. 1870), 494; II (April 1870), 588, 589, 591 (description of Deaf and Dumb Institution).

64 *Contract Record*, 19, No. 20 (1908), 15.

65 CAB, XI (1898), n. pag.

66 CAB, II (1889), 38.

67 *Canada Farmer*, II (1865), 140.

68 *Canada Farmer*, V (1868), 29.

69 Loudon, p. 2.

70 Prisons: Nikolaus Pevsner, *A History of Building Types* (Princeton: Princeton Univ. Press, 1976), p. 163. Notebook on cereal manufacture: Murphy-Moore Collection.

71 Stephen A. Otto to Lynne DiStefano, 12 August 1985.

72 *The Industries of Canada* (Toronto: M.G. Bixby & Co., 1886), p. 48.

73 *The Industries of Canada* (Toronto: M.G. Bixby & Co., 1887), p. 77.

74 Robert Furneaux Jordan, *Victorian Architecture* (Harmondsworth: Penguin, 1966), p. 131.

75 'Cold Iron,' *Rewards and Fairies, The Mandalay Edition of the Works of Rudyard Kipling* (Garden City: Doubleday, Page, 1927), x, part 2, 25.

76 Early history of iron: Eric Arthur and Thomas Ritchie, *Iron* (Toronto: Univ. of Toronto Press, 1982), pp. x-xi. Cort: Arthur and Ritchie, pp. 3–4. Darby, St. Pancras, Crystal Palace: Roger Dixon and Stefan Muthesius, *Victorian Architecture*, 2nd ed. (London: Thames and Hudson, 1985), p. 94. Chicago: Thomas Ritchie, *Canada Builds* (Toronto: Univ. of Toronto Press, 1967), p. 260.

77 Dixon and Muthesius, pp. 96 ff., 102.

78 *CAB*, XIII (1900), 48.

79 Christopher Hobhouse, *1851 and the Crystal Palace*, 2nd ed. (London: Murray, 1950), pp. 112–13, 95.

80 *The Great Exhibition of the World's Industry* (London: John Tallis, 1851?), p. 100.

81 Hobhouse, p. 109.

82 Quoted in Arthur and Ritchie, p. 163.

83 Van Norman, Hamilton Blast Furnace, imports: George Cleghorn Mackenzie, 'The Iron and Steel Industry of Ontario,' *Report of the Bureau of Mines*, 1908, 190–94, 197, 201. First World War: *Bureau of Mines*, 1915, 27.

84 Leonard: *Free Press*, 7 Aug. 1926. McClary's: *Advertiser*, 3 July 1882.

85 *Dominion Mechanical and Milling News*, Feb. 1884, p. 7.

86 The London Steel Works appears only once in a city directory, in 1883.

87 *Proceedings*, 12 Feb. 1875. Quotation: *Free Press*, 27 Sept. 1875.

88 Specification Book, Murphy-Moore Collection; *Free Press*, 18 Nov. 1882. Quotation: L.N. Bronson, '100 Years Ago,' *Free Press*, 17 Sept. 1980.

89 Specification, H.C.R. Becher Papers, Regional Collection.

90 McBride, 'not an inch of woodwork': *Advertiser*, 2 Oct. 1873. 'Scientific men': *Free Press*, 22 Sept. 1873.

91 *The Industries of Canada* (1887), p. 96.

92 Dixon and Muthesius, p. 102.

93 On glass technology: Kenneth M. Wilson, 'Window Glass in America,' *Building Early America: Contributions toward the History of a Great Industry*, ed. Charles E. Peterson (Radnor: Chilton, 1976), pp. 150–64; *Encyclopedia Britannica*, 11th ed.; Dixon and Muthesius, p. 139; Ritchie, pp. 269–72.

94 *Free Press*, 9 May 1883.

95 *Advertiser*, 2 Feb. 1869.

96 Specification Book, Murphy-Moore Collection.

97 *London The Forest City* (1906), p. 22. Later works: Directories.

98 Window glass in Canada: Gerald Stevens, *Early Canadian Glass* (Toronto: McGraw-Hill Ryerson, 1967), pp. 70, 107, 109. Crystal Hall: *Free Press*, 22 Sept. 1873. German glass: Specification Book, eg pp. 351, 359, 403.

99 Walker Field, 'A Reexamination into the Invention of the Balloon Frame,' *Journal of the American Society of Architectural Historians*, 2, No. 4 (1942), 3–29. Leslie Walker, *American Shelter: An Illustrated Encyclopedia of the American Home* (Woodstock: Overlook, 1981), p. 124. Ritchie, p. 171.

100 Specification Book, Architectural drawings, Murphy-Moore Collection.

101 Scott, p. 123.

102 Saws, treadle lathe: Walker, p. 130; John I. Rempel, *Building with Wood and other aspects of nineteenth century*

building in central Canada, 2nd ed. (Toronto: Univ. of Toronto Press, 1980), p. 375. Dodd: *Advertiser*, 29 May 1884.

103 *The Industries of Canada* (1887), p. 65.

104 Herbert S. Craig (Vice-President, London Branch, Architectural Conservancy of Ontario), interview by Nancy Tausky, 15 Dec. 1985.

105 *Universal Design Book* has been recently reproduced as *The Victorian Design Book: A Complete Guide to Victorian House Trim* (Ottawa: Lee Valley Tools, 1984). Decorators Supply Co. to John M. Moore, 20 April 1910, Decorators Supply Co.: *Illustrated Catalogue of Composition Capitals and Brackets*, pp. 17, 55, Office of Ronald E. Murphy, Architect.

106 *Bureau of Mines*, 1903, 28.

107 *Bureau of Mines*, M.B. Baker, 'Clay and the Clay Industry of Ontario,' 1906, 10–11; 1904, 15.

108 *Free Press*, 19 June 1851.

109 *Bureau of Mines*, Baker, 1906, 80.

110 Sylvia Hodgman to George E. Walker, Sr. A copy of the note was sent by Walker to Lynne DiStefano on 10 Jan. 1986.

111 Scott, p. 337.

112 Clarence T. Campbell, 'The Settlement of London,' London and Middlesex Historical Society *Transactions*, III, 1911, 13.

113 Ritchie, p. 211.

114 *Bureau of Mines*, Baker, 1906, 44 ff.

115 *Free Press*, 5 Aug. 1868.

116 *Advertiser*, 7 Aug. 1868. Fysh: Directories.

117 *Bureau of Mines*, Robert J. Montgomery, 'The Ceramic Industry of Ontario,' 1930, 4.

118 Ritchie, p. 213.

119 *Bureau of Mines*, Baker, 1906, 80–81.

120 Ritchie, p. 221.

121 Specification, H.C.R. Becher Papers, Regional Collection. Architectural drawings, Murphy-Moore Collection.

122 *Bureau of Mines*, 1912, 29; 1920, 23.

Brick veneer: *Free Press*, 23 Nov. 1889.

123 Scott, pp. 337–38. *Bureau of Mines* reports listed brickmakers each year; by 1923, Phinn Brothers was the only London survivor.

124 Specification Book, Murphy-Moore Collection; *Bureau of Mines*, 1905, 16.

125 *CAB*, X (1897), 35.

126 *Bureau of Mines*, 1930, 7.

127 *Bureau of Mines*, 1930, 7.

128 *Bureau of Mines*, 1905, 17.

129 Montreal Terra Cotta Lumber Company: Ritchie, pp. 216, 217. Clay products in south-western Ontario: *Bureau of Mines* reports, especially those for 1923 (p. 31) and 1930 (Montgomery, p. 138).

130 The building definitely faced with St Marys stone was the Chapter House (*Free Press*, 29 July 1873). The design for St Mary's Church, by Moore and Henry, was strongly influenced by Durand's design for an Anglican church in St Marys. (Architectural drawing, Regional Collection). The St Marys building committee chose another design over Durand's.

131 Custom House: *Advertiser*, 22 Aug. 1870. Becher: Specification, H.C.R. Becher Papers, Regional Collection. Cronyn house: Specification Book, Murphy-Moore Collection. Simcoe Street School: *Advertiser*, 29 Oct. 1888.

132 *Bureau of Mines*, 1905, 15, 16.

133 Classified Business Sections, Directories. On roofing materials: Diana S. Waite, 'Roofing for Early America,' *Building Early America*, ed. Charles E. Peterson (Radnor: Chilton, 1976).

134 *Advertiser*, 19 Sept. 1865.

135 *Bureau of Mines*, 1904, 14; 1903, 29. *The World Book Emcyclopedia*, III (Chicago: World Book, Inc., 1984), p. 256.

136 Smeaton and Aspdin: Ritchie, p. 229; *Bureau of Mines*, P. Gillespie, 'Cement Industry of Ontario,' 1905, 118; On the virtues of concrete: Gillespie, 174, 175.

137 Ritchie, p. 233.
138 Manufacturing cement blocks: Directories. McClary's: *CAB*, XVII (1904), 153–156. Halifax: *CAB*, XVII (1904), n. pag. Kahn system: Ritchie, pp. 245, 247; *Bureau of Mines*, P. Gillespie, 'Cement Industry of Ontario,' 1905, p. 179.
139 *City of London Directory, 1856–7*, p. 262.
140 *Advertiser*, 31 Aug. 1865.
141 Manse: *Free Press*, 28 Oct. 1871. London Club: Specification Book, Murphy-Moore Collection.
142 Collegiate Institute: *Advertiser*, 29 May 1875. City Gas Company: Armstrong and Brock, 'The Rise of London,' p. 94 (see note 5, chap. 1). Houses: Architectural drawings, Specification Book, Murphy-Moore Collection. Arva church: *Minutes* of Building Committee, 1898–1936, 19 July 1898, United Church Archives.
143 *Free Press*, 12 Nov. 1886; *1888–89 City Directory*.
144 Architectural drawings, Murphy-Moore Collection.
145 Collegiate Institute: *Advertiser*, 31 Aug. 1865. Bishop's Palace: *Advertiser*, 2 May 1872. London Club: Architectural drawing, Murphy-Moore Collection. Houses: Architectural drawings and Specification Book, Murphy-Moore Collection.
146 Thomas C. Grattan, *Civilized America* (1859), quoted in Eugene S. Ferguson, 'An Historical Sketch of Central Heating: 1800–1860,' *Building Early America*, ed. Charles E. Peterson (Radnor: Chilton, 1976), p. 168.
147 Ferguson, pp. 172, 173, 182 n. 18.
148 Hodgins, p. 61.
149 *Advertiser*, 29 Oct. 1888.
150 *CAB*, II (1889), 137.
151 *CAB*, IX (1896), 86.
152 *CAB*, IX (1896), 86.
153 Qualifications for membership: *CAB*, III (1890), 41. Examinations: *CAB*, III (1890), 135.
154 *CAB*, II (1889), 138.
155 *AABN*, XXVII (1890), 183.
156 Efforts in the 1890s: W.A. Langton, 'History of the Ontario Association of Architects,' *CAB*, XIV (1901), 85, 86. 1931 act: Raymond Card, *The Ontario Association of Architects 1890–1950* (Toronto: OAA, 1950), pp. 32, 33.
157 OAA: *CAB*, XIV (1901), 85, 86. RAIC: 'A Brief History of the RAIC,' supplied by Robert Hill.
158 *CAB*, XV (1902), 37.
159 *AABN*, XXVI (1889), 38.
160 Goodspeed, p. 981.
161 Toronto Mechanics' Institute: Goodspeed, p. 982. Collegiate Institute, London: 1865 Prospectus, Regional Collection. Robinson's students: *London and Its Men of Affairs* (London, Ont.: Advertiser Job Printing Co., 1915), pp. 114, 115.
162 Materials in the Murphy-Moore Collection. These developments were in part the result of a series of confrontations between builders and architects during the 1880s, in which the builders insisted on greater protection against architects' judgements concerning costs and on the provision of more detailed plans and specifications. See *Advertiser*, 17 Dec. 1881; *Free Press*, 27 Feb. 1888; *CAB*, I (1888), 5.
163 *CAB*, XVII (1904), 37.
164 *CAB*, II (1889), 142, 143.
165 *CAB*, XIII (1900), 28.
166 R. Phene Spiers, *Architectural Drawing* (London: Cassell & Co., 1887), p. 46.
167 1889 Daybook, Murphy-Moore Collection.
168 *CAB*, II (1889), 143.
169 A copy of Spier's book in the office of Ronald E. Murphy, Architect, is signed 'Fred. Henry, 1890.'
170 1912 Daybook, Murphy-Moore Collection.
171 Moore vs. Durand, Chancery Court, 1889, Regional Collection. See chapter 4.
172 1912 Daybook, Murphy-Moore Collection.

173 For Reverend Dean Flannery and Reverend E. Meunier. Architectural drawings, Murphy-Moore Collection.

CHAPTER THREE

1 Minute Book, London Mechanics' Institute, 5 Jan., 6 Sept. 1841, London Room.
2 Erwin Panofsky, 'Et in Arcadia Ergo: Poussin and the Elegaic Tradition,' in Meaning in the Visual Arts (1955; rpt. Garden City: Doubleday, 1957), pp. 295–320.
3 Goodspeed, pp. 980–82. Other sources about Robinson's life as a whole are OLS (1895), 170–71, and OLS (1915), 51–52. The latter account is by John M. Moore.
4 On Rosegarland's history, see Mark Bence-Jones, Burke's Guide to Country Houses: Volume I, Ireland (London: Burke's Peerage, 1978), pp. 245–46. John Neville was Baron of Rosegarland in the time of Henry IV [Mr and Mrs S.C. Hall, Ireland (London: Virtue and Co., n.d.), Vol. II, p. 153 n.]
5 The most detailed account of Young's career is S.G. Morriss, 'Thomas Young,' Dictionary of Canadian Biography, VIII, 959–61.
6 Morriss, p. 959.
7 Quoted in Richard Jenkyns, The Victorians and Ancient Greece (Cambridge: Harvard Univ. Press, 1980), pp. 18–19. On Young and King's College, see Eric Arthur, Toronto: No Mean City, 2nd ed. (Toronto: Univ. of Toronto Press, 1974), pp. 88–92, and William Dendy, Lost Toronto (Toronto: Oxford Univ. Press, 1978), pp. 134–35.
8 The ratio of breadth to height is 2:1; the area between the towers forms a square; the rectangle bounded by the tops of the towers, their outermost walls, and their bases is the Classical Golden Rectangle; and, if one were to draw a vertical line through the centre of the building to a point as high as the towers, that point and the upper corners of the outer walls would lie on the diameter of a circle having a radius equal to the structure's width. On the Golden Rectangle, see H.E. Huntley, The Divine Proportion (New York: Dover, 1970). On Young and the Guelph courthouse, see MacRae and Adamson, Cornerstones of Order, pp. 103–110 (see note 30, chap. 1).
9 Morriss, p. 960; MacRae and Adamson, pp. 110–11.
10 Stephen A. Otto to Nancy Tausky, 30 May 1985; Stephen A. Otto to Nancy Tausky and Lynne DiStefano, 3 Oct. 1985.
11 John C. Howard, Journal, Baldwin Room, Metropolitan Toronto Library.
12 Stephen A. Otto and Marion Bell MacRae, 'Henry Bowyer Joseph Lane,' Dictionary of Canadian Biography, VIII, 485–486.
13 William Robinson, Report [to John Howard?], Fisken Papers, Baldwin Room, Metropolitan Toronto Library.
14 William Robinson to John Howard, n.d., Fisken Papers, Baldwin Room. Fiancée: Lucy Booth Martyn, Aristocratic Toronto: 19th Century Grandeur (Toronto: Gage, 1980), p. 110.
15 Goodspeed, p. 982; Charles Rankin obituary, OLS, 1921, 118–20.
16 Information on Leather supplied by Stephen A. Otto, 29 Aug. 1981.
17 Goodspeed, p. 283; Hamilton Spectator, 28 April 1853.
18 Free Press, 1 May 1860.
19 Goodspeed, p. 226.
20 Free Press, 26 March 1856.
21 Free Press, 26 March 1856.
22 1856–57 City Directory, pp. 262–63, Regional Collection.
23 Free Press, 28 March 1857. Appointed City Engineer: City Council Minutes, 18 May 1857.
24 Free Press, 12 March, 9, 10, 23, April, 7 May 1857; City Council Minutes, 9

March, 6 April, 4 May 1857. Hours: *Free Press*, 28 Feb. 1856.

25 Directories.

26 *Proceedings*, 13 Jan. 1873.

27 'A By-Law To Prevent Wooden Buildings being erected in the thickly settled part of the City of London, and for the further prevention of Fires,' *1856–57 City Directory*, pp. 48–50; Article No. 96, *Charter and By-Laws of the City of London* (1880), p. 42: 'the Chief Engineer shall perform the duties of Inspector of Buildings.' Regional Collection.

28 Immigrant Depot: Department of Public Works, *General Report 1872–1873* (Ottawa, 1874), p. 124. Police station: *Free Press*, 10 Aug. 1873.

29 Amelia Harris Diary, Regional Collection.

30 Goodspeed, p. 285.

31 *Free Press*, 12 Sept. 1865.

32 H.C.R. Becher Diary, Regional Collection.

33 Goodspeed, pp. 396, 399.

34 Amelia Harris Diary, 12 Sept. 1860.

35 H.C.R. Becher Diary, 13 Sept. 1860.

36 *Free Press*, 13 March 1863; 16 March 1863 (*Prototype* quoted in *Free Press* letter-to-the-editor); 14 March 1863.

37 *Free Press*, 31 March 1863; Orlo Miller, *A Century of Western Ontario* (Toronto: Ryerson, 1949), pp. 136–40.

38 *Advertiser*, 29 Oct. 1888; Goodspeed, p. 359.

39 Amelia Harris Diary, 20 Dec. 1861; H.C.R. Becher Diary, 19 Dec. 1861; Amelia Harris Diary, 16 Dec. 1864; Amelia Harris Diary, 3 June 1866.

40 Goodspeed, p. 250.

41 Amelia Harris Diary, 11 Nov. 1865.

42 H.C.R. Becher Diary, 11 Nov. 1865.

43 Fred Landon, *Province*, II, 1081.

44 Amelia Harris Diary, 11 Jan. 1876.

45 *Free Press*, 3 Jan. 1882; Goodspeed, pp. 387–88.

46 Carling's speech: *Free Press*, 19 Dec. 1873. Pigs: *Advertiser*, 29 Oct. 1888. 'Tasty' park: *Free Press*, 3 Jan. 1882.

47 *Advertiser*, 27 Aug. 1874.

48 *Free Press*, 5 July 1869; *Advertiser*, 16 Aug. 1870; *Free Press*, 28 Oct. 1871; *Advertiser*, 1 May 1872; *Advertiser*, 25 Nov. 1874.

49 *Advertiser*, 7 March 1873, 11 April 1876; Amelia Harris Diary, 29 Aug. 1876.

50 *Advertiser*, 27 Aug. 1874, 24 Aug. 1874.

51 *Free Press*, 27 July 1857, 24 Sept. 1858. Collection.

53 Basil F.L. Clarke, *Church Builders of the Nineteenth Century: A Study of the Gothic Revival in England* (1938; rpt. Newton Abbot: David & Charles, 1969), p. 24; Kenneth Clarke, *The Gothic Revival*, 3rd ed. (Harmondsworth, England: Penguin, 1964), p. 81.

54 A.W.N. Pugin, *Contrasts* (1836; rpt. Leicester: Leicester Univ. Press, 1969), pp. 57–58.

55 James F. White, *The Cambridge Movement: The Ecclesiologists and the Gothic Revival* (Cambridge: Cambridge Univ. Press, 1962), pp. 25–47.

56 *Ecclesiologist*, quoted in White, p. 5.

57 Worship Gothicism: quoted in Clark, p. 149. Export: Phoebe B. Stanton, *The Gothic Revival and American Church Architecture* (Baltimore: Johns Hopkins, 1968), pp. 97–98. New Zealand: White, p. 88.

58 Stefan Muthesius, *The High Victorian Movement in Architecture 1850–1870* (London: Routledge & Kegan Paul, 1972), pp. 8–9.

59 'Ecclesiastical Architecture,' *Anglo-American Magazine*, Jan. 1854, p. 20.

60 'On Simplicity of Composition,' *Ecclesiologist*, II (1843), 121.

61 'Ecclesiastical Architecture,' p. 21.

62 Architectural drawings (signed by Robinson), Murphy-Moore Collection.

63 Gavin Stamp and Colin Amory, *Victorian Buildings of London 1837–1887* (London: Architectural Press, 1980), p. 97.

64 In the drawings, the door on the south porch is slightly larger than the main door.

65 Examples: First Presbyterian Church, London; Wellington Street Methodist Church, London; St Andrew's Presbyterian Church, Stratford; Wingham Anglican Church, Wingham.

66 Henry-Russell Hitchcock, *Architecture: Nineteenth and Twentieth Centuries*, 4th ed. (Harmondsworth: Penguin, 1977), p. 278.

67 John Ruskin, *The Seven Lamps of Architecture* (1849; rpt. New York: Farrar, Straus and Giroux, 1984), pp. 46, 28 (Chap. II, Art. xii; Chap. I, Art. x).

68 Mark Girouard, *The Victorian Country House*, 2nd ed. (New Haven: Yale Univ. Press, 1979), p. 56.

69 *Free Press*, 28 Jan. 1856.

70 Alfred, Lord Tennyson, 'The Princess' (1847–1853).

71 Ruskin, *Seven Lamps*, pp. 98–99 (Chap. III, Art. xxiv).

72 Quoted in Dana Johnson and Leslie Maitland, 'Osgoode Hall and the Development of Public Architecture in Canada,' Society for the Study of Architecture in Canada *Bulletin*, 10, No. 4 (1985), p. 17.

73 Robert Kerr, *The Gentleman's House* (1864; rpt. New York: Johnson, 1972), pp. 367, 368, 363.

74 Elizabeth Gaskell, *North and South*, ed. Angus Easson (London: Oxford University Press, 1973), p. 334.

75 See Chap. II, 'The Lamp of Truth,' in Ruskin, *Seven Lamps*.

76 Ruskin, *Seven Lamps*, p. 55 (Chap. II, Art. xviii).

77 John Ruskin, *The Stones of Venice* (London: George Allen, 1903), pp. 347, 348 (Chap. XXVI, Art. i).

78 Tennyson, 'The Epic.'

79 Georg Germann, *Gothic Revival: in Europe and Britain* (London: Lund Humphries, 1972), p. 68.

80 Kerr, pp. 341–42.

81 Quoted in Peter Collins, *Changing Ideals in Modern Architecture 1750–1950* (1965; rpt. Kingston and Montreal: McGill-Queen's Univ. Press, 1967),

p. 119.

82 Collins, p. 119.

83 *AABN*, 15 Jan. 1876, p. 18.

84 *Advertiser*, 29 June 1876.

85 Kerr, p. 341.

86 Collins, p. 98.

87 *Free Press*, 3 June 1865. Cottage: Lot No. 15, 6th Concession, London; *Free Press*, 19 April 1867.

88 John Ruskin, *The Poetry of Architecture* (London: Routledge, 1907), pp. 23, 24, 25, 28.

89 Quotation from the title-page of Samuel Brees, *Rural Architecture* (London: R.A. Sprigg, 1843).

90 Quoted in Peter J. Schmitt, *Kalamazoo: Nineteenth Century Homes in a Midwestern Village* (Kalamazoo: Kalamazoo City Historical Commission, 1976), p. 99.

91 Quoted in Schmitt, p. 101.

92 *Free Press*, 3 June 1875.

93 The Fraser house mantel, no longer installed, was shown to Nancy Tausky by its present owner, Lloyd Needham. Fraser House (520 Dundas Street) by Robinson: *Advertiser*, 20 Sept. 1877; Directories.

94 Architectural drawings for A. McCormick (346 Richmond), R. Darch and M. Gould (342, 344 Richmond), Murphy-Moore Collection.

95 Richard Purdom Fairbairne, Report for Classification, Ontario Public Service, 12 May 1919, Ontario Archives. OLS (1937), 115–17.

96 Goodspeed, p. 982.

97 'Some of London's Earliest Builders and Architects,' *London and Its Men of Affairs*, p. 114. Will of William Robinson, Middlesex Circuit Court Records, Application No. 261, Regional Collection.

98 *Free Press*, 9 Dec. 1878.

99 *Robertson's Landmarks of Toronto* (Toronto: J. Ross Robertson, 1908), p. 59.

100 'The Old Crystal Palace, A Reminiscence,' *CAB*, VIII (1895), 109.

101 *Free Press*, 28 Sept. 1861. Unless

otherwise noted, factual material and quotations regarding the building and the exhibition come from this article.

102 Eric Arthur and Thomas Ritchie, *Iron* (Toronto: Univ. of Toronto Press, 1982), pp. 154, 155; Dana Johnson and Janet Wright, 'Aberdeen Pavilion, Landsdowne Park, Ottawa, Ontario,' Agenda Paper, Historic Sites and Monument Board of Canada; 'Ottawa: The Main Exhibition Building,' *Canadian Illustrated News*, 25 Sept. 1875, p. 197.

103 Loudon, *Encyclopaedia*, p. 965 (see note 41, chap. 1).

104 *Free Press*, 15 June 1955.

105 Goodspeed, pp. 205, 206.

106 *Free Press*, 31 March 1863.

107 'Our Parishes and Churches: No. 10 – Christ Church London, Ont.,' *The Canadian Church Magazine & Mission News*, July 1887, p. 310.

108 'History of the Parish of St Paul's: Address given by Very Reverend G.M. Innes, Rector of St Paul's Cathedral,' n.d., p. 6, Huron Archives.

109 Innes, p. 6; *Free Press*, 31 March 1863. 'Stone forest': R. Furneaux Jordan, *A Concise History of Western Architecture* (London: Thames and Hudson, 1969), p. 148.

110 Church Hall: Margaret Lee, interview by Nancy Tausky, 9 April 1986. Gallery: 'Our Parishes and Churches,' p. 310.

111 Will of William Robinson, (see note 97, above).

112 *Free Press*, 18 Oct. 1864. The original prospectus of the Institute is in the Regional Collection.

113 Murray L. Barr, *A Century of Medicine at Western* (London: Univ. of Western Ontario, 1977), p. 71; J.R.W. Gwynne-Timothy, *Western's First Century* (London, Univ. of Western Ontario, 1978), pp. 82, 134. Unless otherwise noted, information about Hellmuth Boys' College and Western University comes from these books.

114 Hellmuth: Gwynne-Timothy, pp. 1–

126; Alfred Henchman Crowfoot, *This Dreamer: Life of Isaac Hellmuth, Second Bishop of Huron* (Toronto: Copp Clark, 1963). Constitution: Minutes of the College Council, Huron Archives. Cost of Institute: *Free Press*, 24 May 1877. Cost of Huron College: Crowfoot, p. 31. Sweatman: Crowfoot, p. 39; Barr, p. 70.

115 Institute program: Prospectus, Regional Collection. UCC: Richard B. Howard, *Upper Canada College, 1829–1979: Colborne's Legacy* (Toronto: Macmillan, 1979) p. 88. $3,000: *Free Press*, 24 May 1877.

116 Ryerson: Clara Thomas, *Ryerson of Upper Canada* (Toronto: Ryerson, 1969), pp. 89, 90; J. Harold Putnam, *Egerton Ryerson and Education in Upper Canada* (Toronto: Briggs, 1912), pp. 204–31. Botany: J. George Hodgins, *The School House: Its Architecture* (Toronto: Copp, Clark, 1876), p. 19. Facilities: Prospectus, Regional Collection; *Advertiser*, 16 Oct. 1865.

117 *Advertiser*, 31 Aug. 1865.

118 *My Dearest Sophie: Letters from Egerton Ryerson to his Daughter*, ed. C.B. Sissons (Toronto: Ryerson, 1955), p. 203. On school's early success: *Advertiser*, 6 Oct. 1881.

119 Sweatman: Howard, p. 87. Fees: Prospectus, Regional Collection. Sale of property: *Free Press*, 24 May 1877.

120 St John's Chapel: *Free Press*, 19 Oct. 1864; Architectural drawings, Murphy-Moore Collection. Hellmuth Ladies' College: Architectural drawings, Baldwin Room, Metropolitan Toronto Library. Chapter House: *Free Press*, 29 July 1873. St Ann's Chapel: *Advertiser*, 12 Nov. 1877. Western University: *Illustrated London News*, 23 Nov. 1878; *Advertiser*, 19 Dec. 1878.

121 The faculties of Arts, Divinity, and Medicine: Barr, pp. 83, 132; Gwynne-Timothy, pp. 82, 83, 87, 88, 92, 108. Cottage: Barr, pp. 86, 88, 115–136; Gwynne-Timothy, pp. 107, 108.

122 Faculty of Law: Barr, pp. 134, 135.

Buildings in disrepair: *Toronto World*, 11 Dec. 1885. Tile company and foreclosure: Barr, p. 135; Gwynne-Timothy, pp. 131, 134.

123 *Toronto World*, 11 Dec. 1885; 'Summarized Statement of Receipts and Disbursements of the Western University,' signed 'Geo. F. Jewell, Accountant,' Regional Collection.

124 *Free Press*, 24 May 1877; Crowfoot, pp. 62, 63; Gwynne-Timothy, pp. 121, 122.

125 *Free Press*, 3 June 1865.

126 *Historical Atlas of Middlesex*, p. 9; *County of Middlesex Gazetteer*, p. 262; *The City of London and County of Middlesex Directory for 1871–72*, p. 215, Regional Collection.

127 Phyllis Mitchell, ed., *Strathroy Centennial 1860–1960*, p. 66.

128 Need for Town Hall: *Strathroy Age*, 23 Dec. 1870. 1872 loan: Mitchell, p. 65; 1874 by-law: Mitchell, p. 66; Cook, $35: *Strathroy Age*, 21 Aug. 1874; 1928 Town Hall: Mitchell, p. 66.

129 Frances E.J. Rogers, *The History of the Parish of Christ Church Dresden*, p. 1.

130 Rogers, p. 1.

131 Daniel G. Hill, *The Freedom-Seekers: Blacks in Early Canada* (Agincourt, Ont.: Book Society of Canada, 1981), pp. 71–72.

132 Hill, pp. 73–74; Robin W. Winks, *The Blacks in Canada: A History* (New Haven: Yale Univ. Press, 1971), p. 230.

133 Rogers, pp. 2–3; Thomas Hughes Diary, Huron Archives.

134 Robin W. Winks, ed., *An Autobiography of the Reverend Josiah Henson* (Reading, Mass.: Addison-Wesley, 1969), p. 144.

135 Fred Landon, *Western Ontario and the American Frontier* (1941; rpt. Toronto: McClelland & Stewart, 1967), p. 71.

136 Early history of Presbyterianism in London: John M. Gunn, *Almost A Century: A Brief Historical Sketch of St Andrew's United Church*, pp. 13–17; *Presbyterian Year Book 1889*, pp. 68–71,

United Church Archives.

137 Seating, Cost: *Free Press*, 25 May 1868. Building Committee: Unsigned Notebook, Regional Collection.

138 No organ, music controversy: Gunn, p. 26. Scott quotation, Cl.T. Campbell, *Pioneer Days in London* (London, Ont: Advertiser, 1921), pp. 44–45. Durand addition: *Advertiser*, 15 Feb. 1887; architectural drawings, Murphy-Moore Collection.

139 Tender call, *Free Press*, 11 July 1871.

140 *Advertiser*, 3 July 1869; Goodspeed, p. 226.

141 Christina Cameron and Janet Wright, *Second Empire Style in Canadian Architecture*, Canadian Historic Sites, No. 24 (Ottawa: Parks Canada, 1980), p. 13.

142 Cost: *Free Press*, 8 Sept. 1870. Dept. of Public Works: Cameron and Wright, pp. 13–14.

143 *Advertiser*, 21 Feb. 1872; *Free Press*, 11 Aug. 1873; *Free Press*, 20 April 1874.

144 *Advertiser*, 19 Sept. 1873.

145 Architectural drawings, Murphy-Moore Collection. Specification, Department of Public Works: Canadian Inventory of Historic Buildings, Parks Canada. *Free Press*, 5 March 1884 (sketch sent to Public Works), 23 Jan. 1885 (building contract awarded).

146 John K.A. Farrell, 'The History of the Roman Catholic Church in London, Ontario 1826–1931,' M.A. Diss. Western Ontario 1949, pp. 35–38.

147 Farrell, p. 64.

148 Father Joseph P. Finn, interview by Lynne DiStefano, 7 May 1986. Father Finn's report of a conversation with Sister Genevieve, C.S.J.

149 James Reaney, *Handcuffs* (Erin, Ont.: Press Porcépic, 1977), pp. 77–83.

150 Rev. John F. Coffey, *The City and Diocese of London, Ontario, Canada: An Historical Sketch* (London, Ont.: Catholic Record Office, 1885), p. 33.

151 *Free Press*, 14 April 1870. Quoted descriptions from *Advertiser*, 2 May 1872.

152 Goodspeed, p. 314. The exact date is

18 June 1885.

153 Nine are listed in Goodspeed, p. 398.

154 *Free Press*, 21 June 1870.

155 *Free Press*, 3 Oct. 1871.

156 Will of William Robinson, Middlesex Circuit Court Records, Application No. 261, Regional Collection.

157 *Free Press*, 22 Sept. 1873. Quoted descriptions from this article, and from *Advertiser*, 2 Oct. 1873.

158 Nancy Geddes Poole, *The Art of London 1830–1980* (London, Ont.: Blackpool Press, 1984), pp. 21–22.

159 *The Industries of Canada: 1887*, p. 47, Regional Collection.

160 *CAB*, xx (1907), 133.

161 Frederick H. Armstrong, 'John Kinder Labatt (1803–1866),' *Dictionary of Canadian Biography*, IX, 436–37.

162 Goodspeed, pp. 372–73.

163 *Free Press*, 6 March 1874.

164 Brewery social: *Free Press*, 19 June 1874. Cupolas: *Free Press*, 14 Aug. 1875; Kenneth H. Geiger (Technical Development Manager, Labatt's Brewing Company Limited), interview by Lynne DiStefano, 12 May 1986.

165 Albert Tucker, 'John Labatt,' *The Canadian Encyclopedia*, 955.

166 Scott, p. 235.

167 Scott, p. 235.

168 *Advertiser*, 9 Aug. 1880; *Free Press*, 3 Aug. 1882.

169 *Montreal Illustrated 1894* (Montreal: Consolidated Illustrated Co., 1894), p. 322.

170 *Dominion Mechanical & Milling News*, Feb. 1884, p. 6.

171 Scott, p. 236.

172 Barr, pp. 40–44.

173 Goodspeed, p. 248.

174 *Proceedings*, 29 April 1867, Regional Collection.

175 *Advertiser*, 27 March 1873. *Proceedings*, 18 May 1874; 1 June 1874; 6 July 1874, Regional Collection.

176 *Free Press*, 7 June 1875.

177 Charles Roland, 'History of Medicine,' *Canadian Encyclopedia*, 1112–1114.

178 John R. Sullivan and Norman R. Ball, *Growing to Serve ... A History of Victoria Hospital, London, Ontario* (London: Victoria Hospital Corporation, 1985), pp. 23, 26.

179 Sullivan and Ball, pp. 30, 54–55.

180 *Free Press*, 8 Sept. 1874; *Advertiser*, 25 Nov. 1874. Johnston's occupation, tenants: Directories.

181 Specification Book, Murphy-Moore Collection.

182 *Advertiser*, 22 Aug., 25 Nov. 1874.

183 *1874–75 City Directory*, Assessment Rolls, Regional Collection.

184 David Hannah obituary, *Free Press*, 4 Oct. 1921; *1905 City Directory*.

185 Directories.

186 Desmond Morton, *Ministers and Generals: Politics and the Canadian Militia 1868–1904* (Toronto: Univ. of Toronto Press, 1970), p. 38.

187 Miller, *A Century of Western Ontario*, p. 141.

188 Morton, pp. 8–10.

189 Morton, p. 38.

190 Proceedings of a Board of Survey, John B. Taylor, President, 29 Jan. 1875. Dominion of Canada, *Sessional Papers*, 1875, Vol. 6, p. 207.

191 *Proceedings*, 27 April 1874, Regional Collection.

192 *Proceedings*, 3 April 1876.

193 *Advertiser*, 3 May 1876; Mackenzie's militia service, Morton, pp. 28–29.

194 *Advertiser*, 3 May 1876.

195 *Advertiser*, 10 May 1875.

196 *Free Press*, 25 July 1885.

197 *Free Press*, 29 July 1885.

198 Carling to Adolphe Caron, 10 March 1884, Public Archives of Canada. Carling's property: *Free Press*, 6 Jan. 1886. Contract: City of London Registrar's Office, Book No. 1, Third Division, Instrument No. 176, 23 Feb. 1886. Copy provided by A.D. Faulkner, Engineering Officer, Canadian Forces Base, London.

199 L.N. Bronson, 'Selecting site for armory proved lengthy affair,' *Free Press*, 13 June 1979.

200 *St Andrew's Presbyterian Church: Diamond Jubilee 1863–1923*, n. pag.
201 Strathroy *Age*, 14 Dec. 1877.
202 Strathroy *Age*, 19 July 1878.
203 Strathroy *Age*, 14 Dec. 1877.
204 *Free Press*, 8 Aug. 1889.
205 *Advertiser*, 8 Aug. 1889.
206 *Advertiser*, 8 Aug. 1889.
207 *Free Press*, 26 March 1856.
208 *Proceedings*, 7 Sept. 1874.
209 *Proceedings*, 22 Feb. 1875.
210 *Proceedings*, 24 March 1875.
211 *Proceedings*, 5 April 1875.
212 Saunders's analysis: *Proceedings*, 1 March 1875. 'Immigrants of capital': R. Louis Gentilcore and C. Grant Head, *Ontario's History in Maps*, Ontario Historical Studies Series (Toronto: Univ. of Toronto Press, 1984), p. 266.
213 E.V. Buchanan, *London's Water Supply: A History* (London, Ont.: London Public Utilities Commission, 1968), p. 9. *Proceedings*, 13 Aug. 1877.
214 *Advertiser*, 29 Dec. 1877.
215 Carling and Tracy quoted in Buchanan, pp. 14, 22. Cost: Buchanan, p. 19.
216 George Munro Grant, *Picturesque Canada* (Toronto: Belden, 1882), II, 503.
217 *Free Press*, 3 Jan. 1882.
218 John Tracy obituary, *Free Press*, 28 June 1897.
219 Directories
220 Thomas Tracy obituary, *OLS* (1926), p. 109.
221 Ontario, *Sessional Papers*, No. 6, pp. 17, 20.
222 *Advertiser*, 9 Nov. 1870.
223 Ontario, *Sessional Papers*, 1873, No. 58, p. 9.
224 Ontario, *Sessional Papers*, 1873, No. 58, p. 9.
225 Ontario, *Sessional Papers*, 1871–1872, No. 49, p. 9.
226 Ontario, *Sessional Papers*, 1871–1872, No. 49, pp. 11–12.
227 Ontario, *Sessional Papers*, 1873, No. 58, pp. 40–43, 49–58.
228 *Advertiser*, 16 Jan. 1873; 22 Feb. 1873.
229 Ontario, *Sessional Papers*, 1869, pp. 20–21.
230 Ontario, *Sessional Papers*, 1873, p. 14.
231 Tracy in Chicago and Albany: Goodspeed, p. 1029; *Contract Record*, 17 Jan. 1912. Surveying streets: *Free Press*, 24 June 1873. Acting City Engineer: *Proceedings*, June 1, 1874.
232 *Free Press*, 6 Dec. 1878.
233 The firm's advertisement changes to 'Tracy & Durand Architects,' *Advertiser*, 3 Jan. 1880.
234 *Free Press*, 9 Feb. 1882.
235 George Durand obituary, *Advertiser*, 21 Dec. 1889.
236 *Advertiser*, 28 July 1885.
237 *Advertiser*, 28 July 1885.
238 *Free Press*, 14 May 1887.
239 Asylum debate: *Free Press*, 8 July 1891. Praise of Tracy: *CAB*, IV (1891), 56.
240 *OLS* (1926), p. 109.
241 L.N. Bronson, 'Looking Over Western Ontario,' *Free Press*, 1 Jan. 1986.
242 *CAB*, V (1892), 25.
243 Thomas Tracy obituary, Vancouver *Sun*, 31 Oct. 1925.
244 *OLS* (1926), p. 109.
245 *Free Press*, 25 July 1885.
246 'Back from Duty,' *Free Press*, 25 July 1885.
247 *Free Press*, 25 July 1885.
248 *OLS* (1926), p. 109.
249 Goodspeed, p. 330.
250 Robert Cater, interview by Thomas E. Tausky, 15 May 1986.
251 Tracy was elected Vice-President on 8 May 1876, and re-elected on 8 May 1877. Minute Book, Mechanics' Institute, London Room. Masonic parade: *Free Press*, 3 Nov. 1876. Western School of Art: Goodspeed, p. 637.
252 Goodspeed, pp. 282, 380, 405.
253 Vancouver *Sun*, 31 Oct. 1925.
254 *OLS* (1926), p. 110.
255 Vancouver *Sun*, 31 Oct. 1925.
256 Goodspeed, p. 1029.
257 *Free Press*, 19 Dec. 1874; *Advertiser*, 29 June 1876. Subsequent quotations

from *Advertiser* article.

258 James Hole, *An Essay on the History and Management of Literary, Scientific & Mechanics' Institutions* (London: Longman, Brown, Green, 1853), p. 17.

259 Eleanor Show, *A History of the London Public Library*, Occasional Paper No. 4 (London: London Public Library, 1941), p. 3.

260 Minute Book, London Mechanics' Institute, 5 Jan. 1841, London Room; Shaw, p. 6.

261 Shaw, p. 7.

262 'The Purpose of Mechanics' Institutes in Upper Canada and Ontario,' Ontario Library Association pamphlet, p. 9, London Room.

263 Shaw, p. 11.

264 Shaw, p. 21.

265 'The Purpose of Mechanics' Institutes,' p. 4.

266 Shaw, p. 22; 'The Purpose of Mechanics' Institutes,' p. 4.

267 *Advertiser*, 3 Nov. 1876.

268 Minute Book, London Mechanics' Institute, 8 May 1876, 14 Aug. 1876.

269 Edmund Joseph Carty Scrapbook, London Room. A photograph shows the former centre tower.

270 *Advertiser*, 21 Sept. 1877.

271 Shaw, p. 25.

272 Shaw, pp. 27, 34.

273 Robin Harris, *Quiet Evolution: A Study of the Educational System of Ontario* (Toronto: Univ. of Toronto Press, 1967), pp. 48–50.

274 Robert M. Stamp, *The Schools of Ontario, 1876–1976*, Ontario Historical Studies Series (Toronto: Univ. of Toronto Press, 1982), p. 7.

275 Benjamin Cronyn, Jr., speech at opening of London High School, *Advertiser*, 24 Sept. 1878.

276 Goodspeed, p. 293.

277 *Advertiser*, 24 Sept. 1878.

278 *Advertiser*, 14 June 1878.

279 Call for tenders: *Advertiser*, 6 Sept. 1889. Photograph: *Illustrated London Ontario, Canada*, 2nd ed. (1900: rpt. London, Ont.: London Public Library, 1967), p. 77.

280 London Fire Department Scrapbook, 1849–1921; Program, Dedication of Collegiate Institute, 31 March 1922, Regional Collection.

281 *Advertiser*, 10 Sept. 1879; 1883 City Directory, Regional Collection.

282 *Advertiser*, 10 Sept. 1879; *The Industries of Canada: 1890*, p. 62.

283 Goodspeed, p. 845.

284 *Advertiser*, 10 Sept. 1879.

285 Specification Book, Murphy-Moore Collection.

286 A. McCormick, 346 Richmond: *Advertiser*, 16 Sept. 1874. R. Darch and M. Gould, two brick stores, 342, 344 Richmond: *Advertiser*, 3 June 1876.

287 Tillsonburg *Liberal*, Oct. 30, 1902.

288 *Advertiser*, 19 Jan. 1880. Subsequent quotations from this article.

CHAPTER FOUR

1 *Advertiser*, 21 Dec. 1889.

2 *Commercial Industries of Canada: 1890*, p. 60, Regional Collection.

3 James Durand obituary, *Free Press*, 14 Nov. 1890. Information about James Durand's career is drawn from this source; from Goodspeed, pp. 243, 250, 315, 398, 400; and from *Industries of Canada: 1890*, p. 60.

4 Nancy Geddes Poole, *The Art of London 1830–1980* (London, Ont.: Blackpool Press, 1984), p. 24.

5 *Advertiser*, 5 Oct. 1868.

6 Diseases: *Free Press*, 21 May 1870. See also J.T.H. Connor, 'Preservatives of Health: Mineral Water Spas of Nineteenth-Century Ontario,' *Ontario History*, 75 (1983), 136–38.

7 *CAB*, II (1889), 143.

8 Cecil R. Roseberry, *Capitol Story* (Albany: State of New York, 1964), pp. 22–23.

Roseberry's book is a comprehensive account of the buiding of the Capitol.

9 Christopher A. Thomas, unpublished manuscript on Thomas Fuller, p. 9.

10 AABN, 11 March 1876, p. 82.

11 Roseberry, p. 33; AABN, 11 March 1876, pp. 82, 83.

12 'Tormented skyline': Roseberry, p. 22. Cost: Roseberry, p. 7.

13 Thomas Fuller letter, 5 April 1878; W.A. Rice letter, 6 April 1878; Hamilton Harris letter, 14 Feb. 1880. Supplied by Katherine D. Holth (great-grand-daughter of George F. Durand).

14 Fuller letter, 5 April 1878.

15 Goderich: Christopher Thomas, 'Dominion Architecture: Fuller's Canadian Post Offices, 1881–96,' M.A. Diss. Toronto 1978, p. 171. Strathroy and London: Architectural drawings.

16 George Durand obituary, Advertiser, 21 Dec. 1889. This article and the Free Press obituary of the same date are the main sources of information about Durand's life. A CAB article (III, 1890, 4) is a condensed version of the Advertiser obituary, and is said to 'present a portrait of the deceased' through 'the courtesy of Mr Thos. Tracy.'

17 Ingersoll church: Advertiser, 1 March 1878. Federal Bank: Free Press, 6 June 1878 (plans underway); Advertiser, 24 July 1879 (Durand identified as architect). Murray house: Advertiser, 5 March 1878.

18 Tracy and Fairbairne call for tenders: Advertiser, 28 June 1879.

19 Advertiser, 3 Jan. 1880.

20 Advertiser, 10 Nov. 1880; Free Press, 10 May 1883.

21 Advertiser, 24 Oct. 1884, 25 April 1885; Free Press, 29 March 1886.

22 Free Press, 22 April 1878.

23 'Report No. 5 of the Court House Committee,' Minutes of Proceedings of the Council of the Corporation of the City of Toronto (1886), p. 331. Advertiser, 21 Dec. 1889.

24 Advertiser, 21 April 1880.

25 Advertiser, 9 Sept. 1882.

26 Advertiser, 21 Dec. 1889; CAB, III (1890), 4.

27 Moore vs. Durand, Chancery Court, 1889, Regional Collection.

28 1888 Daybook, Murphy-Moore Collection.

29 1888, 1889 Daybooks. Matthews: obituary, Free Press, 13 Dec. 1941.

30 Free Press, 20 Aug. 1889.

31 CAB, III (1890), 4.

32 Advertiser, 21 Dec. 1889; Free Press, 21 Dec. 1889.

33 Free Press, 24 Dec. 1889.

34 Advertiser, 21 Dec. 1889.

35 Goodspeed, p. 637.

36 Three engravings owned by Durand (now in the possession of Katherine D. Holth) were circulated by the Art Union of London, which is named on the works themselves.

37 CAB, II (1889), 140.

38 CAB, II (1889), 41.

39 CAB, III (1890), 4.

40 Will of George F. Durand, Middlesex County Surrogate Court Register, X 464. Regional Collection. Assets: 'Estate of George F. Durand: Summary of Cash Account,' 14 Sept. 1903; supplied by Katherine D. Holth.

41 Sarah Durand obituary: Advertiser, 4 Jan. 1895.

42 James Durand obituary, Free Press, 14 Nov. 1890. George Durand to Ann Durand, 21 Aug. 1874; copy of letter supplied by Katherine D. Holth.

43 CAB, III (1890), 3.

44 Directories.

45 Free Press, 29 March 1886.

46 Donald Creighton, Dominion of the North: A History of Canada, 2nd ed. (Toronto: Macmillan, 1957), p. 362.

47 Advertiser, 18 April 1887; 2 May 1887; 10 May 1887; 28 May 1887.

48 Advertiser, 19 April 1887; CAB, I (1880), 5.

49 Free Press, 4 Jan. 1889.

50 Daybook (1889), Memoranda section,

Regional Collection.

51 William Humber, *Cheering for the Home Team: The Story of Baseball in Canada* (Erin, Ont.: Boston Mills, 1983), p. 39.

52 Harold Seymour, *Baseball: The Early Years* (New York: Oxford Univ. Press, 1960), p. 173. Anson's *Free Press*, 28 Aug. 1877. Goldsmith: Seymour, p. 174.

53 Humber, pp. 39, 44.

54 *Free Press*, 10 Aug. 1878.

55 *Free Press*, 9 Jan. 1880.

56 Goodspeed, pp. 345–50.

57 Goodspeed, p. 358.

58 *Free Press*, 2 April 1910.

59 Frances Ruth Hines, 'Concert Life in London, Ontario 1870–1880,' M.A. Diss. Western Ontario, 1976, p. 1.

60 Hines, pp. 28, 31; Goodspeed, p. 360.

61 Hines, pp. 25–27; Helmut Kallmann, 'Sippi, Charles A.,' 'Sippi, George B.,' *Encyclopedia of Music in Canada* (1981), 872.

62 *Free Press*, 27 July 1885; 29 July 1885; 28 July 1885.

63 Hines, p. 4.

64 Hines, pp. 51–69. Quotation, p. 69.

65 Hines, p. 68.

66 *Advertiser, Free Press*, 19 March 1880.

67 Mary Markham Brown, 'Circuits and Circuiteers' (unpublished article), p. 10. To appear in Ann Saddlemyer ed., *The History of Theatre in Ontario, Volume One: The Beginning to 1914.* Article provided by Kathleen Fraser.

68 *Advertiser, Free Press*, 9 Sept. 1881.

69 Mary Markham Brown, 'The Entertainers' (unpublished article; to appear in *The History of Theatre in Ontario*), *passim.* Mary Markham Brown, Grand Theatre Performance Calendar.

70 Poole, pp. 25, 28–29, 26–27, 53, 51, 63, 43.

71 Roseberry, p. 31.

72 *AABN*, 15 Jan. 1876, p. 19.

73 For example, in a catalogue preceded by an interview with Durand, the reporter (*Advertiser*, 10 Nov. 1880) says

of Thomas Beattie's store: 'the architecture is to be very fine and of the Queen Anne style.' On 3 Aug. 1882, the *Free Press* reporter 'elicited' from Durand 'the following information': of Oakwood, 'the style is Renaissance'; the two schools, Waverley and Endiang are all 'Gothic.' Upper Canada College is described as 'modified Romanesque' at a very early stage of planning (*Free Press*, 19 Dec. 1887); the description uses details that could only have come from the architect. Other references: *Advertiser*, 5 May 1880, 17 Dec. 1888, 4 Oct. 1889.

74 The Gothic Revival is analysed in works by Stefan Muthesius (see Chap. 3, note 58); Kenneth Clark (see Chap. 3, note 57) and Robert Furneaux Jordan (see chap. 2, note 74).

75 *The Ecclesiologist*, 20 (1859), 185, quoted in John Summerson, 'William Butterfield; or the Glory of Ugliness,' *Heavenly Mansions, and other Essays on Architecture* (New York: Norton, 1963), pp. 167, 168.

76 Old English: Girouard, *Victorian Country House*, pp. 71–74; Charles L. Eastlake, *A History of the Gothic Revival* (1872; rpt. Watkins Glen: American Life Foundation, 1979), p. 340.

77 Eastlake, p. 343.

78 'Old English' architects as artists, Taylor quotation: Girouard, *Sweetness and Light: The Queen Anne Movement 1860–1900* (London: Oxford Univ. Press, 1977), pp. 25–27, 15. Shaw: Eastlake, p. 343.

79 John Gloag, Introd., *Hints on Household Taste in Furniture, Upholstery and Other Details* (1878; rpt. New York: Dover, 1969), pp. viii, xxiv. The first two quotations are from Eastlake's preface to the second edition, quoted in Gloag's introduction.

80 *California Architect and Building News*, Oct. 1881, p. 97 and April 1882, p. 49, quoted in Judith Lynch Waldorn, *A Gift to the Street* (New York: St Martin's,

1976), pp. 167, 168.

81 Eastlake, *A History of the Gothic Revival*, pp. 359, 372.

82 J.J. Stevenson, *House Architecture* (London: Macmillan, 1880), I, 331, 330, 335, 336.

83 *AABN*, 21 Oct. 1876, p. 344.

84 Roderick Marshall, *William Morris and his Earthly Paradises* (Tisbury: Compton Press, 1979), p. 216.

85 Elizabeth Aslin, *The Aesthetic Movement: Prelude to Art Nouveau* (New York: Praeger, 1969), front jacket illustration. Sunflower, detail of a piano cover, designed by C.R. Ashbee, c. 1889.

86 Stevenson, I, 381.

87 *AABN*, 2 Nov. 1878, p. 148.

88 *Advertiser*, 10 Nov. 1880.

89 *Advertiser*, 6 June 1878. Portland Block: William H. Jordy, *American Buildings and Their Architects: Progressive and Academic Ideals at the Turn of the Twentieth Century* (Garden City, N.Y.: Doubleday, 1972), pp. 15–18.

90 *AABN*, 27 July 1889, p. 38.

91 *AABN*, 4 April 1885, p. 166.

92 Quoted in Vincent J. Scully, *The Shingle Style and The Stick Style*, 2nd ed. (New Haven: Yale Univ. Press, 1971), pp. xli, xliv.

93 Scully, pp. lvii, lviii.

94 *Advertiser*, 24 July 1879.

95 Girouard, *Sweetness and Light*, pp. 208–223. Henry Hudson Holly, *Modern Dwellings in Town and Country Adapted to American Wants and Climate* (New York: Harper, 1878), pp. 19–21; illustrations: passim.

96 On Richardson, see Jeffrey Karl Ochsner, *H.H. Richardson: Complete Architectural Works* (Cambridge: MIT Press, 1982); Henry-Russell Hitchcock, *The Architecture of H.H. Richardson and his Times* (New York: Museum of Modern Art, 1936).

97 Antoine-Laurent-Thomas Vaudoyer, quoted in David Van Zanten, 'Architectural Composition at the Ecole des Beaux-Arts from Charles Percier to Charles Garnier,' *The Architecture of the Ecole des Beaux-Arts*, ed. Arthur Drexler (New York: Museum of Modern Art, 1977), p. 118. Ecole des Beaux-Arts influence: David P. Handlin, *American Architecture* (London: Thames and Hudson, 1985), pp. 109 ff.

98 *Free Press*, 3 Sept. 1881.

99 Directories.

100 *1886 City Directory*, Regional Collection.

101 *Advertiser*, 12 Oct. 1887. This lengthy article contains the complete text of an auditor's report by George Jewell.

102 Bank of London vs. Charles Murray, Chancery Court, 29 Sept. 1887, Regional Collection.

103 Rocliffe Morton Breckenridge, *The History of Banking in Canada* (Washington: National Monetary Commission, U.S. Senate, 1910), p. 129.

104 *Advertiser*, 6 June 1878.

105 *Advertiser*, 24 July 1879.

106 Jordy, (see note 89 above), pp. 15–18.

107 *Advertiser*, 6 June 1878.

108 Federal Bank of Canada, Specification Book, Murphy-Moore Collection.

109 Breckenridge, pp. 129–130.

110 R.T. Naylor, *The History of Canadian Business 1867–1914* (Toronto: Lorimer, 1975), I, 149.

111 *London The Forest City* (promotional brochure, 1906), p. 25, Regional Collection.

112 *Farmers' and Business Directory for the Counties of Huron, Middlesex and Perth, 1887* (Ingersoll: Union Publishing Co., 1886), III, A35; *Illustrated Historical Atlas of the County of Huron, Ontario* (Toronto: Belden, 1879), pp. 17, 19.

113 *The Huron Expositor*, 18 June 1880.

114 *Dominion Churchman*, 12 Aug. 1880.

115 'Minutes of the Standing Committee of the Incorporated Synod of the Diocese of London,' p. 104. Meeting of 4 Dec. 1879.

116 Mrs Earl Mills, interview by Lynne DiStefano.

117 Joseph McDermott, 'Historical Sketch of the Palmyra Baptist Church,' Histor-

ical Committee of the Baptist Convention of Ontario and Quebec, p. 3; Mildred Congo to Lynne DiStefano, 21 Aug. 1985.

118 McDermott, p. 4.

119 Mildred Congo to Lynne DiStefano, 21 Aug. 1985; Gordon Mills to Lynne DiStefano, 20 Aug. 1985.

120 *Free Press*, 5 Aug. 1880.

121 *Free Press*, 9 May 1881.

122 *Free Press*, 9 May 1881.

123 *Free Press*, 9 May 1881.

124 *Free Press*, 9 May 1881.

125 *Free Press*, 9 May 1881.

126 *Free Press*, 3 Sept. 1881; *Advertiser*, 13 Aug. 1881.

127 *Advertiser*, 13 Aug. 1881.

128 *Free Press*, 24 Feb. 1900; 1967, 1968 City Directories, Regional Collection.

129 William Dendy, *Lost Toronto* (Toronto: Oxford Univ. Press, 1978), p. 93.

130 *Advertiser*, 11 Aug. 1873.

131 Orlo Miller and Brandon Conron, *The London Club: A Century in Light-Hearted Retrospect* (London, Ont.: London Club, 1980), p. 11.

132 Miller and Conron, p. 14.

133 *Free Press*, 7 May 1881.

134 Miller and Conron, p. 25.

135 Miller and Conron, p. 19.

136 Orlo Miller, *The London Club: An Irreverent History* (London, Ont.: London Club, 1954), p. 12. In the revised edition (Miller and Conron, p. 19), 'ugly face' has been changed to 'amiable face.'

137 'Talbot Street,' *Baptist Reporter*, April 1895, p. 216.

138 *Canadian Baptist*, 25 Aug. 1881, p. 5.

139 The seating capacity is marked on Durand's floor plan, Murphy-Moore Collection.

140 Two post-cards, cancelled on 23 April 1908, show the effect of the renovations on the interior and the exterior. The writer, L. Russell, remarks: 'It is one of the prettiest churches here.' Regional Collection.

141 'First Reformed Church – 513 Talbot St.' A one-page description, undated, issued by the present congregation.

142 'Principal's Report,' *County of Middlesex Gazetteer and Directory 1864–65*, p. 30, Regional Collection.

143 Goodspeed, p. 288; 'Superintendent's Report,' *County of Middlesex Gazetteer and Directory 1864–65*, p. 27.

144 Goodspeed, p. 289; Orlo Miller, *St George's School 1852–1952: A Complete History*, p. 9. Miller's account provides a good overview of early public education in London.

145 Dana Johnson, *Going to School in Ontario: The Urban Primary School 1850–1930*, Research Bulletin 213, Parks Canada, p. 4.

146 Miller, *St George's School*, p. 18; Johnson, pp. 2–3.

147 'Superintendent's Report,' p. 28.

148 *The Changing Face of Catholic Education in London 1858–1963: A Study Prepared by the Sisters of St Joseph for the Separate School Board, London, Ontario*, p. 9.

149 *Free Press*, 19 July 1880.

150 The other schools were Central School, East London (later Rectory St. School), Princess Avenue School and Hamilton Road (later Aberdeen) School. They are pictured in *Illustrated London, Ontario, Canada* (2nd ed., 1900; rpt. London Ont.: London Public Library Board, 1967), pp. 81, 82, 83.

151 *Advertiser*, 7 Feb. 1882; John K. Elliott ed., *London Heritage* (London, Ont.: London Free Press, 1972), n. pag., entry #46.

152 *Advertiser*, 29 Oct. 1888.

153 *The Changing Face of Catholic Education*, pp. 9–10.

154 *Advertiser*, 9 Sept. 1882.

155 Frederick H. Armstrong, 'George Jervis Goodhue: Pioneer Merchant of London, Upper Canada,' *Ontario History*, 63 (1971), pp. 217, 229–231; Frederick H. Armstrong, quoted by Joe Matyas in 'The Waverley Mansion,' *Encounter: Sunday News Magazine of the London*

Free Press, 16 March 1986, p. 10.

156 Goodspeed, pp. 253–55; *Free Press*, 6 Dec. 1873.

157 *Free Press*, 6 Dec. 1873.

158 *Advertiser*, 28 Dec. 1874.

159 *Advertiser*, 12 Oct. 1887.

160 Hamilton J. Peck to S.H. Blake, 5 Dec. 1896, Regional Collection.

161 Edward Cronyn to Verschoyle Cronyn, 18 Dec. 1896, Regional Collection; Benjamin Cronyn to Verschoyle Cronyn, 30 November 1896, Regional Collection.

162 *1930 City Directory*, Regional Collection.

163 Photographs of Tovey's drawing, taken by Lynne DiStefano. The original, formerly in the possession of the Shute Institute, appears to have been lost.

164 Frederick H. Armstrong, 'George Jervis Goodhue,' pp. 217–32, passim. Quotation, p. 231.

165 *Advertiser*, 29 Aug. 1980.

166 Goodspeed, p. 340; Miller and Conron, *The London Club*, p. 51.

167 John Lutman, quoted by Joe Matyas in 'The Waverley Mansion,' *Encounter*, 16 March 1986, p. 11; Benjamin Franklin Clarke, 'Case Studies of the London Elite,' M.A. Diss. Western Ontario 1978, pp. 151–61.

168 Katharine Harley (a granddaughter of John Labatt), interview by Nancy Tausky, 28 June 1986.

169 John Lutman, quoted by Joe Matyas in 'The Waverley Mansion,' p. 11.

170 *Free Press*, 3 Aug. 1882.

171 Clarke, pp. 64, 66–69.

172 *Advertiser*, 12 April 1884.

173 Katharine Harley, interview by Nancy Tausky, 28 June 1986.

174 Clarke, p. 70; Albert Tucker, 'John Labatt,' *The Canadian Encyclopedia*; *Advertiser*, *Free Press*, 28 April 1915.

175 *Free Press*, 3 Aug. 1882.

176 Directories; 1881 Insurance Map, Regional Collection.

177 Goodspeed, p. 377.

178 R.T. Naylor (see note 10), II, 171.

179 Goodspeed, p. 257.

180 *1887 City Directory*, 1887 Assessment Roll, Regional Collection.

181 Crawford's death: *1890 City Directory*. Beattie: *Free Press*, 7 Sept. 1911. Apartments: *London Heritage*, n.p., Entry #22.

182 Contemporary evidence is drawn from the following sources: Stratford *Beacon Weekly*, 25 Aug. 1882, 26 Oct. 1883; Stratford *Times*, 30 Aug. 1882.

183 Stratford Water Supply Company difficulties, selling price: *Stratford Beacon-Herald*, 23 June 1932.

184 Goodspeed, pp. 410–11; 'When London East Walked Alone,' *London Centennial Review, 1826–1926*, pp. 69–70.

185 1882 Auditor's Report, East London, Charles Lilley Scrapbook, Edwin Seaborn Collection, Box 4320, Item 55, Regional Collection.

186 Charles Lilley, 'To the Electors of London East,' Lilley Scrapbook.

187 *Advertiser*, 25 Aug. 1883.

188 C.A. Hale, 'Rural, Village and Town Halls in Canada,' *Town Halls of Canada* (Ottawa: Parks Canada), I, 102–105.

189 Goodspeed, p. 499; *Free Press*, 29 May 1937.

190 *Centennial Souvenir, 1858–1958*, Guthrie Presbyterian Church, Melbourne.

191 *Free Press*, 10 May 1883.

192 *Free Press*, 29 May 1937, 26 Dec. 1937.

193 David George Bowyer, *Christ Church, Delaware, Ontario, 1834 to 1984: A Century and a Half of Faith, Worship and Witness*, pp. 1–2, 12–13, 27, 29.

194 *Free Press*, 9 Sept. 1884.

195 David George Bowyer, interview by Nancy Tausky, 7 July 1986.

196 *Free Press*, 3 Jan. 1882.

197 Laing: Goodspeed, pp. 365, 387. Masuret: Goodspeed, pp. 365, 387, 648.

198 *Advertiser*, 24 Oct. 1884; *Free Press*, 29 March 1886.

199 George E. Walker, Sr. to Lynne DiStefano, 10 Jan. 1986.

200 Directories.

201 Assessment Rolls, Regional Collection.

202 Goodspeed, p. 884.

203 Henry Dunn obituary, *Free Press*, 3

March 1898; Directories; Elizabeth Mason (granddaughter of Henry Dunn), interview by Thomas E. Tausky, 9 July 1986.

204 *Free Press*, 29 March 1886. James Street: Architectural drawing, Murphy-Moore Collection. Seamstress: Elizabeth Mason.

205 *Free Press*, 3 March 1898.

206 Date of Dunn's death: *Free Press*, 3 March 1898. Elizabeth Dunn's addresses: Directories, Regional Collection. Other information from Elizabeth Mason, M.W. Foster (present owner of 195 Elmwood Avenue).

207 Kelly Crossman, *The Early Court Houses of Ontario*, Manuscript Report Series No. 295 (Ottawa: Parks Canada, 1978), ii, 400–401; James Anderson, *Perth County Buildings–Stratford* (guidebook, n. pag.), Stratford-Perth Archives.

208 Anderson.

209 W. Stafford Johnston and Hugh J.M. Johnston, *History of Perth County to 1967* (Stratford: County of Perth, 1967), pp. 66–67.

210 'Report of Committee on County Property re County Buildings,' Perth County Council Minutes, 30 Jan. 1885, Stratford-Perth Archives.

211 Perth County Council *Minutes*, 7 Dec. 1887.

212 Anderson.

213 Payment of $1200 to Terra Cotta Company, 'General Expenditure,' Perth County Council *Minutes*, 31 Dec. 1887.

214 Murphy-Moore Collection.

215 One of his signatures is so placed as to suggest a larger role. In the series of six panels across the main part of the façade, where Durand had his signature moulded into the right-hand plaque representing architecture, Plaffehaeit signed the left-hand plaque, associated with the arts.

216 Perth County Council *Minutes*, 28 Jan., 24 June 1887.

217 Stratford *Beacon*, 13 May 1887.

218 Perth County Council *Minutes*, 7, 8 Dec. 1887.

219 Mabel Shirray, *Hensall United Church: An Historical View*, p. 1.

220 'I.S.B.,' 'Half a Century of Service,' *Presbyterian Review*, 20 Oct. 1898.

221 Shirray, p. 2; Percy A. Ferguson, *Witnessing Through A Century: The Story of Carmel Presbyterian Church Hensall, Ontario*, n. pag.

222 Other churches in the same style are: St Andrew's Presbyterian Church, Lucknow; St Philip's Roman Catholic Church, Petrolia; a Baptist church, London East.

223 Victor Lauriston, *Lambton's Hundred Years 1849–1949*, p. 151, Regional Collection.

224 Charles Whipp and Edward Phelps eds., *Petrolia 1866–1966* (Petrolia: Petrolia Centennial Committee, 1966), pp. 26–27, Regional Collection.

225 Masonic Temple, Victoria Hall, St Philip's Roman Catholic Church: Architectural drawings, Murphy-Moore Collection. St Andrew's Presbyterian Church: Architectural drawings, Presbyterian Church in Canada Archives, Knox College, Toronto. Two brick stores for J.L. Englehart: *Advertiser*, 30 April 1878. High School: Daybook, Murphy-Moore Collection.

226 Roger E. Riendeau, 'Victoria Hall: Historical Report,' Architectural History Division, National Historic Parks and Sites Branch, Parks Canada, i, 2.

227 Mayor's speech: Petrolia *Advertiser*, 11 Jan. 1889.

228 Whipp and Phelps, p. 27.

229 Petrolia *Advertiser*, 11 Jan. 1889.

230 Riendeau, i, 3; Whipp and Phelps, p. 28.

231 Petrolia *Advertiser*, 11 Jan. 1889.

232 Whipp and Phelps, p. 42; Petrolia *Advertiser*, 11 Jan. 1889.

233 Dana Johnson, 'Victoria Hall,' *Town Halls of Canada* (Ottawa: Parks Canada, 1981), II, 120.

234 Petrolia *Advertiser*, 11 Jan. 1889.

235 Riendeau, I, 3.
236 Edward Phelps, *Petrolia 1874–1974* (Petrolia: Petrolia Print and Litho Limited, 1974), pp. 9–10.
237 Riendeau, I, 4.
238 Victoria Playhouse Petrolia, brochure.
239 *Proceedings*, 6 July 1874.
240 *Proceedings*, 17 May 1880; 'City of London Election Results, Jan. 3, 1881,' *Proceedings*.
241 *Free Press*, 24 Dec. 1885.
242 *Free Press*, 6 Jan. 1886.
243 *Free Press*, 29 March 1887.
244 *Free Press*, 27, 28 Nov. 1885; *Advertiser*, 28 Nov. 1885; *Advertiser*, 22 March 1887.
245 *Free Press*, 23 May 1887.
246 *Free Press*, 28 May 1887.
247 *Free Press*, 21 Sept. 1887.
248 *Free Press*, 31 Jan. 1927.
249 *Jubilee Souvenir, Knox Presbyterian Church Listowel* (1914), n. pag.
250 *Jubilee Souvenir.*
251 *Advertiser*, 17 Dec. 1888.
252 Upper Canada College Archives. Quoted in Richard B. Howard, *Upper Canada College: Colborne's Legacy* (Toronto: Macmillan, 1979), pp. 146, 152.
253 Howard, p. 117.
254 Howard, p. 13. UCC early history: Howard, pp. 1–29.
255 A Liberal member: Howard, p. 110. Compromise, Howard, pp. 111–12. Dickson: Toronto *Globe*, 15 Oct. 1891.
256 *Free Press*, 25 Oct. 1888.
257 *Advertiser*, 5 Jan. 1888.
258 Kivas Tully was acting as a Consulting Engineer by February 1880. Fred Henry and 'Messrs Strickland and Symons' were also employed. Upper Canada College Minutes, pp. 50, 73, 76, 82–83, 88, Upper Canada College Archives, Univ. of Toronto Archives.
259 Criticisms of Durand's building: Howard, pp. 169, 247. Parkin: Howard, pp. 125–34, 163–67.
260 Goodspeed, p. 400. Durand as president: Directories; James Durand obituary, *Free Press*, 14 Nov. 1890.
261 Sandstone: *Advertiser*, 4 Oct. 1889. F.W. Peel: probably the elder brother of the painter Paul Peel. F.W. Peel was listed in a London City Directory as a 'marble cutter.' In the 1888 Detroit Directory, F.W. Peel advertises 'architectural carving' as one of his twelve specialities. Alice C. Dalligan (Chief, Burton Historical Collection, Detroit Public Library) to Lynne DiStefano, 25 Feb. 1986.
262 Tenants, interior details: *Advertiser*, 4 Oct. 1889.
263 G.A.P. Brickenden, 'The Loan Companies of London,' *London Centennial Review, 1826–1926*, p. 32, Regional Collection.
264 1887 address: 1982 Stratford *Beacon Herald* Sesquicentennial Edition; 1891 address: Stratford *Herald*, 31 May 1891. All newspaper sources quoted are in the Stratford-Perth Archives.
265 Stratford *Beacon Herald*, 7 June 1941.
266 Stratford *Beacon*, 8 May 1891.
267 Stratford *Beacon*, 8 May 1981.
268 Stratford *Herald*, 13 May 1891.
269 *Commercial Industries of Canada: 1887*, p. 48, *1883 City Directory*. Regional Collection.
270 *Free Press*, 6 Jan. 1886.
271 Goodspeed, pp. 918–19.
272 Architectural drawings, Murphy-Moore Collection. 1881 Insurance Map, City Directories, Assessment Rolls, Regional Collection. *Free Press*, 23 Nov. 1889.

CHAPTER FIVE

1 *Advertiser*, 29 Sept. 1888.
2 Goodspeed, pp. 71–73, 189, 510, 933. Temperance League: Goodspeed, p. 391.
3 E.J. Carty, 'Home of Mayor's Father Still Stands in London,' newspaper article provided by John H. Moore. Employment: Directories.
4 Directories.
5 Marriage date: information provided by

John H. Moore. Oliver McClary: Goodspeed, p. 369.

6 *Advertiser*, 7 Jan. 1889.

7 *Contract Record*, 18 Nov. 1897, 15 March 1899.

8 Stratford *Beacon*, 25 Aug. 1882; Charles Lilley Scrapbook, Edwin Seaborn Collection, Box 4320, Item 55, Regional Collection.

9 John M. Moore Correspondence, Murphy-Moore Collection.

10 John H. Moore, interview by Lynne DiStefano and Nancy Tausky, 5 Nov. 1984.

11 Dennis DesRivieres, 'The Great Enniskillen Swamp: Speculation, Drainage and Settlement,' *Western Ontario Historical Notes* , 26 (1972), p. 27.

12 John M. Moore Correspondence, Murphy-Moore Collection.

13 C.G.E.: *Contract Record*, 15 June 1893; Architectural drawing, Murphy-Moore Collection. London Electric: *Contract Record*, 17 May 1899; Architectural drawing. Bell: *Contract Record*, 12 Oct., 2 Nov. 1898; Architectural drawing. London Street Railway: *Contract Record*, 12 Sept. 1895, 29 May 1901, 25 Oct. 1905. Streetcar design, cigar factories, Empire Brass: Architectural drawings.

14 Corn Flake: Architectural drawing. Biscuit: *Contract Record*, 10 Jan. 1912; Architectural drawing.

15 Articles of Partnership, Murphy-Moore Collection.

16 Murphy-Moore Collection.

17 Andrew Saint, *The Image of the Architect* (New Haven: Yale Univ. Press, 1983), pp. 84–89.

18 *CAB*, XIV (1901), 56; *CAB*, XV (1902), 98.

19 YMCA: *Contract Record*, 15 Aug. 1895, 21 May 1896, 26 Nov. 1896; *Canadian Architect and Builder*, Oct. 1896; Architectural drawing. Masonic Hall: *Contract Record*, 4 April 1900; Architectural drawing. Churches, Houses: Architectural drawings.

20 *CAB*, VIII (1895), p. 28.

21 *Advertiser*, 28 July 1885.

22 *Advertiser*, 27 Nov. 1925; *Free Press*, 1 Dec. 1925.

23 John M. Moore obituary, *Advertiser*, 20 June 1930.

24 Moore advertisement: *Free Press*, 2 Dec. 1925. Election result (Moore 10,118; Wenige 8,587): *Free Press*, 7 Dec. 1925.

25 Acclamation: *Proceedings*, 20 Dec. 1926. Illness: *Proceedings*, 17 March 1927 (leave of absence); 18 Nov. 1927 (return).

26 Moore's performance: Inaugural Address, *Proceedings*, 20 Dec. 1926; Moore obituaries, *Free Press*, 19 June 1930; *Advertiser*, 20 June 1930. Springbank Park: *Free Press*, 19 June 1930.

27 George T. Moore, interview by Lynne DiStefano, 10 July 1985.

28 John H. Moore, interview by Lynne DiStefano and Nancy Tausky, 5 Nov. 1984.

29 *Free Press*, 19 June 1930.

30 UWO: *Construction*, Nov. 1924. Bell: *Journal*, Aug. 1930. Hotel London: *Contract Record*, 28 Sept. 1927; *Construction*, Aug. 1927. London Life: *Contract Record*, 29 Oct. 1924, 24 Feb. 1926; *Construction*, Dec. 1927.

31 *Journal*, March 1927, p. 115.

32 Directories.

33 Architectural drawing, Correspondence, Murphy-Moore Collection.

34 'Exceptional ability': *Advertiser*, 19 June 1930. Activities: *Free Press*, 19 June 1930; *Advertiser*, 20 June 1930.

35 Moore: *Free Press*, 1 Dec., 3 Dec. 1925. Cronyn: *Free Press*, 3 Dec., 6 Dec. 1873.

36 *Free Press*, 3 Jan. 1882, 5 Aug. 1905.

37 Religion: *Census of Canada*, 1871, vol. 1, pp. 92–93; 1901, vol. 1, pp. 202–203; 1911, vol. 2, pp. 60–61. Birthplace: *Census of Canada*, 1901, vol. 1, p. 430; 1911, vol. 2, p. 397.

38 *Free Press*, 1 April 1910.

39 Value of products: *Census of Canada*, 1911, vol. 3, xiv. Industries: *Census of*

Canada, 1901, vol. 3, pp. 194–95;
1911, vol. 3, pp. 258–59.

40 *Advertiser*, 18 June 1907.

41 *Census of Canada*, 1911, vol. 1, p. 554.

42 *London The Forest City* (1906),
Regional Collection. *Free Press*, 5 Aug.
1905.

43 'Railroad city': London *News* Anniver-
sary Number, June 1897. Grand Trunk:
R.T. Naylor, *The History of Canadian
Business 1867–1914* (Toronto: Lorimer,
1975), II, 111. C.P.R.: *Free Press*, 23
April, 9 May 1910.

44 *Free Press*, 5 Aug. 1905.

45 *Free Press*, 29 March 1900.

46 *Free Press*, 27 March 1900.

47 *Illustrated London Ontario, Canada*,
2nd ed. (1900; rpt. London, Ont.: London Public Library, 1967), pp. 175–76.

48 *Free Press*, 2 March 1900.

49 *Advertiser*, 25 April 1896.

50 'British to the backbone': *Free Press*,
19 Sept. 1911. McClary: *Free Press*, 31
Aug., 7 Sept., 9 Sept. 1911. Union
Jack: *Free Press*, 22 Sept. 1911.

51 *Free Press*, 17 May 1907. Cf. 'South
London Enjoying a Real Building Boom,'
Free Press, 3 July 1914. West London:
Free Press, 1 April 1910.

52 *Advertiser*, 8 May 1896. Cf. 'More
Asphalt,' *Advertiser*, 15 May 1896.

53 *Advertiser*, 5 May 1896.

54 Street Railway: Armstrong and Brock,
'The Rise of London,' p. 94 (see note 5,
chap. 1). Electrification: Fred Landon,
Province, II, 1076. Cronyn: Verschoyle
Cronyn Correspondence, Regional
Collection.

55 Armstrong and Brock, p. 94.

56 *Free Press*, 9 March 1900.

57 W.R. Plewman, *Adam Beck and the
Ontario Hydro* (Toronto: Ryerson, 1947),
pp. 39, 52.

58 *Free Press*, 30 Nov. 1910.

59 Plewman, *passim*. Cf. 'One of London's
Self-Made Men: Hon. Adam Beck,
M.P.P., Thrice Mayor of the City,' *Free
Press*, 5 Aug. 1905.

60 *Free Press*, 10 July 1899.

61 *Free Press*, 6 July, 12 July 1899. Cigar-
makers: *Free Press*, 3 June 1910.

62 *Free Press*, 10 July 1899.

63 Ross speech: *Free Press*, 23 Dec. 1899.
Election results: *Advertiser*, 2 Jan.
1900. The *Advertiser* said that 'he is a
good business man and ... he will make
a good alderman.'

64 'Fifty-Nine Years as a City,' *Free Press*,
3 Aug. 1914.

65 The same reversal takes place in the
Advertiser, from 'Canada and War,' 1
Aug. ('it does not indicate patriotism
on Canada's part to become excited) to
'Canada's Place,' 3 Aug. ('Canada will
bear its share in effort and sacrifice').

66 Volunteers: *Free Press*, 8 Aug. 1914.
Boer War analogy: *Free Press*, 30 July
1914.

67 *Free Press*, 4 Aug. 1914.

68 Quoted in Gwendolyn Wright, *Building
the Dream: A Social History of Housing in America* (1981; rpt. Cambridge:
MIT Press, 1983), p. 109.

69 Wright, p. 98.

70 Gwendolyn Wright, *Moralism and the
Model Home: Domestic Architecture and
Cultural Conflict in Chicago 1873–1913*
(Chicago: Univ. of Chicago Press, 1980),
p. 116.

71 *Free Press*, 27 May 1902.

72 *CAB*, VIII (1895), 65; XVI (1903), 32.

73 *CAB*, XI (1898), 106.

74 *CAB*, VIII (1895), 65.

75 *CAB*, VIII (1895), 42.

76 Helliwell: *CAB*, XI (1898), 107, 106.
Newton: *CAB*, VIII (1895), 42.

77 *CAB*, VII (1894), 125; VIII (1895), 10.

78 *CAB*, XI (1898), 108.

79 *CAB*, XIX (1906), 59.

80 C.E. Schermerhorn, *House Hints*,
quoted in *CAB*, XIX (1906), 59.

81 Toronto newspaper: quoted in *AABN*,
11 Jan. 1890. 'Queen-in-Anne-ity': *CAB*,
V (1892), 56.

82 Charles Wagner, *The Simple Life* (Toronto: Briggs, 1904), pp. 3, 17. Roosevelt
quoted in David E. Shi, *The Simple
Life: Plain Living and High Thinking in*

American Culture (New York: Oxford Univ. Press, 1985), p. 183.

83 Shi, p. 186.

84 Marcus Whiffen, *American Architecture Since 1780: A Guide to the Styles* (1969; rpt. Cambridge: MIT Press, 1981), pp. 167–71. McKim: Andrew Saint, *The Image of the Architect* (New Haven: Yale Univ. Press, 1983), p. 82.

85 Alistair Service, *Edwardian Architecture: A Handbook to Building Design in Britain 1890–1914* (London: Thames and Hudson, 1977), pp. 60–73; Virginia and Lee McAlester, *A Field Guide to American Houses* (New York: Knopf, 1984), pp. 321–41.

86 Arts and Crafts in the US, *Craftsman*: Shi, pp. 190, 191.

87 Vincent J. Scully, Jr., *The Shingle Style and the Stick Style*, 2nd ed. (New Haven: Yale Univ. Press, 1971), 71–112.

88 Shi, p. 187.

89 Whiffen, pp. 173–77; Richard Oliver, *Bertram Grosvenor Goodhue* (New York: Architectural History Foundation and Cambridge: MIT Press, 1983), pp. 52–54.

90 Shi, p. 187.

91 *CAB*, IX (1896), 38.

92 *CAB*, XIV (1901), 202.

93 *CAB*, XVI (1903), 34.

94 Quotations from Dick's lecture and exchange with Henry from *CAB*, X (1897), 14–17.

95 *CAB*, XII (1899), 121.

96 *CAB*, IX (1896), 68.

97 Percy Nobbs, 'Canadian Architecture,' in Adam Shortt and Arthur G. Doughty eds., *Canada and Its Provinces: A History of the Canadian People and Their Institutions* (Toronto: Publishers' Association of Canada, 1913), XII, 675.

98 John H. Moore, interview by Lynne DiStefano and Nancy Tausky, 5 Nov. 1984. The McKenzie homestead, one of the very first buildings in the London area, was destroyed as a practice exercise by a local fire department in 1985.

99 John R.W. Gwynne-Timothy, *Western's*

First Century (London, Ont.: Univ. of Western Ontario, 1978), p. 161.

100 *Journal*, July-August 1925, p. 128.

101 Gwynne-Timothy, pp. 242–43.

102 Spier, tour, Gothic: *Sherwood Fox of Western: Reminiscences by William Sherwood Fox* (Toronto: Burns and MacEachern, 1964), pp. 135–36.

103 Moore as main architect: James J. Talman and Ruth Davis Talman, *'Western' – 1878–1953* (London, Ont.: Univ. of Western Ontario, 1953), pp. 101–02; Architectural drawings, Office of Ronald E. Murphy, Architect. Moore on Board: Moore obituary, OLS, (1931), p. 134. Moore's gift: Fred Landon, 'New Buildings of the University of Western Ontario,' *Construction*, November 1924, p. 335. Adams: Fox, p. 136.

104 Fox, p. 135; Landon, p. 332.

105 Hazel Woods, 'A Brief History of the Dorchester Presbyterian Church,' typescript supplied by the author, p. 1.

106 Mrs Harold H. Ross, *North Dorchester: A Century Past to Present*, p. 71. Goodspeed, p. 491.

107 Tenders called by Moore for Presbyterian Church: *Advertiser*, 11 April 1889. Methodist Church: Building Committee Minutes, Methodist Church, 29 June 1888, United Church Archives.

108 By-law No. 375, Town of Walkerton, 26 Aug. 1890.

109 Excerpts from *County of Bruce 1867 Directory* and *Illustrated Atlas of the County of Bruce 1880*, supplied by Dale E.A. Wilson, Executive Secretary-Treasurer, Heritage Walkerton; Bruce *Herald*, 29 Jan. 1891.

110 Ralph Greenhill, Ken MacPherson and Douglas Richardson, *Ontario Towns* (Ottawa: Oberon, 1974), n. pag.

111 Bruce *Herald*, 29 Oct. 1891. Dale E.A. Wilson, telephone interview by Lynne DiStefano, 20 May 1986.

112 By-law No. 400, Town of Walkerton, 18 March 1892.

113 *1868–69 City Directory*, Regional

Collection; *OLS* (1935), 93–94.

114 *1895 City Directory.*

115 Sarah Catherine Lewis, interview by Lynne DiStefano, 23 July 1986.

116 *OLS*, p. 93.

117 *Free Press*, 4 May 1887.

118 *OLS*, p. 93.

119 1889 Daybook, Murphy-Moore Collection.

120 Articles of Partnership, 14 Nov. 1891, Murphy-Moore Collection.

121 *CAB*, VIII (1895), p. 64.

122 *CAB*, XII (1899), p. 17; XIII (1900), p. 1.

123 *Free Press*, 6 June 1902.

124 *Free Press*, 17 June 1896. Andrew Durand, George's brother, was another signer for the Liberals.

125 Margaret Archibald, *By Federal Design: The Chief Architect's Branch of the Department of Public Works, 1881–1914* (Ottawa: Parks Canada, 1983), pp. 5–7, 25, 30–31.

126 *Advertiser*, 2 Feb. 1905.

127 Quoted in L.N. Bronson, '1905 opening of London armory colourful affair,' *Free Press*, 6 Feb. 1980.

128 Mrs Paul L. Dawson, interview by Lynne DiStefano, 23 July 1986. Information in this paragraph from Mrs Dawson and Sarah Catherine Lewis. Henry's daughter Dorothy, who survives in poor health, was also interviewed.

129 *Advertiser*, 27 May 1890.

130 Goodspeed, pp. 519–20.

131 *Advertiser*, 26 June 1890; *Seventy-Fifth Anniversary 1890–1965: St George's Church*, Huron Archives; *Free Press* obituary, 23 Aug. 1938, quoted in *Seventy-Fifth Anniversary.*

132 Glencoe *Transcript*, 17 Sept. 1891.

133 *History of Burns' Church, Mosa* (Alvinston: Alvinston *Free Press*, 1941), pp. 6–7, 14.

134 Elsie M. Pomeroy, *William Saunders and His Five Sons* (Toronto: Ryerson, 1956), p. 5.

135 Pomeroy, pp. 32–37, 72–76; *Free Press*, 2 June 1986.

136 William Saunders obituary, *Free Press*,

28 June 1943.

137 Pomeroy, passim.

138 Pomeroy, pp. 96–97.

139 *Free Press*, 28 June 1943.

140 Pomeroy, pp. 4, 114; *Free Press*, 28 June 1943.

141 Pomeroy, p. 97.

142 Thomas G. Whiskard obituary, *Free Press*, 8 April 1919.

143 *Free Press*, 1 June, 2 June 1902.

144 *Free Press*, 23 March, 29 March 1900.

145 *Advertiser*, 7 April 1919; *Free Press*, 8 April 1919; Directories, Regional Collection.

146 Patricia G. Skidmore, *Brescia College 1919–1979* (London, Ont.: Brescia, 1979), p. 10.

147 R.C. Struthers obituaries, *Advertiser*, *Free Press*, 19 Nov. 1926; *1881 City Directory.*

148 *Free Press*, 5 Aug. 1905; London Industrial Edition (1903), p. 2, Regional Collection; *Free Press*, 2 March 1900.

149 Cf. the Franklin MacVeagh House, the J.R. Lionberger House, and the Sir Hubert Herkomer House [Jeffrey Karl Ochsner, *H.H. Richardson, Complete Architectural Works* (Cambridge: MIT Press, 1982), pp. 391–93, 407–08, 414–17].

150 Fred Landon, *100 Years 1834–1934* (London, Ont.: E. Leonard & Sons, 1934), p. 6, Regional Collection.

151 Quoted in D.A. Trumper, 'The Business Policy Evolution of E. Leonard and Sons' (1935 undergraduate essay), p. 21, Regional Collection.

152 'Testimonials of the Peerless Self-Oiling Engine,' E. Leonard & Sons Catalogue 40A, Regional Collection.

153 *CAB*, VI (1893), 113.

154 *100 Years 1843–1934*, p. 15.

155 Directories.

156 Murray G. Ross, *The YMCA in Canada: The Chronicle of a Century* (Toronto: Ryerson, 1951), pp. 3–4; Goodspeed, p. 355.

157 Ross, p. 20, describes church affiliation as 'the kiss of death' for YMCAs. 1873:

Goodspeed, p. 355.

158 Minute Book, YMCA, 28 Feb. 1895. Regional Collection.

159 Minute Book, YMCA, 12 Aug. 1895. The Minute Book records Henry's presence at Board of Trustees' meetings on at least thirteen occasions, from 23 Sept. 1895 to 4 Dec. 1896.

160 Minute Book, 24 Sept. 1895.

161 See Ochsner, pp. 114–23.

162 Architectural drawings, Murphy-Moore Collection. Jubilee Hall: Minute Book, 3 April, 9 April 1897.

163 Classes: Minute Book, 4 Oct. 1897; Business College: Minute Book, 29 June 1896; Architectural drawings.

164 New York *Times*, 11 Nov. 1893.

165 *Letters of Bret Harte*, ed. Geoffrey Bret Harte (Boston: Houghton Mifflin, 1926), p. 459.

166 Mary Markham Brown, Grand Theatre Performance Calendar.

167 Fred Landon, 'Memorial for an actress,' *Free Press*, 1 Oct. 1966.

168 Landon, *Free Press*, 1 Oct. 1966.

169 Mausoleum factual details from CAB, x (1897), 127.

170 Charles H. James, ''A Church Built on Hallowed Ground,'' *Huron Church News*, Dec. 1965, p. 4, Huron Archives.

171 James, p. 4.

172 CAB, IX (1896), 11.

173 St John's: 'Auspicious Inauguration,' unidentified newspaper article in St John's Church History, Huron Archives. St Matthew's: James.

174 'Auspicious Inauguration.'

175 Goodspeed, p. 517.

176 Floreen Ellen Carter, *The Place Names of Ontario* (London, Ont.: Phelps Publishing, 1984), II, 1041.

177 Building Committee Minutes, Arva Methodist Church, United Church Archives.

178 Moore: Building Committee Minutes, 23 Nov. 1898. 'Square': Building Committee Minutes, 9 Feb. 1898.

179 Jennie Raycraft Lewis, 'History of the Arva United Church – 1857 to 1957,' in *History of Three Churches: Arva, Hyde Park, Melrose* (Toronto: United Church of Canada, n.d.), p. 7, United Church Archives.

180 Cy Warman obituary, *Free Press*, 7 April 1914.

181 *Advertiser*, 7 April 1914.

182 John H. Lutman and Christopher L. Hives, *The North and The East of London: An Historical and Architectural Guide* (London, Ont.: City of London, 1982), p. 5.

183 Scully, p. 130.

184 *Free Press*, 7 April 1914.

185 *Advertiser*, 4 March 1912.

186 *Free Press*, 9 April 1914.

187 Directories.

188 Directories.

189 Directories.

190 Floor-plan: Architectural drawings, Murphy-Moore Collection. James O'Donnell: Directories.

191 *Advertiser*, 3 July 1882.

192 *Dominion Mechanical & Milling News*, Feb. 1884, p. 6.

193 Scott, p. 142; Fred Landon, 'John McClary,' *Province*, III, 150.

194 *Free Press*, 5 Aug. 1905.

195 Scott, p. 141.

196 CAB, XVII (1904), 153–56. All factual details from this article, and from Architectural drawings.

197 *Free Press*, 4 May 1907.

198 *Free Press*, 5 Aug. 1905.

199 *Free Press*, 5 Aug. 1905.

200 *Free Press*, 13 July 1914.

201 *Free Press*, 25 April 1986.

202 *Free Press*, 26 June 1986.

203 J. Vicar Munro obituary, *Free Press*, 28 Dec. 1936; *Journal*, Jan. 1937, p. 18.

204 CAB, III (1890), 41.

205 Jeanne Arnold (Deputy Registrar, Ontario Association of Architects), interview by Lynne DiStefano, 14 Jan. 1986.

206 Murphy-Moore Collection.

207 Directories.

208 State House: Alan Gowans, *Images of American Living: Four Centuries of*

Architecture and Furniture as Cultural Expression (1964; rpt. New York: Harper & Row, 1976), p. 118. Baldwin, Pennington: Henry F. Withey and Elsie Rathburn Withey, *Biographical Dictionary of American Architects* (Los Angeles : Hennessy and Ingalls, 1970), pp. 33, 467.

209 Partnership Agreement, John M. Moore and John V. Munro, 25 March 1908, Murphy-Moore Collection. Extensions, 1 March 1910, 1 March 1912.

210 Memorandum of Agreement, 22 Feb. 1913, Murphy-Moore Collection.

211 Directories.

212 *Free Press*, 28 Dec. 1936; *Journal*, Jan. 1937, p. 18; Directories.

213 Ellen Southem, interview by Nancy Tausky, 13 March 1986.

214 Directories.

215 Whiffen, pp. 183–90.

216 *Free Press*, 4 May 1907.

217 Ontario Furniture Co., *Catalogue of Furniture and House Furnishings* (1915), London Room.

218 Arthur E. McClary obituary, *Advertiser*, 23 Feb. 1920.

219 Fred Landon, *Province*, III, 36.

220 Architectural drawings, Murphy-Moore Collection; Directories.

221 Scott, p. 92. Further information about cigar-making, including McDonald's

testimony, from Scott, pp. 92–105.

222 *Free Press*, 5 Aug. 1905.

223 Directories; Scott, p. 105.

224 Scott, pp. 96–98.

225 *1918 City Directory*.

226 Directories.

227 The firm of Siskind Cromarty has also done an excellent restoration of the Nathaniel Reid Cottage (Chap. 3).

228 *Free Press*, 23 March 1910.

229 'Memorandum Concerning Residence at 90 Central Avenue,' Diocese of London Archives.

230 Robinson and Tracy call for tenders, *Advertiser*, 7 Jan. 1875. 'Firbrae': Thomas Kent obituary, *Advertiser*, 4 March 1912.

231 See Gustav Stickley, *Craftsman Homes*, 2nd ed. (1909; rpt. New York: Dover, 1979).

232 Jay and Jane Jeffery, interview by Nancy Tausky, 12 Aug. 1986.

233 Previous owners Dr and Mrs John H. Walker, interview by Lynne DiStefano, April 1984.

234 An advertisement for 'The Great Dissolution Sale' (*Free Press*, 4 Jan. 1915) describes Arthur Keene as 'New Proprietor of Keene Bros.'

235 Directories.

236 *Free Press*, 4 Jan. 1915.

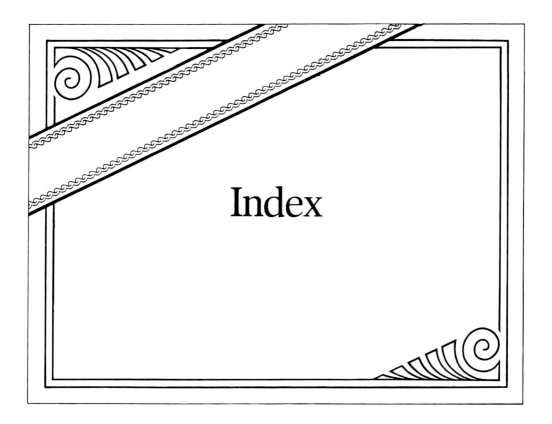

Index

This book
was designed by
WILLIAM RUETER RCA
and was printed by
University
of Toronto
Press